Capitalism, Alienation and Critique

Studies in Moral Philosophy

The titles published in this series are listed at *brill.com/simp*

Capitalism, Alienation and Critique

Studies in Economy and Dialectics
(Dialectics, Deontology and Democracy, Vol. 1)

By

Asger Sørensen

Edited by

Lisbet Rosenfeldt Svanøe

BRILL

LEIDEN | BOSTON

This publication, and the research that made it possible, has been generously supported by Aarhus University Research Foundation, Denmark.
Support has also been received from the Project: Public Sphere and Emerging Subjects (FFI2016-75603-R, AEI/FEDER, UE), Ministry of Economy and Competitiveness, Spain.

Library of Congress Cataloging-in-Publication Data

Names: Sørensen, Asger, 1960- author.
Title: Capitalism, alienation, and critique : studies in economy and
    dialectics / by Asger Sørensen ; edited by Lisbet Rosenfeldt Svanøe.
Description: Leiden ; Boston : Brill, 2019. | Series: Dialectics, deontology,
    and democracy vol. 1 | Series: Studies in moral philosophy, ISSN 2211-2014
    ; VOLUME 13 | Includes index.
Identifiers: LCCN 2017057559 (print) | LCCN 2018006888 (ebook) | ISBN
    9789004362420 (E-book) | ISBN 9789004362413 (hardback : alk. paper)
Subjects: LCSH: Capitalism. | Alienation (Philosophy) | Critical thinking. |
    Dialectic.
Classification: LCC HB501 (ebook) | LCC HB501 .S7748 2018 (print) | DDC
    335.4--dc23
LC record available at https://lccn.loc.gov/2017057559

Typeface for the Latin, Greek, and Cyrillic scripts: "Brill". See and download: brill.com/brill-typeface.

ISSN 2211-2014
ISBN 978-90-04-36241-3 (hardback)
ISBN 978-90-04-36242-0 (e-book)

This book is printed on acid-free paper and produced in a sustainable manner.

To Britta Harboe Olsen

∴

Contents

Preface

The work presented in this book has stretched over many years. Allow me therefore to extend a general expression of my gratitude to all the people, circles and networks, not to forget all the institutions, organizations and technology, maintained and governed by innumerable people, and paid for by even more, without which this work would not be worth presenting. Over the passing decades, this plurality of material, corporal and ideal entities has collectively enabled me to work on these matters that I hold so dear, refining and developing my ideas, and without this totality, the material results of all my good intentions would be far less interesting and readable.

At least, this is the conclusion I would argue, empirically as well as normatively. The social division of labour cannot but add to the quality of specialized academic work. Hence, the romantic ideal of the thinker – always male, sitting all by himself in his attic (or his mountain cabin), alone with his thoughts, supplied only with quill, paper and candle – could not be further from the realities of modern day academics. And so it should be; for me there are no regrets regarding professional specialization of intellectual work and the possibilities provided by technological globalization, i.e. the internet. If only we could have had it without capitalism…

The academic acknowledgements regarding specific chapters are placed in the Acknowledgements section below. Here I will simply thank those wonderful people who stood by me and helped me keep up my good spirits, especially in the final phases of completing the manuscript for this first volume of *Dialectics, Deontology and Democracy*.

Allow me to thank my editor, Lisbet Rosenfeldt Svanøe, for her highly competent work and friendly assistance, allowing me to focus on the content without worrying too much about matters of form, and even providing me with valuable suggestions and philosophical insights to refine my arguments along the way. A special thanks also to Eskil Riskær, who generously read the volume as a whole prior to production, contributing not only to the proofreading, but also to the structure and the precision of the argument.

The spring term 2016 at University of Sussex was where this volume really took form. Thanks to Gordon Finlayson, the local faculty decided to award me the title of Visiting Research Fellow, and with such an esteemed title came all kinds of facilities provided by the School of History, Art History and Philosophy (HAHP), the Department of Philosophy and the Centre for Social and Political Thought (SPT). Included was thus an office, a series of seminars and conferences, some very accommodating and able philosophical colleagues – apart from Gordon, I would in particular like to thank Anthony Booth, Mahon O'Brien and Darrow Schecter – and the helpful staff at the HAHP office. Thanks to all of them, to Gavin the porter, and especially to Jeanette, Jackie and Sheila who hosted me at the guesthouse at the Institute of Development Studies (IDS).

Still, my deepest gratitude when it comes to Sussex goes to Gordon, director of SPT, and his remarkable wife Blaire. They greeted the lone rider upon arrival, provided him with a bicycle, and saw to that he was alright throughout the three month stay – Gordon even took the time to take me to the cricket field and explain the intricate details of this very British sport!

Of course, nothing compares to my own wife Britta who, on the one hand, originally encouraged me to undertake the work that I am in the process of presenting here and who has supported it actively from start to finish, but who, on the other hand, retains a healthy scepticism with regard to professional philosophical reflections and those who spend too much time on such activities. Behind every man ... This book is for her!

Frederiksberg
August 2016

Acknowledgements

As my work with these themes has developed and matured over the years, so has my academic practice of acknowledging helping hands, minds and institutions. Especially when it comes to the older texts included in this compilation, I am therefore likely to have forgotten many of the people that I owe a lot for their contributions along the way. I am sorry about this, and can only hope they will forgive me these omissions due to youthful negligence, ignorance and – some may add – a flawed character.

•••

The **Introduction** was in a draft version made public at my homepage at www .academia.com in June 2016. Thanks a lot to Mogens Chrom Jacobsen who generously provided many helpful suggestions and corrections, as well as to Joaquín Valdivielso and Andres Felipe Hurtado for their comments.

The **Presentation** was also made public as a draft at my homepage at www .academia.com in June 2016, and I am grateful for comments and corrections by Joaquín Valdivielso.

The **Interlude** has not been published before. Also in this case, however, a draft version was made public in June 2016 at my www.academia.com homepage, and regarding this work I am grateful for comments, critique and corrections received from, in particular, Mogens Chrom Jacobsen, but also from Anders Ramsay, Joaquín Valdivielso, Luise Li Langergaard and Karsten Mellon Hansen. Part of the argument was presented and discussed in July 2016 at my PhD course at *Universidad de la Laguna*, Tenerife, Spain. Thanks to Maria José Guerra Palmero for the invitation and the pleasant stay, and thanks also to Maria José, Gabriel Bello and the rest of the participants for inspiring discussions.

Some of the basic arguments were presented in Danish already in 2010, in the chapter "6. Kritisk teori" in Michael Hviid Jacobsen, Kasper Lippert-Rasmussen & Peter Nedergaard (eds.), *Videnskabsteori*, pp. 168–195 (København: Hans Reitzel). A much extended version was published as "7. Kritisk teori" in the 2nd edition of the said book, 2012, pp. 245–87, and finally an abridged and thoroughly revised version as "7. Kritisk teori" (now co-authored with Luise Li Langergaard) in the 3rd edition of the book, 2015, pp. 251–86. I am grateful for comments, critique and corrections to this work in Danish, which I have received at various stages from Anne-Marie Eggert Olsen, Heine Andersen, Jonas Jakobsen, Kasper Lippert-Rasmussen, Lars Theil Münster, Luise Li Langergaard, Martin Laurberg and Per Jepsen. Thanks also to Jan Riis Floor who originally, in 1980, introduced me to the Critical Theory of Horkheimer and Habermas, not because of philosophical inclination, but out of duty, since in those years it was considered essential reading. Thanks, finally, to Jan Ulrik Dyrkøb and Flemming Juhl who in the autumn 1987 – independently of each other, but in the same semester and at the same university (University of Copenhagen) – both gave their own course on Horkheimer and Adorno's *Dialectic of Enligthenment*; to Gitte Pedersen, with whom I was to write a joint essay, for good discussions, and to Ole Thyssen who had the grace afterwards to explain to me and discuss not only the reasons for his marking, but also various crucial issues related to the content.

Chapter 1 was originally published as "Value, Business and Globalisation – Sketching a critical conceptual framework", *Journal of Business Ethics*, Vol. 39, No. 1–2, 2002, pp. 161–67. Allow me to express my gratitude to Juan-Carlos Siurana for the invitation to rework my presentation at the 14th Annual Conference of the European Business Ethics Network (EBEN), Valencia, 12th Sept. 2001, to an article in this special issue of *Journal of Business Ethics*, together with a very exclusive selection of contributions to the conference. It became my first publication in what at the time was recognized as an A-journal within this field, and I am also grateful for Juan-Carlos's editorial comments and suggestions. The article was presented at Roskilde University in December 2003 and reprinted in Jacob Dahl Rendtorff (ed.), *Værdier, etik og socialt ansvar i virksomheder – Brudflader og konvergens* (Roskilde University: Center for Værdier i Virksomheder. Institut for Samfundsvidenskab og Erhvervsøkonomi, 2003), pp. 168–77. A Danish translation forms Chapter 7 in my *I lyset af Bataille – politisk filosofiske studier* (København: Politisk Revy, 2012), pp. 160–70.

Chapter 2 was originally published as "On a Universal Scale. Economy in Bataille's General Economy", *Philosophy of Social Criticism*, Vol. 38, No. 2, 2012, pp. 169–97. Thanks to the anonymous reviewers for helpful suggestions and especially to the editor-in-chief, David Rasmussen, for granting me the favour, upon my humble pleas, not to shorten the article even though it was recommended by the reviewers. An early version was presented at Chinese Academy of the Social Sciences (CASS) in Beijing, September 2009. Thanks to Zhou Zuiming for the invitation, to Li Jian for translating the lecture, and to the participants for comments and questions. A presentation was also scheduled at the annual conference on Philosophy and the Social Sciences, Prague, May 2010, but due to institutional obstacles I had to stay at home. An abridged version translated by Li Jian was published in Chinese in CASS's journal, *Foreign Theoretical Trends*, as "在普遍的尺度上——巴塔耶一般经济学中的经济", 国外理论动态, No. 2, 2012, pp. 17–25.

A very early version of the argument was published in Danish as "I universets målestok. Om økonomi i Batailles generelle økonomi", *Agora* (Norway), No. 3,

2005, pp. 111–38. Thanks to editor-in-chief, Ragnar Braastad Myklebust, both for the invitation to contribute to the special issue on Bataille and for helpful suggestions. Also thanks to the anonymous reviewer. I owe a lot to people who have commented on and criticized earlier Danish drafts of the article. An early exploration of the theme was presented in Iceland, July 2004, in study circle eight under Nordic Summer University (NSU), "Critique and Analysis of Society under Global Capitalism". A draft of the argument was presented, firstly, at the philosophical Autumn Academy at University of Southern Denmark in October 2004 (thanks to Lars Binderup for the invitation!), and, secondly, in the above-mentioned NSU circle in March 2005 in Lund. I would like to express my gratitude to the participants for a lot of inspiration, especially in the NSU circle to Anders Ramsay, Ingerid Straume, Leif Thomsen and Anders Lundkvist. In relation to the final phase of the work in Danish, I would like to thank especially Luise Li Langergaard, to whom I owe the structure of the argument that is also maintained in the English language version. The early Danish version is reprinted as Chapter 10 in my book *I lyset af Bataille – politisk filosofiske studier* (København: Politisk Revy, 2012) pp. 238–65.

Chapter 3 was first published as "Dialectics – a commentary to Singer: 'Global business and the dialectic'", *Human Systems Management*, Vol. 21, 2003, pp. 267–69. Thanks to Alan Singer for initiating the email exchange that sparked the arguments presented in this note and for facilitating the publication at a time when I had no idea how all this worked.

Chapter 4 has been published as "The Inner Experience of Living Matter. Bataille and dialectics", *Philosophy & Social Criticism*, Vol. 33, No. 2, 2007, pp. 597–615. The same text was also published with the same title in Asger Sørensen, Morten Raffnsøe-Møller and Arne Grøn (eds.), *Dialectics, Self-consciousness, and Recognition* (Malmö: NSU Press, 2009), pp. 89–112. I would like to express my gratitude to Søren Brier for an extensive commentary, to Anne-Marie Eggert Olsen to whom I owe the present structure of the argument and to Thomas Basbøll who generously provided the original language revision. A draft version was published as *The Inner Experience of Living Matter. Bataille and dialectics*, Working Paper No. 2 (Department of Management Politics and Philosophy, Copenhagen Business School, 2006). The article was presented in May 2007 at the conference on Philosophy and the Social Sciences in Prague. The argument has been presented twice at Nordic Summer University, firstly in an early version in February 2004 in Oslo in study circle eight, "Critique and Analysis of Society under Global Capitalism", and, secondly, in the final version in July 2007 in Uppsala in circle four, "Pauses – Shadows – Holes". Thanks to the participants for comments, critique and corrections. A Danish translation forms Chapter 12 in my *I lyset af Bataille – politisk filosofiske studier* (København: Politisk revy, 2012), pp. 288–307.

Chapter 5 was first published as "Contradictions are Theoretical, neither Material nor Practical. On Dialectics in Tong, Mao and Hegel", *Danish Yearbook of Philosophy*, Vol. 46, 2011, pp. 37–59, published in 2014. I would like to thank Finn Collin as editor of the journal and the anonymous reviewer for helpful suggestions and comments. Originally, the paper was occasioned by a visit by Tong Shijun at the School of Education, Aarhus University in September 2009, where a seminar was held on "Dialectics" in the research unit for Political, Ethical and Religious Development (PERD) and I must express my gratitude to Jakob Soelberg for the references to Mao that proved to be essential for the argument. The argument was later presented in March 2010 at the annual meeting in the Danish Philosophical Association at the said School, just as elements of the argument were presented in a guest lecture on dialectics at the School of Architecture, Royal Danish Academy of Arts, March 2012. I would like to thank Dag Petersson for the invitation to lecture at the Academy and the participants at all the occasions for stimulating comments and criticism.

An early version was submitted in 2012 to *International Critical Thought*, published by Routledge and the Chinese Academy of Social Sciences (CASS), and I thank both Marek Hrubec for the invitation and the two anonymous reviewers for comments, critique and suggestions. One of the reviewers, however, was clearly offended by the article and made the following comment, quoted in verbatim: "The article argues that Mao's dialectics and Chinese traditional dialectical thinking are practical and naive materialist, which is common sense to those who were cultivated by Western philosophy. But it is not the truth. The great thinkers such as Martin Heidegger wish to seek inspiration in Chinese Taoism. The advantage Chinese thinking has over Western thought is she is conscious of 'nothing', and this is a kind of transcendent consciousness which is different from western religion. So it has some of Eurocentrism to argue easily that Chinese dialectical thinking is simple and instrumental". Still, the recommendations were to accept the article with revisions, which I of course made, but then suddenly, months later in 2013, during the final copy-editing phase, i.e. at the brink of publication, I received an email from Deputy Editorial Director Liu Zixu, CASS, that the editors had decided the article "cannot be published as it is", apologizing "for presenting this decision and reviewing results at the very late stage. The initial reviewing focused too much on the title itself and missed the sutlety [sic!] of the content. We would still love to publish it, if the content is consistent with the title and the part on the Chinese philosophy is theorized to enable a solid foundation for the comparison". I of course offered to change the title once more, but the answer was that "the title is only one of a number of things that lead to our decision, so we won't be able to take the easy solution of a different title". The specification of my faults, however, was never provided, and that was a lesson for me, i.e. realizing the different academic cultures around the world in spite of years of globalization and ambitions of international cooperation. I would therefore like to thank those involved in the process for the lesson learned.

Chapter 6 has been published as "Not Work, but Alienation and Education. *Bildung* in Hegel's *Phenomenology*", *Hegel-Studien*, Vol. 49, 2015, pp. 57–88, 2015. I would like to thank Anniina Leiviskä, Carl-Göran Heidegren, Darío González, Jørgen Huggler, Peter Wolsing and the anonymous reviewer for helpful comments, critique and corrections. Thanks also to the editor at *Hegel-Studien*, Johannes-Georg Schülein, for many important corrections and especially for a relevant reference to *Wissenschaft der Logik*. Also, without the patience of generations of students, especially on the graduate programme in Philosophy and Business Economy at Copenhagen Business School, and continuous conversations over the years on Hegelian themes with Anne-Marie Eggert Olsen, Arne Grøn, Carsten Friberg, Dag Petersson, Per Jepsen and Thomas Schwarz, I would not have been able to maintain literacy in relation to Hegel's *Phenomenology of Spirit* for so long. My original introduction to the *Phenomenology* took place back in 1984, when I followed a course offered by Arne Grøn, two hours a week for fifteen weeks; however, on the day of the examination I decided not to show up, since I still did not understand enough of what it was all about. Again in 1987, Arne offered the course on the *Phenomenology*, but this time with four hours a week, and with all these lectures under my belt I finally reached the point of daring to show up at the examination day, passing the test however without distinction. Thanks to Arne for these unforgettable experiences and for having the courtesy to honour me a few years ago by asking to borrow my original notes from back then when, after many years, he was to repeat the course.

Thanks also to Ingerid Straume for commissioning and commenting on the chapter in Danish ("Hegel. Bevidsthed, fremmedgørelse og sprog" in Ingerid Straume (ed.), *Danningens filosofihistorie* (Oslo: Gyldendal, 2013), pp. 197–211.), which in part laid the foundation for the present chapter and benefitted a lot from the generous comments of Jørgen Huggler. Further thanks for an inspiring discussion to those who attended my guest lecture on Hegel and *Bildung* at the University of Jena, May 2013, and to Hartmut Rosa and David Strecker for making it possible. Thanks finally to those who attended and discussed my presentations on this subject at the Nordic Summer University (NSU) Winter Symposium, University of Turku (Finland), February 2012 (thanks especially to Carl-Göran Heidegren for some very enlightening comments); at the annual meeting in the Danish Philosophical Association, University of Southern Denmark, March 2013 (thanks especially to Jørgen Hass for a very illuminating, and extensive, comment!); at the 14th Biennial Conference of the International Network of Philosophers of Education (INPE), University of Calabria (Italy),

August 2014; and at the first international congress of *Red Española de Filosofía* (REF) [The Spanish Philosophy Network], *Universitat de Valencia* (Spain), September the same year. An announced presentation at the second congress of the *Asociación Latinoamericana de Filosofía de la Educación* (ALFE) [Latinamerican Association of Philosophy of Education], *Universidad de la República* (UdelaR) (Uruguay), May 2013, never took place – it was one of the last sessions; the convenor did not show up and neither did the rest of the presenters. Finally, the overall argument was presented in its entirety in July 2016 at my PhD course at Universidad de la Laguna, Tenerife, Spain. Thanks to Maria Jose Guerra Palmero for the invitation, and to her, Gabriel Bello and the PhD students for questions and comments.

A short preliminary presentation of the general argument has been published in the proceedings of the NSU symposium ("Alienation, language and freedom. A note on *Bildung* in Hegel's writings", *Nordicum-Mediterraneum* (Iceland), Vol. 7, No. 2, 2012 (4 pp., Web)), and in an almost unchanged version in the proceedings (on CD-rom) of the said ALFE congress ("Alienation, language and freedom. On *Bildung* in Hegel's writings (extended summary)" in Andrea Diaz Genis *et al.* (eds.), *20 Congreso Latinoamericano de Filosofía de la Educación* (Montevideo: Dpto. de Historia y Filosofia de la Educacion, Instituto de Educacion, Facultad de Humanidades y Ciencias de la Educacion, UdelaR and ALFE, 2013)). An early, but abridged, version of the whole argument with some detail was published in the proceedings of the INPE conference (*"Bildung* in Hegel's *Phenomenology.* Acute alienation" in Stefan Ramaekers and Philippe Noens (eds.), *Old and new generations in the 21st century: Shifting landscapes of education* (The Site Committee of the 14th Biennial Conference of the INPE, 2014), pp. 274–285.). A translation of this text by Darío David González, "Extrañamiento agudo. *Bildung* en la *Fenomenologia* de Hegel", appeared in *Fermentario* (Uruguay), vol. 9, 2015 (Web). An unrevised draft version of the present argument has been published in the proceedings of the REF congress (*"Bildung* in Hegel's *Phenomenology.* Acute Alienation and Education" in Cinta Canterla (ed.), *Sección temática 8: Historia de la filosofía* (vol. IX in Antonio Campillo y Delia Manzanero (eds.), *Los retos de la Filosofía en el siglo xxi. Actas del I Congreso internacional de la Red española de Filosofía* (Valencia: Publicacions de la Universitat de Valencia (PUV), 2015)), pp. 63–80.

Chapter 7 has not been published before, but a draft has been accessible at my homepage at www.academia.com since early 2015. Thanks for extensive comments, critique and corrections to Alessandro Ferrara, Maja R. Ekebjærg, Per Jepsen and Søren Gosvig Olesen. The final version was sent to *Philosophy of Social Criticism* early 2016, and even though it was shortly after withdrawn, I received an extensive comment by an anonymous reviewer, for which I am very grateful. Thanks to the editor, Zhuoyao Li who decided to let me have the comments anyway! A heavily edited and abridged version, about half the length of the present chapter, and with a new introduction, various additions in the text and some for me completely unknown references, has been published as Chapter 2, "The Role of Dialectics in Marcuse" in Terry Maley (ed.), *One Dimensional Man 50 years on: The Struggle Continues* (Halifax: Fernwood Press, 2017), pp. 40–56. Thanks to the editor for the invitation and for his engaged editorial work, and thanks to the two anonymous reviewers for helpful suggestions.

An early draft of the chapter was presented at the 7th annual Critical Theory conference at Loyola University Chicago, Rome, Italy, and at a research seminar at the School of Education, Aarhus University, Copenhagen, in May and June 2014 respectively. More mature versions were presented February 2015 at the annual meeting of the Danish Philosophical Association at Aarhus University; in May 2015 at the conference on Philosophy and the Social Sciences in Prague, and in July 2016 on my PhD course at Universidad de la Laguna, Tenerife, Spain. Thanks to colleagues and students attending these sessions and commenting on my presentations, especially to Alessandro Ferrara, Lars-Henrik Schmidt, Maria José Guerra Palmero and Gabriel Bello. In particular at Tenerife, the discussion among the PhD students was very lively and stimulating. A special thanks to James T. Richardson for providing me with the reference to Koestler at a Nordic Summer University conference dinner in Vilnius, Lithuania, March 2014 and to Hans Siggaard Jensen for the reference to David Lodge. Thanks also to my post-graduate students in the programme Philosophy of Education, who have over the years engaged in discussing Marcuse, both in class and in essays, and have demonstrated to me that Marcuse is indeed relevant for the understanding and critique of contemporary capitalist society.

The **Postscript** has not been published before, although – once again – a draft version was made public at my homepage at www.academia.com in June 2016. I would like in particular to thank Bernat Riutort and Mogens Chrom Jacobsen for extensive and generous comments, as well as constructive critique and corrections. Thanks also to Joaquín Valdivielso and Luise Li Langergaard for helpful and encouraging comments. Some of the elements of the argument were touched upon in a guest lecture at Copenhagen Business School in February 2014 called "Critique of capitalism – reasons and varieties": thanks to Jacob Dahl Rendtorff for the invitation and to those attending for comments and questions.

•••

Language revision has been provided generously by the faculty of ARTS and the School of Education, both Aarhus University, in the former case facilitated by Nicholas Wrigley, in the latter by Simon Rolls. Introduction, Interlude, Post-script, Acknowledgements and the Chapters 1–6 were revised by William Frost, Last Word Consultancy, whereas Preface, Presentation and Chapter 7 were revised by Simon himself. Chapters 1–5 were revised after the original jour-nal publication; in some cases, the texts in the present versions are therefore slightly changed in relation to the originals.

Little of all this would have been possible without the generous support of my employer, the Danish School of Education, and, more in general, Aar-hus University (AU). Apart from time specifically dedicated to research and all kinds of supporting infrastructure, such as language revision, travel allow-ances, bookkeeping, etc., the AU Research Foundation provided the means to stay in Sussex in the form of a Mobility grant, administered by the AU faculty of ARTS, just as the same Foundation has supported the publication of the present work financially.

Thanks finally to Johanna Sjöstedt and the board of Nordic Summer Univer-sity for organizing Giorgio Baruchello's review of the present publication, to Giorgio for the review, and to Thom Brooks for accepting to publish my work in the Brill series *Studies in Moral Philosophy*.

Abbreviations

The indication of standard references does not always imply that the studies have been carried out using these editions. In some cases, they have been added only afterwards for convenience.[1]

AA   Immanuel Kant, *Gesammelte Schriften* [Akademieausgabe], ed. Königlich Preußische Akademie der Wissenschaften and Berlin-Brandenburgische Akademie der Wissenschaften (Berlin: Reimer 1900–21 (vol. 1–29) and de Gruyter 1922).

CP   Tong Shijun, *Chinese Philosophy: Practical Reason and Dialectical Logic* (Bergen: Filosofisk Institutt, Universitetet, 1989).

DA   Max Horkheimer and Theodor W. Adorno, *Dialektik der Aufklärung* (1947), in GS_A 3.

DDD   Asger Sørensen, *Dialectics, Deontology and Democracy*, vol. I–III.

DN   Pedro Montes, *El desorden neoliberal* (1996), 3rd ed. (Madrid: Trotta, 1999).

EC   Paul A. Samuelson, *Economics*, 10th ed. (Tokyo: McGraw-Hill Kogakusha, 1976).

EI   Jürgen Habermas, *Erkenntnis und Interesse* (1968), 2nd ed. (Frankfurt a.M.: Suhrkamp, 1973).

ER   Georges Bataille, *L'Érotisme* (1957), in OC_B x, ed. Francis Marmande and Yves Thévenieau (Paris: Gallimard, 1987).

ER_E Georges Bataille, *Eroticism* (1957), trans. Mary Dalwood (London: Penguin, 2001).

GS_A Theodor W. Adorno, *Gesammelte Schriften* (1970–86), vol. 1–20, ed. Rolf Tiedemann, together with Gretel Adorno, Susan Buck-Morss and Klaus Schultz (Darmstadt: Wissenschaftliche Buchgesellschaft, 1997).

GS_H Max Horkheimer, *Gesammelte Schriften*, vol. 1–19, ed. Alfred Schmidt and Gunzelin Schmid Noerr (Frankfurt a.M.: Fischer, 1985–96).

GW_H G.W.F. Hegel, *Gesammelte Werke*, ed. Deutsche Forschungsgemeinschaft, Nordrhein-Westfälische Akademie der Wissenschaften and Hegel-Archiv (Hamburg: Felix Meiner, 1968-).

KM   Axel Honneth, *Kritik der Macht* (1986), 2nd ed. (Frankfurt a.M.: Suhrkamp, 1989).

---

1   The works of Plato and Aristotle are, regardless of the edition, referred to using, respectively, Stephanus and Bekker numeration.

MEW   Karl Marx & Friedrich Engels, *Werke*, vol. 1–43, ed. Institut für Marxismus-
            Leninismus beim Zentralkomitee der Sozialistische Einheitspartei
            Deutschlands (SED) (vol. 1–42) and Institut für Geschichte der Arbeiterbe-
            wegung (vol. 43) (Berlin: Dietz Verlag, 1956–1990).

N_GW   G.W.F. Hegel, *Nürnberger Gymnasialkurse und Gymnasialreden (1808–1816)*,
            in GW_H 14, ed. Klaus Grotsch (Hamburg: Felix Meiner Verlag, 2006).

N_TWA   G.W.F. Hegel, *Nürnberger und Heidelberger Schriften 1808–1817*, in TWA 4.

OC_B   Georges Bataille, *Œuvres complètes*, vol. I–XII (Paris: Gallimard, 1970–88).

ODM   Herbert Marcuse, *One-Dimensional Man. Studies in the Ideology of Ad-
            vanced Industrial Society* (1964) (Boston: Beacon Press, 1968).

ONC   Mao Tse-Tung, "On Contradiction" (1937), in Mao, *On Practice and Contra-
            diction*, ed. Slavoj Žižek (London: Verso, 2007).

PHG_GW   G.W.F. Hegel, *Phänomenologie des Geistes* (1807), in GW_H 9, ed. Wolfgang
            Bonsiepen and Reinhard Heede (Hamburg: Felix Meiner Verlag, 1980).

PHG_H   G.W.F. Hegel, *Phänomenologie des Geistes* (1807), ed. Johannes Hoffmeister
            (Hamburg: Felix Meiner Verlag, 1952).

PHG_HW   G.W.F. Hegel, *Phänomenologie des Geistes* (1807), in Hegel, *Hauptwerke
            in sechs Bänden,* vol. 2 (Darmstadt: Wissenschaftliche Buchgesellschaft,
            1999). Page numbers follow the pagination of PHG_GW.

PHG_TWA   G.W.F. Hegel, *Phänomenologie des Geistes* (1807), in TWA 3.

PHS   G.W.F. Hegel, *Phenomenology of Spirit*, trans. A.V. Miller (Oxford: Univer-
            sity Press, 1977).

PM   Georges Bataille, *La Part maudite. Essai de économie générale. 1. La con-
            sumation* (1949), in OC_B VII, ed. Thadée Klossowski (Paris: Gallimard,
            1976).

POM   Anders Lundkvist, *Hoveder og Høveder. En demokratisk kritik af det private
            samfund. I. Privatejendom og markedsøkonomi* (København: Frydenlund,
            2004).

PW   Max Horkheimer, "Zum Problem der Wahrheit" (1935), in GS_H 3.

S_M   Herbert Marcuse, *Schriften* (1978–89), vol. 1–9 (Springe: zu Klampen Ver-
            lag, 2004).

TKH   Jürgen Habermas, *Theorie des kommunikativen Handelns* (1981), vol. 1–2
            (Frankfurt a.M.: Suhrkamp, 1988).

TKT   Max Horkheimer, "Traditionelle und kritische Theorie" (1937), in GS_H 4.

TWA   G.W.F. Hegel, *Werke in 20 Bänden. Theorie Werkausgabe*, ed. Eva Molden-
            hauer and Karl Markus Michel (Frankfurt a. M. : Suhrkamp, 1970).

• • •

All quotations from non-English sources were translated by the present author (consulting published translations when available).

Introduction

It all begins with an experience. It can be the experience of pity, rage or anger, or anxiety, all of them the result of being confronted with human degradation and suffering, wondering how this can be possible, knowing very well that often sufficient resources are ready at hand, and realizing that a lot of people, maybe even most people, know about this, but nevertheless somehow they prefer to turn the blind eye to all the mess, or simply give up, probably precisely because they cannot cope with experiencing social reality after all. Or, alternatively, it can be an experience of the kind that engenders for the individual self such excitement, joy or desire, or just pleasure, that everything else does not seem to matter, creating an enthusiasm so overwhelming that it, however, also tends to make one private, insensitive or just careless in relation to one's surroundings – indifferent to whether fellow beings are in pain or not, simply being satisfied with how things are developing for oneself.

The point is that ignorance or misrecognition, being just preoccupied with oneself, whatever the roots and flavour, can become habitual, and that this self-centeredness is a threat to social relations and thus to the coherence of society. The problem is well-recognized and discussed in various forms of social critique – among them the kind of Critical Theory I was raised with intellectually – both recently by Axel Honneth and originally, decades ago, by Max Horkheimer and Theodor W. Adorno, the latter two being preoccupied with the authoritarian coldness and lack of compassion demonstrated by the bourgeois persona.

This was never just a matter of personal traits or qualities. Hence, instead of thinking in terms of psychology, one has to move from social psychology to sociology and social philosophy. Some societies are more prone to engender personal coldness than others, i.e. some societies either demand or provoke more self-centred ignorance than others. For a nobleman of the 19th century, such as Alexis de Tocqueville, the relevant contrast was between aristocracy and democracy, the latter being more equalitarian and individualist than the former.[1] For me, however, as indicated by the qualification 'bourgeois', it is the capitalist class society that stimulates and actively fosters such mutual indifference, idealizing the individual entrepreneur and the economic man, thus legitimizing inequality, exploitation and ultimately real material poverty. In both cases, the problem is the emergence of a modern society without the social cohesion of

---

1 See, e.g., Alexis de Tocqueville, *Democracy in America* (1835), trans. James T. Schleifer (Indianapolis: Liberty Fund, 2010), vol. 2, Ch. 2, pp. 287–88.

the traditional society, hence alienating people from the society they are supposed to feel part of by the all too visible examples of blatant injustice.

The outset is thus real experiences of real injustice and alienation. Of course, these realities are perceived, as all experiences are, but they are perceived as real, i.e. as having a real material impact, both on the subjects perceiving the injustices, thus feeling sad or outraged, and on the objects, i.e. the human beings who are first being treated unfairly or even indecently, having to give up in despair their work, home, belongings, or even their food, then having to survive on the mercy of class society, gradually loosing self-respect and willpower, i.e. the strength to fight for their own dignity, eventually becoming degraded in a way that makes them less to be pitied than despised by those having had the fortune to be able to maintain and refine their humane tastes and appetites.

Hence, I will insist that injustice and alienation are something all too real in contemporary capitalist society.[2] In other words: the misdeeds of capitalism are the truths taken for granted beforehand. Wealth is unevenly distributed; it is not due to any kind of merit or deserts, and there is nothing noble about poverty and misery. However, it is a source of both comfort and hope that some people, in spite of all the hardship experienced, for some even in generations, manage to uphold themselves morally as well as aesthetically. It is for this reason that it is still worth criticizing capitalism. Capitalism produces injustice and alienation by appealing to what is less than human, thus corrupting and holding down those qualities of human beings which ought to be nurtured. These glimpses of humanity remind us that humanity, in spite of all, has survived as potentially human since its outset long before history, and therefore it is reasonable to continue fighting for its further and maybe even full realization. It is simply part of being human.

A   Cultural Marxism: Economy and Dialectics

It is sentiments such as these that have motivated the reflections presented in this book, even if they seem rather diverse. They express a horizon that today might best be called a kind of cultural Marxism. Such a horizon was widespread among intellectuals and scholars in the 20th century up until, at least, my generation, resulting in the belief that perceptions and experiences such as those just referred to are to be understood, at least partly, as a consequence of, and thus characteristic of, a particular economic system with a logic that has

---

2   See, e.g., Hartmut Rosa, *Alienation and Acceleration* (Malmö: NSU Press, 2010).

a specific historical birth and therefore, as a specific historical formation, may also be imagined to be overcome and eventually disappear.

This cultural Marxism may be understood in the same sense one speaks of cultural Christianity or Islam, i.e. as loosely connected communities sharing commonplaces and presuppositions even without having read the relevant holy scriptures, and even if some of the members are very critical about the commonplaces in question.[3] Defining traits of this shared cultural horizon is a special sensitivity to socially inflicted human suffering, a strong emphasis on the importance of the material aspects of what Charles Taylor has characterized as "ordinary life",[4] i.e. trivial down-to-earth issues such as work and economy, as well as the presupposed historicity of our current societal predicaments.

What it takes for granted, further, is that the present societal totality can be understood through dialectics as one system, and therefore that the actual social injustice encountered in the present society should not be considered as merely arbitrary. It is further assumed that what is human-made may also be changed, best through concerned and coordinated efforts by human beings, i.e. through politics. Therefore, it is worth considering and discussing our current societal situation, hence conducting social and political analysis as well as criticism to enable us to change our living conditions in a reasonable way, i.e. through some kind of social democracy involving the population at large, i.e. also ordinary people, so to say. However, within this cultural horizon, politics is to be understood in a rather broad sense, being open to all kinds of activities, parliamentary as well as extra-parliamentary, governmental as well as non-governmental, including such practices that today would often be labelled as terrorism, seeing in radical revolts the possible germs causing hope for revolutionary change.

Within this broadly defined cultural horizon, one finds various strands of Critical Theory, each emphasizing different aspects of human reality thus perceived. Ever since I started working on these questions, I have taken for granted the pervasive influence of the material living conditions forced upon us, though not thinking of it as totally determining the content and thus the possibilities of human consciousness. Assuming the possibility, in some sense, of freedom in both thought and action, I have nevertheless constantly been interested in the dynamics and causal logic of capitalist economy as a system, and many have been the cases where I have simply referred to these matters as part

---

3   See for instance my account of the classical anarchist critique of Marxism in Asger Sørensen, *I lyset af Bataille – politisk filosofiske studier*, ed. Johannes Sohlmann, Rævens sorte bibliotek (København: Politisk Revy, 2012), Ch. 14.

4   Charles Taylor, *Sources of the Self* (Cambridge Mass.: Harvard University Press, 1989), Part III.

of a critique of some ideology, be that ethical, political or educational.[5] Along-side with such studies, I have therefore also, from time to time, tried to dig a little deeper into the substance of the capitalist system. Within a horizon as the aforementioned, at least two elements become crucial: economics and dialectics. Compiled in the present volume are thus seven chapters, two on Economy and five on Dialectics, constituting respectively Part One and Part Two.

Hence, as a whole, the book is an investigation into two essential pillars of what I take to be the common horizon for much critical thought, at least for the cultural Marxism that I consider typical for my generation of north-western scholars.[6] The argument underlying all of the texts is that somehow humanity needs to reconsider, locally as well as globally, culturally as well as socially and politically, how we organize our common interaction with our-selves, our fellow human beings and with nature, i.e. how we produce, how we consume and how this 'we' is to be constituted. This is arguably becoming more urgent every day, thus approaching what in often called a 'burning plat-form'. What we have to deal with are big questions, and I would be silly to claim to provide any final answers; still, that should not keep us from asking such questions. Everybody can see that the world is in a serious crisis, economically as well as ecologically, and something radical must be done. As I argue, there is no doubt that capitalism is one of the essential factors responsible for the emerging disaster. It is therefore necessary to criticize it thoroughly in order

---

5   For some recent examples, see Asger Sørensen, "The *Law of Peoples* in the Age of *Empire*: The Post-Modern Resurgence of the Ideology of Just War", *Journal of the Philosophy of Inter-national Law* 6, no. 1 (2015), pp. 19–37; "Cosmopolitan Democracy and the State. Reflections on the Need for Ideals and Imagination", *Journal of Constitutionalism & Human Rights* 3–4, no. 8 (2015), pp. 8–19; "Cosmopolitanism – Not a 'Major Ideology', but still an Ideology", *Philosophy & Social Criticism* 42, no. 2 (2016), pp. 200–24; "From Critique of Ideology to Politics. Habermas on *Bildung* ", *Ethics and Education* 10, no. 2 (2015), pp. 252–70. These texts will be included in *Justice, Peace and Formation*, i.e. the book that forms volume III of the present work, *Dialectics, Deontology and Democracy*, hereafter referred to as DDD. Hence, what you are reading now is the introduction to DDD I.

6   Unfortunately, this term has been taken up by right-wing radicals to give substance to their conspiracy theories (see, e.g., Jason Wilson, "'Cultural Marxism': a uniting theory for righ-twingers who love to play the victim", *The Guardian*, January 19th 2015). One example is the Norwegian Anders Breivik, who in the years up to his terrorist attack, under a *nom de guerre* and with a fictional publication place, sampled a huge compendium on the challenges for Europe. In the introduction to this work, cultural Marxism is distinguished from traditional economic Marxism and described as one of the main roots of the current sorry state of af-fairs (see *2083. A European Declaration of Independence*, ed. Andrew Berwick (London, 2011), pp. 13–22). Moreover, within this strand of thought, Breivik attributes a crucial role to the Critical Theory of the Frankfurt School (see further below and in the Interlude).

to give rise to ideas for alternative ways to organize humankind. This book is a contribution to this project.

B   The Genealogy of the Texts

As a whole, the present volume commences an extensive topography of the philosophical and social scientific landscape that needs to be traversed in order to criticize consistently and sufficiently late capitalist modernity and contemporary neo-liberalism. To add substance to the overall argument, the two main parts have been supplemented with the present Introduction, a Presentation of the larger project of which the present volume is a part, an Interlude arguing for the continued relevance and validity of classical Critical Theory, and finally a Postscript continuing the critique of political economy.

This being said to emphasize the consistency of the present volume, it must also be said that originally all the main chapters were written independently as standalone articles, each having its special occasion, and not being thought of as possible elements of a book like this. Moreover, they are included in their original form, revised only linguistically, hence with no changes of content or structure in order to add consistency to the overall argument. In principle, each of the chapters can therefore be read in the same way, i.e. independently of the rest; but the claim is nevertheless that even such a reading will introduce to crucial aspects of *Capitalism, Alienation and Critique*.

Furthermore, as already indicated, the two main parts, i.e. Economy and Dialectics, are not coincidental. They may have emerged intuitively, but in hindsight I take them to constitute two crucial elements in the generational horizon, each referring to an essential constituent of Marx's thought, i.e. on the one hand Adam Smith, Ricardo *et al.*, on the other Hegel. Thus, economy and dialectics may be said to define the constellation constituting all the texts presented here.

In both of the two parts, the chapters are compiled such as to make it possible to read them as a continuous philosophical reflection developing themes along the way. Uneven as they are in size, in both parts the texts are ordered chronologically according to the period when the basic research was in fact carried out, and thus in the order in which the basic conclusions were reached, disregarding the time when the texts were revised and eventually published.[7]

---

7   For further details on the origins of the texts, e.g., where they were first published, see the Acknowledgements above.

Being thus aligned in the light of the overall argument, the organization of the texts also reveals another fact they have in common. Both of the articles introducing the two parts thus take as their point of departure the two major subject disciplines taught at business schools, i.e. economics and organizational studies. Hence, it is somewhat ironic, considering the horizon just described, that the first institution to accept my research in academia after the PhD was the Copenhagen Business School (CBS). This being the original context, the two texts are both somehow submissive to the realities of business, allowing the philosophical concepts to be used mainly as tools for purposes ultimately foreign to them. What they reveal, however, is also a certain asymmetry. What I learned at the CBS was that it was in fact much easier for the business community to relate to a left-wing agenda of political economy than to philosophy proper. With leftists, one can negotiate, making the disagreements a matter of money and power, whereas philosophers have an agenda that is even more provoking, not recognizing the priority of individualized needs, desires and greed, thus delegitimizing business activity as such.

For business to take a genuine interest in metaphysics and thus dialectics is even more incomprehensible and thus incommensurable and provocative than diverging on issues concerning political economy. Allowing myself to be defined by dialectics even more than by economy, ultimately a business school could not cater for me. Gradually, my reflections on both these issues grew out of the business context,[8] but today they have found an appropriate setting at the School of Education at Aarhus University (AU). Still, the generosity of the business world, always willing to take a chance for the sake of profit, gave me the opportunity to continue and develop my philosophical investigations, thus ultimately being able to provide concepts for wider uses than merely market competition and capitalist exploitation. The results of this endeavour are what I offer here.

Hence, in one sense this compilation is a collage, and from time to time I have even considered it a *bricolage*, i.e. a pastime hobby project or a daydream, with which I would play in order to escape all the more serious burdens ready at hand in the daily work as a philosopher of education. However, by making the compilation a real project, a logic and a line of thought have emerged, which I hope to reconstruct to appear as persuasive to the reader as I myself think they are. One element of this reconstruction has been presented above, namely the table of contents, demonstrating a line of thought through a sequence of *post hoc* mutually adjusted titles. A second element is the present introduction, the

---

8 For my reflections upon leaving CBS, see Asger Sørensen, "FLØK in memoriam", *Studietidsskriftet*, no. 3 (2009), pp. 86–97.

reading of which I hope has already provided an idea of the project, thus preparing for what is to follow. Hence, having finished reading the Introduction, I hope that you will be eager to continue reading not only the Presentation and the Interlude, but also the main chapters and the Postscript, and that this will eventually confirm the mood that I have attempted to bring you in already here.

C   Critical Theory

Compiling these philosophical works under the title *Capitalism, Alienation and Critique*, and thus making the case for identifying myself with Critical Theory in the sense mentioned above, has made me realize that there was an important element that, although mostly absent, was still taken for granted in the main chapters, namely the very idea of Critical Theory. Before the main articles in the compilation, I have therefore added an Interlude deliniating what I take to be the basic presupposition of the work compiled here, i.e. the classical idea of Critical Theory, arguing that it should not distance itself too far from the basic approach of the first generation, with all the philosophical and political radicalism this implies.

The reason for both the absence and the return of this classical idea of Critical Theory is my somehow troubled relationship to the mainstream tradition of Critical Theory, i.e. the so-called Frankfurt School. Originally, I was presented to Horkheimer's "Traditional and Critical Theory", as well as to Jürgen Habermas's "Knowledge and Human Interest", already in my first semester as a philosophy student at the University of Copenhagen in 1980. Early on in my career, i.e. as a post-graduate student in the mid-1980s, I wrote a rather long essay on Horkheimer and Adorno's *Dialectic of Enlightenment*, including Habermas's and Honneth's attempts to move beyond its *aporias*. This made a lasting impression on me. Still, the impression was initially one of horror and disbelief, not being willing to accept the conclusions of the radical critique of civilization, but still somehow entangled in Critical Theory, thus finding the logic of history and socialization so compelling that I did not see any way out of it.[9]

Reading Georges Bataille became my escape and the subject of my first dissertation, subtitled *Bataille in the light of Hegel, Marx et al.*, i.e. Critical

---

9   For an inside account of the strong impression of despair that could be left by the said *Dialectic* in those days, see the account by the director of the Frankfurt Institute in the 1990s: Helmut Dubiel, "Der Streit um die Erbschaft der kritischen Theorie", in *Ungewißheit und Politik*, ed. Helmut Dubiel (Frankfurt a.M.: Suhrkamp, 1994), pp. 230–47.

Theory.[10] Not being convinced that Habermas's communicative paradigm provided an answer to the worries caused by the said *Dialectic*, I still continued referring to Horkheimer and Habermas in my work, but did not pursue Critical Theory *per se*. Instead, it was through Bataille that I investigated the two generational pillars, economy and dialectics, which can be seen in Part One and Part Two. Bataille was a kind of cross-bred illegitimate child incorporating into his thinking various intellectual traditions, some of which I could already relate to when I discovered him, namely the French Hegelianism stemming from Kojève, as well as psychoanalysis, Dadaism and Surrealism. It was only much later – i.e. after more than two decades – that I returned to the infamous *Dialectic of Enlightenment*, having allowed myself to be commissioned to write a comprehensive introduction to Critical Theory.[11] This became an opportunity to look more closely into the basic matters again, and it settled a lot of issues, making me more at ease with classical Critical Theory and stimulating, for instance, my recent studies of Herbert Marcuse.

Most of my original work on these matters was carried out in Danish. Addressing now an international audience, what I am reconstructing in the Interlude below is therefore somehow an anachronism, i.e. an idea of Critical Theory that would have been advocated around 30 years ago, but which I must admit I still hold dear. The Interlude is the most recently written text in the compilation, so when it comes to basic textual studies of classical Critical Theory, there is a slip from the middle of the 1980s until rather recently. Thus, passing from the Interlude to Part One or Two on the one hand means leaping forward around 15 years, say from 1986 until 2001, when Chapters 1 and 3 were in fact written. However, it also means moving 15 years backwards, namely from the time of the completion of the present Interlude and back to 2001.

The studies presented in the compilation in fact stretch over more than three decades, going back to when I first entered university. However, the actual research and the writing of the first four chapters only dates back to my time at CBS, whereas the last three chapters are due to the generosity of my present employer, AU, as is the rest of the book.

---

10   See my dissertation for the Danish *mag.art.* degree, Asger Sørensen, *Suverænitet. Bataille set i lyset af Hegel, Marx & Co., mag. art.*-thesis (København: Filosofisk Institut, Københavns Universitet, 1992). See also Sørensen, *I lyset af Bataille*, Ch. 3, which was originally published in 1994, summarizing the main argument of the dissertation.

11   See Asger Sørensen, "Kritisk teori", in *Videnskabsteori: i statskundskab, sociologi og forvaltning*, ed. Michael Hviid Jacobsen, Kasper Lippert-Rasmussen, and Peter Nedergaard (København: Hans Reitzel, 2010), pp. 168–95.

D   Critique of Capitalism and Political Economy

Making the compilation a project, there was another thing that struck me, namely the unevenness mentioned earlier. As a work on *Capitalism, Alienation and Critique*, it did not give the critique of political economy the room I actually think it deserves. Being conceived within the horizon of cultural Marxism, somehow all the works collected in the present volume presuppose a critical understanding of capitalism as an economic system. However, only in a few cases have I directly made this explicit, namely in the works collected in Part One, and even in those works the critique is somehow displaced in relation to traditional Marxist critique of political economy. The reason is that my critique of political economy drew a lot of conceptual inspiration from another tradition.

Until WW I, German economics were deeply influenced by the so-called historical school,[12] but since then this approach has mainly migrated to disciplines such as history and, especially in France, sociology. In Germany, it meant that economy was primarily studied as 'national economy', and in Denmark this expression has survived until today, at least in colloquial academic language. As such, it signifies a practically orientated discipline just like classical political economy, aiming to assist a government in choosing measures regarding the economy of a nation to ensure its prosperity and continuous wealth. In this tradition, however, one is more prone to consider not just empirical evidence but also historical accounts, criticizing rationalist models based on the idea of *homo economicus*, i.e. the idea of an economic man as an instrumentally rational egoist, assumed in what was back then known as Manchester economy.

It was critique of political economy with roots in this approach that I encountered in the writings of Bataille, presenting what he called the 'general economy' in contrast to the 'restricted' economies modelled on the basis of the idea of *homo economicus*. Being conditioned generationally and culturally to criticizing capitalist economy, this immediately caught my attention, remaining one of the main reasons for my continued interest in his thinking, realizing only much later the possible conceptual complicity with post-modern capitalism.[13] Bataille led me to his predecessors; first of all, the ethnologist

---

12   See, e.g., Harald Hagemann, "Concluding Remarks", in *The German Historical School and European Economic Thought*, ed. José Luís Cardoso and Michalis Psalidopoulos, Routledge Studies in the History of Economics (Oxon & New York: Routledge, 2016), pp. 223–36.

13   See further below, Ch. 2, Sect. C.

Marcel Mauss and his classical "Essay on the Gift",[14] but also to the economic historian of British utilitarianism, Elie Halévy and the most important figure in this tradition, Émile Durkheim, whose first important work was precisely a presentation of the German critique of Manchester economy.[15]

In spite of the cultural and generational conditioning just mentioned, i.e. the cultural Marxism, it was through this French tradition of economic thinking that I obtained my basic knowledge of political economy, as well as sociology and, most recently, education.[16] However, even though the aim of the economic critique of Durkheim *et al.* clearly was meant to be moral and political, their positivism also implied a critique of the scientific and metaphysical shortcomings of the dominant economic thinking, namely the reductionism perceived in it, and this theoretical critique often came to overshadow the practical issues.

Thus, acknowledging that capitalism throughout the decades of globalization has achieved a discursive hegemony making it seem almost incontestable, I have found it appropriate to indulge in a more classical political critique of capitalist economy as inherently unjust. Hence, instead of continuing Durkheim's and Mauss's moderate political and moral critique, I will now come out of the closet and again pursue a more radical political agenda. At the business school, I was a bit hesitant to follow my critical inclinations; now, I am well-established as associate professor at a classical university and can let go without fearing repercussions – I hope![17]

Of course, I cannot reconstruct the actual intuitive ideas about political economy assumed in my studies decades ago, but even with lots of hindsight and many philosophical studies, I believe that many of my original misgivings about capitalism and political economy are still both intact and valid. I have therefore allowed myself the privilege to write a long Postscript attempting

---

14   My studies in Danish on Bataille, including a chapter-long intermezzo on Mauss, are found in Sørensen, *I lyset af Bataille*, First Book, pp. 39–307.

15   See Émile Durkheim, "La science positive de la morale en Allemagne", *Revue philosophique de la France et de l'étranger* xxiv (1887), pp. 33–58, 113–42 and 275–84.

16   See Asger Sørensen, *Den moralske virkelighed* (Malmö: NSU Press, 2012), which contains my Danish language studies into Durkheim's ethics and sociology of morality from 1997–1999. In the present context, these themes will be dealt with in the texts collected in DDD II, *Discourse, Value and Practice*. On Durkheim, politics and education, see Sørensen, "Durkheim: The Goal of Education in a Democratic State is Autonomy", in *Politics in Education*, ed. Peter Kemp and Asger Sørensen (Paris/Berlin: Institut international de philosophie/Lit Verlag, 2012), pp. 183–98, which will be included in DDD III, *Justice, Peace and Formation*.

17   This theme I will return to in DDD III, Part Three.

to offer a follow-up on Part One, providing some contemporary critical perspectives on political economy, thus trying to make up for my neglect so far regarding these basic issues that I hold as constitutive for Critical Theory, hoping that it will eventually be only the first of such attempts.

E The Project

To be mentioned is also that the present compilation is planned as volume one out of three, together assembling a wide selection of my English language studies in practical philosophy and appearing here as a trilogy under the common title *Dialectics, Deontology and Democracy*. Hence, before the Interlude on Critical Theory, and immediately after the Introduction, I will present the overall idea behind this three-volume project, thus introducing in a systematic way some common themes in the work collected under the said title.

F Presenting the Texts

Ultimately, however, an introduction must introduce directly the work that is collected in a volume such as this. Having now sketched the genealogical logic of the present volume, and its setting within a larger project, I will therefore briefly present the sequence of works that constitute the first part of the trilogy.

The **Presentation** explains the basic idea of the title *Dialectics, Deontology and Democracy* as pointing to three different, but equally valid, obligatory and necessary ways of relating to social reality: the first through *dialectics*, stimulating critique and imagination as to how things could be different; the second through *deontology*, recognizing the duties of being human, but precisely therefore also questioning various claims to validity; and finally the third through *democracy* realizing that social reality ultimately rests only on human practice and that for this reason we can change things to the better if we really want to. Not that it is easy, though, but it is our duty as human beings.

The **Interlude** of the present volume argues for maintaining Critical Theory in its most classical version, i.e. as the programme for critical social science proposed by Horkheimer and Marcuse, allowing philosophy to play a crucial role for science as a political practice. Science must strive to attain the truth, but ordinary social science, i.e. science describing existing empirical realities, cannot describe the truth of society, since true society, and thus freedom, justice and equality, has still not been realized. Critical Theory thus makes a case for science to engage in emancipatory activities that can be considered liberating, theoretically as well as practically. In a capitalist society, the truth of which is injustice and alienation, theory must be critical rather than affirmative, but dialectical thinking means the possibility to point beyond critique.

Unfortunately, the pessimist philosophy of history proposed in *Dialectic of Enlightenment* seems to have overwhelmed not just its authors but also later generations of Critical Theorist. Against Habermas, I argue that the proposed shift to a communicative paradigm is neither necessary nor fortunate for Critical Theory. Communicative action is not likely to succeed without a, if not prior then at least synchronic, gain of consciousness, which the critique of political economy provides very well. Moreover, Habermas's dichotomy between instrumental and communicative action weakens the link to the critique of political economy and thus the project of a radical and transformative critique of capitalist society. Being almost a contemporary with Honneth, I admit that he conveys very well the sentiments caused by the reading of the said *Dialectic*. Still, against Honneth it is argued that reducing Critical Theory to social philosophy might maintain the critique as radical and material, pointing to life being damaged by capitalist modernity, but it nevertheless threatens to make the critique politically impotent due to its very radicality, thus being incapable of suggesting an organized political transformation of the existing social order.

The **seven main chapters** are, as mentioned, divided into two parts, Economy and Dialectics, both introduced by articles written at the business school: one offering a conceptual reflection on value in economy, the other discussing dialectics prompted by an interest in organisational issues. Within the cultural horizon mentioned above, one can say that I depart from an ambition to understand the dynamics of globalized capitalist economy in terms of political philosophy, turning instead to a more classical philosophical ambition, namely to look into the very idea of dialectics as a crucial element in knowing the truth of society, i.e. both understanding and criticizing the current social order, and developing emancipatory and liberating proposals.

In the first part, **Chapter 1** is, on the one hand, true to the cultural Marxism described above, demonstrating sympathy for the organized riots and protests against capitalist globalization that took place by the end of the last millennium. Still, on the other hand, after an Interlude hailing the basics of Critical Theory, arguing for the continued relevance of the positivist tradition of Durkheim *et al.*, it may seem a strange place to begin the critique of political economy. For me, however, due to my long detour over Bataille, this became the possible point of departure for a research project on the concept of value, aiming to accommodate both the business settings and the traditional

ambitions of the cultural Marxism, being at the same time a normative exploration and a critique of political economy.[18]

The argument departs from the fact that value is a basic concept in economics, ethics and sociology. Locke made labour the source of value, whereas
Smith referred to an ideal exchange, and Kant specified that commodities only
have a market price, no intrinsic value. I then distinguish between two modern concepts of value: one that is economic, trying to explain value in terms
of utility, interest or preferences; and one that is ideal, values to be ends in
themselves. On this basis, Durkheim constructed his theory of value, which
was elaborated by his followers Mauss and Bouglé, and further by Bataille.
Their line of thought provides a comprehensive concept of value that can insist on the necessity of value creation in both an economic and a social sense.
Employing the theoretical possibilities of this tradition makes it possible to
develop a conceptual framework that can be used to criticize neo-liberalism,
big business and the effects of globalization, while at the same time defending
the moral value of everyday business, calling attention to the social quality of
small concrete markets, and offering an affirmative sociological understanding
of the anti-globalization protests.

Chapter 2 analyses Bataille's idea of a general economy in relation to political economy. In the first section, I present the critical perspective on economy
that is necessary in order to appreciate Bataille's conception of general economy, i.e. the critique by Durkheim *et al.* The second section present the general economy, firstly considered in a macro-perspective, which comprises the
whole of the universe, secondly in a micro-perspective, where the subjective
aspect of economy is maintained as non-objectified desire and inner experience. In the third section, I turn to the general economy as it was explicitly
intended, namely as a political economy. First, I argue that the suggestions Bataille himself presents are apolitical in an ordinary sense of politics, and that
this can be shown to be due to conceptual slides between nature and society
and between history and ontology. I then sketch some post-modern attempts
to legitimize, respectively, capitalism and communism by referring to general
economy, arguing, however, that Bataille can escape both agendas, since he
maintains the important distinction between need and desire. Although Bataille's conception of economy thus reminds us of aspects often overlooked
by economy in an ordinary sense, it also contains some serious aporias, which
means that it cannot constitute the theoretical basis for a new general political

---

18   For reflections on preparing this unfinished project, see Asger Sørensen, "Om værdien
        af værdi i etik og moral – nogle indledende overvejelser", *Filosofiske studier* 24 (2008),
        pp. 281–301. See also DDD II, Part Two.

economy, as Bataille had hoped. This conclusion constitutes the outset of the return in the Postscript to a more traditional critique of political economy, criticizing contemporary economics primarily in relation to the injustice that they cause.

In the second part, **Chapter 3** introduces the idea of dialectics, giving a short reply to a suggestion that dialectics could be useful for organization studies in providing means to understand ambiguities, contrasts, paradoxes, dilemmas and value-differences. As an answer to the implications of this suggestion, dialectics is presented in a very classical philosophical way, i.e. taking it all the way from Plato and Aristotle to Hegel and Marx, emphasizing the aim of truth and the Hegelian idea in the *Phenomenology of Spirit* of substituting abstract scepticism with determinate negation. It is emphasized that, traditionally, dialectics is not just one scheme of thought among others, providing convenient tools for analysis, but the one and only way to achieve true knowledge. The employment of dialectics would thus reveal the conflicts experienced in organizational studies to be merely apparent and, in principle, able to be done away with by employing dialectics in a comprehensive sense, aiming at the truth of reality as a whole.

Chapter 4 addresses the dialectical aspect in the work of Bataille that is often neglected. At the suggestion of Foucault and Derrida, Bataille is most often even taken to be a non-dialectical thinker. However, as I argue, Bataille worked intensely with Hegel's ideas, his thought was expressed in Hegelian terms, and both his epistemology and ontology can be considered a determinate negation of Hegel's position in the *Phenomenology*. This I argue, firstly, by analysing Bataille's notions of the 'inner experience' of the consciousness, and, secondly, by showing how Bataille extends dialectics to the natural, non-human realm, even conceiving of the link between the human and non-human as dialectical in itself. However, once we see the dialectical nature of his theoretical stance, we are also struck by a conspicuous vagueness in his practical conception of where society ought to be going.

Chapter 5 takes as its point of departure a concept of dialectics held by Tong Shijun that can also be found in Mao's writings and in classical Chinese philosophy, understanding dialectics as mainly practical and material. Having presented Mao's idea of dialectics, I argue that Tong is ambivalent in his attitude to dialectics in this sense, and for this reason he recommends contemporary Chinese philosophy to focus more on formal logic. In contrast, I argue that with another concept of dialectics, Tong can have dialectics without giving up on logic and epistemology. This argument is substantiated through an analysis of dialectics discussing different interpretations of Hegelian dialectics found in the Marxist tradition, in particular those emphasizing an ontological idea of dialectical-material change. Instead, I advocate the epistemological dialectics of Hegel's *Phenomenology*, leading consciousness from skepticism to the freedom achieved through alienation in *Bildung*, i.e. formation or education. In a final note, I dismiss the idea that this discussion is about eastern versus western philosophy, maintaining that it is about politics, arguing that the vitalism often implied by dialectical materialism is too lenient towards a form of capitalism ruled by chance.

Chapter 6 offers an answer to some recent attempts to revive Hegel's social and political thinking, combining *Bildung* with freedom as it is presented in the *Philosophy of Right*. However, making *Bildung* the explicit point of departure reveals the *Phenomenology* to be the most relevant reference. Reading the famous dialectics of the master and the servant, it has been common to highlight how Hegel conceptually associates the working on an object with *Bildung*. However, Hegel consistently fails to use the word '*Bildung*' in this context. Instead, he uses '*Bilden*'. Hence, it may very well be that for Hegel, the thing is formed according to the labourer's idea, and that consciousness is formed through the work, but that does not mean that consciousness achieves *Bildung*. The most comprehensive philosophical reflections on *Bildung* in the *Phenomenology* are found in Chapter 6, "The Spirit". Here, *Bildung* is closely intertwined with alienation, and in such a perspective freedom might not reconcile itself that easily, neither with reason nor with the state nor even with society. As acute alienation, being split and torn apart, *Bildung* becomes the condition for realizing and expressing the truth of modern society, thus creating the possibility of critique. Further, *Bildung* as a phenomenon is not solely linked to the individual human being. Spirit is first of all realized as a people and a family, and as such spirit has political importance. *Bildung*, however, presupposes not only the experience of alienation, but also the expression of it. Language is thus a necessary condition for *Bildung*. *Bildung* requires higher education. A close reading of the account of *Bildung* in Hegel's *Phenomenology* thus negates many interpretations of dialectics and philosophy of history in the slipstream of 20th century Marxism.

Chapter 7 argues that dialectics is indispensable for a Critical Theory aiming to provide a comprehensive critical understanding of modern capitalist society, taking as the prime example of such an understanding Marcuse's *One-Dimensional Man*, the occasion being the 50th anniversary of its publication in 2014. By way of introduction, three remarks are offered, the first on the importance of dialectics for my generation, the second on the way Marcuse understood it, and the third on his peculiar standing within Critical Theory. The main argument reconstructs Marcuse's analysis of one-dimensional thought as the typical ideology encountered in late modernity, criticizing empiricism and ordinary language philosophy for their affirmation of the existing social order. Instead, Marcuse insists on employing the dialectics of Plato to maintain not only the contrast of appearance with reality, but also the transgression of the former as a necessary condition for the emergence of the latter.

Due to Hegel, dialectics remains critical, both in terms of knowledge and in terms of history, now enabling the negativity to suggest potentials for the historical future. For Marcuse, through dialectical thinking Critical Theory can thus carry the critique of capitalist society into the imagination of a future of non-aggression in relation to both other human beings and the rest of nature, employing a reason that transgresses instrumental rationality and enables society to realize a technology of pacification instead of spending resources on destructive military technology. Marcuse thus connects dialectics, negativity and history, just as he offers an account of how dialectical thinking also entails the possibility of imagining liberation and an alternative way of being human. As a whole, the argument presented here can be considered a continuation of the argument from the Interlude about the importance of the original insights, thus claiming the necessity of dialectics for Critical Theory, and this last point also indicates why *Dialectics* in the present volume is used in the titles at two levels, i.e. both in the title of Part Two and in the general title of the trilogy.

The **Postscript** takes up the critique of political economy left at the end of Part One, carrying the theoretical reflection on economy into the practical realities of 21st century globalized capitalism. As a critical theorist, I take for granted that the material sufferings taking place all over the world to a large extent have their causes in the existing economic system. I thus assume that there is something called capitalism that can be assessed as generally unjust, and that it can be understood as a human made system, thus in principle possible to change and outlive historically.

Providing substance for such assumptions about economy, however, implies the unveiling of several layers of ideology, all of which point in the direction of supporting the main pillars of capitalism, i.e. that the free market is for the good of everybody and that property must be private. I therefore present one of the main theoretical underpinnings of economics, the theory of comparative advantage and the critique of it as ideology. I also argue that we are facing an offensive with actors believing in what they are doing, although it is difficult to decide whether the stimulation of selfish greed is a political agenda or simply what it appears to be, i.e. outright egoism. Finally, I go into some detail concerning the neo-liberal critique of neo-classical economics, which I take to be the biggest ideological challenge in the contemporary political struggle for social justice and political freedom. Assisted by monetarist economics, neoliberalism has managed to create the material preconditions for its own relevance, i.e. the globalized capitalism constantly in the process of eliminating political, social and cultural restrictions, one of the results being a speculative financial market beyond imagination. These material realities make it increasingly difficult to fight capitalism. But we have to do that nevertheless!

Presentation: Dialectics, Deontology and Democracy

The three words in the title, i.e. *Dialectics, Deontology and Democracy*, refer to the three overall themes of each of the three volumes constituting this work, each thus focusing on a basic way of relating normatively to our societal reality. Hence, the philosophical claim is that we *ought* to relate to our societal reality in all of these ways, i.e. through dialectics, deontology and democracy, and that democracy, as the final stage, is only achievable through citizenship education. As a whole, the work presented here is an argument for *Democracy*, but the final political philosophical argument is only generated through critical discussions of selected aspects of the current human predicament as they are manifested within social and moral philosophy, i.e. through *Dialectics* and *Deontology*. The normative *ought* is therefore constituted by and intertwined with a speculative *is*.

The individual disciplines (social philosophy, moral philosophy and political philosophy) are usually considered in isolation, each focusing on concepts they in particular hold dear (respectively, e.g., alienation, duty, and justice) in their own typical manner (critical, principled, realistic). My ambition with these volumes is to bring together these aspects and perspectives and present them in a developmental sequence, arguing that, through citizenship education, we may indeed be formed as human beings with a viable future on earth. Addressing both politics and education, the argument thus seeks to transcend the impotency of both social critique objectifying capitalism and of ethical universalism beyond communal practice, demonstrating the apolitical liberalism inherent both in the idea of a social reality governed by super human natural laws and in the idea of universal and inalienable pre-political rights.

The order of the three core terms thus signals a progression in the constitution of the argument and in how one ought to relate normatively, but also in the way I have handled such issues philosophically over the past decades. Hence, the argument addresses the broad field of practical philosophy comprising the following three elements:

I   Dialectics

When social reality is experienced as something out of our control, and maybe even both unjust and alienating, one has to examine this reality more closely, attempting to lift the veil and reveal the conceptual logic, perhaps in the process detecting law-like regularities – e.g. economic, natural, historical or logical – governing this reality. When faced with social reality as it presents itself under capitalism, one must conclude that this is not the true society, and that a science committed to the truth must transcend mere description and contribute to the realization of the true society; i.e., a society without injustice and alienation. Ensuring that social science and philosophy retain this indispensable ambition is the task of classical Critical Theory, and this is facilitated by arguing dialectically. This task is unfolded and exemplified in the present volume, *Capitalism, Alienation and Critique*, and especially in the chapters of Part Two below.

II   Deontology

Even when relating to social reality in the way described above, when experiencing despair confronted with alienation and injustice, when feeling burnt out and depressed, to be human means to aspire to be virtuous and to acknowledge one's duties: in Greek *deon*. Morality is constituted by normative experiences of wanting to do something that requires an effort and may even conflict with one's immediate personal interest or desire. However, although we all know this, it is unclear what provides the practical validity of such willed duties, i.e. their binding force. Hence, human practice gives rise to both claims and questions regarding the validity of morality and ethics: some referring to reason, discourse or human nature; others to traditional morality or ethical experiences. Some claims to validity are clearly ideological in the classical sense; nevertheless, ethics and morality cannot be ignored, and this is the theme explored in volume II, *Discourse, Value and Practice*.

III   Democracy

No matter how alone we are, no matter that alienation and morality are always experienced individually, at a basic level, our social reality consists of a collectivity of human practices. The existing political economic order and the ruling morality are human made and could therefore also be otherwise. Still, it is in no way given that changes will be to the better. Therefore, it is essential that we all engage politically in our social reality, ideally as citizens in a democracy, keeping in mind the issues raised in relation to dialectics and deontology, but transcending impotency and despair by participating actively in education, politics and the creation of peace among human beings. This is explored in volume III, *Justice, Peace and Formation.*

Thus, there is no question that we *ought* to relate to our societal reality in all of the ways mentioned. However, the question is whether we, as a totality of human beings on this planet, *can* cope with this comprehensive task. Even when considered from within an affluent society protected by a certain degree of social conscience and effective exclusionary walls, it is clear that humanity faces severe challenges: social, ethical, political and economic, as well as environmental. The present work as a whole seeks to contribute to the establishment of credible normative frameworks enabling us to comprehend conceptually, and hopefully also to cope with, the current human predicament, while remaining painfully aware that such an ambition may in fact be overly presumptuous.

•••

The three volumes of *Dialectics, Deontology and Democracy* are each composed of a series of standalone studies which, in composite, aims to provide an enhanced conceptual understanding of the respective ways of relating to society: socially, ethically and politically. Accordingly, each volume will bear its own title and can be read as a standalone work, with its own preface, table of contents, introduction, etc. Only the subtitle and volume number—and texts such as the present Presentation—indicate the volume's role in the overall argument. The texts selected as components for this intellectual endeavour cannot claim to comprise an exhaustive exploration of dialectics, deontology and democracy. They do, however, provide analysis and philosophical discussion of a number of key contemporary challenges facing humanity. Together, they aim to provide a fruitful and wide-ranging orientation for further political argument. Let me present the content of each of the three volumes in a little more detail.

I   Capitalism, Alienation and Critique. Studies in
        Economy and Dialectics

At the beginning of the 21st century, capitalism has become truly global, ideologically as well as materially. This makes classical Critical Theory more relevant than ever, and it is therefore the subject of a lengthy presentation and discussion in this volume. Even more, however, this globalization demands serious reflection on *economy*. This is attempted by examining the critique of political economy offered by Durkheim, Mauss and Bataille, in light of classical Critical Theory, as well as relating it both to the ideas of contemporary Marxist thinkers such as Hardt and Negri and to contemporary neo-liberal economic thought.

Furthermore, the way of relating to a social reality conditioned by capitalism is analysed in terms of *dialectics*, discussing conceptually basic ideas such as inner experience, alienation and contradiction with reference, primarily, to Bataille, Hegel, Tong Shijun and Marcuse. In a social philosophical perspective, social reality, although created by human beings, has achieved an objective independence which conditions materially and ideologically the very way of being human. According to Hegel, *Bildung* as formation of consciousness cannot help being alienating, haunted by the material contradictions in politics and economy within modernity, but only such a consciousness can utter the truth. In such a perspective, the critique of political economy also becomes a critique of ideology. This first volume concludes by providing such a critique through an extensive study of contemporary economic thinking.

II   Discourse, Value and Practice. Studies in Ethics and Morality

Critique of capitalism implies claiming certain ideals. This is the point of departure for *discourse* ethics, in one version arguing for transcendental pragmatics as the strategy for grounding the validity of duties and ideals. Another approach which still merits consideration is provided by traditional anthropology, just as it can be argued that moral sociology must be taken into consideration. This explorative discussion is conducted with reference to, among others, Kemp, Apel, Bataille, Durkheim and Bauman. Considering the classical distinction between deontology and teleology, the claim is that the critique of the greatest happiness principle must not lead to contractarianism presupposing selfish actors. This would mean relinquishing ethics, as is argued in relation to Bentham, Broad, Frankena and Rawls.

Furthermore, according to Moore, it can be argued that utilitarianism presupposes moral realism, although this metaphysical grounding encounters a serious obstacle in the vagueness of the idea of *value*. In fact, the Aristotelian reference to *practice*, formation and reason appears attractive if supplemented with an understanding of societal structures and recalcitrance. Considering the role of emotions, communicative rationality is preferred. Again, however, the need for a supplement is stressed: namely a critique of ideology grounded in the acknowledgement of the inescapable materiality, and thus precariousness, of human life. This is argued with reference to, among others, Lovibond,

Vetlesen, Dussel and Habermas, concluding that a critique of deontological ethics is acceptable only if it implies compassion and solidarity with those unable to fulfil the demands of duty. Finally, an epilogue reflects on some of the presuppositions and lacunae of the discussion.

III   Justice, Peace and Formation. Studies in Politics and Education

Accepting the legitimacy of a radical critique of capitalist modernity poses serious challenges to political philosophy and philosophy of education. Politics assumes that human beings are able to take responsibility, that they can arrive at reasonable decisions on collective issues and that such decisions may have considerable influence on their common future. This is presupposed by the very idea of government, be that monarchical, aristocratic or democratic. Hence, political philosophy must transcend both the impotent social critique of capitalism as an objectified entity and the heteronomous ethical universalism, hereby demonstrating the liberalism inherent in both the idea of a social reality governed by transcendental divine or natural laws and the idea of inalienable, pre-political human rights. Furthermore, the idea of democracy must transcend liberalism and be incorporated in a comprehensive theory of *justice*. These points are argued with reference to, among others, del Águila, Rawls, Habermas, Forst, Chomsky and Foucault.

Democracy is also a core issue when it comes to peace, the ideal of which is undermined by the idea of just war as advocated by Walzer and Rawls. Referring to Hardt and Negri, Rawls's *Law of Peoples* is thus criticized as part of his *Political Liberalism*. Moreover, it is argued that the idea of democracy beyond the nation state demands ideal imagination, referring in this context to Kant, Habermas, Held, Scheuermann and John Lennon. Still, the ethical ideal of cosmopolitanism is criticized as an ideology that sustains capitalism; instead, Kant's *peace* project, with its combination of republicanism, federalism and world citizenship, is presented as a promising framework for a balanced global political and legal order. Main references in this argument, other than Kant himself, are Rawls, Pogge, Beck and Bauman.

Regarding democracy as a constituent element of justice means that not just citizenship as the right to have rights, but also civic education and *formation* become central political issues. For the social and political *Bildung* of human beings to become democratic citizens, the goal is to enable them to cope with alienation. Referring to Habermas and Durkheim, this must be reflected in the norms for ethics, politics and pedagogy. However, as a critical reminder, I argue that under the current regime of neo-liberal New Public Management, public universities, even in apparently well-established democracies, are no longer able to uphold the ideals of academic freedom and freedom of research. Finally, this critical situation of modernity is the point of departure for summing up the main conclusions concerning justice, peace and formation, arguing that the realization of a genuine social democracy presupposes citizenship education.

•••

Having presented the overall argument at this level of abstraction, I must admit that I myself find the scope alarming! With such a comprehensive project, there is a very real risk that the result will be both superficial and inconsistent. However, it is too late to back out now, having brought myself and the project to the brink of completion. I can only appeal to the principle of mercy and hope that the constitutive elements in and of themselves are found to be persuasive and worthwhile, and that the reader may therefore grant the project as a whole the benefit of the doubt.

Interlude: Arguing for Classical Critical Theory: Horkheimer, Marcuse *et al.*

Outside the office, capitalism is running amok. The university is struggling for survival on the market conditions that have already subdued the rest of society. Globalization has reached the outmost corners of the world, exploiting human beings, societies and nature – and it is difficult to see a way out. Sad as it may seem, however, this is not the first time the prospects of humanity have looked gloomy; in such situations, it is important to have critical conceptual tools to be able to reconstruct the logic below the surface, making it possible through criticism to argue for and imagine the realization of something better. This is the role of Critical Theory.

Many have tried to define Critical Theory, making up all kinds of theoretical constructions.[1] My approach here will be as simple as it is radical, namely going back to the roots, consulting the texts in which Critical Theory was defined by the founding fathers, arguing that they still provide valuable insights worth maintaining for 21st century Critical Theory.[2] The name Critical Theory is normally traced back to a now classical article from 1937, Horkheimer's "Traditional and Critical Theory" and the discussion published later the same year between Horkheimer and Marcuse, "Philosophy and Critical Theory".[3] These texts appeared in the now legendary journal of the Institute for Social Research, *Zeitschrift für Sozialforschung*, i.e. the Journal for Social Research, or *Studies in Philosophy and Social Science*, as it was renamed in US exile before closing down in 1941 after only nine volumes.

Horkheimer's article was one in a series of essays, providing reflections aimed at developing a cross-disciplinary social research programme that recognized the constitutive roles of what in Germany is called *Wissenschaftstheorie,* i.e. theory of science, and philosophy at large. Before arriving at the term 'Critical Theory', the programme was for a long time presented under the heading 'Materialism', thus recognizing more explicitly the allegiance to Marxist thought, but leaving it open as to how this allegiance should be

---

1   For a brief overview and some references, see Ch. 7, Sect. A.
2   This project is continued in Ch. 7.
3   See Max Horkheimer, "Traditionelle und kritische Theorie", *Zeitschrift für Sozialforschung* VI, no. 2 (1937), pp. 245–94 and Max Horkheimer and Herbert Marcuse, "Philosophie und kritische Theorie", *Zeitschrift für Sozialforschung* VI, no. 3 (1937), pp. 625–47.

© KONINKLIJKE BRILL NV, LEIDEN, 2019 | DOI 10.1163/9789004362420_004

specified. The programme was proclaimed already in 1931,[4] when Horkheimer took on the positon as both the director of the said institute and professor in social philosophy at Frankfurt University. This marked the beginning of the Frankfurt School. However, already in early 1933, the Nazis closed down the Institute, Jews were banned from the universities, and the Institute went into exile. The original idea of Critical Theory was therefore developed in the USA, i.e. not in Frankfurt. After the end of ww II, however, the original German positions were recreated, and since then they have been the institutional backbone of Critical Theory.

•••

In its most original form, Critical Theory poses as a theory of science or, as it is more commonly put in English, a philosophy of science, and in particular a philosophy of the social sciences. As such, Critical Theory is characterized by privileging the social sciences and providing them with a special epistemological role as sciences. While positivism and critical rationalism do not recognize any fundamental distinction between the sciences, Critical Theory emphasizes that the social sciences must commit themselves to the truth in a much more comprehensive sense than what is usually the case. Critical Theory must not limit itself to simply describing social reality as it is, but also contribute to realizing society as it should be, thus realizing the true society. Critical Theory is theory that consciously criticizes existing social injustice and alienation as false, and that is also the case when it poses as theory of science.

The word 'critique' is said to stem from the Greek word *krinein*, which means something like "in a qualified way to differentiate, assess, select and decide",[5] and a critique of something therefore also implies an analysis and an assessment of it. Critical Theory can be said to understand 'critique' in at least two ways. First, there must be critique in the political and social sense, where the point of departure is Marx's critique of political economy. Here the basic point

---

4   See Max Horkheimer, "Die gegenwärtige Lage der Sozialphilosophie und die Aufgaben eines Instituts für Sozialforschung" (1931), in Horkheimer, *Gesammelte Schriften*, vol. 3, ed. Alfred Schmidt (Frankfurt a.M.: Fischer, 1988). Reference to Horkheimer's *Gesammelte Schriften* will hereafter be indicated as GS$_{\mathrm{H}}$.

5   Claus von Bormann, "Kritik", in *Historisches Wörterbuch der Philosophie*, ed. Joachim Ritter (Darmstadt: Wissenschaftliche Buchgesellschaft, 1976), vol. 4, p. 1249.

is to show how the bourgeois attempt to realize the classical liberal ideas about politics and economy by necessity will result in societal suffering and injustice. Second, Critical Theory also recognizes the use that Kant makes of the word in his famous *Critique of Pure Reason*. Here, we get an analysis of human experience in order to assess the limits of knowledge and science. It is this analysis that lays the ground for what became theory of knowledge and later, i.e. in the 20th century, theory of science. It is worth emphasizing that in both senses critique is crucial for a normative aspiration, i.e. both when the ambition is political and epistemological.

Critical Theory is characterized by employing both these senses of critique, emphasizing the importance of critique for social and political thought as well as for theory of knowledge. It is this feature that gives Critical Theory its special touch, extending the critique employed in theory of knowledge to the critique of capitalist relations of production, thus radicalizing Kant's critique of knowledge to social critique and critique of ideology. The double perspective of critique implies a simultaneous claim to both scientific and political validity.

In one sense, such a double perspective is already present in Marx's critique of the utopian socialists and his critique of the ideology of liberal political economy, Marx himself being inspired by radical materialist *philosophes* of the Enlightenment such as d'Holbach and Helvétius to asses and to evaluate ideas in terms of their origins, revealing religion as deceit and the ruling ideas as mainly in service of the rulers.[6] That the two senses are already "inseparably united"[7] by Marx is emphasized by Rüdiger Bubner, who, however, also points out the ambiguity of this feature; knowledge that falls short of "ideal knowledge" is "not knowledge at all", but even if our everyday society is far from the "ideal society", it is still a society. There is clearly a difference between Kant's "critique of knowledge" and Marx's "critique of ideology", the former contesting the truth in relation to theoretical criteria, whereas truth in the latter case is "disclosed" in order to propel "practical action".[8]

For Horkheimer, having written his habilitation on Kant's third critique, a critical programme for philosophy of social science must as theory of science contain an even stronger and more explicit element of epistemology, i.e. a theory of knowledge that takes up the fundamental logic of the knowing subject. As David Rasmussen has stressed, it is this "epistemological turn" that marks

---

6   See, e.g., Christopher L. Pines, *Ideology and False Consciousness: Marx and his Historical Progenitors* (SUNY Press, 1993), pp. 33, 45–60.

7   Rüdiger Bubner, "Habermas's Concept of Critical Theory"(1982), in *Critical Theory*, ed. David M. Rasmussen and James Swindal (London: Sage, 2004), vol. 2, p. 49.

8   Bubner, ibid., p. 60.

Critical Theory as distinct in relation to the "Marxian orthodoxy".[9] Still, beyond the theory of knowledge, the feature just mentioned also implies a strong and comprehensive notion of scientific truth, negatively manifested in the idea of ideology critique as revealing the falsity of beliefs that present themselves as universally valid, but in fact only benefit the particular holders of those beliefs.

This original epistemological framework was adopted and developed in the 1960s by Adorno, assisted by Habermas and, for instance, Albrecht Wellmer. Today, however, Habermas has in his sparse work on epistemology come closer to traditional theory of knowledge,[10] and when it comes to Honneth there is very little to indicate any interest at all in theory of knowledge or science. Instead, the focus in contemporary mainstream Critical Theory is on political and social philosophy, the former with Habermas as the main protagonist, whereas Honneth emphasizes the latter.[11] However, even recognizing the specific German roots of Critical Theory, today it has, not least thanks to the organizational efforts of Habermas, Honneth *et al.*, developed into an international research community,[12] which is well-established at certain universities, has its own preferred journals and meets regularly at more or less exclusive seminars and conferences all over the world. Hence, Critical Theory can still be reproduced in the classical sense, posing as theory of science and ideology critique, although this sometimes takes place far away from Frankfurt, as in the case of Enrique Dussel.[13] The marginal standpoint again shows it epistemological worth;[14] hence, in the centre, both the ideas of critique and criticism as well as that of Critical Theory have become less unequivocal.[15]

In the following, I will build up my basic case for classical Critical Theory by first presenting some of the traits of Critical Theory as they were initially conceived of by Horkheimer, Marcuse and Adorno, thus first sketching the basic idea of Critical Theory (A), then demonstrating the significance of philosophy

9   David M. Rasmussen, "Critical Theory and Philosophy" (1996), in *Critical Theory*, ed. Rasmussen and Swindal, vol. 2, p. 10.

10   See, e.g., Jürgen Habermas, *Wahrheit und Rechtfertigung* (Frankfurt a.M.: Suhrkamp, 1999).

11   See, e.g., Rainer Forst *et al.*, *Sozialphilosophie und Kritik* (Frankfurt a.M.: Suhrkamp, 2009).

12   See, e.g., Rasmussen and Swindal, *Critical Theory*.

13   See, e.g., Enrique Dussel, "El programa científico de investigación de Karl Marx", in *Los retos de la Globalización*, ed. Francisco López Segrera (Caracas: UNESCO/CRESALC, 1998), pp. 185–217.

14   See, e.g., Asger Sørensen, "Dussel's Critique of Discourse Ethics as Critique of Ideology", *Public Reason* 2, no. 2 (2010), pp. 84–101, which will conclude Part Two of DDD II, *Discourse, Value and Practice*.

15   See, e.g., *Was ist Kritik?* ed. Rahel Jaeggi and Tilo Wesche (Frankfurt a.M.: Suhrkamp, 2009).

for Critical Theory (B), and finally discussing the idea of dialectics, recalling the status it had in the first decades of Critical Theory (C). Having thus saved the essentials of classical Critical Theory, I will present the restoration of Critical Theory as theory of science that Adorno and especially Habermas were responsible for in the 1960s, stressing the fruitful critique of both positivism and Marxism, but criticizing Habermas's ambition to establish a new communicative paradigm for Critical Theory (D). Honneth, however, accepts this communicative turn, but for him it becomes part of an unfortunate argument for interpreting the very idea of Critical Theory as essentially social philosophy, which I will therefore also criticize (E). Finally, to sum up, I will claim the continuous relevance of classical Critical Theory, thus practising and advocating Critical Theory through the presentation of the basic conceptual schemes of my highly distinguished comrades in arms.

A   Classical Critical Theory

When Critical Theory claims validity as theory of science, it implies a critique of traditional theory of knowledge. The idea of a critical theory of course presupposes the existence of a theory that is not critical, and this is what Horkheimer names Traditional Theory. Crucial for Critical Theory is understanding theory as part of societal development. In this role, theory ought to contribute to raising the consciousness of society about the fundamental structure of capitalism, thus also contributing to the fight for social justice and against unnecessary suffering. And theory is necessary, since one cannot immediately know what is right and what is wrong, neither in nature nor in society. The argument thus proceeds through an account of the theory of knowledge and Traditional Theory to the fight for justice and the necessity of a critical theory.

i   *Science and Knowledge*
The idea of a theory of science goes back to at least Rudolf Carnap, who defined it as "the logical-empiricist theory of knowledge".[16] The point of departure for theory of knowledge is scepticism, as we for instance know it from Descartes or Hume. The point is that knowledge requires truth and certainty, but that we have good reason to be sceptical about sense experience, since the senses are known to deceive. As Hume emphasizes, there is always good

---

16   Rudolf Carnap, "Logical Foundations of the Unity of Science", in *International Encyclopedia of Unified Science*, ed. Otto Neurath, Rudolf Carnap and Charles W. Morris, vol. 1, no. 1 (1938), p. 42.

reason to think twice over what the senses tell us.[17] Deception and mistakes, however, are also possible when it comes to the most reasonable and rigidly logical thinking. Even if knowledge can be traced back through a strictly logical constitution to clear and reasonable intuitions, what appears as completely clear and evident can nevertheless lead to contradictions and paradoxes.[18] For Hume, the conclusion is that, as a default attitude, one has good reason to be sceptical and doubt everything one believes to know.

It is this way of thinking that Kant, on the one hand, recognizes as having awoken him from his "dogmatic slumber";[19] on the other hand, however, he also considers it a "scandal for philosophy and human reason in general".[20] The sceptical attitude may be warranted when it comes to the emancipation from dogmas, speculative thought constructions and other kinds of mysticism, but taken to its limit, it would make it impossible to believe anything at all, not even what we consider validated by science, and therefore it is a scandal. That is the reason why Kant makes the attempt to answer Hume's scepticism with a *Critique of Pure Reason*, thus analysing and reconstructing the kind of reasonable thinking that is supposed to provide the foundation of scientific knowledge. Kant wants to demonstrate that there may be good reasons to be sceptical, but that there are also good reasons to believe something: namely, if it can be considered scientific and true.

Kant's critique is the basis of what we consider as theory of knowledge. Hence, theory of knowledge is not an empirical theory about experience as it is commonly understood. It is a philosophical theory about how to justify that human experience does provide the possibility of knowledge that is both scientific and true. That does not mean that everything we believe to know is thereby true and scientific; part of it is simply beliefs, and even if some of them happen to be true, that does not mean that they are also scientific. Thus, the challenge for theory of knowledge after Kant is how to successfully affront dogmatic faith as well as the potentially damaging principled doubt of scepticism. Only on this condition can scientific knowledge be thought of as possible, and it is theory of knowledge in this sense that after Carnap is continued

---

17   See, e.g., David Hume, *Enquiry Concerning Human Understanding* (1748/77), in Hume, *Enquiries* (Oxford: Clarendon, 1972), p. 151.

18   See Hume, *ibid.,* p. 157.

19   Immanuel Kant, *Prolegomena zu einer jeden künftigen Metaphysik, die als Wissenschaft wird auftreten können* (1783), in Kant, *Werke in sechs Bänden*, ed. Wilhelm Weischedel and Norbert Hinske (Darmstadt: Wissenschaftliche Buchgesellschaft, 1983/98), vol. III, p. A 13 (AA IV, 260).

20   Immanuel Kant, *Kritik der reinen Vernunft* (1781/87), in Kant, *Werke in sechs Bänden*, vol. II, p. B XL.

under the heading 'theory of science'. To maintain the awareness of this origin, I prefer to continue using the Germanic expression, while acknowledging that it can sound somewhat awkward in English. As theory of knowledge is not a descriptive theory of the acquisition of knowledge understood as an empirical psychological process, neither is theory of science a descriptive theory of science as an empirical phenomenon, be that historical, social or psychological.[21]

As it is well-recognized, for Kant the idea of critique also had social, cultural and political aspects, aiming for liberation and emancipation, encouraging people to dare trusting their own judgement and not always that of the authorities.[22] Perhaps less known, however, is that many logical positivists and empiricists also had strong leftist leanings. However, as Fred Rush puts it, for Critical Theory the latter could only be "'accidental' radicals".[23] In the comprehensive societal perspective adopted by Critical Theory, even when considered as a part of a general Enlightenment project, both theory of knowledge and theory of science still exhibit disturbing internal splits. Horkheimer thus draws attention to Descartes, for whom the radical methodological doubt and uncertainty about reality is accompanied by an apparently unshaken certainty in the dogmas of the catholic faith. Another example is Kant, for whom the radical scepticism concerning theoretical and scientific matters goes together with a "naïve belief in standalone stiff principles", e.g., about the right to private property. As Horkheimer puts it, cautiousness and suspended belief in science goes hand in hand with "childish faith in the Bible",[24] and that ought to make one wonder why this is so.

Inspired by Marx's historical materialism, Horkheimer directs his attention towards the material and economic conditions. Science and its theories are part of the societal totality, and that also goes for theory of knowledge and theory of science. Horkheimer follows Marx in considering science as

---

21   For a more detailed argument, see Asger Sørensen, *Om videnskabelig viden. Gier, ikker og ismer* (Frederiksberg: Samfundslitteratur, 2010), pp. 12–17; in fact, this is the argument of the whole book!

22   See, e.g., James Gordon Finlayson, "Political, Moral, and Critical Theory. On the Practical Philosophy of the Frankfurt School", in *The Oxford Handbook of Continental Philosophy*, ed. Brian Leiter and Michael Rosen (Oxford: Oxford University Press, 2007), pp. 633–36.

23   Fred Rush, "Conceptual Foundations of Early Critical Theory", in *The Cambridge Companion to Critical Theory*, ed. Fred Rush (Cambridge: Cambridge University Press, 2004), p. 22.

24   Max Horkheimer, "Zum Problem der Wahrheit" (1935), in GS_H 3, p. 280. In the present chapter, the following page references are indicated in brackets in the text as PW, nn.

primarily societal "forces of production".[25] As it is well-known, such forces of production are always found within the totality of the societal organisation of production, i.e. what Marx calls the "relations of production",[26] and the dynamics of history is due to contradictions between these two elements. What is interesting in this context is a remark made later by Adorno that science can also be considered relations in this sense.[27] For Critical Theory, science is thus societal in more than one sense, i.e. both as part of the technical capacity of society for production and as a part of the societal consciousness accompanying production, i.e. a conscious and material element in the economic, social and political totality of society.

According to Horkheimer, the development of science is not only about expanding our knowledge; as forces of production, the sciences have also increased our technological control of nature, but this control is, due to the capitalist relations of production, individual and therefore without plan. However, that this is the case is ignored because ordinary theory of science does not take into account the social aspect of science, thus expressing a philosophical consciousness reflecting the social position of the bourgeoisie. Hence, for Horkheimer, we have good reason to suspect philosophical theory of knowledge and science to be defective and untrue as a form of consciousness.

ii   Traditional Theory

As mentioned, Critical Theory defines itself by opposing Traditional Theory. For Horkheimer, a traditional idea of scientific research is that it aims to formulate a theory as the best possible unity of propositions about a given object field:

> The fewer the superior principles in relation to the consequences, the more perfect is the theory. The real validity of the theory consists in the agreement between the sentences deduced and the factual events.[28]

---

25   See, e.g., Karl Marx, *Das Kapital*, vol 1 (1867), in Marx & Engels, *Werke*, vol. 23 (Berlin: Dietz Verlag, 1974), p. 54 (references to Marx & Engels, *Werke* will be indicated as MEW); see also Max Horkheimer, "Bemerkungen über Wissenschaft und Krise" (1932), in GS$_{\text{II}}$ 3, p. 40.

26   See, e.g., Marx, *Das Kapital*, vol. 3, ed. Friedrich Engels (1894), MEW 25 (Berlin: Dietz Verlag, 1974), p. 260.

27   Theodor W. Adorno, "Einleitung zum 'Positivismusstreit'" (1969), in Adorno, *Gesammelte Schriften*, ed. Rolf Tiedemann (Frankfurt a.M.: Suhrkamp, 1972), vol. 8, p. 283. Reference to Adorno's *Gesammelte Schriften* will be indicated as GS$_{\text{A}}$.

28   Max Horkheimer, "Traditionelle und kritische Theorie" (1937), in GS$_{\text{II}}$ 4, p. 162. In the present chapter, the following page references are indicated in brackets in the text as TKT, nn.

According to Horkheimer, this formal aspect of theory is independent of the epistemological origin of the fundamental principles. Some, such as John Stuart Mill, may thus refer to empirical induction as the way to obtain the fundamental principles, while others like Edmund Husserl would point to the intuitive grasping of the phenomenon as constitutive, and still others may, as the French philosopher of science Henri Poincaré, consider the principles as merely arbitrary conventions (TKT, 164).

Traditional Theory is clearly what is typically assumed in the sciences, and in this perspective the most perfect example of a science is mathematized physics. Traditional Theory assumes it to be its primary task to explain the facts of the real world, and to explain means here to subsume under a relevant law. The fall of bodies is thus explained when one can apply a theory such as the law of the fall of bodies and thereby calculate quantitative relations between acceleration, speed, drop and gravity, where the result calculated is in agreement with the factual measurements. The ambition for Traditional Theory is to construct a universal scientific system, where the distinction between the different sciences has been made obsolete, since one can reduce propositions about different object fields to a common set of premises. In the social sciences, the traditional conception of theory and the inspiration from the sciences means that one will, to a large extent, attempt to rationalize and quantify logical implications to become mathematical operations, such as is the case in economics.

To many scientists, this is the essence of theory, also today. However, as Horkheimer argues, this is only the immediate task for theory, not the essential. He acknowledges that the traditional conception of theory reflects a real experience of scientific activity, but this experience is only part of the truth. The traditional understanding of theory can be said to reflect unreflectively science, as it is practiced in the secluded sphere that it is confined to as the result of the social division of labour in bourgeois society. In other words, Traditional Theory does not say anything about the world in which science takes place and is constructed. It says nothing about what theory means to human existence as such. To put it simply, Traditional Theory expresses a restricted and thus defective understanding of science, i.e. it does not bring forth what is essential about the object matter studied.

A theory is a logical ordering of our knowledge in a hypothetical system, and what Horkheimer would like to stress is that it is precisely this ordering that makes it possible for the disclosure of facts to become fruitful for technological purposes and developments. To understand the nature of theory, it is necessary to include the understanding of the societal function of theory. As he puts it:

> Neither the application of theory on matter nor the influence of matter on theory is merely an internal scientific process, it is also societal. The relations of hypotheses to facts are ultimately accomplished in the industry, not in the heads of the learned community (TKT, 170).

Hence, basic research into molecular chemistry will be accomplished as medicine to be sold on the market, just as theoretical physics brought us nuclear power as well as bombs, and mathematics the computer and the internet. If the understanding of theory does not take into account these matters, i.e. the importance of scientific work on theories for the historical development of the capitalist forces of production, the understanding of theory becomes "ideological" (TKT, 169) and, therefore, according to Marx, false.[29] Hence, Horkheimer considers the traditional conception of theory as an expression of "the false consciousness of the bourgeois scholars" (TKT, 171). By ignoring economic and technical aspects of science, Traditional Theory becomes ideological and thus functions as legitimizing the existing order of society, including the privileges allotted to traditional scholarly work, assumed to be purely theoretical and beyond values and interests.

Adopting this almost ideal typical Marxist perspective, Critical Theory understands Kant's analysis of human experience in a rather untraditional way. For Kant, the forms of perception (time and space) as well as the categories of reason (unity and multiplicity, causality etc.) are necessary transcendental conditions for the synthesis that transforms the plurality of sense impressions to knowledge. The faculties of human experience thus play a very active role in the construction of scientific knowledge; for Horkheimer, that means that experience and knowledge can be understood in terms of work and production. The epistemological synthesis that according to Kant is provided by the transcendental subject is in fact work done by real historical human beings. That also means that our knowledge about the world, including the knowledge created in the social sciences, could have been created much differently (see TKT, 183). Thus, for Critical Theory, the role of the social sciences is to change both science and society, realizing the true societal reality characterized by justice and non-alienation.

---

29   See Karl Marx and Friedrich Engels, *Die deutsche Ideologie* (1845–46), in MEW 3 (Berlin: Dietz, 1990), pp. 13–14.

iii   *History and the Struggle for Justice*

For Critical Theory, it is crucial that social science considers society in its totality and as a result of a historical development. The development of the societal totality is understood in continuation of Marx's historical materialism,
history thus being driven forward by societal contradictions and antagonisms.
However, it is important to emphasize that for Critical Theory there is no automatic non-human mechanism in history. On the contrary, what is decisive
is that real human beings collectively and consciously undertake the responsibility to realize the vision of a reasonable society; only as a conscious goal
can this realization become historically necessary. Hence, 'necessary' in this
context means necessary for the survival of humanity, not necessary in a me-
chanic, logical or metaphysical sense. As Marcuse stresses, there are no auto-
matics that guarantee the transition from capitalism to socialism.[30] It is only
the realization of freedom and happiness that makes this transition necessary.
According to Marcuse, that was also Marx's point since such a transition for
him means coming to consciousness, which again means that society can be
governed with reason: "If capitalism is negated, the social processes will no
longer be subjugated to blind natural laws".[31]

This conception of history has at least two implications. The first is political, implying that historical conflicts and struggles do not necessarily lead to
anything better. Such conflicts can also make civilisation take retrograde steps,
which, according to Horkheimer, was what happened in the 1930s, especially
in Europe, and which is what some of us fear may also be what we are witnessing today when otherwise modern societies around the world employ
authoritarian measures to avoid the material consequences of globalized capitalism. Thus, what we see is the deliberate curtailment of basic civil, political
and even human rights, both in relation to citizens and foreigners, e.g., creating
walls of barbed wire against refugees or exporting them to off-shore camps, all
to counter the immigration produced by the exploitation and wars set in motion by the rich world. According to Horkheimer, capitalism can be said to have
been beneficial to human development for a long period, but at least in 1937
that did not seem to be the case anymore and that added to the argument for
the necessity for changing the fundamental form of society.

---

30   See Herbert Marcuse, *Reason and Revolution. Hegel and the Rise of Social Theory* (1941),
        2nd ed. (London and New York: Routledge, 2000), p. 318 (Herbert Marcuse, *Vernunft und
        Revolution*, in Marcuse, *Schriften*, vol. 4 (Springe: zu Klampen Verlag, 2004), p. 279). Refer-
        ences to Marcuse, *Schriften* will be indicated as S_M.

31   Marcuse, *Reason and Revolution*, 2nd ed., p. 317 (S_M 4, 278).

The other consequence has more to do with Critical Theory considered as theory of science. Hence, according to Horkheimer, the difference between traditional and critical theory is not as much "a difference in the objects as in the subjects" (TKT, 183), i.e. not as much a difference in society as the object matter as the subjects that constitute society and those who study it scientifically. The aim of Critical Theory is to make all of those involved in society gain consciousness about the fundamental structure of capitalism and its implications.

Hence, the transition from capitalism to socialism demands raising the consciousness of people about reality, and Critical Theory contributes to this process. This means, however, that the concepts of the theory do not get their confirmation from a description of the existing society, as the different types of positivists would normally take it. Marx's categories of 'class', 'exploitation', 'surplus value', 'profit', 'pauperization' and 'break down' are all part of a conceptual whole that presupposes the idea of society's "change to the right" (TKT, 192) society.

Thus, Critical Theory in this classical form is not just aiming to change this or that specific disparity in capitalist society; the aim is to establish a completely new organisation of societal labour *per se*. As Douglas Kellner tells the story, Horkheimer was radicalized due to his "extreme sensitivity to suffering, especially of the working class".[32] He was, therefore, unequivocal in his commitment to socialism, relentlessly attacking bourgeois society, capitalism and imperialism, denouncing the "world wide system of organized exploitation" and the "property system" as being responsible for "immeasurable sufferings" and "poverty in its crudest forms",[33] as well as "a brutalization of personal and public life", "where children go hungry", while "the hands of the fathers are busy turning out bombs".[34] In this perspective, Critical Theory was simply perceived as the "intellectual aspect" of the "emancipation" of the "proletariat" (TKT, 189).

iv   *The Necessity of Theory*

To Horkheimer, however, the development of Critical Theory does not mean that the proletariat will be brought to know the truth about capitalism without intermediaries. On the contrary, the theorist whose task it is to contribute to the realization of a society without injustice can easily find herself or himself in opposition to ruling ideas and opinions that are widespread among the proletariat. According to Horkheimer, that is precisely the reason why Critical

---

32   Douglas Kellner, *Critical Theory, Marxism and Modernity* (Cambridge: Polity Press, 1989), p. 237.

33   Horkheimer in Kellner, *ibid.,* p. 15.

34   Horkheimer, "Materialismus und Moral" (1933), in GS_II 3, p. 135.

Theory is necessary; if the necessary knowledge was given immediately for those who are in need of it, then there was no need for the critical contribution.

Horkheimer emphasizes that Critical Theory is just as demanding and strict in its deductions as traditional theories from the different kinds of what may be called normal science, when they address their particular subject area. "Also a critical oppositional theory must extract its propositions about real issues from universal concepts and through them let these issues be represented as necessary" (TKT, 202). That is precisely what Marx does in *The Capital* when he deduces necessary traits of capital accumulation from the analysis of the commodity as a universal concept.

Still, Critical Theory does not ignore time as do the steps in a deductively ordered structure (TKT, 207). As mentioned, Horkheimer thinks of Critical Theory as a continuation of Marx's historical materialism, thus thinking of the contradictions of capitalism as leading to the development of socialism and communism. However, the essential implication of connecting theory to time is not that one can theoretically construct historical periods that correspond to parts of the theoretical construction, as it arguably happens in Hegel's *Phenomenology of Spirit* and even more pronouncedly in Marx's historical materialism. What is essential is that by admitting and even emphasizing temporality, Critical Theory can take into account the continued change of its theoretical assessment of society, insisting that this change is conditioned by the conscious involvement of Critical Theory in the real historical process. Horkheimer denies that this changes the validity of the theory, and neither does the historical development shake the scientific certainty.

> The strength of the theory is derived from the fact that the fundamental economic structure of society, the class relation in its most simple form, and thereby the idea of its sublation, remains the same up through all societal vicissitudes (TKT, 208).

It is this fundamental class structure that Critical Theory insists on bringing forth in the analysis of the societal totality. If one only focuses on singular phenomena, the risk is that one is blinded and mystified by the small details. Only if one keeps in mind the overall perspective, i.e. considers the totality, is it possible to grasp what is essential about the subject matter at hand. Horkheimer sharply denounces what he perceives as "hostility towards what is theoretical *per se*". Critical thinking is the precondition for a transformative activity, and without theory there is no critique. He even goes as far as claiming that hostility towards theory in general is due to an unconscious fear, namely that theoretical thinking could reveal one's hard-earned adjustment to reality as "misguided and superfluous" (TKT, 206).

Hence, theory is unavoidable. By the transition from the present form of society to a future form, human beings must collectively create themselves as a conscious subject and actively determine their own life-form. Since the future does not exist, such a determination must of course be speculative and involve imagination; resistance against theory therefore means inhibiting human emancipation and liberation. Hence, Critical Theory does not refuse the validity of Traditional Theory altogether. A major task for Critical Theory is to screen the existing society and to reconstruct it employing traditional theories developed in the existing sciences. Without this basic theoretical work, there can be no hopes for "a fundamental improvement of human existence" (TKT, 207). This work, however, is only necessary, not sufficient. As Horkheimer concludes, in our historical epoch, i.e. capitalism, true theory must be critical rather than simply affirmative (see TKT, 216).

To sum up, Critical Theory in its most classical form basically poses as a theory of science, i.e. a normative program for multi- or cross-disciplinary social science about the modern society. As Horkheimer already emphasized in his 1931 inaugural lecture, it employs and addresses, apart from philosophy, especially the empirical scientific work of sociology, political economy, history and psychology.[35] As such, it insists that society must be studied critically and in its totality. Critical Theory is therefore not a collection of particular critical theories; it is to be understood as *the* Critical Theory of society *per se*. It further insists that the research of the social sciences should make itself part of a social and political practice that through consciousness raising activities aims at the sublation of injustice, suppression and alienation.

B   Philosophical Social Research

Critical Theory is a programme for how to conduct social science and social research, namely as an analysis that always takes into account the whole of society in its totality. As Helga Gripp emphasizes, a totality in this sense is not just the sum of all of the parts; rather, it is the continuous dialectical mediation between the universal and the particular.[36] Critical Theory aims at realizing a reasonable society, and reason is, as Marcuse accentuates, "the fundamental

---

35   See Horkheimer, "Die gegenwärtige Lage der Sozialphilosophie", in GS_H 3, p. 29.
36   See Helga Gripp, *Jürgen Habermas* (Paderborn: UTB Schöningh, 1984), p. 12.

category of philosophy".[37] For classical Critical Theory, universal concepts such as reason and freedom thus play a crucial role, and this role gains even more substance when we take a look at the conscious adoption and development of Hegel's comprehensive concept of truth, adding further credibility to the idea of investigating society in its totality.

i   *Reason, Freedom and Imagination*

Philosophy is by nature idealist, subsuming existence under thought, and it is precisely because philosophy thinks ideally about reality as such, that reason must be considered a critical instance in relation to the existing realities, i.e. the world as it is given for us. Certainly in what Horkheimer and Marcuse would call 'bourgeois philosophy', e.g., in the philosophy of Descartes, Hume and Kant, reason is typically perceived as something individual. However, as Marcuse argues:

> [In] this reason there is also a concern for the rights of the individual, i.e. for that in the individual that is more than an economic subject, for that which has to give up confronted with the totality of exchange in society. Idealism has at least wished for thought to remain pure.[38]

Thus, in spite of its frequent use of a Marxist vocabulary, classical Critical Theory is not materialist in the sense that everything is determined by the dialectical interplay between forces of production and relations of production. On the contrary, both consciousness and reason are accorded substantial roles. Still, Critical Theory recognizes Marx's critique of political economy, taking for granted that the apparently free production and circulation of goods presuppose the exploitation of the surplus value provided by the workers in the production process. Marcuse points out Marx as a prime example of a critique of the societal relations as a whole, i.e. a critique of "a society, the totality of which is determined by economy to such an extent that the uncontrolled economy dominates all human relations, thus where economy comprises everything non-economic".[39] In such a society, even indispensable needs, i.e. needs necessary for life, are typically evaluated in relation to contingent budgetary circumstances of the daily business economy. In such a society, doctors and nurses are made redundant if the hospital budget indicates a shortage of liquidity, no

---

37   Herbert Marcuse, "Philosophie und kritische Theorie" (1937), in s_M 3, p. 228.

38   Marcuse, ibid., p. 232.

39   Ibid., p. 236.

matter how many patients are waiting, and even, as we witness it nowadays, when the health service is public.

Instead of such an economically rational but socially pathological society, i.e. instead of capitalism, as we know it, Critical Theory wants to realize a society that is reasonable in the sense that economy is subjugated to the needs of the individuals of the society and not the other way around. However, since society is still far from realized as reasonable in that sense, according to Marcuse it is not only Critical Theory that is in opposition to the established order but also philosophy, which by its very nature must insist on reason. The point is that through philosophy insights are expressed, where the truth content "rises way above what is conditioned by society".[40] Hence, it is indispensable for Critical Theory as part of its social research to take an interest in the truth content of philosophical concepts.[41]

As a prime example of a crucial philosophical concept, Marcuse takes the idea of the human being as essentially reasonable, thus demanding freedom and considering happiness its highest good. It is due to this "universal character" of the idea that it acquires the "power to drive forwards".[42] Demanding happiness, freedom and reason is not restricted to this or that individual person. What is demanded is that all human beings should be realized as reasonable, free and happy individuals, accepting the basic thought of Marx that the freedom of each human being is dependent on the freedom of all human beings. Thus, Marcuse's point is that these philosophical ideas make it obvious that we are living in a society, where the basic constitution is opposed to the universal realization of such ideas. A market does not appeal to the individual as reasonable, but to desire. Individuals' greed and anxiety are what drive a capitalist society, not the power provided by the intuitive validity of universal ideas. Hence, when it comes to science and research in contemporary capitalist society, academic freedom and the traditional strive for truth are facing severe challenges, the tendency thus being to favour strategic research where the results can be privatized and made useful on competitive commercial markets in the so-called knowledge economy. Traditional publicly financed science that makes its efforts known and accessible to the public, thus facilitating through open access the general utility of its results, is increasingly under pressure.

Living in a society as we know it, what is immediately given is an unjust and thus false or untrue arrangement of society. Thus, to be able to formulate the truth of universal concepts such as reason and freedom, Critical Theory has to

---

40   Ibid., p. 240.

41   See ibid., p. 239.

42   Ibid., p. 243.

transcend what is merely given by experience. Marcuse stresses that "in our present reality" we have to "maintain as goal what is not yet present".[43] That is, however, not possible to do as conceptual thinking, since concepts according to Kant are formed in the meeting between sense perception and understanding. Instead, we must rely on what Kant names the "capacity of imagination", i.e. imagination or fantasy. It is this faculty that enables us to think anew what is not already given. Marcuse emphasizes that it is only the power of imagination that enables us to formulate what really is of interest for us as human beings, i.e. the famous questions formulated by Kant: "What can I know? What shall I do? What dare I hope?"[44] and, finally, the later addition, "What is man?"[45]

> Without [imagination,] philosophical thought would be retained in the present or in the past, cut off from the future, i.e. from the time that, as the only one, connects philosophy with the real history of humanity.[46]

Horkheimer also stresses the importance of imagination (see, e.g., TKT, 216). It is imagination that forces human consciousness beyond the limitations of experience. Hence, in spite of the official title "social research", as well as the long track record of empirical social research conducted by the Institute both before and especially after WW II, at the most fundamental level Critical Theory finds itself left to search for the truth in the universal notions provided by philosophy and not in the given social reality. According to the research programme as it was formulated initially by Horkheimer, the social research must be multi- or cross-disciplinary, but since thought has been privileged as the only real place where we have a chance of grasping the truth of a just society, in practice social and political philosophy is of paramount importance to the Critical Theory of modern society.

ii   *Truth*

For Critical Theory, it is crucial to retain the classical goal of scientific research, i.e. to provide the truth about the subject matter in question. Hence, this is also the goal that must guide the efforts of social science and social research. However, since the true society, i.e. the society without injustice and alienation, does not yet exist, social science and research must contribute to a historical

---

43   Ibid., p. 244.

44   Kant, *Kritik der reinen Vernunft*, p. B 833.

45   Marcuse, "Philosophie und kritische Theorie", p. 238.

46   Marcuse, ibid., p. 246.

development that can be expected to realize the true society. However, truth, just as reason and freedom, is one of those basic philosophical concepts that Critical Theory must take issue with, and for Horkheimer it is Hegel who provides the most fruitful point of departure.

Horkheimer thus refers to Hegel's initial and rather traditional determination of truth as the "accordance between knowledge and object" (PW, 292). To Hegel, however, such an accordance cannot be considered an isolated event. The experience, the knowledge and thus the truth of an object is only possible through knowledge of the whole of the totality. "The truth is the whole",[47] as Hegel famously puts it. For Critical Theory and in particular for Horkheimer, this means that ordinary empirical observation of something considered part of existing social reality can only be of limited importance and that it can never in itself earn the label "truth". This is the reason why Critical Theory insists on always taking into account the societal totality as a whole. However, as Horkheimer stresses following Hegel, this does not mean that the truth of the whole is something completely different from that of its parts. The truth is "the complete process of thought that comprises all the limited representations, each accompanied by the consciousness of their limitation" (PW, 286).

The truth of a subject matter has to state what is essential about it, and it is for Horkheimer precisely due to its deficiencies in this regard that Traditional Theory is untrue. At most, Traditional Theory can state something about what is immediately perceived, but that is not what is essential, and therefore it can only be false. Similarly, with regard to society: The existing society, i.e. that which can be immediately experienced, is deficient as a society. The very idea or concept of society implies justice in some sense and that is in plain contradiction with the contingencies of the jungle law that is allowed to rule the free market. Competitive capitalist society does not express what is essential about a society and therefore it is false as a society. According to Marcuse, Marx's point was precisely that the sufferings of the proletariat demonstrated the falsity of existing bourgeois society. Thus, the proletariat shows us that "truth is not realized".[48]

Social science and research cannot renounce on the standards of truth. At a purely verbal level, Critical Theory can therefore agree with, say, Max Weber

---

47   G.W.F. Hegel, *Phänomenologie des Geistes* (1807), ed. Johannes Hoffmeister (Hamburg: Felix Meiner Verlag, 1952), p. 21 (alternatively, see TWA 3, 24, which refers to *Phänomenologie des Geistes*, in Hegel, *Werke in 20 Bänden*, ed. Eva Moldenhauer and Karl Markus Michel (Frankfurt a. M.: Suhrkamp, 1970), vol. 3, p. 24).

48   Marcuse, *Reason and Revolution*, 2nd. ed., p. 261 (s_M 4, 232).

when he stresses how a researcher must strive towards truth and objectivi-ty.[49] It is only when Weber demands that social research must consist in value free description of existing social phenomena, that Critical Theory protests. Instead, a comprehensive idea of truth is proposed, reflecting the two aspects of the critique mentioned earlier, i.e. being normative with regards to both science and politics. It is this demand that implies that social science and re-search must involve itself in social and political practice, realizing the truth of society through the sublation of unnecessary social suffering. What is im-portant to stress is that this demand is not about what people are obliged to do as private citizens; rather, it is about their duties as social researchers. Or, to put it differently, it is not a matter external to social science; it is what it takes to do social scientific research, including, I would add, social and politi-cal philosophy.

C   The Grandeur and Decline of Dialectics

As it should be clear by now, Critical Theory is characterized by insisting on a close relationship between social science and philosophy, being especially fond of German idealism. The point of departure is Kant's theory of knowl-edge, but taking seriously Hegel's critique of Kant as well as Marx's critique of Hegel means thinking through the programme for a theory of knowledge and science in terms of dialectics. As David Rasmussen puts it, Critical The-ory thus draws simultaneously on two strains of German philosophy, i.e. one that emphasizes reason as constitutive, where the other focuses on reason as transformative.[50]

Dialectics is considered crucial from the very beginning, but the understand-ing and thus the assessment of dialectics undergoes a dramatic change already in the first decades of Critical Theory. First, following Hegel, Horkheimer and Marcuse consider dialectics as the core of a method that contains principles for explaining conceptually both consciousness and history, and the Institute already in the early 1930s planned to "write a definitive book on dialectics".[51] As time passed, however, the basic idea of dialectics was transformed, and in the famous *Dialectic of Enlightenment* from 1947 Horkheimer and Adorno

---

49   See, e.g., Max Weber, "Die 'Objektivität' sozialwissenschaftlicher und sozialpolitischer Erkenntnis" in Weber, *Gesammelte Aufsätze zur Wissenschaftslehre* (Tübingen: J.C.B. Mohr, 1988), p. 184.

50   See Rasmussen, "Critical Theory and Philosophy", p. 5.

51   Kellner, *Critical Theory, Marxism and Modernity*, p. 245.

seem to let dialectics become the inescapable logic of history rolled out behind our backs, determining a destiny of humanity not at all desirable, and that in spite of our efforts, or actually worse: *because* of our efforts as human and thus rational beings. For many, including the most important proponents of contemporary Critical Theory such as Habermas and Honneth, the latter idea of dialectics has been of pivotal importance and to a large extent responsible for their different ambitions to reform Critical Theory. In order to claim the continuous relevance of classical Critical Theory, it is thus crucial to consider this issue. First, an account of some of the basics of Hegel's dialectics, then the way it was radicalized by Critical Theory, and finally the *Dialectic* leading to the *Eclipse of Reason*.

i   *Scepticism and Determinate Negation*

As mentioned already, Horkheimer perceives a fundamental split in tradition-al theory of knowledge and science: on the one hand, any theory is consid-ered with scepticism as merely subjective and relative; on the other, a truth is accepted dogmatically as something absolute and definitive. As an answer to this split, he refers to Hegel who offers a different set of basic concepts for the understanding of scientific work and method, namely the links between truth, time and totality sketched above. Hegel can be said to be sceptical towards the scepticism that is taken for granted by traditional theory of knowledge and sci-ence. Instead, he develops the idea of the determinate negation.

When perception, experience, knowledge or science is put in doubt and thus denied its immediate validity, this process can be described as a nega-tion. Hegel's point is that it is always something determinate that is negated in this way, not anything else. The experience of a negation does not imply that one should doubt and be uncertain about everything, such as seems to be the conclusion of Descartes, Hume and Kant. Formally speaking, that would be a logical error, namely the same error that can be found in all inductivist reason-ing. At most, a negation can tell you something specific about the case or sub-ject matter considered. A negation is therefore not just determinate, but also determining, since it leads to a better understanding of the case in question. A negation is therefore conducive to knowledge, since the experience of the ne-gation, i.e. of realizing that an original proposal was false, must be considered a positive result in terms of knowledge.

Hence, as Horkheimer emphasizes, a negation does not imply the rejection of what is negated (see PW, 286). A scientific insight can be false simply by be-ing limited, and in this case a negation can mean a further elaboration of the original insight. Because of the negation, we now know more about the subject matter than before it took place. This is what Hegel expresses by describing the negation as a sublation: eliminating while at the same time preserving.[52] The truth now experienced thus rests on the premise that a former experience was false, and this restricted experience is therefore a condition for the truth now accepted. As Horkheimer points out, such a process of experience does not eliminate particular limited or partial aspects of the experience, quite the contrary. The aspects negated are preserved in the sublation as what Hegel calls "moments",[53] i.e. as operating parts of the resulting truth.

A determinate negation means that consciousness has made an experience about a particular case and therefore that this case to a larger extent is experienced in its truth. As part of the same process, a formation or an education of consciousness has also taken place.[54] Thus, consciousness can be said to have matured by having done, or had, an experience. Neither the case experienced nor consciousness is given once and for all. As a point of departure, consciousness forms a concept of the subject matter towards which it directs its attention. This concept is then developed by being realized either theoretically or practically in reality, and in this process its particularity is revealed, and thus its limitations. By the negation experienced, it becomes clear that concept and object are not in accordance after all, i.e. they do not agree. Thus, consciousness has not obtained true knowledge in the process. This complex experience, however, i.e. both realizing that truth was not obtained in the process, but nevertheless accepting the content of the experience as a fact, becomes the basis for consciousness constructing a new concept about the object or case in question, which then again will be the target of critique and further precision, the result being that the concept and hence the knowledge is refined even more in relation to reality.

According to Horkheimer, for a presentation of a subject to become scientific, all of its details must be subjected to a scrupulous and strict conceptual critique. Only in this way can "the progressive experiences of instances of one-sidedness" result in the "progressive inclusion of them in the complete picture of the whole" (PW, 285). It is this process of experience that classical Critical Theory in continuation of Hegel understands as a dialectical movement and that is proposed as a way to think of scientific method. As Adorno later remarks, for Hegel the dialectical movement is understood as a comprehensive principle for the explanation of reality,[55] and Hegel can therefore categorize his

---

52   See Hegel, *Phänomenologie des Geistes*, p. 90 (TWA 3, 94).

53   Hegel, *ibid.*, p. 73 (TWA 3, 78).

54   See *ibid.*, p. 67 (TWA 3, 72–73) See further below, Ch. 6.

55   See Adorno, "Einleitung zum 'Positivismusstreit'", in GS$_A$ 8, p. 289.

philosophical masterpiece, *The Phenomenology of Spirit*, as the first part of his system of science, namely the "science of the experience of consciousness".[56]

Thus endorsing Hegel's idea of the determinate negation, Critical Theory may at first sight appear simply to be in line with the critical rationalist idea of falsification, first developed by Karl R. Popper in the same period. This is, however, not the case. Popper adopts the traditional idea of scepticism also taken for granted by Descartes *et al.*, thus expecting the falsification process to eliminate what is on trial completely as simply an error, i.e. as downright false and nothing more. This means proposing the test process to start from the absolute beginning every time. The falsification is not understood to provide a positive result to lay the foundation for and thus determine further experiences on the way to realize the truth. For Popper, by negating, no knowledge is achieved of that which is negated, and nothing is therefore preserved in the sublation.

ii   *Radicalizing Hegel's Dialectics*

The idea of dialectical development also has implications for what we understand by reason. Critical Theory considers human being as reasonable being. That does not mean that every single empirical human being is reasonable, but we all have a potential to become reasonable that can be actualized. For Critical Theory, it is in particular due to Hegel that philosophy has been brought beyond the unfruitful opposition between human reason and an unreasonable reality. After Hegel, the world does not have to make itself manifest as a "secretive arrangement". Reality can become reasonable and there is therefore no reason to "despair" over "practical helplessness" (PW, 286). When Hegel states that what is reasonable is real and what is real is reasonable,[57] that does not mean that the in fact existing reality is reasonable, but that it has the potential to become so. Reason is a possibility for every human being, but it can only be realized completely as part of a reasonable society.

It is to this historical process that social science and research must contribute, which is done by revealing how modern capitalist society is fundamentally contradictory, antagonist and thus conflictual. Radicalizing Hegel's understanding of reason and reality thus adds to Critical Theory's argument for the importance of social science. Under the right circumstances, human beings can show themselves to be reasonable; the problem is that the dynamics of desire and anxiety encouraged by capitalist free market economy are not conducive to the realization of such circumstances. Intuitively, people always find it reasonable collectively to establish associations and unions, for instance

---

56   See Hegel, *Phänomenologie des Geistes*, p. 74 (TWA 3, 80).

57   See G.W.F. Hegel, *Grundlinien der Philosophie des Rechts* (1820), in TWA 7, 24.

to provide basic provisions and infrastructure in society. However, the possibility to prosper individually because of recognized private property right, i.e. the possibility to claim as legitimate possession that which the collective has been deprived of, fosters greed and undermines such intuitive sociability. This is the logic used to destruct housing associations, collective transport, public education, mutual insurance etc., putting it all on shares and thereby bringing it on the form of a commodity.

The radicalization of Hegel is also manifest when it comes to epistemological issues. Here it is important to stress that Critical Theory, by adopting the Hegelian scheme of thought, has broken with some crucial traits of traditional theory of knowledge and science. Answering the epistemological scepticism, i.e. that we in principle cannot trust any kind of knowledge, Hegel thus transcends the logical point of departure and adopts an ontological approach, understanding consciousness and the experiential process as existing and unfolding in reality. His claim is that even if our knowledge about some given subject matter is always uncertain, still the process of experience gradually creates knowledge that is more secure. Hence, real existing experience and knowledge are processes that happen in time.

The Hegelian answer to the split and relativism of bourgeois philosophy, including positivism and critical rationalism, is therefore that the temporal formation of experience can ultimately result in the absolute and true knowledge of reality. However, as Horkheimer points out, this idea simply reproduces the relativism in a different shape. According to Hegel, all the representations realized so far can be included in this formation process where experiences are sublated to become new experiences, and nothing can really be said to be downright false in this process, since all representations contribute to the progressive process of knowledge. This tolerance in relation to all earlier representations and conceptions, acknowledging them as merely conditioned and limited, implies for Horheimer that all past is juxtaposed. As he puts it: "Destitution and misery is sanctioned", and "heroes of the revolution" is put on equal terms as "generals from the victorious counter-revolution" (PW, 290–91). In spite of the fruitfulness of Hegel's dialectics as methodology, for Horkheimer it nevertheless ultimately comes to express the same bourgeois relativism as the theory of knowledge, and in relation to the ruling powers, this implies an ideological affirmation that Critical Theory must investigate critically.

Still, it is through Hegel that Critical Theory is provided with concepts to think of the truth as the result of a real process of experience that is stretched out over time. Further, conceiving of the experiential process as dialectical also means that consciousness can be understood through the process of becoming conscious of itself as conscious. And Hegel does not leave it at that. Employing human consciousness as a model, Hegel conceives of the whole of reality, human as well as natural, as being which through history, i.e. with time, becomes conscious of itself. For Hegel, reality can thus become self-conscious as mind or spirit when a unity is created of self-consciousnesses, each by themselves free and independent, i.e. as it is famously put, when "I am the we and we are the I".[58] It is from this persuasive philosophical idea that Hegel, Marx and classical Critical Theory think of history as one total development, making it possible to think of humanity as a whole collectively coming to consciousness about itself as humanity. In the common Marxist interpretation, this means that workers all over the world should organize internationally, uniting themselves as members of unions and, thereby, raising their specific consciousnesses of the role of the proletariat as the revolutionary subject of history.

However, as Horkheimer underlines, for Critical Theory, dialectics is both material and unfinished. Still, he insists that this does not imply that dialectics must give up the possibility to provide the truth. When the truth is the whole, then the truth is historical and in principle incomplete, being thus true in a sense beyond both absolutism and relativism. Through the determinate negation, it is revealed what is merely one-sided and relative, both in the thoughts of ourselves and those of others, and for that purpose there is no need for a "super historical and thus overwrought concept of the truth" that ultimately stems from the "concept of God" (PW, 295).

Historically, the principled incompleteness means the confirmation of certain truths for Critical Theory will depend on "historical processes yet not completed". Even fundamental categories such as "history, society, progress, science", yes, even "dialectics itself", can in fact change their meaning completely, since they are all only a "moment" in the actualized "totality of knowledge" (PW, 309–10). Hence, even though Marx has provided us with a concept of the end of history as the reasonable society, and even though we must think of it as realizable in real time, recognizing the insights of Kant *et al.*, and wanting to leave a space open for future political thinking, we are cut off from knowing the details of that end.

iii   *The Eclipse of Enlightenment*
Even granting classical Critical Theory all the charity and credit it deserves for such an ambitious project, it is clear that there are tensions that not only have to be confronted, but also dealt with. I see no problem in retaining the basic critique of political economy and the ideology critique, even though

---

58   Hegel, *Phänomenologie des Geistes*, p. 140 (TWA 3, 145).

both have been widely criticized. As Joseph Heath mentions, there are those who perceive the very idea of ideology as insulting the intelligence of the supposed holders of ideological and thus false beliefs, typically the "working class, women, or the subaltern".[59] Against the perceived "paternalistic tone",[60] one can argue that, in many cases, people can have good reasons to "participate in maintaining and reproducing institutions under which they are oppressed or exploited".[61] Instead of attributing the participation to some set of false beliefs about "their 'real' interests",[62] Heath calls attention to the classical dichotomy between "*our* interest" and "*my* interests",[63] i.e. the "free-rider incentive"[64] that may tell me to let the others assume the burden of culture and civilisation. As he rightly emphasizes, in real life there is real competition, and this may imply that people reproduce practices that are not in their long-term interest to sustain. Due to their upbringing in capitalist class society, they may adapt to rules not in their interest, not being able to imagine the better possibilities, or they may have good reasons to fear the alternative: "having a bad set of rules is often better than having no rules".[65] As Heath mentions, people may also have very good reasons not to engage in revolutions, such endeavours being surely "risky business",[66] personally as well as politically.

Still, being suspicious about revolutions does not mean that politics as a collective enterprise makes no sense. Popular solidarity can still have an effect in relation to capitalism, namely to backup and legitimize state regulation of the dynamics of economy. That was the way various kinds of social democrats and social liberals built up the welfare states in the 20th century. Recognizing that the oppressed or exploited in fact have real collective interest in a capitalist class society, and that they may best protect these interest through a collective effort, it is worth proposing remedies for the selfish and destructive free-rider attitude. The classical means in such a project is raising consciousness individually and collectively, i.e. character building through education and organization, in families, schools, unions and associations. It may be that some are offended by being told they have been fooled and deceived by their superiors,

---

59   Joseph Heath, "Problems in the Theory of Ideology" (2001), in *Critical Theory*, ed. Rasmussen and Swindal, vol. 4, p. 64.

60   Heath, ibid., p. 73.

61   Ibid., p. 63.

62   Ibid., p. 80.

63   Ibid., p. 69.

64   Ibid., p. 78.

65   Ibid., p. 76.

66   Ibid., p. 70.

or that they should not themselves fool or deceive, but others are happy to learn in order to avoid being victim to excessive individualism.[67]

I also would like to defend the necessity of employing ideal concepts, the comprehensive concept on truth, and the idea of experiential knowledge and truth based on the determinate negation, i.e. the idea forwarded by Darrow Schecter as only knowing capitalist society completely "while fundamentally changing it".[68] However, in hindsight, the optimism regarding the possibilities of realizing a just society in some relatively near historical future was clearly founded on shaky grounds. As Habermas has argued, the historical materialist dialectics between forces and relations of production "transformed itself into pseudo-normative statements about an objective teleology of history"[69] and such a scheme of thought is clearly not tenable.

Still, being a real materialist and precisely not subjugated to any preconceived idealist schemes of historical progression, one has to leave open the possibility of the realization of a just society. Humanity does, in fact, have not only the potential, but also the inclination to be both compassionate and reasonable. It is a remarkable fact that human reason and morality have survived all kinds of calamities throughout history; thus, the rumours of them having passed away are greatly exaggerated. Therefore, I do not think it unrealistic to leave Critical Theory where Horkheimer left it in 1937, i.e. before the outbreak of ww ii and the discovery of Auschwitz *et al.*, only skipping the belief stemming from Marxist orthodoxy that justice can somehow be predicted or expected to be realized in some nearby future. Such a stance would bring back Critical Theory from the totalizing critique of civilization to the political critique of capitalism. Still, the ideals as well as the critique may be considered radical, but it is only by retaining the ideal idea that we can hope to bring about at least some improvement; giving up on ideals and believing only a worst-case-scenario may very well prove to become a self-fulfilling prophecy.

Thus, relieved as Critical Theorists of the burden of having to prove that the ideal future can be realized imminently, let us turn to how Horkheimer and Adorno thought of the *Dialectic of Enlightenment*. It is common to consider it as a displacement towards a pessimist philosophy of history and a radical critique of civilization. The dialectics of enlightenment thus signify

---

67   These are themes I will discuss in DDD III, *Justice, Peace and Formation.*

68   Darrow Schecter, *The Critique of Instrumental Reaon from Weber to Habermas* (New York and London: Continuum, 2010), p. 84.

69   Jürgen Habermas, *Theorie des kommunikativen Handelns* (1981) (Frankfurt a.M.: Suhrkamp, 1988), vol. 2, p. 561. In the present chapter, the following page references are indicated in brackets in the text as TKH 2 (or 1), nn.

a logic in the historical development from myth to enlightenment, claiming that enlightenment will, by necessity, eventually pass over or return to myth.[70] According to Horkheimer and Adorno, human beings have always had to choose between submitting to nature or subjugating it (see DA, 49). It is the distance between subjugator and subjugated that creates the possibility of a relation between subject and object (see DA, 25–29). Behind the scientific relation to nature, we find a practical relation that is determined by an implacable fight. Science is, just as technology and labour, merely a way that we as human beings subjugate nature with our consciousness.

The point of departure for Horkheimer's *Eclipse of Reason*, also from 1947, is that reason, following Hegel, can be considered objectively present in reality. This objective reason corresponds to a subjective reason, and for Horkheimer it is obvious that this subjective reason in the modern capitalist society becomes an instrumental reason.[71] Reason is instrumental when it restricts itself to choosing the best means available to achieve a selfish goal, and through calculus optimizing operationally the achievement. It is this type of reason that Weber categorizes as "goal-rationality",[72] i.e. purposive or means-end rationality. The point for Horkheimer and Adorno is that the subjectivity in reason is determined by valuing as higher one's own goals than apparently objectively given social necessities, for instance by cheating others. As they put it: "Cunning is nothing else than the subjective display of the objective falsity of the victim" (see DA, 69–70), i.e. of being victimized. As Gordon Finlayson stresses, what we see here is a "deep change" in the "assessment of rationality; the very rationality that they had hitherto assumed was the solution now became the origin of the problem that was to be addressed".[73]

According to Horkheimer and Adorno, the enlightened western societies develop science as well as technology and thus subjective reason, making possible an increased human mastery over nature, the effect of which is the liberation of human being from nature. The problem, however, is that human being is itself also nature. When domination means subjugating nature, it also implies the subjugation of human beings themselves. Thus, domination is also liberating, constituting the restraint necessary for the realization of autonomy. However, more importantly for Horkheimer and Adorno, domination also implies

70   See Max Horkheimer and Theodor W. Adorno, *Dialektik der Aufklärung* (1947), in GS_A 3, p. 25. In the present chapter, the following page references are indicated in brackets in the text as DA, nn.

71   See Max Horkheimer, *The Eclipse of Reason* (New York: Oxford University Press, 1947), p. 6.

72   Max Weber, *Wirtschaft und Gesellschaft* (1921–22) (Tübingen: Mohr Siebeck, 1972), § 2.

73   Finlayson, "Political, Moral, and Critical Theory", p. 648.

not being able to regard other people on equal terms as reasonable and independent individuals, but only as creatures that have to be submitted to force. Increased subjective enlightenment and, thus, increased subjective reason, i.e. instrumental rationality, mean that, no matter how good the intentions, due to the logic of enlightenment we will eventually have barbaric sociality and inhumanity.

The *Dialectic of Enlightenment* is a necessary dialectical logic that is developing behind the backs of the real reasonable beings of the world. Dialectics is no longer considered a methodological possibility for science, and nor is the determinate negation acknowledged as a principle of explanation in a liberating social science through the knowledge of society in its totality. On the contrary, the dialectical process carried through by the "determinate negation" is now considered as the "totality in system and history" that leads to "the absolute" and declines into "mythology"; even though Hegel escapes the "positivist decay", enlightenment becomes "totalitarian as only a system can be" (DA, 40–41). The only hope left lies in the paradox that the enlightenment, "in control of itself and coming to power, can break through the limitations of the enlightenment" (DA, 243).

Horkheimer and Adorno emphasize that "freedom in society is inseparable from enlightened thought" (DA, 13), but enlightenment carries the seeds of its own destruction, and without recognizing the retrograde and destructive aspects of Enlightenment, one cannot claim to know the truth of it. In the process, Horkheimer and Adorno thus dismissed the optimism inherent in Marx's historical materialism as well as his critique of political economy; they even tried to conceal that it had ever been there by systematically changing the vocabulary of the argument before publication, substituting 'capitalism' with 'the existing conditions', 'capital' with 'economic system', and 'capitalist extorter' with 'industrial tycoon' etc.[74]

This is, of course, only a superficial symptom of something more fundamental. As Moishe Postone demonstrates, at stake are some basic conceptual transformations that ultimately determine the idea of the historical transformation. Basic for Marxism is that the relationship between forces of production and relations of production are considered contradictory and that this conditions the possible historical transformation of capitalism to socialism. Thus, a principled conflict is assumed between the necessities of industrial technology and the essentials of capitalism, i.e. market and private property. It is this basic contradiction that Horkheimer still maintains in 1937, thus being

---

74 See Rolf Wiggerhaus, *Die Frankfurter Schule* (1986), 2nd ed. (München: Deutscher Taschenbuch Verlag, 1988), pp. 446–47, see also Kellner *Critical Theory, Marxism and Modernity*, pp. 110–11.

able to think that the historical transformation is still possible, although not probable at the time,[75] and that Critical Theory is meaningful in contributing to the consciousness about this contradiction, as it manifests itself in various cultural spheres, e.g., science.

The crucial move is Friedrich Pollock's argument for the possibility of 'state capitalism', i.e. a post-liberal capitalist order that apparently maintains private property and markets, thus is still antagonistic, but fundamentally leaves the distributional coordination to the state, thus balancing production and distribution.[76] Analysing the Nazi economy in Germany, Stalin's USSR and Roosevelt's New Deal in the USA, Pollock distinguishes between a totalitarian version and a democratic version. As Postone reconstructs the logic of the argument, in both cases the political sphere takes precedence over the economic sphere, and therefore there are no laws governing the economic development, neither within capitalism nor beyond capitalism, i.e. in history. With the "primacy of the political",[77] there are no longer contradictions between the forces and the relations of production, only societal antagonism, i.e. class conflicts, and therefore the basic dynamics of historical materialism is given up. Whereas the economic sphere contained a logic that could transgress capitalism, this is not the case in the political sphere. Instead, there are only different versions of a bureaucratic "command hierarchy operating on the basis of a one-sided technical rationality".[78]

What is worrying, according to Pollock, is that in state capitalism both private property and the market have given way to a rational planning suitable for industrial production, but that this has not led to emancipation.[79] As Postone argues, this becomes even worse, since the notion of labour becomes reduced to an activity essentially, i.e. beyond history, associated with instrumental rationality and, therefore, in no way "the locus of freedom".[80] Still, there is much worth criticizing in capitalism, but the critique can no longer become a determinate negation of a social order referring to inherent contradictions. What Pollock developed was an idea of capitalism that is still an antagonistic and repressive social totality, i.e. an exploitative class society, but essentially

---

75   See Moishe Postone, "Critique, State, and Economy", in *The Cambridge Companion to Critical Theory*, ed. Rush, p. 183.

76   See Postone, ibid., p. 173.

77   Ibid., p. 171.

78   Ibid., p. 167.

79   Ibid., p. 174. See also further below in the Postscript, sect. A.

80   Ibid., p. 181.

non-contradictory and therefore without "an immanent dynamic".[81] As Post-one concludes, what is left for Horkheimer is simply to insist on the indeterminacy in the principled difference between concept and reality,[82] thus retaining the trans-historical freedom to criticize modern civilization, but without any prospects of transformation.

Finally, as a sequel to this transformation of the philosophy of history and the displacement of the critique of capitalism into a critique of civilization, Horkheimer also sharpens the critique of positivism and, in particular, pragmatism. Hence, the latter is taken to claim that "our ideas are true, because our expectations are satisfied and our actions successful". Pragmatism is thus the ideology of a society where there is no time to "remember or reflect",[83] i.e. the American society. Its ideal is, like the rest of the industrialized society, "efficiency", and since it reduces reason to just an "instrument" and disregards "the speculative capacity of reason", pragmatism is simply "anti-philosophical".[84]

This is where many have seen the tragic end of classical Critical Theory and from which point Horkheimer did not write anything of importance anymore. Auschwitz demonstrates that the totalizing subjective instrumental reason has prevailed in relation to our fellow human beings, making us guilty of violating something very basic in ethics that Kant synthesized under the heading the Categorical Imperative, i.e. that one must never treat another human being as merely a means, always regarding her or him also as a goal.[85] This being the case, Stefan Gandler rightly calls attention to the curious lack of interest in discussing the role of anti-Semitism in the *Dialectic of Enlightenment*.[86]

Be that as it may, Wellmer speaks for many when he concludes that after the *Dialectic*, Critical Theory can only conceive of itself as an impotent protest against an "apocalyptic system" of "alienation and reification".[87] For Habermas, the philosophy of history sketched in the *Dialectic* implies a "catastrophic view" of the relationship between "mind and nature", juxtaposing "self-preservation" and "self-destruction" (TKH 1, 509–10). As Marcuse remarked, "the less a society is rationally organized and directed by the collective efforts of free men, the

---

81   Ibid., p. 190.

82   See ibid., p. 187.

83   Horkheimer, *The Eclipse of Reason*, pp. 43–44.

84   Horkheimer, *ibid.,* pp. 50–52.

85   See, e.g., Immanuel Kant, *Kritik der praktischen Vernunft* (1788), in Kant, *Werke in sechs Bänden*, vol. IV, p. A 156 (AA V, 87).

86   See Stefan Gandler, *Fragmentos de Frankfurt* (México: Siglo XXI, 2009), p. 114.

87   Albrecht Wellmer, *Kritische Gesellschaftstheorie und Positivismus* (Frankfurt a.M.: Suhrkamp, 1969), p. 54.

more it will appear as [...] governed by 'inexorable' laws".[88] Hence, despair and alienation facilitate objectification, and one could argue that this is what Horkheimer and Adorno fell victim to in their transformation of the idea of dialectics. As it is generally recognized, Adorno and Marcuse ultimately came to disagree sharply on the idea of Critical Theory and especially the role played by dialectics.[89]

D   Rethinking Critical Theory

It is a good hermeneutical principle to try understanding the work under scrutiny better than its creator. As Heath notes, one problem of ideology critique is that when the truth has been told, both about the false beliefs in fact held and the real interest that should be pursued, and nothing happens, then what? One answer may be that the critique was, after all, not radical enough, i.e. that it did not get to the roots, and was, therefore, not persuasive. This may foster "a vicious cycle of theoretical self-radicalization, in which critics respond to an increasing irrelevance of their theories by further radicalizing them", in the end making Critical Theory "increasingly baroque, increasingly obscure, and of course, increasingly unlikely to change anything".[90]

It may be argued that this is what happened with classical Critical Theory during its first decade. From a politically motivated Marxist critique of capitalism, it ended up as a totalizing critique of modernity and civilization. It adds to the tragedy of Horkheimer that he even toned down further his original allegiance to Marxism, replacing, for example, 'class domination' with 'social injustice', when his early essays were republished in the late 1960s.[91]

However, not being prone to despair and pessimism in the same way as the Schopenhauerian inventor of Critical Theory, I would like to maintain some of the original radical insights, thus insisting on the possibility of enlightenment, education and a consciousness suitable for furthering social democracy.[92] As I argue, I will retain most of the original conception of the Critical Theory of

---

88   Herbert Marcuse, *Reason and Revolution. Hegel and the Rise of Social Theory*, 3rd ed. (Boston: Beacon Press, 1960), p. 315; quoted from David Held, *Introduction to Critical Theory* (Berkeley and Los Angeles: University of California Press, 1980), p. 172.

89   See, e.g., Held, *Introduction to Critical Theory*, pp. 356–58; about some of the tensions between the founding fathers, see, e.g., Wiggerhaus, *Die Frankfurter Schule*, pp. 383, 439, 515–18.

90   Heath, "Problems in the Theory of Ideology", p. 81.

91   See Held, *Introduction to Critical Theory*, p. 440.

92   Reflections on such issues are collected in DDD III.

science, although, as many others, skipping the historical materialism that facilitates the belief that somehow we will all live to see the realization of the reasonable society, thus taking seriously the original claim that materialist dialectics is indeed, not just as David Held puts it "unconcluded",[93] but in principle inconclusive, both in regards to science and history.

Thus, when it comes to dialectics, it can be maintained as a method of thinking about reality that attempts to grasp reality in change and motion, as Gadamer puts it.[94] Employing the idea of the determinate negation, dialectics can continue to be considered a temporal principle of not just explanation and scientific knowledge, but also experience, critique and thus assessment of especially human and social reality. By means of dialectics, we can thus make a case for both social science and philosophy to aim for a dynamic accordance between concept and case as well as subject and object, i.e. for the progressive realization of a society with still less injustice and alienation. As Horkheimer puts it: "The process of knowledge involves real historical willing and acting as well as experiencing and conceiving. The latter cannot progress without the former".[95]

After WW II, however, the ambitions of classical Critical Theory were, I would claim,[96] primarily maintained by Marcuse, choosing eventually to stay in the USA and being widely recognized for remaining rather consistent philosophically in spite of the turbulences of life.[97] In Germany, however, what has now become the mainstream tradition of Critical Theory, i.e. the successors of Horkheimer and Adorno in Frankfurt at the Goethe University and the Institute for Social Research, took a different turn. Within Critical Theory, one can, therefore, discuss who are the legitimate heirs, and for a contemporary critical theorist in exile such as Gandler, the choice is in essence between the interior and the exterior, i.e. between those who were educated by the "(ex) Nazis", e.g., Habermas, Honneth and Helmut Dubiel, or "the exiled, the dead and the excluded".[98] Still, being a bit uncertain as to the latter, in the rest of this chapter I will mainly engage critically with the former, i.e. the German mainstream tradition of Critical Theory.

---

93   Held, *Introduction to Critical Theory*, p. 178.

94   See reference below, Ch. 4, Sect. A.

95   Horkheimer, "Zum Problem der Wahrheit", quoted in Held, *Introduction to Critical Theory*, p. 191.

96   See below, Ch. 7.

97   See, e.g., Held, *Introduction to Critical Theory*, p. 73.

98   Gandler, *Fragmentos de Frankfurt*, p. 116.

In the post-war reconstruction of Critical Theory, the first step, i.e. Adorno's and Habermas's revival in the 1960s, is largely congruent with the classical approach, at least until the latter took it upon himself to redefine Critical Theory through a communicative paradigm. The second step, i.e. Honneth's turn – some would say *return* – to social philosophy, is also problematic, or so I will argue in the next section. In the rest of the present section, I will let Adorno state the radical presuppositions for a Critical Theory of modern society; I will then sketch Habermas's critique of, first, positivism and, second, Marxism, all of which I still take to be basically valid as ways of grasping the issues dealt with. This leads up to the famous ideas of, first, *Knowledge and Human Interest* and, second, the *Theory of Communicative Action*, progressively arguing for the replacement of the allegedly monological philosophy of consciousness with an intersubjective approach.

i   *Critique of Positivist Theory of Science*
According to the *Dialectic* of Horkheimer and Adorno, social domination was at the heart of traditional science: "Even the deductive form of science reflects hierarchy and coercion. [...] To the individual, domination appears to be the universal, as reason is in reality" (DA, 38). As Adorno continues to emphasize in the 1960s, the Critical Theory of society originates from philosophy, and just as philosophy distrusts the phenomena, Critical Theory distrusts "the façade of society".[99] Thus, for Critical Theory it is still important to emphasize the difference between the traditional and the critical approach to social science, and therefore there is also good reason to continue the dispute with positivism.[100] According to Adorno, the basic societal reality is contradictory. The ideals of clarity and exactness promoted by positivism thus pose a threat to the possibility of acquiring knowledge about what is in fact the case.[101] When the subject matter to be experienced and known is complex, the demand of simplicity and regularity is not necessarily ideal.[102] According to Adorno, what is essential of society is hidden, but it nevertheless determines the facts, i.e. the law that history so far has followed. This essence, however, is an "un-essence", debasing and threatening the lives of human beings, but it is precisely when the

99   Theodor W. Adorno, "Soziologie und empirische Forschung" (1957), in GS$_A$ 8, p. 196.
100   See, e.g., Theodor W. Adorno *et al.*, *Der Positivismusstreit in der deutschen Soziologie* (Darmstadt: Luchterhand, 1969) and Hans-Joachim Dahms, *Positivismusstreit* (Frankfurt a.M.: Suhrkamp, 1994).
101   See Theodor W. Adorno, "Zur Logik der Sozialwissenschaften" (1962), in GS$_A$ 8, p. 548.
102   See Adorno, ibid., p. 553.

contradiction makes itself manifest that what is essential can be experienced and thus known.[103]

Insisting on the prospects beyond such a radical and critical understanding of modern society, in *Theory and Practice* from 1963 Habermas draws a line back to the classical enlightenment project of emancipation. The basic idea is that emancipation is made possible through the scientific knowledge of the mechanisms of compulsion forced upon us by reality, such as they are depicted, for instance, by Adorno. Hence, by employing scientific insights even as radical as these, one can argue for the possibility of a human practice based on reason.

What disturbs Habermas about the practice of the existing modern society is that the material basis of societal life has become a functionally entangled system of research, technology, production and administration that as a whole appears as overwhelming and completely "confused".[104] Thus, already decades ago, the point could be made that one can no longer separate technical and political questions; this situation has become even more acute with modern information technology, often making it impossible to judge whether facilities at public websites are due to the technological possibilities and limitations of computerized machines or the logic of what is considered just and fair according to law.

In the modern capitalist society, science tends to be reduced to merely forces of production, and as such it cannot be relied upon to provide reasons for answers to the most pertinent practical questions,[105] i.e. questions of ethics and politics. This development is reflected in the understanding of science expressed in 20th century theory of science, primarily in the positivist idea of objective knowledge. Habermas thus continues Horkheimer and Adorno's argument that theory of science, as well as social science, must focus on the embeddedness of science in the general structures of capitalist society, i.e. the forces and relations of production.

Worth mentioning is a difference noticed by Wellmer within the field that we call theory of science. On the one hand, we have the logical positivists who like Carnap are involved in reconstructing scientific language focusing on the meaningfulness of propositions; on the other hand, there is Popper's critical rationalism intending a logical-methodological reconstruction of the research

---

103   See Theodor W. Adorno, *Negative Dialektik* (1966), in GS$_A$ 6, p. 169.

104   Jürgen Habermas, *Theorie und Praxis* (1963/71), 2nd ed. (Frankfurt a.M.: Suhrkamp, 1974), p. 309.

105   Habermas, *ibid.,* p. 308.

process *per se*.[106] Hence, where the logical positivists use semantics to issue methodological recommendations on how to acquire knowledge, critical rationalism formulates requirements to knowledge and logics that determine science as the practice of critical examination of the results of a contingent process of inquiry. For Critical Theory, however, both are basically expressions of positivism because they only relate to what is present, i.e. the positively given phenomena. Logical positivism and critical rationalism are both the result of the split in the theory of knowledge developed in what Horkheimer called bourgeois philosophy, i.e. Descartes, Hume *et al*. Thus, positivism is characterized by not letting science discuss the relationship between representation and substance, or concept and object, as suggested by the dialectical methodology of Hegel, Marx *et al*.

Hence, traditional theory of science is positivist, but according to Habermas it is at the same time objectivist. Experience and knowledge are processes that have both a subjective aspect and an objective aspect, but logical positivists as well as critical rationalists demonstrate a notorious aversion to reflecting positively on the subjective conditions for knowledge. Hence, Popper is said to stress only that scientific theories must correspond with independent facts,[107] but such an objectivism breaks with the classical theory of knowledge where human consciousness is recognized as a constituent element of knowledge.

Habermas traces this objectivist break with theory of knowledge back to Ernst Mach, who was a crucial inspiration for the logical positivists. For Mach, there are only facts that are immediately given and objective. Such facts are considered "elements" that are constituent building blocks for both "the corporal world and the hypostasized sensations of consciousness". The object of science is thought of as "facts structured by laws",[108] and Habermas thus considers Mach's objectivist positivism a fully developed "ontology of facts" (EI, 109).

Popper's acceptance of such a positivist objectivism means that he ignores crucial preconditions of scientific propositions and theories, i.e. the linguistic, cultural and societal aspects of science, just as he fails to demonstrate any consciousness of the possibility of using theoretical information technologically.[109] However, as has been stressed several times, science is a force

---

106   See Wellmer, *Kritische Gesellschaftstheorie und Positivismus*, p. 16.

107   See, e.g., Jürgen Habermas, *Zur Logik der Sozialwissenschaften* (Frankfurt a.M: Suhrkamp, 1970), p. 45.

108   Jürgen Habermas, *Erkenntnis und Interesse* (1968/73), 2nd ed. (Frankfurt a.M.: Suhrkamp, 1977), p. 91. In the present chapter, the following page references are indicated in brackets in the text as EI, nn.

109   See Habermas, *Zur Logik der Sozialwissenschaften*, p. 51.

of production, and as practice it therefore has a specific inherent knowledge interest, namely the technical domination of its object. Habermas recognizes that positivism, in spite of its objectivism, can provide a critique of ideology in relation to metaphysics of value and phenomenological ontology, but it remains a critique that is "reduced",[110] instrumental, and thus ultimately open to interpretation in terms of technique and machinery.

Even worse, however, is the fact that Popper ends up defending a kind of decisionism, detaching decisions from any kind of rationality. His criticism of metaphysical dogmatism thus implies a choice for which he does not think there can be given reasons, namely the choice between "knowledge and faith".[111] This he considers ultimately an irrational choice, but for Habermas this is not acceptable for a theory of science that claims to provide the foundation for a critically rational scientific theory and practice.

For Critical Theory, the fundamental irrationality of critical rationalism is the consequence of the progressive instrumentalization of reason in modern capitalist society. Still, Habermas insists on thinking theory in continuation of the classical enlightenment project. It must be possible to carry through theory by the inherent interest of reason in genuine authority, autonomy of action, and emancipation from dogmatism,[112] but since contemporary societal reality only does little to promote theory in this sense, at present there is no alternative to Critical Theory. According to Habermas, the goal for Critical Theory must be to think of the will as enlightened, thus saving interests from becoming merely subjective and securing decisions from pure arbitrariness and contingency.[113] Thinking through the relationship between knowledge and interest thus becomes crucial for Habermas's understanding of Critical Theory.

ii   *Knowledge and Interest*

In his inaugural lecture in 1965, "Knowledge and Interest" (i.e. human interest), Habermas emphasizes how Husserl's phenomenology can be regarded as a critique of the objectivism just sketched. Husserl's analysis of consciousness makes it clear that the objects have their origin in our pre-scientific lifeworld, and that it is the subject that gives the object its meaning. Still, Habermas argues that Husserl also falls into objectivism, although of a different sort,

---

110   Habermas, *Theorie und Praxis*, pp. 318–20.
111   Habermas, *ibid.*, p. 328.
112   See *ibid.*, p. 310.
113   See *ibid.*, pp. 315–16.

since his concept of theory remains traditional,[114] such as was also argued by Horkheimer.

Continuing the restoration of Critical Theory in the book *Knowledge and Human Interest* from 1968, Habermas revisits the fundamental preconditions of the original project, i.e. Hegel's critique of Kant's theory of knowledge and Marx's critique of Hegel's idealism. According to Habermas, an objectivist typically assumes that a subject goes out in the world and meets things that objectively are out there, just waiting to be known. In contrast to this model, through Hegel we get the idea of knowledge as an objective result of a real gain of consciousness of an object, where work plays a crucial role. Hence, the subject processes the matter at hand according to an idea that the subject can recognize in the resulting object as its own.[115] Further, Hegel makes it clear that work is not just crucial for the consciousness and knowledge of an object; it is also a fundamental condition for the formation of the self-consciousness of the subject. The realization, and thus the knowledge, of the importance of work makes the subject conscious of her or his own potential as a human being.

Continuing this line of thought, the young Marx makes production the fundamental human activity, since a human being can be said to produce itself, its family, its surroundings, and its consciousness.[116] Following Horkheimer, Habermas thus argues that Marx provides us with all the premises to radicalize Hegel's critique of the theory of knowledge in a materialist direction (see EI, 43). Still, he criticizes Marx for totalizing work and production as the essential human practice, claiming that Marx interpreted Hegel's idea of work too instrumentally, thus being led to reduce reflection to be understood as merely a kind of instrumental action. As Habermas argues, Marx does not distinguish the logical status of science from that of critique, and therefore Marx simply "understands the concept of reflection according to the pattern of production" (EI, 59–61).

Habermas recognizes that Marx in some instances indicates awareness of the crucial distinction between work and interaction (see EI, 71). In spite of the attempt to subsume by definition the totality of societal practice under the concept of production, Marx ultimately recognizes that the coherence in the relation between production and distribution, as well as institutionalized relations of power, rest on an "interaction mediated by symbols" (EI, 75).

---

114   See Jürgen Habermas, "Erkenntnis und Interesse" (1965), in Habermas, *Technologie und Wissenschaft als >Ideologie<* (Frankfurt a.M: Suhrkamp, 1969), pp. 151–53.

115   See Hegel, *Phänomenologie des Geistes*, ed. Hoffmeister, p. 149 (TWA 3, 153–54). Below, in Ch. 6, I discuss the implications of Hegel's concept of work for education and formation.

116   See Marx and Engels, *Die deutsche Ideologie*, in MEW 3, pp. 21–23.

Even though Marx thus provides the possibility to distinguish between tech-nical "knowledge of production" and practical "knowledge of reflection", Habermas still thinks that these distinctions are much better developed in the theological writings of the young Hegel where they are constitutive for a "dia-lectics of morality" (EI, 77). It is this analysis that leads Habermas to distinguish between "instrumental action" and "communicative action". Instrumental action is the answer to the external pressure of nature, thus determining the control exercised by the forces of production over nature. In contrast, communicative action is the answer to the suppression of one's own inner nature. While the liberation from the external powers of nature happens through the creation of useful technological knowledge, the emancipation from inner compulsion can only succeed to the extent that the interaction of society is organized as a "communication free of dominance" (EI, 71–72).

Habermas emphasizes that knowledge is both an instrument for survival and a transgression of this instrumentality.[117] Thus, as it is well-known, be-side the knowledge guiding interest of the empirical-analytical sciences, i.e. technological control, according to Habermas, there is also a practical knowl-edge guiding interest, namely understanding that constitutes the historic-hermeneutical sciences, i.e. arts and humanities. Of importance for Critical Theory is the idea of a third such interest, namely the interest in liberation or "the emancipatory knowledge interest",[118] being inherent and thus constitutive for the social sciences as well as for philosophy. It is these material interests that make the various forms of scientific activity meaningful as conscious hu-man practices, apparently discarding as ideology the traditional truth claims of science. Still, so far I think Habermas remains within the framework of clas-sical Critical Theory, conducting ideology critique of positivism and develop-ing the critique of political economy with an insistence on the importance of collective interaction besides production. However, by his own account, this is not the case in the next stage of the restoration project.

iii   *The Communicative Paradigm*
Habermas's work from 1981, *The Theory of Communicative Action*, is a milestone in Critical Theory, both continuing and breaking with these discussions related to theory of science. Habermas insists that the idea of communicative action is a critical standard for societal theory (see TKH 1, 7), and that implies that so-cietal theory must be thought of in a different way. Hence, as is well-known, he argues for the necessity of leaving behind the premises connected to subject

---

117   See Habermas, "Erkenntnis und Interesse", p. 162.
118   Habermas, ibid., p. 155.

philosophy or philosophy of consciousness that so far, he claims, had been the foundation on which Critical Theory was built, such as it was demonstrated by Horkheimer's account of the dialectical progression towards true knowledge. Instead, Critical Theory is now supposed to depart from a paradigm of communication theory: decisive for a normative position is neither knowledge in the traditional sense (as known from Kant, Carnap, Popper etc.), nor the formation of consciousness through experience (Hegel, Marx, Horkheimer etc.), i.e. neither constitution nor transformation. What is crucial is rational argumentation and emphatic "mutual understanding", i.e. the reciprocal understanding that can occur in communication free of dominance under ideal circumstances. Habermas thus displaces the basic presupposition from a subject-object-relation to an ideal subject-subject-relation.

The "paradigm shift to a communication theory" (TKH 1, 518) has two steps. For the first, Habermas can draw on an implicit normativity inherent in classical Critical Theory, interpreting Adorno's idea of "reconciliation" as "undistorted intersubjectivity" that implies an "understanding inherent in the reciprocal and free recognition" (TKH 1, 523). The second step is the "linguistic turn" of the "subject philosophy" that leads to a more comprehensive "communication theoretical turn", and this is what marks the real "*caesura*" (TKH 1, 531–32), i.e. the paradigm shift. To explain his motivation in everyday terms, Habermas relates his experiences associating with other people. This has given him reason to hope that "successful interaction" can be the foundation for an "undamaged intersubjectivity". Such civility, or "friendliness", as he calls it, does not exclude conflicts, but it may transform them, providing them with "humane forms".[119] The *Theory of Communicative Action* is thus to provide Critical Theory with a "normative foundation" beyond the "untenable [...] philosophy of history" (TKH 1, 583).

The ideal of interaction through communicative action occasions analyses of the basic logic in different types of rational discourse. Discourses are rational when it is possible to argue and thus provide reasons for taking a particular stand; this is the case not only within the fields of technical instrumentality and ethical practicality, but also in aesthetical critique, psychotherapy, and artistic utterance. They are all "symbolic utterances" connected to "validity criteria" (TKH 1, 44), i.e. demands the validity of which can be claimed as universal norms. Most fundamental for a successful discourse is that it is understandable; beyond this, however, one can distinguish between theoretical discourses that demand truth and applicability (as in science), practical discourses that

---

119   Habermas in Horst Holzer, *Kommunikation oder gesellschaftliche Arbeit? Zur Theorie des kommunikativen Handelns von Jürgen Habermas* (Berlin: Akademie Verlag, 1987), p. 15.

demand normative righteousness (as in ethics, and, one can add, politics and pedagogics), and finally therapeutic discourses that demand subjective sincerity or earnestness. In all three cases, the idea is that a specific type of rational discourse claims validity by being related to universal normative requirements specific for that particular type of discourse.

Hence, Habermas no longer determines Critical Theory as a programme for social science stressing materialist dialectics or an emancipatory knowledge guiding interest. Instead, he proposes a framework that is still explicitly normative, but where validity is now dependent on clear discursive reasoning rather than the attainment of consciousness. Hence, the *Theory of Communicative Action* provides an "ahistorical" reconstruction of the "reasonable content of anthropologically deeply embedded structures" of "action and understanding" that can be detected in the "intuitive knowledge of competent members of modern societies" (TKH 1, 561–62).

Habermas's experience of successfully associating with other people can thus be translated into a substantial idea of the "lifeworld" beyond what was proposed by Husserl. Husserl originally understood the lifeworld according to his philosophy of consciousness, namely as the pre-scientific epistemological condition for the construction of the meaningful objects of scientific knowledge.[120] Instead, Habermas employs the interpretation provided by the sociologist Alfred Schütz, understanding the lifeworld as the totality of what defines "mutual understanding" (TKH 2, 192). What is now considered crucial for Critical Theory is the idea of a pre-scientific lifeworld where people as speakers and listeners can become understandable for each other when communicating about matters, whether they originate in the objective, social, or subjective world. Hence, the lifeworld is the instance of interacting through communication mediated by symbols, all the time being orientated towards emphatic mutual understanding and relating to the relevant validity criteria.

As a contrast, Habermas develops the idea of the "system" that includes the economy and the bureaucracy, i.e. capitalism and the state. The system is characterized by functioning by means of the steering media of money and power, thus being determined by instrumental and strategic action. For Habermas, an action is strategic when it is orientated instrumentally towards egoistical results, and further in its calculation exploits the rationality of other actors involved in the process (see TKH 1, 385). Habermas stresses, however, that both lifeworld and system are necessary for a modern society.

---

120   See, e.g., Edmund Husserl, *Die Krisis der europäischen Wissenschaften und die transzendentale Phänomenologie* (1935–36), in Husserl, *Husserliana*, vol. VI (Haag: Martinus Nijhof, 1962), pp. 48–49.

While the lifeworld provides the framework for cultural reproduction, the system is where the material reproduction of society takes place, and Habermas recognizes the latter as "a kind of sociality without norms" (TKH 2, 455).

The lifeworld is the condition of a communication free of domination, i.e. a human interaction not distorted by the system. According to Habermas, Critical Theory must criticize the "colonialization of the lifeworld by the system" (TKH 2, 522), as he famously phrases it, since it damages human interaction. The normative foundation for this critical project is to be worked through in a "communicative ethics" (TKH 2, 147), i.e. what later became known as "discourse ethics"; the basic idea being that ethical values can only claim universal validity as moral norms, if they can be made acceptable for all possible participants of a practical discourse.[121]

This strong condition for moral righteousness makes it possible for Habermas to hold on to the claim that the demand is "analogue to truth".[122] Both theoretical and practical discourses are said to have cognitive content, the only difference being the relation to the world. Whereas for the theoretical discourse employing the criterion of truth must acknowledge a reference exterior to itself, i.e. the objective world, this is not the case for the practical discourse relating to the moral validity claim.[123] On the other hand, the practical discourse is the place for "opinion and will formation",[124] and in his recent discussion of the relation between theory and practice, Habermas brings back into prominence the Aristotelian idea of practical philosophy, i.e. philosophy preoccupied with questions concerning the "wise conduct of life",[125] in particular ethics and political philosophy.

Ultimately, Habermas thus reaffirms the epistemological outset of Critical Theory, i.e. that science must commit itself to the truth and that this implies being engaged in realizing the true society, adopting reasonable principles, and securing justice. Even though he denies that the practical philosophy of Aristotle can claim validity under "modern conditions for post-metaphysical thinking",[126] it is nevertheless as practical philosophy that Critical Theory has developed recently under his guidance, namely as political philosophy and philosophy of law.

---

121   See, e.g., Jürgen Habermas, *Moralbewußtsein und kommunikatives Handeln* (Frankfurt a.M.: Suhrkamp, 1983), p. 103. For further discussions of discourse ethics, see DDD II.

122   Habermas, *Wahrheit und Rechtfertigung*, p. 103.

123   See *ibid.*, p. 296.

124   *Ibid.*, p. 314.

125   *Ibid.*, p. 320.

126   *Ibid.*, p. 321.

iv   *Making a Case for Classical Critical Theory*

While I appreciate much of the work Habermas has done in political philosophy,[127] I do not find his argument for a paradigm shift persuasive. In fact, I find it detrimental to the whole idea of Critical Theory that I am trying to defend here. However, if what we are dealing with is indeed a paradigm shift, this kind of criticism should not cause any concern on the side of Habermas, since the idea of a paradigm shift implies that we then face each other from incommensurable positions, which by definition cannot be bridged by any argument. My hunch, however, is that this is not the case. Still, Habermas' use of such an expression signals the acceptance of positivist premises that should have been left in the past. I will, therefore, not treat this change as paradigmatic; from the perspective of Critical Theory, in this case I think Habermas is simply wrong, and I will therefore leave out this allegedly fundamental part of his program.

First of all, I do not see why the correct insistence of communicative interaction and reflection as a supplement to human work has to lead to an almost hostile takeover of the latter by an alleged paradigm shift totalizing the former. By Habermas's own account, he was originally inspired to this move by the theological writings of the young Hegel, i.e. a philosopher of consciousness if ever there was one. In particular, I do not see why the two approaches, i.e. that of communication and that of work, cannot supplement each other, together accounting for a necessary though not sufficient sequence in the progression towards the reasonable society that is on the top of the agenda for most versions of Critical Theory.

Moreover, if we take seriously that the lifeworld is a constituent part of the real social world, I find it unconvincing that communicative action should play such a crucial role in achieving the desired consensus free of dominance without there being secured beforehand some substantial gain of consciousness, i.e. some degree of civilization and civility, and the latter has so far brilliantly been provided by social and political movements based on the critique of capitalism and of the ideology sustaining it, i.e. trade unions, social democracies and various left-wing grass-root organizations. The prospects of communicative action to have by itself such substantial progressive effects are even more unlikely, since Habermas accepts the system as necessary for the material reproduction of modern society.

---

127   See, e.g., Asger Sørensen, "From Critique of Ideology to Politics. Habermas on Bildung", *Ethics and Education* 10, no. 2 (2015), pp. 252–70, and "Cosmopolitan Democracy and the State. Reflections on the Need for Ideals and Imagination", *Journal of Constitutionalism & Human Rights* 3–4, no. 8 (2015), pp. 8–19. Both texts will be included in DDD III.

All this must, of course, be the object of further inquiry and discussion, and in fact this has already been the case.[128] However, let me add that just as Held, I find it strange to insist so strongly on the distinction between production and interaction.[129] The result is that the distinction between communicative and instrumental action becomes too definitive, restrictive, and reductive. It seems to me an overreaction that may have its roots in the absolutized opposition between human being and nature from the *Dialectic of Enlightenment*. There is no reason why we could not think of the human relation to nature in non-instrumental terms, but this is simply denied and ridiculed by Habermas, for instance in his critique of Marcuse.[130] However, as Held rightly remarks, "[w]hy should an attitude to our own body or to aspects of the external environment which is, for example, contemplative or playful, have no cognitive status?"[131] Thus, I suspect that Habermas overreacts due to traumas inherited from Horkheimer and Adorno.

Hence, by making the distinction so absolute and identifying work simply with labour, Habermas arrives at the same point as Horkheimer; namely, ultimately reducing work to mere instrumental action. Thereby, Habermas loses sight of the comprehensive Hegelian idea of work that propels the Marxist critique of both the alienation of the workers under capitalism and the exploitation of the surplus value they provide, just as it is this idea of work that for Marx carries through the idea of free creativity to the realm of freedom beyond the realm of necessity. This means that the links from Critical Theory to the critique of capitalism and political economy are seriously weakened. By his own account, Habermas "never felt at home"[132] in political economy, and in the *Theory of Communicative Action* he even reaches the point of foreswearing critical evaluation and normative judgements of "totalities, forms of life and culture [...] as a whole" (TKH 2, 562),[133] thus calling into question general critique such as that of political economy and capitalist modernity.

---

128   See, e.g., Arne Johan Vetlesen, *Menneskeverd og ondskap. Essays og artikler 1991–2002* (Oslo: Gyldendal Norsk Forlag, 2003), waging this critique, forcefully and in a comprehensive way. Or, see my review: Asger Sørensen, "Book review: Arne Johan Vetlesen: Menneskeverd og ondskap", *Sats* 5, no. 2 (2004), pp. 141–47, which has been translated into English to be included in Part Two of DDD II.

129   See Held, *Introduction to Critical Theory*, pp. 390–92.

130   See below Ch. 7, Sect. D.

131   Held, *Introduction to Critical Theory*, p. 393.

132   Habermas in Matthew G. Specter, *Habermas: an Intellectual Biography* (Cambridge: Cambridge University Press 2010), p. 209.

133   See also Finlayson, "Political, Moral, and Critical Theory", p. 670.

Finally, lumping together capitalist economy and the state under the heading 'the system' is simply too typical of that particular epoch, i.e. the 1960s and 70s. Moreover, Habermas thereby accepts the negative concept of the state as simply the locus of power that is often an integral part of both Marxist and liberal ideology, thus legitimizing dismantling the political states that throughout the 20th century were able to counter capitalism. Habermas corrects this mistake later in his political philosophy, i.e. in *Between Facts and Norms,* where he endorses a republican account of the state in tune with a modern understanding of political rights and democracy;[134] so why not question the fundamental idea of a paradigm shift that was partly responsible for this mistake? Even Habermas can fall victim to *Zeitgeist* and ideology!

E   Critical Theory as Social Philosophy

This brings me finally to discuss Honneth's idea of Critical Theory that deconstructs Critical Theory as theory of knowledge and science, instead identifying strongly with a particular idea of social philosophy. Whereas Habermas was raised intellectually as Adorno's assistant, Honneth came to Critical Theory from the outside, attempting like many of us in the 1980s a critical appropriation of classical Critical Theory from the available texts. His *Critique of Power* thus exemplifies very well what was then considered the canonical sequence in the Critical Theory reading list, i.e. pre-war Horkheimer, *Dialectic of Enlightenment,* and post-war Adorno.

For Honneth this initially, i.e. in his 1983 dissertation, leads to an extensive analysis of Foucault's social philosophy and, in particular, his theory of power, emphasizing how much Foucault has in common with the authors of *Dialectic,*[135] which I recognize as a typical move in this period; however, I will not discuss that aspect in this context. The point here is that only in the second round, i.e. in 1986, is Habermas finally brought in as the "best chance" (KM, 224). Where Habermas thus allowed himself to be preoccupied by some of the same problems as discussed in classical Critical Theory, i.e. the discussion of theory of knowledge and science reconstructed in the previous sections, Honneth relates philosophically to the very idea of Critical Theory, just

---

134   See, e.g., Axel Honneth, "Critical Theory in Germany today" (1996), in *Critical Theory,* ed. Rasmussen and Swindal, vol. 4, p. 14.

135   See Axel Honneth, *Kritik der Macht* (1986), 2nd ed. (Frankfurt a.M.: Suhrkamp, 1989), pp. 19–21. In the present chapter, the following page references are indicated in brackets in the text as KM, nn.

as I have done in the present analysis, only that we differ when it comes to the conclusions.

Feeling thus somehow on level, at least in generational terms, I will therefore discuss and criticize some of the steps in Honneth's appropriation in order to retain Critical Theory in a more classical form. The point of departure is Honneth's analysis of the classics, but most space is given to his analysis of Habermas, where I will criticize Honneth's initial displacement of the epistemological critique of the positivist theory of science as being already social philosophy. In the last round, I will criticize Honneth's recent attempts to reduce Critical Theory *per se* to social philosophy, as if Critical Theory was only about the social critique encountered in philosophy, and not at the same time a critique in both the political and the scientific sense. Completing my own reappropriation in this way, I hope to save the fundamental equivocality of critique inherent in classical Critical Theory, claiming the validity of critical social research according to both political and scientific standards, i.e. to both Marx and Kant, as well as to Hegel.

i   *From Theory of Science to Cultural Critique*

In the analysis of Horkheimer's original idea of Critical Theory, Honneth calls attention to the acceptance of the basic Marxist philosophy of history as the material dialectics between forces and relations of production. His point is that Horkheimer in fact recognizes the significance of theoretical critique and social struggle, and therefore the actual concept of practice employed must be more comprehensive than what is offered by historical materialism (see KM, 23). According to Honneth, Horkheimer is not aware of these implications, and therefore he maintains a reductionist understanding of history in terms of societal domination of nature, as it becomes manifest in the material production necessary to sustain society. This social understanding of human practice is on the individual level supplemented with the understanding of needs and drives provided by psychoanalysis, making socialization also a question of dominating nature. However, for Honneth, this narrow understanding of human action implies a sociological deficit in the interdisciplinary Critical Theory of society (see KM, 26). Referring to Weber, Honneth affirms that sociology is about describing social action, but with Horkheimer's very limited understanding of social practice sociology can at most become an "auxiliary discipline" (KM, 40). This weakens the project of Critical Theory as combining "particular scientific" investigation into the capitalist society with "philosophical diagnosis of the times" (KM, 27).

For Honneth, it is precisely in the perspective of such a philosophy of history that *Dialectic of Enlightenment* marks a radical inversion. Where Critical

Theory, following Hegel and Marx, was originally able to regard history as moving forward in the direction of enlightenment, reason, and justice, history is now conceived of as a process ultimately realizing "the total domination" (KM, 48), expressing the "experience in philosophy of history" of a "reverse history of the species" (KM, 49); Honneth remarks that this history of "civilizational decline" to a "remarkable extent is in agreement with" (KM, 54) the conservative cultural criticism of those days, including that of Heidegger. The continuous progress in societal domination of nature is just considered the "cover page of a parallel process of decline", making human beings ever-more "alienated" in "relation to their nature" (KM, 60).

The technical-instrumental relation to nature is assumed to prevail socially in the domination of the suppressed classes (see KM, 66), and the analogy between domination of nature and social domination does not leave much room for "a domination supported by consensus" (KM, 67), such as it is conceived of in democracy. Thus, in other words, Honneth agrees with Habermas's basic intuition, i.e. that what is missing in classical Critical Theory is the possibility to conceptualize interaction, and, as it is well-known, Honneth also in his work on communication directs his attention to the writings of the young Hegel; hence, as the "early Habermas", he directs his attention to the "early Hegel" and the "early Horkheimer".[136] Doing this, Honneth can be said to accept the first step of Habermas's communicative turn, criticizing subject philosophy and emphasizing the idea of an undistorted intersubjectivity; the second step, i.e. the paradigm shift implied in criticizing philosophy of consciousness and endorsing the linguistic turn, he ignores. In relation to Habermas's final *Theory of Communicative Action*, Honneth can thus be said to expand the idea of communication beyond verbal argument, and through his habilitation thesis this eventually, in 1992, became the *Struggle for Recognition*.[137]

ii   *From Epistemological Anthropology to Social Philosophy*

On the basis of this analysis, Honneth is very accommodating towards Habermas's basic idea of rethinking Critical Theory in terms of both production and interaction, and it is in discussion with Habermas that he develops his own approach to Critical Theory. Honneth thus offers a "historically orientated inquiry"[138] into how Habermas's idea of knowledge guiding interests leads to the formulation of a Critical Theory of society that does not depend on a problematic philosophy of history.

---

136   Honneth, "Critical Theory in Germany today", p. 12.

137   See Axel Honneth, *Kampf um Anerkennung* (1992) (Frankfurt a.M.: Suhrkamp, 1994).

138   Axel Honneth, "Nachwort" (1988), in KM, p. 380.

According to Honneth, Habermas follows Horkheimer in regarding scientific knowledge as necessarily tied to "pre-scientific situations of interest" (KM, 230), and such situations are determined by what Honneth chose to call "the world orientations of human beings in practical life" (KM, 232). Habermas is thus quoted to claim that "the interest in sustaining life through societal work confronted with the force of natural circumstances" for the "human species" has been "constant".[139] For Honneth, this means that the human being "is universally submitted to a technical world orientation" (KM, 238), and with this turn from epistemological "transcendentalism" to philosophical anthropology Habermas is thus lead to the idea of an inherent "technical knowledge interest" (KM, 239) in the sciences.

Honneth calls attention to the fact that the critique of positivism is neither a critique of science as such nor of the positivist interpretation of it. Critical Theory merely argues that scientific practice must imply the possibility to relate to reality not just in technological terms, but also "beside that" (KM, 240) in terms of critique. Habermas's acceptance of Popper's critical rationalism makes Honneth accuse the former of "methodological dogmatism" (KM, 241). For Honneth, the significance of Popper's post-empiricist theory of science is that it recognizes the communicative research community as of constitutive importance for scientific knowledge (see KM, 235), enabling Habermas already in his theory of science to recognize "another kind of human action" (KM, 244). To this is added the inspiration from the hermeneutics of Gadamer, making it possible for Habermas to think of interaction as determined mainly through the linguistic communication used by individuals, assuring themselves and each other of being part of "a community of action orientation and ideas of value". This is what enables us to manage "the collective task of material reproduction" (KM, 245).

Honneth considers philosophical anthropology a "very fruitful and helpful tradition",[140] and it probably influences his interpretation of Habermas. For the latter, human being thus sustains existence through both production and interaction. Besides the natural sciences, Habermas stresses the importance of the sciences that investigate the meaningful reality, i.e. cultural and social sciences, arts and humanities. Hence, the "empirical-analytical sciences" are embedded in a "practical understanding of the word" characterized by the "compulsion to process nature in an instrumentally rational way", whereas the "hermeneutical sciences are embedded in a practical understanding of the world, in which human beings are subject to the constant compulsion

139   Habermas in KM, p. 238.
140   Honneth, "Critical Theory in Germany today", p. 7.

of intersubjective mutual understanding" (KM, 247). For Honneth, the implication of Habermas's discussions of theory of science is "a transcendental-anthropological reflection on the universal societal conditions for the possibility of scientific experience" (KM, 247), and in this sense Habermas's critique of positivism is "always already" a "theory of society" (KM, 265). Rather than "making clear the status of Critical Theory of society within theory of science", Habermas is said to provide the "framework for the construction of social theory" (KM, 230).

Honneth recognizes that Habermas, in contrast to Horkheimer, gradually develops a concept of practice that leaves room for human action beyond material production, thus being able to account for science both in relation to nature and human beings, each with their proper knowledge guiding interest. For both of the latter, however, most pertinent is to determine the special scientific character of critical social research, and, as Honneth argues in his interpretation, this is where Critical Theory ultimately becomes social philosophy, thus displacing itself out of ordinary discussions within theory of science.

Honneth stresses that the critical social sciences, just like the hermeneutical sciences, are anchored in ordinary pre-scientific communication, and their peculiarities are only brought forth when a "pre-scientific process of communication" becomes inaccessible to hermeneutic investigation because of "distortions and blockages" (KM, 263). The difficulties thus become manifest in the confrontation of "the subjectively situated consciousness of the acting individual" with the "empirical social conditions" (KM, 253). These conditions demand an explanation, and this is why Critical Theory for Habermas is a program of "ideology critique", combining the "methods of understanding meaning" (KM, 252) with those of explanation from the empirical sciences, making it possible to account for how it is possible for false beliefs to deceive.

Critical Theory is critical, and this requires some normative standard. Honneth argues that Habermas, by his transformation of theory of science into some kind of anthropological epistemology, claims the foundation of Critical Theory of society to be the very "fundamental conditions of the socio-cultural existence" (KM, 254) of human beings. However, to exist as a human being, it is not enough to exist as a species or a member of society; one also has to develop an individual identity. For Honneth, a "successful formation of identity" depends on a subject being able to "achieve individual autonomy" (KM, 261), the formation of individual character thus having a "societal constitutive function" (KM, 258). Habermas's determination of the emancipatory interest of Critical Theory claims anthropological support from "the peculiar capacity of human rationality". This capacity displays itself in science as a "reflective power" that is "inherent in the consideration of arguments in all discussions" (KM, 255).

Beyond technical knowledge and intersubjective understanding, Habermas thus assumes that science can provide "self-reflection" (KM, 259).

Hence, the scientific research community is ruled by the ideal of the "discussion free of domination" and the "unforced consensus"; as Honneth argues, for Habermas Critical Theory precisely becomes "normative" through the "anticipation" of a situation with "unforced consensus" (KM, 261). It is when the expectations about such a situation are not satisfied that one can experience oneself as alienated in relation to society, and this is the experience that Honneth considers fundamental for social philosophy. Thus, Honneth concludes, Habermas's critique of theory of science is already social philosophy.

iii   Endorsing Rousseau and Marx as well as Nietzsche
Honneth develops this initial displacement further by inscribing Critical Theory *per se* in a tradition of social philosophy. As he argues, from Horkheimer to Habermas Critical Theory is characterized by the idea that individual freedom is only possible if it happens together with a "societal realization" of what can be considered a "reasonable universal". A deviation from this Hegelian-Marxist ideal can, for Critical Theory, only be considered a "social pathology",[141] and for Honneth this line of thought is constitutive for social philosophy.

Honneth calls attention to Rousseau's "critique of civilization" as a prime example of social philosophy, in its "critical diagnosis" contrasting "the natural state of human being" with the "pathologies of the modern life form".[142] Similarly, Marx's "critique of capitalism" is not primarily a question of "injustice", but about "social alienation". In the perspective of a social philosophy, capitalism is pathological as a "social life form, thus bringing human being in contradiction to its essence and divesting it of any prospects of a good life".[143] Having already relegated to the past scientific critique and the standard of truth, Honneth thus emphasizes strongly the social aspect of critique in terms of alienation, sidetracking also the political critique of injustice, i.e. both the distributive questions of social justice in terms of welfare and the questions relating to political autonomy and government.

Hence, in Honneth's version of Critical Theory as social philosophy, the moral and political critique of the injustice produced and reproduced under

---

141   Axel Honneth, "Eine soziale Pathologie der Vernunft. Zur intellektuellen Erbschaft der Kritischen Theorie" (2004), in Honneth, *Pathologien der Vernunft. Geschichte und Gegenwart der Kritischen Theorie* (Frankfurt a.M.: Suhrkamp, 2007), p. 35.

142   Axel Honneth, "Pathologien des Sozialen. Tradition und Aktualität der Sozialphilosophie" (1994), in Honneth, *Das Andere der Gerechtigkeit* (Frankfurt a. M.: Suhrkamp, 2000), p. 16.

143   Honneth, ibid., p. 27.

capitalism is toned down. As he tells the story, there is little mention of Marx's critique of economic exploitation or Rousseau's political philosophy, both of which must be understood in terms of justice. This has consequences for what we can reasonably hope for. Although Honneth is very sensitive to the damaging consequences of modern society on human life, without a philosophy of history, a critique of political economy, or a political philosophy to make a strong and maybe even plausible case for a transformative progression, the rational hope for a fundamentally better world is difficult to sustain. The only thing social philosophy in this sense can offer humanity is the recognition of its sufferings as an understandable reaction to the pathologies of modernity. With capitalism as our final historical destination, Critical Theory will continue to be relevant, since the material conditions for the social critique of alienation will be reproduced indefinitely.

This is the reconstruction of Critical Theory Honneth is proposing, i.e. this is the identity that he finds it appropriate to ascribe to his predecessors in the Frankfurt School. The argument is thus part of a programmatic reconstruction that defines Critical Theory in opposition to both theory of science and political philosophy, and this turn I find deeply problematic and worrying. Hence, as I see it, not only is his interpretation of both Critical Theory and social philosophy distorted; Honneth's move also threatens the scientific legitimacy of Critical Theory as founded in the equivocality already mentioned, weakening it as political critique and leaving its discontent vulnerable to being ridiculed as something that one should simply get over, just like whining and sobbing.

One basic problem is Honneth's endorsement of a line of thought that may appear radical when it comes to critique, but that shuns the idea of science, instead hailing poetic art, self-realization, and creativity, i.e. Nietzsche, Foucault *et al.* In the philosophical and scientific perspective of classical Critical Theory, these thinkers must be considered both metaphysical and positivist, and admitting them as part of Critical Theory means opening up for both dogmatism and relativism. Honneth, however, argues for the exemplarity of Nietzsche's "genealogical analyses", claiming them to be "methodological ideals" for "the social philosophical diagnosis of our age"[144] as they appear in the texts of Horkheimer and Adorno as well as Foucault. Thus, juxtaposing Nietzsche's philosophy of life and French positivism with classical Critical Theory, Honneth even claims that societal critique is only possible if one uses "genealogical research [...] as a detector" for "social transformations of meaning".[145]

---

144 Ibid., p. 31.
145 Axel Honneth, "Rekonstruktive Gesellschaftskritik" (2000), in Honneth, *Pathologien der Vernunft*, p. 69.

As it is commonly recognized, Foucault's radical deconstruction of reason and progress implies relativism in relation to the classical ideals of the Enlightenment,[146] and Honneth admits that by endorsing Nietzsche the problems of social philosophical critique come to a head. Hence, a diagnosis describing something as a social pathology implies "a standard" that can both justify the diagnosis and itself be "justified". However, through the radical critique of Nietzsche, society is for Honneth revealed as a "nihilistic state of ethical arbitrariness", and no standard can therefore "claim objective validity". Confronted with Nietzsche's critique of ideology, Weber tried to claim the ideal of value freedom for social science, but as Honneth rightly notes, this ideal must also make clear how "its validity can be justified".[147] As Nietzsche famously expressed it, the problem is the "value of truth".[148]

I think Honneth's interpretation of Nietzsche is completely wrong. Nietzsche was not a nihilist; as it is well-known, he wanted to revalue all values, thus bringing forth those values that would stimulate life's fulfilment through artistic creativity; furthermore, scientific objectivity and morality are criticized because they are not stimulating in this sense, but in fact inhibit human activity.[149] However, the interpretation of Nietzsche is not interesting in this context. The problem is that Honneth accepts this nihilistic figure as not only the condition of capitalist modernity, but also as necessary conceptual condition for Critical Theory. This is, to say the least, a catastrophe. Honneth thus accepts the complete nihilism as the necessary point of departure, i.e. the condition that any theory must confront, and which makes Critical Theory just one choice among others, depriving it of any necessity, accepting decisionism as a fundamental human condition, i.e. precisely the position that Habermas rightly criticized as the implication of Popper's critical rationalism. For Honneth, the result is that ultimately he cannot but be strongly affirmative towards the existing social order, having only the reconstruction of what is given to rely on. A sad result indeed for what was originally aimed to be a transformative critique of capitalism.

---

146   See, e.g., David Ingram, *Critical Theory and Philosophy* (St. Paul, Minnesota: Paragon House, 1990), p. 200.

147   Honneth, "Pathologien des Sozialen", p. 36.

148   Friedrich Nietzsche, *Zur Genealogie der Moral* (1887), in Nietzsche, *Werke* (1955), ed. Karl Schlechta (Darmstadt: Wissenschaftliche Buchgesellschaft, 1997), vol. II, p. 891.

149   See, e.g., Brian Leiter, "Morality Critics", in *The Oxford Handbook of Continental Philosophy*, ed. Brian Leiter and Michael Rosen (Oxford: Oxford University Press, 2007), pp. 715–21.

iv   *Problematizing Social Philosophy*

As Honneth construes the idea of social philosophy, the societal critique typically has two ways to justify its claims: a substantial philosophical anthropology or an optimistic philosophy of history. Habermas is constructed as an example of the former, while early Critical Theory becomes an example of the latter, arguing that this line of thought was given up with the *Dialectic of Enlightenment*, ultimately understanding "the historical convergence of fascism and Stalinism" as the realization of "totalitarianism".[150] According to Honneth, classical Critical Theory has, up until Habermas, assumed a philosophy of history that can be traced back to Lukács and his "fusion of Marx and Weber". Honneth admits that there are variations, but he claims that the common ground is a "post-idealist" version of the "Hegelian" idea of the "unfolding of the human potential for reason in historical learning processes".[151] Honneth finds the assumptions concerning philosophy of history totally unacceptable today, and since he also finds Horkheimer's idea of social research insufficient, he suggests as a novel orientation of the "critique of society" that it should follow a "'reconstructive' way".[152]

For Honneth, such a reconstructive Critical Theory must imply an immanent critique in the sense that the standard of the critique must be sought in the society in question:[153] "only such principles or ideals hold as legitimate resources for societal critique that already" have been given "shape by the given social order".[154] In this affirmative stance in relation to the existing capitalist society, Honneth maintains that there is a fundamental difference between the critique of social pathology and the "moral philosophical critique of social injustice".[155] Hence, as social philosophy, Critical Theory merely criticizes phenomena in modern capitalist society such as "'split', 'reification', 'alienation', [...] 'nihilism', [...] loss of community', 'disenchantment', 'depersonalization' and 'commodification'".[156] The political project of changing the conditions

---

150   Honneth, "Pathologien des Sozialen", p. 47.

151   Honneth, "Eine soziale Pathologie der Vernunft", pp. 43–45.

152   Honneth, "Rekonstruktive Gesellschaftskritik", p. 59.

153   See Axel Honneth, "Über die Möglichkeit einer erschließenden Kritik" (2000), in Honneth, *Pathologien der Vernunft*, pp. 71–72.

154   Honneth, "Rekonstruktive Gesellschaftskritik", p. 61.

155   Honneth, "Eine soziale Pathologie der Vernunft", p. 32. See also Axel Honneth and Luc Bolsanski, "Soziologie der Kritik oder Kritische Theorie. Ein Gespräch mit Robin Celikates", in *Was ist Kritik?*, ed. Jaeggi and Wesche, pp. 111–13.

156   Honneth, "Pathologien des Sozialen", p. 58.

producing such phenomena, as it has been pursued especially by the late Habermas,[157] is therefore not considered part of Critical Theory.

Implied by such a critique is some idea of a "'normal' or 'healthy'" society, and for Honneth that is a society that "allows its members an undistorted form of self-realization",[158] i.e. a classical liberal way of defining the good society. Honneth emphasizes that it is not enough for societal critique simply to take a normative position; it also has to provide elements to explain the patholo-gies experienced, i.e. a "disclosure of society as a social process".[159] Honneth emphasizes that not every "sensation of injustice" provides a "foundation for critique".[160] There are different levels of social disrespect, and it is only in some of them that the pathological aspects of capitalism as a life form become mani-fest. In these cases, human beings are offended due to "intuitively given ideas of justice", because they expect their "value, honour or integrity" to be respected. Hence, in capitalist society, the pathological "disrespect" occurs when "recog-nition fails to materialize",[161] even though it was both expected and deserved.

It is clear that for Honneth's reconstruction of Critical Theory as social philosophy, the *Dialectic of Enlightenment* plays a crucial part. As he puts it, Critical Theory was from the beginning influenced by a "social theoretical neg-ativism", focusing on the "loss of the conditions of a good or successful life",[162] but with the said *Dialectic* Critical Theory even came to express a "pessimism" that is still reflected in Habermas's analysis of the system's "colonialization of the lifeworld".[163]

Thus, also for Honneth, the *Dialectic* signifies the transformation in Criti-cal Theory from an optimistic philosophy of history emphasizing progress to one of decline. However, Wellmer has recently argued that Horkheimer and Adorno perhaps deliberately employ exaggeration as a method for obtain-ing knowledge.[164] As they put it: "Only the exaggeration is true (DA, 139)". According to Weber, to benefit the scientific investigation an ideal type has to

---

157   This theme I will discuss in DDD III.

158   Honneth, ibid., p. 57.

159   Honneth, "Rekonstruktive Gesellschaftskritik", p. 62.

160   Honneth and Bolsanski, "Soziologie der Kritik oder Kritische Theorie", p. 97.

161   Axel Honneth, "Die soziale Dynamik von Mißachtung. Zur Ortsbetimmung einer kritisch-en Gesellshaftstheorie" (1994), in Honneth, *Das Andere der Gerechtigkeit*, p. 99.

162   Honneth, "Eine soziale Pathologie der Vernunft", p. 31.

163   Honneth, "Die soziale Dynamik von Mißachtung", p. 94.

164   See Albrecht Wellmer, "Über Negativität und Autonomie der Kunst", in *Dialektik der Frei-heit*, ed. Axel Honneth (Frankfurt a.M.: Suhrkamp, 2005), p. 240; see also Per Jepsen, *Ador-nos kritische Theorie der Selbstbestimmung* (Würzburg: Königshausen & Neumann, 2012), p. 40.

be constructed in its conceptual purity as one-sided and "foreign to reality",[165] and acknowledging this, Honneth has argued that maybe after all the *Dialectic* does not have to be read as a pessimist philosophy of history. Instead, we can think of it as a consciously exaggerated ideal type that serves to sharpen the knowledge of the contradictions in the culture of modern capitalist society.[166] However, as he has also pointed out, this interpretation leaves it "open as to which kind of truth claims it can uphold".[167]

Relieved of the burden of historical decline, and only having to care about the contradictions of modern capitalist culture, not society as such, Honneth can to an even larger extent admit existing value and norms as valid by employing the reconstructive method, making it even more difficult to legitimize the radical criticism of capitalism and the political economy sustaining it as ideology in terms of justice. Honneth took Habermas's paradigm shift as his point of departure, but just as the exaggerated insistence on interaction and communication was unfortunate for Habermas himself, this is also the case for Honneth, although in another way, namely by making it difficult for him to escape the narrow framework of mutual and reciprocal relations. Honneth's non-verbal version of the communicative approach thus implies reconstructing valid normativity out of intersubjective relations already restricted and made pathological by the existing social order, again being caught up in the affirmative stand rather than the critical.

Implicit in Honneth's critique of the material damage inflicted by capitalist modernity on human life is a normative idea of living and realizing a full human life. However, limiting Critical Theory to be defined by the existing social reality perceived in this way threatens to render Critical Theory politically impotent. Social philosophy in Honneth's version is at risk of perceiving social reality as something so strange and totalizing that it appears impenetrable for the political actions of individual human beings, thus adding to the existential and corporal experience of discomfort, loneliness, nausea *et al.*, being incessantly forced to choose, but not being able to decide your own destiny.

This perception is, of course, part of the critique of the livelihood in capitalist (post-)modernity, but it is important not to universalize it as a necessary

---

165 Weber, "Die 'Objektivität' sozialwissenschaftlicher und sozialpolitischer Erkenntnis", p. 190 and *Wirtschaft und Gesellschaft*, § 1.

166 See Axel Honneth, "Eine Physiogonomie der kapitalistischen Lebensform. Skizze der Gesellschaftstheorie Adornos", in *Dialektik der Freiheit*, ed. Honneth, pp. 172–73.

167 Axel Honneth, "The Possibility of a Disclosing Critique of Society: the *Dialectic of Enlightenment* in the Light of Current Debates in Social Criticism" (2000), in *Critical Theory*, ed. Rasmussen and Swindal , vol. 2, p. 227.

existential condition of social life in modernity *per se*. That this could easily be the material implication of social philosophy is confirmed by positive versions of social philosophy that are focused on the normative rights and liberties of the individual in relation to the state, adding legitimacy to the freedom of the individual in an almost libertarian way.[168] Social philosophy in this liberal and positive version thus prefers the free dynamics of civil society economy rather than reasonable political deliberations, decisions and actions, because politics will imply the use of state force. But the latter may, because of clashes of class interest, in the end be a necessary step to realize justice. Without admitting the use of legitimate political force, there is little hope of governing, in a reasonable way, the dynamics of desire in society.

Honneth's interpretation of Critical Theory fares even worse when compared with Horkheimer's original idea of social philosophy. As Honneth, Horkheimer was professor in social philosophy, and both the institute and the legendary journal were from the beginning dedicated to social research. As Kellner has pointed out, Horkheimer himself stressed in his 1931 lecture that his chair was in social philosophy and not in political economy as that of his predecessor.[169] However, when Horkheimer was to define the program for social philosophy and research, the ambition was to elucidate the

> fate of human beings, in so far as they are parts of a community, and not mere individuals. It concerns itself above all with the social life of people: state, law, economy, religion, in short, with the entire material and spiritual culture of humanity.[170]

Hence, what Horkheimer originally meant with 'social philosophy' is something very different than what is proposed by Honneth. In Horkheimer's version of social philosophy, it is not primarily about the failed existential relation between the individual and the society, i.e. it is not primarily about alienation; on the contrary, there is plenty of room for political discussions of justice in relation to state, law, and economy. Instead of Honneth's individualist and psychologicalized displacements, at risk of furthering mental impotence, Critical Theory must recall the traditional importance attributed to raising the consciousness of progressive political actors, of empowering the people, thus

---

168   See, e.g., Joel Feinberg, *Social Philosophy* (Englewood Cliffs, New Jersey: Prentice Hall Inc., 1973).

169   See Kellner, *Critical Theory, Marxism and Modernity*, p. 18; see also Horkheimer, "Die gegenwärtige Lage der Sozialphilosophie", in GS$_H$ 3, p. 30.

170   Horkheimer, "Die gegenwärtige Lage der Sozialphilosophie", p. 20.

enabling them to engage politically in democratic decision making and participate in the conscious government of society through the state, rather than leaving societal regulation to impotent ethical individuals pursuing their self-realization at the mercy of impersonal market forces. Fortunately, the tradition of Critical Theory has a lot to offer in this direction, recalling, e.g., the writings of Marx, Marcuse, Habermas *et al.*

F   Conclusion

The philosophy of history has been of overwhelming importance for Critical Theory, not least due to the dramatic shift from the early classical writings to the *Dialectic of Enlightenment*. It obviously made a huge difference to the first generation that were the authors of the shift, in all likelihood being, as Held remarks, "excessively influenced by their experience of fascism and Nazism".[171] However, as I have tried to show, this trauma obviously also had a decisive impact on following generations that either worked together with the authors of the *Dialectic*, as did Habermas, or appropriated Critical Theory primarily through studying the *Dialectic*, as was the case with Honneth.

It is obvious that Critical Theorists from the beginning were motivated and moved by the hope that a better world would materialize in their own life time. In that sense, Critical Theory was clearly political. Horkheimer himself stressed in 1933 that the "ideals" of "materialism" were determined by the "needs in general", and that they should be assessed in relation to "what was possible with the human forces at hand and in a foreseeable future".[172] Traumatic disappointment and frustration have therefore been integral in the theory development since on the early stages. In the cases I have discussed in this Interlude, I think the traumas have to a large extent been responsible for the exaggerated urge to redefine Critical Theory so categorically and unreflexively, as it has been attempted, apparently ignoring the obvious, namely that they have all, in their own way, conducted a series of determinate negations in the most classical Hegelian sense.

Criticizing the philosophy of history has almost become a hallmark of contemporary Critical Theory. As I have shown, for Habermas the critique of the philosophy of history was an essential part of his critique of Horkheimer and Adorno; this was also the case for Honneth, who even radicalized the critique and included Habermas among those targeted; recently, Amy Allen has even

---

171   Held, *Introduction to Critical Theory*, p. 365.

172   Max Horkheimer, "Materialismus und Metaphysik" (1933), in GS_H 3, p. 105.

criticized both Habermas and Honneth for presupposing a normative "left-Hegelian" idea of "historical progress",[173] inscribing Adorno and his "'other' other son – Michel Foucault"[174] to back up her claims. Honneth thus receives a dose of the same medicine that he administered to his predecessors, and the idea of history having one specific direction, be that progressive or regressive, should now finally be something confined to the past within Critical Theory.

However, as I have argued, some of these argumentative moves are simply too categorical and thus ill conceived, e.g., the proposed paradigm shift to communicative action and the totalizing redefinition of Critical Theory as social philosophy. And the main reason is that they pose themselves as paradigmatic or hegemonic discourses aiming to exclude or include the other by definition, not recognizing mutually the specificity, worth and significance of the other, not being willing to join forces and supplement each other. To put it simply, social, moral and political philosophy need each other. The experience of injustice produces alienation, alienation is unjust, and underneath both issues is a capitalist economy producing reification and sustained ideologically by modern political economy, all of which calls for the political organization of victims resisting the material wrongdoings.

When it comes to the political economic agenda, I think both Habermas and Honneth have weakened Critical Theory: the former by having lost the ambition to think through a more radical transformation of the current political economic order, in fact accepting the basics of the liberal democratic ideology sustaining contemporary capitalism; the latter by presenting a critique that, though radical and sensitive to human suffering under capitalism, could be called reduced, i.e. not facilitating conceptually the social engagement to organize politically for real societal change. Indeed, in the wake of Habermas's rethinking of Critical Theory, it got to the point where Dubiel, as director of the Institute of Social Research, could insist that just as there is "no guarantee from philosophy of history" against new "civilizational regressions", "there is no alternative" to "capitalism", "democratic will formation and the rule of law".[175]

Recently, Michael J. Thompson has called attention to this *Domestication of Critical Theory*. From a more traditional Marxist perspective, the "linguistic, procedural, and recognitive turn" can only be perceived as "neo-Idealist".[176]

---

173   Amy Allen, *The End of Progress. Decolonizing the Normative Foundations of Critical Theory* (New York: Columbia University Press, 2016), p. 3.

174   Allen, *ibid.*, p. 16.

175   Helmut Dubiel, *Ungewißheit und Politik* (Frankfurt a.M.: Suhrkamp, 1994), p. 8.

176   Michael J. Thompson, *The Domestication of Critical Theory* (London and Lanham: Rowman and Littlefield, 2016), pp. 2–3.

The basic problem is that contemporary Critical Theory does not pay sufficient attention to "the ways that social pathologies are rooted in social forces that are predominantly grounded in economic logics", relying normatively too much on "norms of social action that cannot possibly maintain their rationality under the pressure of reification".[177] Contemporary Critical Theory presupposes "subjects capable of and looking for a critical, democratic and progressive confrontation with their society and culture",[178] and the basic concepts "alienation, reification, domination, ideology, and so on" are not analysed as "rooted in material forms of social life, but as properties of discourse, recognition, or some other philosophical concern".[179] The reawakening of such idealist assumptions is especially alarming, however, since it takes place at the same time as "a massive integration of social life along neo-liberal lines"[180] and when large scale struggles are few against the "de-democratizing effects of the expansion of inequalities of wealth".[181] The domestication of Critical Theory has, therefore, not only weakened the theory itself but also the struggle it is supposed to be part of.

However, instead of excluding my highly esteemed predecessors by yet another categorical or paradigmatic definition, I invite them all to join hands within Critical Theory, recalling the strengths of our common heritage, i.e. the classical normative theory of science granting a special emancipatory role to the social sciences and philosophy, thus summing up what I have argued, especially in the first two sections. Moreover, in the spirit of Thompson, I also insist on the significance of another constitutive component of classical Critical Theory, i.e. the critique of political economy, at the same time criticizing capitalism and the ideology sustaining it, i.e. some kind of liberalism.[182]

Hence, Critical Theory will retain the equivocality in relation to validity, i.e. striving for the truth both scientifically and politically, striving to realize reason as both constitutive and transformative. Scientific knowledge is not merely a logical relation between subject and object, but a material process of experience taking place in consciousness and society. Reflections on particular issues will always take into account the totality, just as they must be considered parts of a social and political struggle for a society without alienation and injustice, i.e. as liberating both the mind and the body to realize a

---

177   Thompson, *ibid.*, p. 26.

178   *Ibid.*, p. 6.

179   *Ibid.*, p. 27.

180   *Ibid.*, p. 10.

181   *Ibid.*, p. 6.

182   This I will return to in the Postscript below and in DDD III.

reasonable and compassionate society. In such a struggle theory, science and research are necessary – just as are rhetoric, political skills and organisational talents – since not everybody can be expected to see through the veil of ignorance created by culture industry and ideology at large. For the same reason, Critical Theory cannot do without philosophical reflection and concepts, relying both on analysis, deduction and imagination.

Taking into account the totality of reality, while at the same time engaging both theoretically and practically, makes necessary a comprehensive idea of the truth, and for this purpose Hegelian dialectics is well-suited as a methodological framework, being able to grasp through its basic concepts both theoretical and practical experiences as well as the material and ideal aspects of both. The truth of society is that the true society still does not exist; therefore, Critical Theory must contribute to realizing this truth. For the same reason, it must also reveal what is false in society as it is, i.e. social pathologies such as alienation and injustice, exploitation and suppression. Hence, truth is not merely a correspondence between theory and empirical data.

Through this classical critical approach, it becomes obvious that besides the concepts of work and production, an analysis of a practice realizing the truth must also conceptualize human interaction and communication. Furthermore, adopting this approach implies a critique of traditional theory of knowledge and science as it is displayed in phenomenology, phenomenalism, empiricism, variations of positivism, critical rationalism, pragmatism etc., showing how the apparent focus on what is merely given is rooted in a naïve objectivism; this critique obtains further substance by determining the emancipatory knowledge guiding interest of critical social science and philosophy. Hence, in contemporary capitalist society at the beginning of the 21st century, there is a lot to do for classical Critical Theory.

PART ONE

Economy

∵

CHAPTER 1

An Alternative Agenda for Political Economy: Durkheim *et al.*

The concept of value is central to many discussions in economy, philosophy and sociology. Particularly in relation to business ethics, the concept of value is of the utmost importance, being one of the conceptual nodes that link ethics and economics.

I would like to present some reflections on the concept of value, inspired by a tradition in theoretical thought that normally does not receive much attention: the French positivism of Émile Durkheim (1858–1917) and his followers. Durkheim drew on classical French and British political and social philosophy as well as the German social sciences and economics of the late 19th century;[1] that is, the tradition that coined the term 'national economics' in opposition to both classical political economy, including Karl Marx (1818–1883), and the neo-classical mathematization of economy.

Today, this line of thought is largely ignored, not only by economics but also by philosophy and sociology. Philosophy considers Durkheim to be part of the sociological tradition,[2] whereas in sociology he is not considered scientific in a modern sense, but rather read as a classic,[3] i.e. a philosophical predecessor more occupied with ethics than sociology proper.[4] However, if we accept Amartya Sen's general conclusion, stating that economics is not only about maximising personal profits,[5] this tradition offers a normative conceptual framework for reflecting further on these matters.

---

1   See Émile Durkheim, "La science positive de la morale en Allemagne", *Revue philosophique de la France et de l'étranger* xxiv (1887), pp. 33–58, 113–42 and 275–84; Durkheim, *Montesquieu et Rousseau, précurseurs de la sociologie* (1892), trans. A. Cuvillier, 2nd ed., Petite Bibliotèque Sociologique Internationale (Paris: Marcel Rivière, 1953); and Durkheim, *De la division du travail social* (Paris: Félix Alcan, 1893); see further on Durkheim in DDD II, *Discourse, Value and Practice,* especially, Part One, and DDD III, *Justice, Peace and Formation,* Part Three.

2   See Jan Rohls, *Geschichte der Ethik* (Tübingen: J.C.B. Mohr, 1991), pp. 396–97.

3   See, e.g., Niklas Luhmann, "Arbeitsteilung und Moral. Durkheims Theorie", in Durkheim, *Über die Teilung der sozialen Arbeit* (Frankfurt a. M.: Suhrkamp, 1977), pp. 17, 27.

4   See George Gurvitch, *La vocation actuelle de la sociologie* (1957–63) (Paris: P.U.F., 1963), vol. II, p. 175.

5   Remark at the Fourteenth Annual Conference of the European Business Ethics Network (EBEN), Valencia, Sept. 12th 2001, i.e. the day after 9–11.

With concepts taken from this tradition, I will argue that

(a)   we can understand that the market both presupposes and creates moral
      values, rather than economic value only. Therefore, we can defend mar-
      ket economics and business in principle.
(b)   we can criticize globalization for expressing and reinforcing an ideology
      of the free market, which abstracts the idea of the market from its proper
      social context. It promotes economic value as the ideal value above all,
      interprets value as personal preferences and believes the law of demand
      and supply to be a natural law, valid for all times and places, for individu-
      als, nations and the global economy.
(c)   we can defend business on a human level but attack the effects of
      globalization, the concentration of capital and the unlimited financial
      speculation.
(d)   we can attack neo-liberalism as socialists without falling into the trap of
      the central commissarial planning of the economy, like yesterday's com-
      munist regimes and today's European Union.
(e)   we can defend the nation state without becoming national chauvinists;
      what we defend is the humane size of the community in question, not
      the nation as such.
(f)   we can recognize morality as a strong human force, understand the soci-
      etal function of morality and ethics and interpret what is happening in
      the world, especially in connection with summits like the ones in Seattle,
      Davos, Prague, Gothenburg and Genoa.

The current political conflict is not – I will argue – a conflict between different
sets of values; rather, it reflects a clash between two different concepts of value:
the ideal value, which is created by strong social interaction, and the economic
value, which indicates social interaction reduced to almost nothing.

    Not only business ethics but business in general should support the popular
protests against globalization. The unregulated flow of capital and commodities tends to accumulate economic values in big multi-national corporations;
this process destroys the moral values that are necessary for the free market
and the creation of values in small-scale businesses. The values accumulated
by big businesses are a threat to values in general.

A   Economics

Today, economics is often seen as a technical discipline dealing with generating value as a means to realize various ends. The scale of violence employed by

the authorities against the anti-globalization protests, however, indicates that something more is at stake. Protecting the leaders of the current economic system with barricades (Gothenburg), *agent provocateurs* (Barcelona) and guns (Genoa) indicates either a cynical protection of interests and privileges, or that the economic system is not just seen as a means to generate money but also bestowed with an intrinsic value.

In classical political economy, value is a function of labour. This idea was originally introduced by the father of liberalism, John Locke (1632–1704). The intrinsic value of nature, he says, is almost none; what constitutes the greatest part of value is labour. Labour transforms nature into useful things, things to be enjoyed, and that creates value.[6]

However, Locke notes, most things useful to human beings have short duration, and man's capacity for labour is also limited. Together, that puts a limit to how many things and how much land it is meaningful to gather, and thereby, a limit to social inequality. However, gold and silver have long duration, which makes accumulation possible, even though as materials they are "little useful in the life of man".[7] The value of gold and silver thus rests exclusively on the common consent of men, and social inequality can therefore, according to Locke, be said to rest on the tacit consent regarding the value of such metals, i.e. money.

Adam Smith (1723–1790) makes explicit the distinction between value in use and value in exchange, employing the famous example of the use value of water and the exchange value of diamonds.[8] However, whereas Locke considers use value to be the real value and a result of labour, Smith defines labour as the "real measure of the exchangeable value". This exchange value determines "the real price" or "the natural price" in a "universal" way, "at all times, and at all places". Labour determines the real exchange value, but, as was the case for Locke, this "market price" is not considered the real price. The market price is only nominal, not a function of the ideal value.[9]

Immanuel Kant's (1724–1804) conception of value is based on the same premises: valuable is that which can be enjoyed and used by man, although Kant does not mention the role of labour in the creation of value. Kant makes a distinction between the "direct value" of various natural and artificial goods and the value of money as only "indirect". Kant considers money a commodity that represents all commodities, which must imply that commodities in general – as commodities – only have indirect value; the price of a commodity

---

6 See John Locke, *Two Treatises of Government* (1698) (Cambridge University Press, 1988), §40–43.
7 Locke, *ibid.*, §50.
8 See Adam Smith, *The Wealth of Nations* (1776) (New York: Random House, 1937), Book 1, Ch. 4.
9 See Smith, *ibid.*, Ch. 5.

is simply the public verdict on the indirect value of the commodity in question, that is, the market price.[10]

Neo-classical economy intends to do away with all kinds of idealism and politics in economics in an attempt to make economics a scientific discipline modelled after the positivist conception of physics. First, the conception of use value is modified by the idea of diminishing marginal utility of the last object acquired. Second, this substitution of use value, "total utility", by relative utility is followed by a redefinition of utility, which solves the paradox of diamonds and water conceptually: if something is in demand, it is useful.[11] That makes use value *per se* irrelevant in economic discussions, and since the exchange value is determined only by demand and supply, the exchange value is the same as the market price.

This development makes the distinction between price and value irrelevant to economics, and in the 20th century the concept of value was to a large degree replaced by the twin concepts of price and utility. Hence, economists in the western world—political leaders and businessmen alike—have been theoretically schooled to ignore other kinds of value than that which can be expressed through the market price. In short, exchange value is price, and use value is demand.

B   Values Today

In light of the above, value is not much of a subject in economic theory today. Philosophy, on the other hand, can distinguish between two typical conceptions of value:

·   The liberal-empiricist conception of value as empirical use value held by Locke, which has been closely linked to the development of economics and held by many philosophers and sociologists in the western world. This concept reduces value to personal interest, utility, preference, desire, emotion, feeling, etc.
·   The liberal-idealist conception of value as something ideal, worthy of attention in itself, which was developed on the basis of the concepts of use value held by philosophers like Smith, Kant and Marx.

---

10   See Immanuel Kant, *Metaphysik der Sitten* (1785) (Leipzig: Felix Meiner, 1945), §31 (AA 6, 287–89).
11   See Paul A. Samuelson, *Economics*, 10th ed. (Tokyo: McGraw-Hill Kogakusha, 1976), pp. 433–38.

This duality was the point of departure for Durkheim more than a century ago, and it is – I believe – equally valid today, at least as a promising alternative approach to understanding the concept of value. The ideal conception played an important part in philosophy, especially in the first third of the 20th century, for neo-Kantians like the sociologist Max Weber,[12] the phenomenological critic Max Scheler[13] and the father of analytical ethics, G.E. Moore.[14] Today, this conception of value is not commonly employed in academic disciplines, but in the general public, and in theology, it is still a widely held conception.

C   Creative Collectivity

Durkheim begins by criticising the conception of value based on empirical use value. Value is ascribed to something enjoyable and useful for the individual. However, value is also something that transcends my personal preferences, something ideal and objective that cannot be controlled.[15] Which things are bestowed with value might be more or less coincidental, but the moment such values have been created, individuals cannot change them at will. This holds true not only for what is considered ideal values but also for even the most unstable exchange values. Hence, values express something more than just personal interest, preferences and utility.

However, understanding value in terms of collective utility – as in utilitarianism and welfare economics – is no solution, since it cannot account for the value ascribed to luxury and symbols.[16] The paradox of water and diamonds is a perfect example. As mentioned, this paradox was solved conceptually by the neo-classics by redefining use value as 'in demand'. Durkheim and his followers however, ignore this solution, allowing diamonds to maintain a value in themselves that is not just a function, neither of the marginal utility, nor of the dynamics of the market in general.

In the concept of national economy, one of Durkheim's students, Celestin Bouglé (1870–1940), finds an economic conception of value that cannot be

---

12   See Max Weber, *Wirtschaft und Gesellschaft* (1921–22) (Tübingen: J.B.C. Mohr, 1990), §§ 2–4.

13   See Max Scheler, *Der Formalismus in der Ethik und die materiale Wertethik* (1926) (Bern: Francke, 1980).

14   See G.E. Moore, "The conception of Intrinsic Value" (1922), in Moore, *Principa ethica*, revised ed. (Cambridge: Cambridge University Press, 1993), pp. 260–98. For an analysis of Moore's ethics, see DDD II, Part Two.

15   See Émile Durkheim, "Jugement de valeur et jugement de fait" (1911), in Durkheim, *Sociologie et philosophie* (Paris: P.U.F., 1996), pp. 118–19.

16   See Durkheim, *ibid.*, pp. 124–25.

reduced to individual interest. A nation, or more—generally—a collective, has different interests than individuals, for instance maintaining the natural resources and creating institutions for everyone's good. Moreover, as Durkheim had already showed—and as Sen mentions—the economy of the liberal market presupposes a moral and legal framework that recognizes the value of contracts, justice and fairness,[17] and this is exactly what the collective provides.

The concept of value as understood by neo-classical economics and *homo economicus* is not sufficient. It turns economics into a theory of maximising individual profits, which—as Bouglé notes—makes theft the most rational economic action: stealing maximizes profit and minimizes cost.[18] The reason why this consequence is not drawn in economic theory is precisely because economic value is not the only value recognized by economics. Without the recognition of alternative values, liberal economy would be ruled by the law of the jungle, resembling the state of nature as described by Thomas Hobbes (1588–1679).

Having dealt with empirical use value and utility, Durkheim develops a sociological interpretation of the idealistic conception of value. Values are ideal and objective in relation to each individual because they are of collective—rather than individual or metaphysical—origin.[19] The interaction between individual human beings creates something exterior to themselves, which in turn becomes relatively independent of each individual. All these products of collective activity are equally real, although some are material – like buildings and coins—whereas others are immaterial—like morality and religion. According to Durkheim, a value is such an immaterial product of the collective mind.[20]

This explains the objectivity of values without supposing anything like Smith's extra-terrestrial metaphysics; still, we need an explanation of the ideality of values, i.e. the normative force, with which values meet us as individuals. This, Durkheim explains through the variation in the intensity of collective interaction. Ideal values are created by the euphoria of crowds, where the participants forget themselves and let their individualities be fused

---

17   See Durkheim, *De la division du travail social*, pp. 225–39; see also Asger Sørensen, *Sandheden er rød – og gid etikken var ligeså!* 2nd ed., PhD-thesis (København: Københavns Universitet, 1999), pp. 292–93, and Sørensen, *Den moralske virkelighed* (Malmö: NSU Press, 2012), p. 234.

18   See Celestin Bouglé, *Leçon de sociologie sur l'évolution des valeurs* (Paris: Arman Collin, 1922), p. 103.

19   See Durkheim, "Jugement de valeur et jugement de fait", p. 132.

20   See Durkheim, ibid., pp. 136–39.

into the crowd. Living as a human being, Durkheim states, is acting, and action is expenditure, i.e. giving.[21] Values are created by collectively giving yourself up to the collectivity, which is then represented symbolically in the values.

In that sense, value is neither a direct function of utility—be it individual or collective—nor a function of exchange in a market. Value is not created by labour but by collective activities where the economic rationality is spending not accumulating. Bouglé tries to reinforce this conception of value by reconstructing the history of value as a process of both centrifugal differentiation and centripetal unification. From a primitive concept of value, which includes economic, moral, religious and aesthetic aspects, we get the split between economic and non-economic values. Nonetheless, Bouglé insists on the fundamental unity of economic and non-economic values.[22] Moreover, this unity is demonstrated by Durkheim's nephew, Marcel Mauss (1872–1950), in his analysis of donation: in every kind of economic exchange, other values are not only presupposed but also created; the market was never—and is never—just a matter of individual material interests. The free market and *homo economicus* are mere abstractions that serve ideological purposes.[23]

D   Accumulation and Expenditure

Georges Bataille (1897–1962), a rather unorthodox reader of Mauss, chose a dialectical approach to the study of the opposing aspects of value, but without trying to reconcile the apparent contradiction. He refuses to do away with the oppositions between the individual and the collective and between accumulation and consumption. Both contradictions are equally real in the life of human beings in a society, and both are dialectical contradictions, united as contraries where neither can be understood without the other, both being determined by their opposites.[24]

---

21   See ibid., pp. 133–36.

22   See Bouglé, *Leçon de sociologie sur l'évolution des valeurs*, pp. 92–96.

23   See Marcel Mauss, "Essai sur le don: Forme et raison de l'échange dans le société archaïques" (1923–24), in Mauss, *Sociologie et anthropologie* (Paris: P.U.F., 1999), pp. 272–75; see also Asger Sørensen, "Marcel Mauss. Kvinder, høfligheder og talismaner: Gaven som fuldstœndig social kendsgerning", in *Tradition og fornyelse i sociologien*, ed. Michael Hviid Jacobsen, Mikael Carleheden, and Søren Kristiansen (Ålborg: Ålborg Universitetsforlag, 2001), pp. 78–79 (or Asger Sørensen, *I Lyset af Bataille – politisk filosofiske studier* (København: Politisk Revy, 2012), Ch. 5, pp. 124–26).

24   See Asger Sørensen, "At tage fat om ondets rod. Batailles radikale civilisationskritik", in *Excesser – om Georges Bataille*, ed. René Rasmussen and Asger Sørensen (Århus: Modtryk, 1994), p. 191 (or Sørensen, *I lyset af Bataille*, Ch. 3, p. 72–73).

On this basis, Bataille developed the concept of general economy in contrast to political economy, which he calls restricted. Political economy is preconditioned by the twin premises of natural scarcity and *homo economicus*. Both these premises, however, are wrong and ideological. Nature is full of resources and man wants to give, not just to acquire.[25] Political economy creates a system of false beliefs, which legitimize acting solely with the purpose to maximize personal profits.

Bataille's approach makes it possible to describe the social life of human beings as a historic process, always oscillating between two equally necessary, albeit impossible, ideal types:[26] the individual who only accumulates, i.e. the Calvinist workaholic,[27] and the collective that only consumes—in orgies, revolutions or wars.[28] An individual who only consumes is an exception, like the king or the artist;[29] a collectivity that only accumulates is equally extreme, like the Soviet Union in the 1920s and 30s.[30]

Consummation makes accumulation valuable as a means, but only the individual or collective expenditure without any apparent economic advantage can be valuable as an end. Economic values, money, are only potential or – in Kant's words – indirect values, representing the power to spend, i.e. to create values. The ideal values pursued in life all represent expenditure, whereas the so-called economic values represent accumulation; there is no historic or transcendent goal beyond these in life, and no way to reconcile them.[31] Nature, on the other hand, is rich and fertile, and the capacity of human beings to work and multiply exceeds by far the need to gather food and reproduce the population.[32]

---

25   See Georges Bataille, *La Part maudite. Essai de économie générale. 1. La Consumation* (1949), in Bataille, *Œuvres complètes* (oc$_B$), vol. VII, ed. Thadée Klossowski (Paris: Gallimard, 1976), pp. 28–33; see also Asger Sørensen, "Georges Bataille: At tage ved lære af fascismen: Mellem modstand og analyse", in *Tradition og fornyelse i sociologien*, ed. Jacobsen, Carleheden and Kristiansen, p. 244 (or Sørensen, *I Lyset af Bataille*, Ch. 6, pp. 143–45).

26   See Georges Bataille, *La Souveraineté* ('1954'), in oc$_B$ VIII, ed. Thadée Klossowski (Paris: Gallimard, 1976), p. 377.

27   See Bataille, *La Part maudite*, p. 119.

28   See Bataille, *La Souveraineté*, p. 277.

29   See Bataille, *ibid.*, p. 248.

30   See Bataille, *La Part maudite*, p. 157.

31   See Bataille, *La Souveraineté* , p. 322; see also Asger Sørensen, "Praktisk filosofi i lyset af Georges Bataille – om lighed, etik og menneskelighed", in *Den ene, den anden, det tredje. Politisk identitet, andethed og fællesskab i moderne fransk tænkning*, ed. Carsten Bagge Laustsen and Anders Berg-Sørensen (København: Politisk Revy, 1999), pp. 206–07 (or Sørensen, *I lyset af Bataille*, Ch. 4, pp. 107–08).

32   See Bataille, *La Part maudite*, pp. 42–43.

History shows that societies have employed this energy to accumulate material wealth. Bataille is able, however, to give a few historic examples of societies which, for a period of time, have maintained an equilibrium of the two processes. This shows the fallacy of the two above-mentioned premises: that natural resources are scarce and that society necessarily is preoccupied with accumulation. The best example is Tibet before the Chinese seized control, where an enormous proportion of the men, i.e. up to 25%,[33] lived in celibacy and without contributing at all to the production of material wealth; the whole system was sustained by ideal values, which legitimized religious expenditure.

E   Towards a Creative Period

On a world-wide scale, there are probably relatively more unproductive people today than in ancient Tibet – some poor and some very rich, becoming even richer every day. The world is still rich, but the wealth is unequally distributed, and the prevalent ideology is clearly not sustainable anymore.

A traditional ethical analysis might interpret the current political conflict as a conflict of values, e.g., between freedom and equality. What I have proposed is to think in terms of different concepts of value rather than just different values. The first conception understands values in an exclusively economic sense, while at the same time interpreting economics as the free pursuit of individual profit and accumulation. The second conception understands values as a more general concept for what is considered valuable in itself by the collective rather than what is profitable only for individuals.

In a Durkheimian perspective, the fight against globalization could be taken as the beginning of one of those creative periods in human history, when intensified human interaction carries people beyond themselves, recreating disinterested, collective values and – ultimately – giving rise to reform or revolution directed against individual accumulation of economic values. In the crowds and during heated discussions, ideal values are recreated, i.e. values that have the double aspect of being both imperative and desirable to those involved in the process.

As Durkheim explains, when ideal values are experienced most intensely, they substitute reality, and people actually believe that paradise can be realized on earth.[34] Examples of these periods are the Reformation, the Renaissance, the French revolution and the revolutionary periods of the 19th and

---

33   See Bataille, *ibid.*, p. 104.
34   See Durkheim, "Jugement de valeur et jugement de fait", p. 134.

20th centuries, the last being the revolutions that caused the Soviet Union and the Eastern bloc to collapse. The euphoria over the collapse of communist systems might be seen as bestowing ideal value upon the basis of the ideology of the free market, the human rights and the freedom to pursue personal profit, i.e. economic value.

As Adorno argues, Durkheim does not recommend revolutions, quite the opposite.[35] What he wanted was to reconcile the social contradictions expressed through the contradictions of the concept of value. However, by monopolising and reducing the concept of value, liberal economy and politics create an ideology that encourages human beings to evaluate their actions only in terms of personal advantage. That in itself has provoked both socialists and conserva- tives since the French revolution, but in the current economic situation the effects of this ideology are not only provoking; they are actually life-threatening.

F   Fight Globalization

The economic system and the ideology – capitalism and liberalism – reinforce each other in a process where the changing of material conditions legitimizes reinforcing the ideology, just as the reinforced ideology legitimizes attempts to change the material situation. Ideologically, liberal politics liberate the economic decision-making from moral values. Thus informed, economic behaviour condenses market dynamics, considering only economic value, i.e. profit, to be true value, thus optimizing exploitation, ignoring social inequality, liberating personal and institutional greed, and gradually legitimizing the rational economic ideal of theft mentioned above.

Theft can be considered an individual reaction to a social problem. However, when these problems were addressed politically by the anti-globalization movement, it was met with a more violent reaction from the police than most criminals experience.

Why all the violence initiated on behalf of our democratic system? Are the political leaders in bad faith, afraid of being exposed as legitimizing large-scale theft, or are they in good faith, fighting for their ideal values? I have no answer.

---

35   See Theodor W. Adorno, "Einleitung zu Emile Durkheim *Soziologie und Philosophie*" (1967), in Adorno, *Gesammelte Schriften* (GS$_A$), ed. Rolf Tiedemann (Frankfurt a.M.: Suhrkamp, 1972), vol. 8, p. 249; see also Asger Sørensen, "Durkheims ansats til en etik for det moderne samfund – og en metodologisk kritik af den filosofiske etik", in *Sociologien om velfærd – gensyn med Émile Durkheim*, ed. Anni Greve (Frederiksberg: Roskilde Universitetsforlag, 1998), p. 79.

What I do know is that the violence did not begin with the summits; the first strike was made by a political system that promotes an ideology which makes economic value the only value, while at the same time allowing this value to slip through the fingers of the majority of the world population, leaving as its trace only a worn-out body forced to sell itself to be exploited day after day, provided it can still work at all.

Globalization creates inequality, civil unrest, criminality and terror.[36] The existence of global corporations proves the ideology of free exchange in a free market to be a lie. Big-business and the ideology conceiving of the law of supply and demand as a natural law undermine the general faith in the moral values of the concrete market and of private property, and thereby the general conditions for private enterprise.

Small-scale business can be both sustainable and socially responsible; as Mauss shows, the local market creates both economic and non-economic values. Business should support the anti-globalization movement and fight the ideology that makes money the only value. As John Locke taught us: recognizing money as value is the precondition for accumulation and inequality, and brought to an extreme this will ruin business *per se*.

---

36   See, e.g., Pedro Montes, *El desorden neoliberal*, (Madrid: Trotta, 1999).

CHAPTER 2

From Restricted Economy to General Economy – and Back: Bataille

In the wake of discussions following the publication of Hardt and Negri's *Empire* in 2000, there has been a remarkable resurgence of interest in the expression 'general economy'. The notion of a general economy can be traced back to, at least, Rousseau's article on economy in the French *Encyclopaedia* from 1755, where it signifies what has later become known as political economy, namely knowledge of the laws necessary to govern the 'household' of a state.[1] From this original sense, however, the reference of 'general economy' can be displaced to include almost every aspect of human and social life,[2] and it is well-known that the expression has been discussed in a similarly broad sense by Derrida and Baudrillard.[3] It is also known that these discussions draw heavily on the ideas of Georges Bataille,[4] and in commemoration of the 50th anniversary of the death of Bataille, this article analyses his notion of general economy.

Bataille's theoretical work was published under the title *La Part maudite. Essai de économie générale*,[5] which has adequately been translated into *The*

---

1   See Jean-Jacques Rousseau, "Economie ou Œconomie", in *Encyclopédie, ou Dictionnaire Raisonné des Sciences, des Arts et des Métiers*, ed. Denis Diderot and Jean le Rond d'Alembert (Paris, 1755), vol. 5, pp. 337–38. Available @: http://www.taieb.net/auteurs/Rousseau/economie .html.

2   See, e.g., Akseli Virtanen, "General Economy: The Entrance of Multitude into Production", *Ephemera* 4, no. 3 (2004), pp. 212–13.

3   See, respectively, Jacques Derrida, "From Restricted to General Economy: a Hegelianism without Reserve" (1967), in Derrida, *Writing and Difference*, trans. Alan Bass (London: Routledge, 1978), and Jean Baudrillard, "When Bataille attacked the Metaphysical Principle of Economy", in *Bataille: A Critical Reader*, ed. Fred Botting and Scott Wilson (Oxford: Blackwell, 1998).

4   See, e.g., respectively, Asger Sørensen, "The Inner Experience of Living Matter: Bataille and Dialectics", *Philosophy & Social Criticism* 33, no. 5 (2007), pp. 599 ff (or below, Ch. 4, Sect. A—where, however, I have some reservations about Derrida's reading of Bataille), and Paul Hegarty, *Jean Baudrillard: Live Theory* (London: Continuum Press, 2004) (or the review, William Pawlett, "Book Review: Symbolic Exchange and Beyond", *International Journal of Baudrillard Studies* 3, no. 1 (2006)).

5   Georges Bataille, *La Part maudite. Essai de économie générale. 1. La Consumation* (1949) in Bataille, French *Œuvres - i.e. oe in one letter complètes,* vol. VII, ed. Thadée Klossowski (Paris: Gallimard, 1976). In the present chapter, the following page references to *La Consumation* are indicated in brackets in the text as PM, nn. References to a volume in *Œuvres complètes* will be indicated as OC_B nn.

© KONINKLIJKE BRILL NV, LEIDEN, 2019 | DOI 10.1163/9789004362420_006

Accursed Share. An Essay on General Economy.[6] The explicit point of departure for Bataille's general economy was political economy (see PM, 19), but in spite of this, the notion of economy eventually developed by Bataille is quite far from economy in the ordinary sense. In the light of the discussions mentioned above, this article is therefore dedicated to improving the understanding of the relationship between economy in an ordinary sense and economy in Bataille's much broader sense. There are three main questions guiding this investigation: what is economy, what does Bataille mean by 'economy', and how can Bataille's understanding of economy contribute to the ordinary understanding of economy?

Before we get to that, let me say a few words about the textual basis of this investigation. The first part of *The Accursed Share* was published in 1949 with the subtitle *1. La Consumation*, i.e. *'1. The Consummation'*. Work on Part two, *L'Histoire de l'érotisme*, i.e. *'History of Eroticism'*, was first dropped in 1951, then recommenced in 1954, and eventually given up again the same year.[7] Work on Part three, *La Souveraineté, i.e. 'The Sovereignty'* took place in the same period but was also given up in 1954.[8] Bataille died in 1962, and the second and third parts did not appear as publications in his lifetime. Thus, for a long time it was common to refer to the only part published, the first part, as simply *La Part maudite*, i.e. *The Accursed Share.*[9] However, in the 1970s this misunderstanding became obvious with the posthumous reconstruction and publication of part two and three in Bataille's collected works vol. VIII that was based on the

---

6 Georges Bataille, *The Accursed Share*, vol. I–III, trans. Robert Hurley (New York: Zone Books, 1991 (vol. I) & 1993 (vols. II–III)).

7 See Thadée Klossowski, "Notes" (1976), in OC$_B$ VII, pp. 470–71. It was, however, only given up as part of *The Accursed Share*. In 1957, Bataille published the 1954 version as a book in a single volume under the title *L'Érotisme* (see Francis Marmande, "Notes", in OC$_B$ X, ed. Francis Marmande and Yves Thévenieau (Paris: Gallimard, 1987), p. 689), not mentioning the original context of the text.

8 See Thadée Klossowski, "Notes", in OC$_B$ VIII, ed. Thadée Klossowski (Paris: Gallimard, 1976), pp. 523, 592–93.

9 This misunderstanding was supported by the second French edition of Bataille's *La Consumation*, which was simply given the title *La Part maudite* (Paris: Minuit, 1967), i.e. *The Accursed Share*. The text was introduced by Jean Piel, but the introduction did not explain the change of title, nor anything about Bataille's original intention with the three volumes of *The Accursed Share*. The subsequent German, Spanish and Swedish translations of *La Consumation* are based on this edition – as is indicated by their titles: *Der verfemte Teil*, in *Das theoretische Werk*, trans. Traugott König and Heinz Abosch (München: Rogner & Bernhard, 1975); *La parte maldita*, trans. Francisco Muñoz de Escalona (Barcelona: Icaria, 1987); and, *Den fördömda delen* (1949), trans. Johan Öberg (Stockholm & Stehag: Brutus Östling, 1991). Given that Piel's introduction is even included in the Spanish edition, the misunderstanding has gained a strong international foothold.

original manuscripts,[10] and finally, in the 1990s, all three parts were published in English.[11]

What is really important about this story, however, is that the scope of the original project indicates that Bataille had a much broader concept of economy than the traditional one; in Bataille's general perspective, the latter is simply to be labelled "restricted economy" (PM, 33). This must be emphasized from the outset and kept in mind, especially since in this article the interpretation and analysis will focus mainly on the first part of *The Accursed Share*, *The Consummation*, or maybe just *The Consumption*. The reason for this is simply that it is in this first part Bataille most systematically discusses economy in both the ordinary and his own general sense. In spite of what has just been emphasized – the general title covering all three parts and general economy thus comprising also eroticism and sovereignty – focus in the following will mainly be on economy as discussed in the first part, *The Consumption*, alias *La Part maudite*.

In the first section, I sketch some limitations of the basic concepts of economy with which it is necessary to be acquainted in order to understand Bataille's conception of general economy (A); first, a political critique of the principles of classical political economy and neo-classical economics (i), and then a critique of neo-classical economics regarding their scientific shortcomings (ii). These critiques are radicalized by Bataille's idea of a general economy, and in the second section I present the main theoretical aspects of this idea (B). First economy is considered in a macro-perspective, which comprises the whole of the universe (i); second, in a micro-perspective, where the subjective aspect of economy is maintained as non-objectified desire and inner experience (ii). The third section analyses Bataille's general economy as it was explicitly intended, namely as a political economy (C). First, I argue that Bataille's own suggestions are apolitical in an ordinary sense of politics (i), and that this can be shown to be due to some conceptual slides between nature and society, and between history and ontology, which are symptomatic for Bataille's undecided relationship to politics (ii). I then compare Bataille's general economy with post-modern attempts to legitimize, respectively, capitalism and communism – both of

---

10   See Georges Bataille, *L'Histoire de l'érotisme* ('1951'), in OC_B VIII, ed. Thadée Klossowski (Paris: Gallimard, 1976), pp. 7–165, and Bataille, *La Souveraineté* ('1954'), in OC_B VIII, pp. 243–56.

11   Nevertheless, the English translation, which contributed to placing *La Consumation* in its right context, also refers to the French 1967 edition as the original text (see *The Accursed Share*, vol. I, p. 4); i.e., neither the original 1949 edition, nor the text as it was published in the collected works in 1976. The misunderstanding can therefore be difficult to avoid, even when attempting to refer to the original text (see, e.g., Miwon Kwon, "The Art of Expenditure", in Cai Gou-Qiang, *I Want to Believe*, ed. Thomas Krens and Alexandra Munroe (New York: Guggenheim Museum, 2008), p. 73).

which refer to the general economy – arguing that Bataille can escape them both, since he maintains the important distinction between need and desire (iii). Nevertheless, even though Bataille reveals important aspects of economy viewed as a kind of political economy, the general economy of *The Accursed Share* must be considered an inconsistent and thus unsuccessful project, which is probably the reason why he gave it up despite the text being almost complete.[12] As often emphasized, it can be difficult to unite a theoretical point of view with practical intentions, just as it is difficult to overcome the abyss between the subjective and the objective perspective. Nevertheless, my final remark stresses that this is exactly the reason that I find it worth maintaining that in practice we overcome theoretical contradictions every day (iv).

A   The Limitations of Economy

The ordinary use of the word 'economy' is ambiguous in a way that one has to explicate, but also to accept. The word 'economy' can signify both a real part of the empirical world – i.e. an object or a case – and the field of studies directed towards such empirical matters.[13] Economy as a discipline can therefore be said to deal with economy as its object matter,[14] and it typically does so in the sense that its aim is practical, namely to govern the economy. In more specialized contexts, the latter sense is often labelled 'economics',[15] but that does not rule out the ambiguity completely.[16] Common for both of the senses mentioned is the reference to the resources needed by human beings to sustain and live their lives. It can thus be said that in a modern society, economy as a practical discipline plays a crucial role in the way economy develops as object matter. The ambiguity in the use of the word 'economy' reminds us, first, that economy as object matter signifies the procurement, creation, distribution, circulation and consumption, or disappearance, of the resources necessary

---

12   I have discussed this issue in more detail in Asger Sørensen, *Suverænitet. Bataille set i lyset af Hegel, Marx & Co.*, mag. art.-thesis (København: Filosofisk Institut, Københavns Universitet, 1992), pp. 117–35, but I have not published anything about it so far in English, and I do not know of other discussions of this particular issue.

13   See, e.g., Carsten Fenger-Grøn and Jens Erik Kristensen, "Behovet for en kritik af den økonomiske fornuft", in *Kritik af den økonomiske fornuft*, ed. Carsten Fenger-Grøn and Jens Erik Kristensen (København: Hans Reitzel, 2001), p. 20.

14   See, e.g., Fenger-Grøn & Kristensen, ibid., p. 15.

15   See, e.g., Paul A. Samuelson, *Economics*, 10th ed. (Tokyo: McGraw-Hill Kogakusha, 1976), p. 3.

16   See Samuelson, *ibid.,* where 'economics' is defined as 'political economy'.

for human life; second, that the optimal use of these resources requires a systematic investigation of the processes or activities in which they are used, i.e. economy as an empirical, theoretical and practical discipline; and, third, that these two aspects of economy cannot and should not be separated completely. These premises are accepted by ordinary economic thinking and the critique of political economy (i), but they are contested by the sociological critique of neo-classical economy (ii), and this is Bataille's point of departure.

i   *A Political Critique of Economy*

Metaphysically speaking it is clear that nothing can be created out of nothing, that nothing can disappear completely, and that theoretically one can consider economy as a subject matter in a purely scientific way. In the practical perspective, it is equally clear that resources are created, and that some resources are accessible while others are not. Since the demands of human beings in principle are almost insatiable, the accessible resources are always limited, and the point of departure for ordinary economic thinking is therefore the so-called 'law of scarcity'.[17] Ordinary economic thinking is rooted in the discipline of political economy, a basis for which is Aristotle's famous distinction between '*oikonomía*', which signifies the practical skill and know-how required to use the resources of a household in the best way possible, and '*chremastitiké*', which signifies private business set in motion only in order to become rich, not considering any natural limitations.[18] This distinction between household and business – that is, between reasonable government of common resources and rational calculus of private opportunities of profit – is traditionally considered fundamental for economic thinking.[19] Today, however, it is considered to be of less importance,[20] probably because the public moral valuation of private business oriented towards profit is much more positive than only a few decades ago.[21]

This change in the relative valuation of the two aspects of economical activity is reflected in the development from the classical theory in early liberalism

---

17   See Poul Nyboe Andersen, Bjarke Fogh and Poul Winding, *Nationaløkonomi* (København: Einar Harcks forlag, 1952), pp. 14–15.

18   See Aristotle, *Politics*, trans. B. Jowett, in *The Complete Works of Aristotle*, ed. Jonathan Barnes (Princeton NJ: Princeton University Press, 1984/1995) , vol. 2, *Pol.* 1257–58.

19   See, e.g., Max Weber, *Wirtschaft und Gesellschaft* (1921–22) (Tübingen: J.B.C. Mohr, 1990), pp. 43–53 (Part 1, Ch. II, §§ 8, 10 and 11); see also Andersen, Fogh and Winding, *Nationaløkonomi*, p. 13.

20   See, e.g., Shaun Hargreaves Heap *et al.*, *The Theory of Choice* (Oxford: Blackwell, 1992), pp. 245 ff.

21   See Fenger-Grøn and Kristensen, "Behovet for en kritik af den økonomiske fornuft", pp. 21 ff.

of value as relative to labour, where value signifies utility and is created by the producer, to the neo-classical understanding of value as market price, where value is created by every single consumer's willingness to pay.[22] This development means that economy changes from being a matter of what is good for human beings in an objective perspective to being defined by what can be considered attractive in a subjective perspective; that is, in the perspective of the individual actor. In both cases, however, we are dealing with an activity that is ruled by a want, and as an overall definition of economy we can therefore safely employ Bataille's definition of economy as the activity of searching for what we are missing.[23]

Such an understanding of economy, however, gives rise to various questions. First of all, the 'we' employed in the definition is not a simple entity. A state or government can be in opposition to its citizens, and, put more generally, every collective unity of people, that is, a society, group, family, etc., can be in conflict with other collective entities as well as human individuals. In Adam Smith's classical political economy, the conceptual solution to such conflicts was a combination of the famous idea of the invisible hand and a less famous emphasis on the double nature of human beings as both selfish and altruistic.[24] In relation to this solution, however, Karl Marx can be said to remind us that all historical societies so far have been characterized by the contradiction between some very specific groups of people, namely what can be called the classes of society. Classes are defined by their relation to the means of production. A class society is a society where some classes are in possession of acknowledged property rights to the means of production,[25] and having such a right means that these classes can prevent other classes from pursuing what they are missing. In other words: in a class society, some classes can exclude

---

22   See, e.g., Asger Sørensen, "Value, Business and Globalization – Sketching a Critical Conceptual Framework", *Jounal og Business Ethics* 39, no. 1–2 (2002), pp. 162–63 (Ch. 1 above, Sect. A).

23   See Georges Bataille, "[Ebauche d'avant propos]" (Sketch to a Preface) ('1954'), in OC$_B$ VII, p. 472. This note was meant as an addition to the preface in the new edition of *La Consumation* as Part one of the complete edition of *La Part maudite*. As mentioned above in the introduction, this edition was planned to be published in 1954, but was given up. Nothing indicates, however, that Bataille changed his mind on the subjects analysed here. See also below, note 43, 56, 98 & 99.

24   See, e.g., James Ottesen, "Adam Smith's Marketplace of Morals", *Archiv für Geschichte der Philosophie* 84, no. 2 (2002), pp. 208 ff.

25   See Karl Marx, *Das Kapital*, vol. 2 (1885), in Marx & Engels, *Werke* (MEW), vol. 24 (Berlin: Dietz Verlag, 1973), pp. 37–38; see also, e.g., Anders Lundkvist, *Hoveder og Høveder. En demokratisk kritik af det private samfund. I. Privatejendom og markedsøkonomi* (København: Frydenlund, 2004), pp. 45 ff.

other classes from participating sufficiently in the economic activity, which will eventually lead to the death of people from the latter classes.

In the further scientification of economic thinking as it happened in the development of neo-classical economy, this societal fact was typically ignored and with it also the issue of political conflict, i.e. the question of who the 'we' of economy really are. Instead, the classical liberal trust in the moral sense of human beings and God's foresight was replaced by a trust in economy as a mechanical equilibrium system, where the stability was secured by an infinity of mutually counteracting bumps or pushes.[26] The point of departure for this neo-classical way of thinking was that the smallest unit in an economic system is the single economic actor. This actor must calculate in an instrumentally rational way the optimal use of resources as well as possibilities of profit, and the criterion for success is the greatest possible wealth. One can consider such an actor as an individual consumer who rationally optimizes his or her private preferences; as an ideal type, this actor is called "the economic man" or "*homo economicus*".[27]

Such an actor always acts in his or her own personal interest in the form of instrumentally rational, selfish actions, and the measure of such actions is always the goal. A goal can be considered an expected result, and a result then as the effect of an activity,[28] and if this effect is considered in physical terms, it is a bump or a push. Again, such a bump is the result of a movement, which is driven by the kinetic energy of subjective desire. The interesting conceptual slide in this way of thinking is the gradual omission of the human intention passing from goal to result and effect. It is this displacement that makes possible the objectification of the subjective perspective in neo-classical economy and, with it, that economy as a whole can be considered a mechanical system inherently aiming at equilibrium, which again makes possible the mathematization that characterizes the established economic science today.[29]

---

26   See Karl-Heinz Brodbeck, *Die fragwürdigen Grundlagen der Ökonomie* (Darmstadt: Wissenschaftliche Buchgesellschaft, 2000), pp. 36–58.

27   Heap *et al.*, *The Theory of Choice*, pp. 62 ff.

28   A similar displacement can be detected in the development from teleological ethics to consequentialism (see, e.g., Asger Sørensen, "Deontology – born and kept in Servitude by Utilitarianism", *Danish Yearbook of Philosophy* 43 (2008), p. 90 (included in Part Two of DDD II, *Discourse, Value and Practice*), and Asger Sørensen, *Forskning, etik, konsekvens. Et filosofisk stridsskrift* (København: Politisk Revy, 2003), pp. 34–42). Both historically and conceptually, these displacements are closely interrelated (see, e.g., Élie Halévy, *The Growth of Philosophical Radicalism* (Boston, MA: Beacon, 1955), pp. 264–81).

29   See, e.g., J. Steven Winrich, "Self-Reference and the Incomplete. Structure of Neoclassical Economics", *Journal of Economic Issues* xvii no. 4 (1984), pp. 987 ff and Alexander

With this objectification of individual human action and the entire economical activity of society, the established economic science can ignore the
societal conflicts of classes; one can even, in a political economy perspective,
criticize the scientification of neo-classical economy for covering up, in practice, such political contradictions. The dominant neo-classical micro-economy
pretends to be merely scientific; in reality, however, it also functions as a
political ideology. Neo-classical economy is thus unambiguous in its support
of the basics of capitalism, namely the acceptance of economic man as the
legitimate model for all economic action and thinking, in business as well as in
households, both in business economy and political economy.

ii   *A Critique of Neo-classical Economy in terms of Science*

Apart from the well-known political critique of neo-classical micro-economy,
the displacement mentioned above can also be criticized for being insufficient
in making economy scientific. Such a critique can be noticed in, for instance,
the writings of Émile Durkheim;[30] however, it is only in Marcel Mauss's eth-
nography that this critique really gains momentum. Mauss studied anthropological narratives and descriptions of exchange in primitive societies, and in
these reports he did not find any markets in the classical economic sense, just
as there were no commodities or economic men in the strict sense in these exchanges. According to Mauss, in an empirical scientific perspective it is much
more correct to speak of systems for exchanging gifts. A gift can be considered
a complete societal performance, meaning that even though the exchange of
gifts of course is economic in the ordinary sense, it also has social, moral and
religious significance. *Homo economicus* cannot be encountered in primitive
societies, just as one cannot find the moral man of duty or the scientific man.
From the very beginning, human actions have been more than just economically rational, and they still are. Therefore, according to Mauss, calculating the
intentions of economic man does not seem to be the best point of departure
for economy as an empirically based science.[31]

Rosenberg, "What is the Cognitive Status of Economic Theory", in *New Directions in Economic Methodology*, ed. Roger E. Backhouse (London: Routledge, 1994), pp. 223 ff.

30   See Émile Durkheim, *Ethics and the Sociology of Morals*, trans. Robert T. Hall (New York:
Prometheus Books, 1993), pp. 60 ff.

31   See Marcel Mauss, "Essai sur le don: Forme et raison de l'échange dans le société
archaïques" (1923–24), in Mauss, *Sociologie et anthropologie* (Paris: P.U.F., 1999), p. 272;
see also Asger Sørensen, "Marcel Mauss. Kvinder, høfligheder og talismaner: Gaven som
fuldstœndig social kendsgerning", in *Tradition og fornyelse i sociologien*, ed. Michael Hviid
Jacobsen, Mikael Carleheden, and Søren Kristiansen (Ålborg: Ålborg Universitetsforlag,
2001), p. 79 (or Asger Sørensen, *I Lyset af Bataille – politisk filosofiske studier* (København:
Politisk Revy, 2012), Ch. 5, pp. 126–27).

Some of the theoretical problems caused by the neo-classical reduction-ism were apparently overcome by the Keynesian economy that dominated economic thinking from after WW II and until the middle of the 1970s. It was considered to be very powerful in terms of empirical explanation and could therefore legitimately assert itself scientifically as well as politically.[32] That, however, also meant that it was affected very strongly by the stagflation cri-sis of the 1970s, since allegedly it could neither account for the crisis nor pro-vide the tools to deal with it.[33] As a replacement for Keynesian economy, most economists chose to return to variations of neo-classical micro-economics, and until very recently – i.e. until the financial crisis that began in 2008 – the model of *homo economicus* has been the unchallenged point of departure for political thinking and the understanding of society as such. Typically, the re-construction has begun with a focus on the individual preferences of one actor, and from considerations concerning the rationality of individual choices one has proceeded to the logic of society as a whole via game theoretical reasoning concerning the interactive choices of a plurality of actors.[34]

There is, however, a rather widespread agreement that micro-economy can-not be said to fulfil the criteria normally required for something to be called a science. Micro-economy cannot provide precise predictions that can be veri-fied or falsified,[35] and neither in relation to Kuhn's nor to Lakatos's theories of science can it be considered a science.[36] It is therefore reasonable to ask what cognitive status micro-economy is supposed to have; here, the best bid seems to be that micro-economy is simply a formalization of contract theory,[37] i.e., a formalization of the core elements of the political ideology of capitalism. For Mauss it was obvious that even though economic man could not empirically be found in our past and only to a very limited extent in his present, it could very well be our future,[38] and today, after decades of neo-liberal ideological hegemony, there is even more reason to fear such a fate.

If one prefers a political economy with a scientific basis, there is still very good reason to criticize micro-economics with its objectification and math-ematization of economic activity, presuming the existence of the ideal typical

32   See Samuelson, *Economics*, pp. 205 f.

33   See, e.g., Samuelson, *ibid.,* pp. 856 f.

34   This way of thinking is, for instance, reflected in the structure of the book by Heap *et al.* mentioned above, *The Theory of Choice.*

35   See Rosenberg, "What is the Cognitive Status of Economic Theory", pp. 216–17.

36   See Daniel M. Hausmann, "Kuhn, Lakatos and the Character of Economics", in *New Directions in Economic Methodology,* ed. Backhouse, p. 205.

37   See Rosenberg, "What is the Cognitive Status of Economic Theory", pp. 232–33.

38   See Mauss, "Essai sur le don", p. 272.

homo economicus. That the preference rationality of *homo economicus* is a normative ideal and thus not to be found in reality has, for instance, been emphasized by Jon Elster.[39] In order to be scientific, one might just as well – or even with better reasons – investigate empirically the economic interchange as a societal and social whole, as was done by Durkheim and Mauss; and this is the point of departure for Bataille's general economy. Bataille thus shares Mauss's critique of the idea of economic man (see PM, 71),[40] and it is within such a scientific perspective that Bataille can notice how economic science has satisfied itself with simply generalizing on the basis of an isolated situation, namely the actions of *homo economicus.* Economic man always directs his actions towards a well-defined goal, and Bataille emphasizes that economic science, by idealizing this situation as a general model for economy, ignores the energy that facilitates economic activity, and more generally the flow of energy in living matter (see PM, 30 f). A proper understanding of energy is, as it will become obvious below, of crucial importance to a material conception of economy such as Bataille's.

B   Economy in a Broader Sense

Bataille considers ordinary economic thinking, including both political economy and the neo-classical scientification of economy, as an inappropriate reduction that is both empirically and theoretically deficient. He therefore distinguishes between such a 'restricted economy' and his own 'general economy'. In the latter, resources, production, circulation, growth and value are thought of not only in relation to the societal or private economy, but also in relation to the economy of nature and the universe. Overall, this constitutes economy in the very broad sense mentioned in the first section above, namely as our search for what we are missing.

When Bataille focuses on the resources necessary for human life, it is the ontological necessity that becomes important, and within such a theoretical perspective, the traditional practical aims of economy are placed in brackets. From the very outset, Bataille's perspective entails a displacement, since such a theoretical perspective means that material resources are not merely useful

---

39   See Jon Elster, *Juicios salomónicos* (1989), trans. Carlos Gardini (Barcelona: Gedisa, 1995), p. 11.

40   For an interesting analysis of the asymmetrical relationship between Bataille and Mauss, see Jean-Christophe Marcel, "Bataille and Mauss: a Dialogue of the Deaf?" *Economy and Society* 32, no. 1 (2003), pp. 141–52.

things or commodities but primarily forms of accessible energy: "Essentially wealth is energy; energy is the basis and measure of the production".[41] In the first of the following two sub-sections I sketch the way in which economy according to Bataille must be considered on a universal scale. In this perspective, wealth is resources and resources are energy. Animals and plants are energy, which our labour can make disposable. We can devour plants and meat and thus appropriate the energy expended in our labour efforts. Energy is the basis and measure of all production and the general economy must therefore account for the flow of energy through the universe, through nature and through society (i).

As described above, economy in the ordinary sense is normally about the practical handling of human resources. Distinction is made between micro-economy and macro-economy, where the former deals with the perspective of the single economic actor, whereas the latter assumes a management perspective on a larger collective unit, typically society as a whole. A macro-economy in Bataille's theoretical sense, however, comprises an objectified descriptive account of the energy as such and all of its movements on earth, i.e. the flow of energy in everything earthly going from the physics of the earth to the political economy of human society through the biological, the social and the historical, affecting the conscience and therefore ultimately thought, science and philosophy. Bataille can therefore allow himself to remark that the object of the general economy is not completely separated from its subject (see PM, 20), and it is the subjective aspect of the general economy that is analysed in the second sub-section. It is shown how Bataille presents a micro-economy that takes the subjective desire as its point of departure, but that does not objectify it as kinetic energy; instead, it attempts to preserve the experience of the desire and its objects as inner experiences (ii).

i   *The Flow of Energy*
In its most basic sense, science requires that a phenomenon is shown to be governed by laws. In the first part of *The Accursed Share* Bataille therefore presents those laws, which are valid for the objective basis of the general economy. Natural laws are normally assumed to be universally valid, and this is also the case here. When Bataille speaks about 'the scale of the universe', it is to be understood quite literally, i.e. that the laws of the general economy are also valid for suns, planets and their mutual relations. For earth as a whole, the

---

41   Georges Bataille, "L'Économie á la mesure de l'univers", (1946) in OC$_B$ VII, p. 9.

ultimate source of wealth is the sun, which both produces and reproduces us. Hence, with its radiating surplus it causes us to be alive and thereby calls forth our surplus of life energy. When seen from earth, the radiance of the sun is unilateral in its expenditure; in this radiance, energy is expended and lost without any calculation, without any retribution (see PM, 34 f).

Following the principles of the theory of relativity, Bataille considers energy as matter in liquid form. As living organisms on the surface of the earth, we are mere passages where the surplus energy of the sun is accumulated and made accessible for a time – in the form of matter – for earthly growth and activity. Energy is only accessible in this sense, if a difference can be created between heat and cold; this difference is created by the sun and the release of accumulated energy. The difference, however, disappears again through the earthly exploitation of the energy. It is this movement of consumption that Bataille initially focuses on. According to the second law of thermodynamics, what happens because of the temperature differences on earth can be considered just one stop on the course of the energy headed for the infinite tepidness of the universe. According to Bataille, as part of the growth of living matter on earth, we are thus involved in delaying the flow of the energy, but when the limits of growth are reached, all of the non-accumulated energy will be lost into the universe.

Earth receives and accumulates energy radiated from the sun, creating an abundance of more or less accessible forms of energy. The living matter obtains life by consuming energy from this abundance provided by the sun, but this consumption only accumulates more energy. In principle, the living matter will exploit the abundance of energy to extend itself as much as possible,[42] which means that it will accumulate and grow as much as physical conditions, such as space, allow. It will use as much energy as possible for growth, while the rest will be lost in the form of heat. The immediate limit to the growth of an individual is spatially given by other individuals, whereas the absolute limit is the size of the biosphere of the earth. The pressure of life extends life to all parts of accessible space, which means that if some location experiences a temporary extinction of life – for instance, because of a forest fire – then life will start invading again immediately after the fire has been extinguished. The pressure of life is like a steam kettle, always ready to explode (see PM, 36 f). Neither growth nor reproduction were possible if plants and animals did not dispose of surplus energy, and it is the pressure of this surplus that ultimately

---

42   See Bataille, ibid., p. 11.

can be expressed through explosive violence. Thus, in the general perspective, the economic problem is always, how life can consume the surplus energy that is the result of the biological activity supported by the donations of the sun.[43]

The essential pressure of life has carried it beyond various relative limitations. Plants are extreme: they use almost all their energy on growth and reproduction; the functionally necessary energy is insignificant. With tall trees, life has overcome the immediate lack of space at the global surface, but there is nevertheless an absolute spatial limit to the growth of plants. One solution to this problem is the development of higher-order organisms that accumulate energy by destroying plants without themselves growing to the same extent. The growth of those eating replaces the growth of those being eaten, but that also means that the overall growth rate of life is reduced, and that a larger part of the energy will therefore be lost. Herbivore animals develop at a slower rate than eatable plants, and for Bataille the consumption by living organisms of living matter is therefore clearly a lavish use of energy. Herbivore animals find energy reserves in plants, carnivore animals in herbivores, and the nutrition is primarily used for growth, secondarily for activity, and then for sexual reproduction.

The extravagant development of colours and shapes in the life of plants and animals, the invasion of space by insects and birds, and not least the development of carnivores all contribute to the dissipation of energy (see PM, 169 f). Nevertheless, the sun and the biological processes of life always produce a surplus in the individual organism as well as in life as a whole. For Bataille, the decisively new thing about the human being is that it is the answer to the surplus problem of life in general.[44] The human being is part of this life, including its labour and technique, but while the essence of life is to accumulate energy and thus produce an even greater surplus, the essential for the human way of being is to consume, i.e. to liberate the energy of the universe for its final loss. Through its very activities, the human being liberates much more energy than it can accumulate by itself. As an organism, the human being is in itself a luxury, i.e., an extravagantly complicated and – in relation to the continued existence of life – completely superfluous result of life's own surplus energy. On top of this, the human being also has the special ability to make the energy

---

43   See Georges Bataille, "[Ebauche à l'Introduction théorique]" ('1954'), in OC$_B$ VII, p. 476. This unpublished sketch was meant as an addition to the introduction of the first part of *La Part maudite. 1. La Consumation* in the contemplated 1954 edition. See also note 23 above and note 99 below.

44   See Bataille, "L'Économie á la mesure de l'univers", p. 14.

accumulated on earth, i.e. wood, coal, oil, water and wind, accessible to human use and thereby increase its own wealth of resources (see PM, 42 f).

When the human being appeared on earth, the space was already filled with life, and it was therefore necessary to find new means of making room for another organism. The solution became the specifically human way of organizing and consciously exploiting dead matter, and Bataille can therefore consider labour and technique to be a modality of the extension of life. Energy resources are transformed through human beings and their animals to substances of nutrition, and the technical know-how is constantly increasing. Every new technique, however, has a double effect in relation to the human being and human society as living unities: a new technique consumes an important part of the surplus energy of living nature, but through this consumption an even bigger amount of accessible energy is provided. The development of the means of production has made possible an extension of the elementary movement of growth beyond its former limitations. This development can be said to have strengthened the living matter with 'annex apparatuses', composed of immense amounts of dead, and thereby inert, matter, and by doing so it has increased the energy resources we have at our disposal.

According to Bataille, capitalist accumulation inhibited the luxurious expenditure of feudalism, but WW II marked the provisional limit to the capitalist development of the means of production. Surplus leads to an increase in the means of production, which leads to further growth and even more surplus; but for every living system there is a final limit to growth in relation to the surroundings. War is an example that shows how the constant accumulation of energy under capitalism created a pressure that finally exploded in the most comprehensive orgy of destruction in human history. The pressure of the excess energy, however, was also relieved in a more peaceful way through the general rise in the standard of living that took place during the war. More and more people became employed in the service sector, wages increased and the working hours were reduced (see PM, 42 f).

For Bataille, the increasingly smaller demand for labour manifests itself as unemployment in capitalist societies. This indicates that in order to use the excess energy, it is no longer sufficient to invest energy in producing more equipment and increasing production in general. The idleness of unemployment, however, only represents a passive solution to the surplus problem, and Bataille argues that this kind of crisis will be worsened to the extent that the human being distances itself from active solutions. Luxury represents such an active solution; it is considered an evil only because economy in the ordinary sense assumes the universal validity of the law of scarcity and thus considers the world as constituted by poverty and in need of productive labour. For Bataille, the problem is quite the opposite: the world is sick of wealth, and the apparent scarcity is only a sign of the misuse of energy.[45] As Bataille sums up:

> The living organism, in a situation determined by the play of energy on the surface of the globe, ordinarily receives more energy than is necessary for maintaining life; the excess energy (wealth) can be used for the growth of a system (e.g., an organism); if the system can no longer grow, or if its excess cannot be completely absorbed in its growth, it must necessarily be lost without profit; it must be spent, willingly or not, gloriously or catastrophically (PM, 29).

Bataille's macro-perspective on economy thus leads to a theoretical account of the objective basis for economic activity in the flow of energy in earthly life. This account is based on what today can be considered general knowledge stemming from physics, chemistry and biology, and as such it is quite uncontroversial in a contemporary ecological perspective.[46] In relation to economy, however, it is still controversial. As a science, neo-classical economy objectified human desire as energy, making it possible to use the mechanics of classical physics as a model for further scientific development.[47]

The reason why Bataille's general macro-perspective is still relevant today is that economy as a science has not changed very much since then, and to the extent it has, it has actually become even more objectifying since the 1970s, as indicated in the first section. That there are limits to growth, materially as well as economically, was already indicated in the same decade by the Club of Rome – something that gave rise to a heated debate in the global intellectual public.[48] Nevertheless, apparently that did not affect mainstream economics. Only relatively few contemporary economists have attempted to systematically

---

45   See Bataille, ibid., p. 15.

46   See, e.g., Erik Christensen, "Det økologiske økonomiparadigme", in *Kritik af den økonomiske fornuft*, ed. Fenger-Grøn and Kristensen, pp. 175–76, and Jesper Hoffmeyer, *Samfundets naturhistorie* (Charlottenlund: Rosinante, 1982), pp. 13–14.

47   See, e.g., Brodbeck, *Grundlagen*, pp. 33–40, who shows how mechanics served as an ideal for classical political economy.

48   See Donella H. Meadows, Dennis L. Meadows and Jørgen Randers, *Limits to Growth: A Report for the Club of Rome's Project on the Predicament of Mankind* (New York: Universe Books, 1972). One of the major contributions to the Danish debate was Inger Christensen, Niels I. Meyer and Ole Thyssen, *Vækst*, ed. Inger Christensen, Niels I. Meyer, and Ole Thyssen (København: Gyldendal, 1979).

incorporate reflections on externalities such as the objective biological conditions of economic activity in economy proper, and even fewer have ventured into the development of something that could be called bio-economy or ecological economy.[49] As macro-economy, Bataille's general economy therefore still has something to bring to economy in the ordinary sense, and this is also the case regarding his micro-perspective.

ii   *Desire and Inner Experience*

According to Bataille, economy can be considered as our search for what we are missing. In a practical perspective, we focus on the 'we', as was done in the first section. In a theoretical perspective, however, this definition makes it relevant to ask more closely about the 'what', e.g., whether we always know what we are missing, or what the relationship is between the 'what' we are searching for and the 'what' we are missing. Humanity as a whole can thus be seen as wanting something which no specific human being or group is actually looking for, since nobody knows about this want. If we consider the flow of energy through human beings, our objective interests as living human beings in a society can be in contradiction with our individual, subjective desire. We are not always conscious about our objective needs, neither is the desire always clear and unambiguous, and on the unconscious level it can even be hard to distinguish between needs and desire. In economic contexts, however, it has typically been considered sufficient to distinguish between objective needs, which can be conscious or unconscious, and subjective desire, which is always conscious and may coincide with the objective needs, be they conscious or unconscious.

Ordinary economic thinking normally chooses to regard this potential contradiction as part of the political issue concerning the distribution of power and wealth mentioned above. As a collective unit, a society can thus be said to have objective needs that can be expressed as its preferences, and in a democratic society these preferences must be made reconcilable with the subjective preferences of the citizens, which also expresses their desires as a whole. Hence, the idea is that the individual preferences of the citizens can be aggregated into a sum, which expresses the united preferences of the society. However, the principles behind such an aggregative construction have been shown to be, if not contradictory, at least deeply problematic.[50] Furthermore, if the conscious subjective preference of the single individual human being does not necessarily express its objective needs, and if neither needs nor desire can be

---

49   See, e.g., Christensen, "Det økologiske økonomiparadigme", pp. 175–76.
50   See, e.g., Heap *et al.*, *The Theory of Choice*, pp. 212 ff.

expressed adequately as preferences, the theoretical problems become even greater. In short: if desire does not reflect need, and neither reflects preferences, then how do we know *what* we are missing?

For Bataille, the opposition between need and desire is not a difference that will disappear as a result of, for instance, enlightenment, scientific investigations, better technology or more democracy. This opposition is simply an essential trait of being human. Desire does not direct itself towards the same objects as needs. The point of departure for Bataille in this analysis is the Marxist critique of capitalist society put forward by his contemporaries, which emphasizes how capitalism reifies the human being by transforming human labour to a mere commodity.[51] For Bataille, this critique is radicalized by Friedrich Nietzsche, who considers human degradation to be inherent in the transformation of human activity to goal-oriented work. Simply by working, you make yourself a tool for the survival of yourself or others, thereby reducing yourself to a slave.[52]

The Marxist critique of capitalism as a historical formation to be overcome by history is therefore radicalized to a general critique of civilization, directed towards society as such,[53] although Bataille still focuses on modern, industrial society (see PM, 123–35).

In the general economy, Bataille wants to connect the objectively given material aspects of economic activity with the subjectively given inner life; that is, he also understands energy in the subjectively given form, namely as the inner experience of desire. This means that for the general economy, "a human sacrifice, the construction of a church or the gift of a jewel is no less interesting than the sale of wheat" (PM, 19). The character of desire means for Bataille that if economy is about what we are missing, economy cannot consist only in production and circulation of things, just as economical problems cannot be considered only theoretical or technical problems. Ordinary economic thinking can consider human actions as commodities, i.e. as things, and it is precisely because of this reduction of human life that ordinary economy is 'restricted'. For Bataille, only by introducing the subjective desire in economic thinking can it be made clear that the human being cannot be objectified as a thing.

---

51   A typical example is the analysis by Georg Lukács, *Die Verdinglichung und das Bewußtsein des Proletariats*, in Lukács, *Werke*, vol. II (Neuwied: Luchterhand, 1968), pp. 257–397.

52   See Friedrich Nietzsche, *Jenseits von Gut und Böse* (1886), in Nietzsche, *Werke* (1955), ed. Karl Schlechta (Darmstadt: Wissenschaftliche Buchgesellschaft, 1997), vol. II, p. 732.

53   See, e.g., Asger Sørensen, "At tage fat om ondets rod. Batailles radikale civilisationskritik", in *Excesser – om Georges Bataille*, ed. René Rasmussen and Asger Sørensen (Århus: Modtryk, 1994), pp. 198 ff (or Sørensen, *I Lyset af Bataille*, Ch. 3., pp. 81 ff).

For a human being itself, life is not about being a thing but about being sovereign, i.e. being free in the moment experienced, independent of any task to be completed (see PM, 177).[54] There is for Bataille an irreducible and principled opposition between the objective needs of the human being *per se* and this subjective desire towards being sovereign, and only with the introduction of such a desire in economy is it possible to seriously begin thinking of economy as a general economy.

If economy is our search for *what we* are missing, but our subjective desires do not reflect our objective needs, *we* cannot in principle know *what* we are missing. This means that economy, both theoretically and practically, must be thought of more generally than is usually the case. It is not enough to solve the inherently unsolvable problem of preference aggregation mentioned above. When Bataille speaks of economy, he does not only mean something more than, and different from, both classical political economy and neo-classical economy; he also means something more than what is claimed by the economic sociology and ecological economy mentioned above. Bataille brings matters to a head by saying that in our economic activity, we are searching for a good that in the end must escape us, because the complete satisfaction of the subjective desire, i.e. the sovereign and without any compromise unproductive pleasure, would result in a drainage of all accessible resources and therefore ultimately and quite literally in death. In a certain sense, we are very well aware that our desire for sovereignty is self-contradictory, and we can therefore be said subjectively as well as objectively to be separated from this good that we desire by the awareness produced by the anxiety of actually having this desire satisfied.

It is because of this dynamical and contradictory structure that Bataille has chosen to call his work on economy *The Accursed Share*.[55] The point is that no matter how far one organizes one's life and doings in a rational, goal-orientated and reasonable way, no matter how much one is objectified, there is always something left that does not allow itself be sublated. That we are going to die, for instance, is an incontestable, objective fact, but still we can never subjectively be reconciled with it. As Bataille remarks, we are actually lying to ourselves, when we curse death (see PM, 41). Death is objectively part of life, and Bataille's general economy is precisely about those objects of our subjective inner experience which most clearly signal to us that we cannot expect

---

54 See also Asger Sørensen, "Om arbejdets patologi – og suverænitetens mirakuløse umenneskelighed if. Bataille", *Psyke og logos* 26, no. 2 (2005), pp. 739 ff (or Sørensen, *I Lyset af Bataille*, Ch. 9, pp. 222 ff).

55 See Bataille, "[Ebauche d'avant propos]", p. 472.

the continuity typically promised us by religion, i.e. those objects that show us decay and death where we would have preferred to see life continued into eternity. These objects are, in a Christian perspective, the accursed leftovers of reality, but they are also objects of desire – at one and the same time both attractive and repulsive. The point for Bataille is that because these objects are perishable and thus only transitory, instead of cursing them we could in principle choose to adore and love them for the very same reasons, and as such subjectively reconcile ourselves with the objective flow we are part of: the infinite movement of consumption departing from the radiation of energy from the sun.[56]

Bataille's intention with the general economy is thus to reconcile the world of decay with the inner life and subjective experiences of the human being. In a material sense, he considers the perishable world to be part of the general flow of energy, which constantly demands consumption and loss, and which ultimately will lead to the destruction of all the resources we can accumulate. According to Bataille, however, this movement can be described independently of the inner life of the human being,[57] and the general economy can therefore be introduced through an ordinary scientific description of the objective basis of the inner life, as done in the first part of this section. To fulfil the ambitions behind the general economy, however, it is necessary not just to reconstruct discursively the logic of the inner life, as is done in *The History of Eroticism* and *Sovereignty*. It is also necessary to construct texts that adequately express the genuine inner experiences, and this is what Bataille attempted to do in his aphoristic work *La summa athéologique, The Atheological Summa*. Never completed either, this work was planned to include, among other texts, *The Inner Experience, Guilty* and *On Nietzsche*.[58] The present article, however, remains within the discursive reconstructions of the general economy as it is presented in *The Accursed Share*.[59]

---

56   See Georges Bataille, "Le mouvement général de l'ouvrage" ('1954'), in OC$_B$ VIII, p. 535. This unpublished sketch was meant to be the preface to the 1954 edition of the whole of *The Accursed Share*. See also notes 23 and 98.

57   See Bataille, ibid., p. 536.

58   See Thadée Klossowski, "Annexe 6" (1976), in OC$_B$ VI, p. 365. For a recent and very precise reading of Bataille primarily based on these texts, see Bruce Baugh, "Bataille: Negativity Unemployed", in Baugh, *French Hegel: From Surrealism to Postmodernism* (New York and London: Routledge, 2003), pp. 71–92.

59   This is also the case with my articles on the subject matters more closely related to volumes two and three of *The Accursed Share*, i.e. the above mentioned "The Inner Experience" (Ch. 4 below) and "Om arbejdets patologi" (Sørensen, *I Lyset af Bataille*, Ch. 9).

What is important to Bataille is that there is always a surplus of energy, and that economy, understood as our search for what we are missing, is in itself an activity supported by this surplus. Only from a restricted point of view can there be necessity and scarcity, and it is therefore an inadmissible reduction when the restricted economy considers human beings as isolated beings constantly fighting against each other over resources. According to Bataille, the general movement of energy being filtered through life can be seen to animate the human being with energy, and the sovereign actions of human beings can be identified in this unstoppable flow of energy towards the final loss. Sovereignty is the subjectively given, i.e. the inner experience of desire that devotes the human being to glorious deeds, which, however, in an objectified and productive perspective can only be considered useless consumption (see PM, 31).

It is precisely this idea of an excess of energy in both the subjectively and objectively given which, according to Bataille, distinguishes general economy from economy in an ordinary sense. The general economy investigates the bubbling and boiling of life, which is caused by the circulation and passage of energy in everything living, i.e. in plants, animals and human beings, including their inner experiences.[60] Human beings must simply be considered part of life, i.e. part of the movement of energy that leaves the sun and comes down to earth, and in this theoretical perspective, everything within the historical and social reality of human beings is merely a delay in the flow of the energy. The specifically human way of being, however, also includes something subjectively given, namely the lived inner experiences of individuals, and it is in these inner experiences that some objects can be presented as cursed or damned. Hence the title, *The Accursed Share*.

C   An Unpractical Political Economy

The theoretical-empirical perspective on economy makes it possible for Bataille to see donations of gifts and squandering with excess resources where ordinary economists see scarcity and barter between instrumentally rational egoists. In a political economy, however, theoretical analyses must be followed up by practical recommendations, and this is also the case in Bataille's general economy. As mentioned in the introduction, Bataille considered *The Accursed*

---

60   Bataille actually reconstructs the sexual reproduction as if – and it is 'as if'- even primitive sexed organisms could be attributed to inner experiences (see Georges Bataille, *L'Érotisme* ('1954', 1957), in OC$_B$ X, pp. 100 ff; see also Sørensen, "The Inner Experience", pp. 604–05 (Ch. 4 below, Sect. C).

Share a work about political economy, i.e. a piece of practically orientated macro-economic thinking, and the theoretical analysis of the general economy must therefore be able to argue for a specifically political organization of the economy. His general recommendation to get rid of the problematic surplus by giving gifts allows him to make some apparently very explicit political statements on a global scale, but since he does not relate to anything more limited than the world economy, and since he is not concerned with justice, his recommendations are beyond what would normally be termed the political sphere (i).

I will argue that to this disappointment can be added that the whole idea of the general economy is based on some very problematic conceptual slides between the natural and the societal level, and between what is ontologically necessary and what is merely historical. With his way of conceptualizing human reality, Bataille tends to disregard what is specifically political in this reality, and therefore he also seems to give up on ideals concerning the government of society (ii). What is even worse, apparently the type of actual political economy best supported by the general economy is the kind of *laissez-faire* liberalist economy recommended by the modern inheritors of classical political economy, namely the post-modern neo-liberals. However, it can be argued that ultimately Bataille's general economy does not support a globalized capitalist economy, since it maintains the fundamental distinction between needs and desire, which facilitates the critique of capitalism (iii). The attempt to handle conceptually this opposition – together with those between theory and practice, objectivity and subjectivity, nature and society and ontology and history – is a philosophical project that makes the general economy an impressive idea of dialectical thought but also, in all likelihood, almost impossible as a practical political project (iv).

i   *The Ontological Necessity of the Gift*

In the global macro-perspective, the economic activity of the human being is driven by nature's movement of consumption. The sun creates an excess of energy that is accumulated *in* earth, and *on* earth the ordinary growth of life accumulates even more energy. Until now we have lived well without knowing the laws and principles governing this movement, and according to Bataille this ignorance has not affected the movement as such. The point is, however, that Bataille does not believe it is possible in the long run to maintain a conflict between the movements of the universe and those of human beings. The reason for our failure in solving our immediate problems is allegedly this basic ignorance and the resulting lack of reconciliation, and if the human accumulation is not reconciled with energy's movement of consumption, the result will be a catastrophe.

The general economy conveys that the energy must be lost in the end without any return, whether we want it or not. The political point for Bataille is that we can decide whether this will happen with or without our consent. We can decide whether we want to give gifts or not – that is, whether the loss is going to happen in an honourable way or in a catastrophic way. It is up to us to decide whether human beings through their actions should demonstrate their desire to be sovereign, i.e. demonstrating themselves as being animated by the movement of consumption, or whether we should simply wait for the movement to cause a societal explosion in the form of a war (see PM, 29 ff). According to Bataille, in a decisive moment – lasting only a very short while – we can choose if we want to let our actions be governed by the laws of the universe or not; if we do not choose to act in the right way, the long-term consequences will be disastrous. The steam in the kettle will always get out.

A practical perspective is, as mentioned in the first section, always limited. The limitation, however, does not have to restrict itself to a single household or organization, city state or nation; it can also be limited in the ambitious way that Bataille limits the general economy, namely to humanity as a whole, i.e. as the unity of all specifically human inhabitants of the surface of the earth. If the general economy is to be understood as a political economy, the world population must be understood as one big household to be ruled by a world government; in fact, Bataille was involved in the public discussion concerning such a government just after WW II.[61]

Regardless of the form of political rule, the general economy tells us that war can only be prevented, if the rich countries donate their surplus to the poor countries. In pre-industrialized societies, the surplus is used for festivals and useless monuments like pyramids and cathedrals. Modern societies have used the surplus on providing welfare, which makes life easier, and increasing the relative amount of time for leisure. That, however, has not been sufficient to spend the excess. In the 20th century, the greatest part of the excess has been left to the kind of loss that takes place in wars, which have grown to catastrophic proportions. For Bataille, it is the recognition of this fact that must imply a Copernican turn of the economy, i.e. a transformation of the restricted economy into a general economy. The global economic development demands that the USA disregards profit in some parts of its economic activities

---

61   See Georges Bataille, "Le gouvernement du monde" (1949), in OC$_B$ XI, ed. Francis Marmande and Sibylle Monod (Paris: Gallimard, 1988), pp. 402 ff.

and donates commodities without return (see PM, 32 f); the economy of the USA is simply – in the eyes of Bataille in 1949 – the most explosive living mass ever seen in history (see PM, 161).[62]

With such an economic analysis, Bataille can be quite satisfied with the political development in those years. At that time, many considered the establishment of the United Nations a step towards a world government,[63] and the USA did in fact organize its global economic politics in a way that could be considered consistent with Bataille's recommendations. This was the time when the USA – after the summit in 1944 at Bretton Woods – was one of the major driving forces behind the establishment of global economic institutions such as the World Bank and the International Monetary Fund, to which it also contributed the main part of the financial basis, just as it committed itself to large-scale political-economic schemes such as the Marshall Plan and the Truman doctrine. Considered as a whole, Bataille regards this development as revolutionary since it renounces "the rule that capitalism is based on" (PM, 164), namely profit; accordingly, what happens is that commodities are donated without any compensation.

The political goal of these initiatives was obviously to revitalize the global economy, which was supposed to be in the objective interest of every single individual. However, because of the uncertainty regarding the actual outcome of these political initiatives, Bataille can emphasize that the plans entailed a large element of gambling (see PM, 168). Bataille also finds it remarkable that the initiatives take into account collective yields, meant to answer collective needs, and that the provision of financial credit is transformed from a business into a societal function (see PM, 167).

Considered as a whole, Bataille finds it substantiated that the world was dealing with a negation of the basic principle of capitalism, i.e. the idea of the isolated, egoistical, instrumentally rational calculus of private profit, and that this negation points in the direction of a totally different principle, namely the communist principle: from everyone according to their means, to everyone according to their needs.

For Bataille, the aid to Europe from the USA after WW II becomes an illustration of the general point, namely that it is necessary to expend. The assumption of the instrumental egoism of 'economic man' cannot, neither in theory nor in practice, constitute the basis of political-economic interventions

---

62   For the same reason, today Bataille would probably be very preoccupied with the economic development in China.

63   See, e.g., Hans Kelsen, *The Law of the United Nations* (New York: Praeger, 1950); here cited after Michael Hardt and Antonio Negri, *Empire* (Cambridge, MA: Harvard University Press, 2000), pp. 5–6, 416.

on a global scale. Bataille nevertheless considers the USA an almost classical, even ideal typical, capitalist society and therefore asks how it was possible to gather political support for financing general global schemes. Based on the premises presented, the answer can only be: the fear of the Soviet Union. Bataille thus sees perfectly clearly that the global economic interventions of the USA could be regarded as a grand-scale economic warfare against the Soviet Union, and he emphasizes that the politics of the communists is a crucial factor in the development of world economy. It was the pressure from the communists that made it necessary to introduce the kind of politics that raised the standard of living in the western world and thus necessitated a fundamental change in economy.

Bataille stresses that this kind of welfare politics catches the USA in the conflict between defending the ideal of free enterprise and arguing for the necessity of the state. The very tension between communism and capitalism, i.e. what became known as the 'cold war', results in an economic development of the same kind as that which resulted from the two world wars: freedom of spirit, relaxed relations between human beings, and the development of state enterprises and public services. The result as a whole will, according to Bataille (still in 1949) be a 'dynamic peace', which will basically be maintained by the threat of war and the continued armament in both camps (see PM, 174 ff). In spite of this material basis, it will primarily express itself as a competition between types of economic organization (see PM, 162), i.e. between the constant, primitive accumulation in the communist world and the reluctant accumulation in the modern bourgeois world (see PM, 148 ff).

Here, Bataille pinpoints the basic tensions found in the political economy after WW II, and he understands that implementing the Keynesian economic programmes will create the foundation for what we know today as the European welfare societies. In his general economical perspective, Bataille is positive towards the redistribution of material resources by the state. It is, however, not primarily because the welfare society would be a more just social order, but because in such societies there is a better balance between accumulation and expenditure than in the communist societies at that time, which were biased towards accumulation. Despite Bataille's strong and consistent political engagement on the left-wing,[64] his economic thinking can be

---

64 Bataille has at various occasions been accused of fascism, but this, I have argued, is a totally misleading characterization (see Asger Sørensen, "Georges Bataille: At tage ved lære af fascismen: Mellem modstand og analyse", in *Tradition og fornyelse i sociologien*, ed. Jacobsen, Carleheden and Kristiansen, pp. 255–56 (or Sørensen, *I Lyset af Bataille*, Ch. 6, pp. 157–59)).

characterized as almost apolitical – maybe even anti-political[65] – or beyond good and evil, as Nietzsche would have phrased it.

ii   *Between Sociology and Ontology*

In this theoretical perspective, it is worth taking a closer look at Bataille's general economy. In relation to the critiques of political economy carried out by Durkheim, Mauss and Marx, the general economy represents a crucial displacement, respectively, from the societal to the natural level, and from the historical to the ontological. The ordinary conception of wealth in terms of money, capital and value is extended in the general economy to comprise all resources, which are then interpreted as accumulated energy. Correspondingly, a displacement takes place from the ordinary economic talk about exchange of commodities and circulation of goods to Bataille's description of the movement of the energy in the resources; that is, its flow through everything living. It is these displacements from economy to ecology that make it problematic to strive for unlimited profit, accumulation and growth in economy and provide the reasons for Bataille's recommendation to expend the excess.

The displacements, however, are not complete. What happens is rather a constant sliding back and forth, meaning that Bataille does not distinguish clearly between economic profit in terms of money, surplus production in the form of commodities and excess energy, just as he does not distinguish clearly between gifts, consumption and loss. As Bataille sees it, surplus is in every respect a problem for human life. The continuous back and forth displacement, however, has some problematic consequences. It means, for instance, that it is the truth of the laws of life's movement of consumption that should be acknowledged and given as reason for actions at the societal level rather than the laws of economy or society as such. Bataille quite clearly believes that his analyses of pre-industrial societies, such as the Aztecs before the Spanish conquest and Tibet before the Chinese invasion, are sufficient basis for understanding the dynamics of modern industrial societies and giving them political recommendations (see PM, 47).

The movement of energy is regarded by Bataille as an "eternal necessity" (PM, 31), but we can nevertheless, as mentioned above, choose how to relate to it, i.e. whether it should be accumulated until the point of exploding or be expended and squandered away before then. Bataille does not, however, go into much detail about who the 'we' really are; as will become clear in the following, that is because Bataille does not actually have much of an idea about how society should be organized politically. When Bataille is moralizing, he

---

65   See Antonio Campillo, *Contra la economía* (Granada: Comares, 2001), p. 4.

appeals to the acknowledgement of the natural ontological necessity rather than the societal or historical necessity. Furthermore, the knowledge of this necessity is regarded as motivating in itself, meaning for the human being that neither its will nor actions are bound causally by the eternal necessities of nature. Bataille thus maintains a rather traditional liberal concept of freedom, which also shines through in his general economy.

With regard to economy, Mauss considers generous interchange of gifts to be the empirically original form of exchange. Interchange of gifts presupposes a higher degree of inequality than both barter and sharing, and the result of the interchange of gifts is typically a reinforcement of the inequality, since the donor in exchange attains higher social status and thereby power, whereas the recipient loses on both scales.[66] Mauss is thinking of himself and is also recognized as a socialist, but nevertheless he believes that morality and politics should be based upon such a generosity.[67] This way of thinking practically is taken over by Bataille, again with a clear conscience – i.e. consciousness – about what giving gifts presupposes and implies (see PM, 73 ff). Bataille radicalizes the structural inequality to the extreme, considering the sun to be the ultimate donor and conceiving of political economy only in the global perspective of a world government; however, whereas Durkheim and Mauss consider society at large as analogous to an organism that demands reasonable yet also authoritarian government,[68] Bataille considers sovereignty to be the essence of every single human being and societal life to be inherently reifying. Bataille thereby sharpens the Marxist critique of capitalism as well as the classical liberal contradiction between individual and society, and even though he does not regard equality as politically significant, as is the case with traditional liberals and socialists,[69] he clearly distances himself from authority as a legitimate principle of government.[70]

---

66   See Mauss, "Essai sur le don", pp. 152 ff.

67   See, e.g., Sørensen, "Marcel Mauss", pp. 84 ff (or Sørensen, *I lyset af Bataille*, 132 ff).

68   See, e.g., Sørensen, ibid., and Asger Sørensen, "Durkheims ansats til en etik for det moderne samfund – og en metodologisk kritik af den filosofiske etik", in *Sociologien om velfærd – gensyn med Émile Durkheim*, ed. Anni Greve (Frederiksberg: Roskilde Universitetsforlag, 1998), pp. 79 ff.

69   See, e.g., Asger Sørensen, "Praktisk filosofi i lyset af Georges Bataille – om lighed, etik og menneskelighed", in *Den ene, den anden, det tredje. Politisk identitet, andethed og fællesskab i moderne fransk tænkning*, ed. Carsten Bagge Laustsen and Anders Berg-Sørensen (København: Politisk Revy, 1999), pp. 211–12 (or Sørensen, *I Lyset af Bataille*, Ch. 4, pp. 113–15).

70   See, e.g., Georges Bataille, "Vers la révolution réelle" (1936), in OC_B I, ed. Denis Hollier (Paris: Gallimard, 1970), pp. 426–28; see also Sørensen, "At tage ved lære af fascismen", pp. 254 ff (or Sørensen, *I lyset af Bataille*, 156 ff).

However, without accepting authority it is not possible to create politics in an ordinary sense; that is, no regulation of social life can take place. The result is that, as a political economy on the normal political scale, the general economy turns out to be almost equivalent to a very liberal market economy, i.e. an economy with few limitations. In Adam Smith's classical liberalism, the societal rule primarily takes place at the individual level, since every human being is gifted with the ability to have moral sympathies. The strong moral appeal of the general economy shows that for Bataille, the main regulatory instrument is also the morality of the individual. Apparently, he imagines that a fundamental change can be achieved in the moral outlook of every individual, so that they will not only accumulate but also consume. As mentioned, the general economy makes Bataille favour bourgeois society over communist society, not because of justice but because of the flow of energy. What is really worrying, however, is that his prime examples of societies in ideal balance with regard to the flow of energy, i.e. pre-Columbian societies in America and Tibet before the Chinese invasion, are societies with strongly authoritarian forms of government, which does not seem to bother Bataille that much. Even though Bataille considers his general economy a political economy, apparently he is not worried by the various forms of political government a society can take, i.e. monarchy, aristocracy or democracy.

The apolitical perspective of Bataille's general economy seems to go hand in hand with an apolitical understanding of social reality as a whole. Such a way of understanding social reality is characteristic of the early Protestant liberals, who subscribed to the idea of a single individual facing the absolute. This absolute is primarily God and secondarily the state, but ultimately it can be the market when it has been hypostasized as a self-sustaining entity, as is the case in neo-classical economy. The ideal typically gained from this way of thinking is freedom in the negative sense of 'freedom from'. What is missing in such an understanding of social reality is the importance of all the institutions of a modern society, which mediate politically between the absolute and the particular at various levels. Recognizing the value of such intermediary institutions, as Durkheim did,[71] typically spurs ideals about a 'freedom to', i.e. freedom to participate in the civic rule of society.[72] The point is that in spite of the

---

71   See, e.g., Émile Durkheim, *Leçons de sociologie* (1950) ['1890–1900'] (Paris: P.U.F., 1997), pp. 99–100, 129–30; see also Anni Greve, "Velfærdsstatens sociologi – les corps intermédiaires", in *Sociologien om velfærd – gensyn med Émile Durkheim*, ed. Greve, pp. 48 ff.

72   See, e.g., Will Kymlicka, *Contemporary Political Philosophy. An Introduction*, 2nd ed. (Oxford: Oxford University Press, 2002), p. 295.

critique directed against both fascism and communism, Bataille does not stress any ideal in relation to how society should be governed, the reason probably being that he never got over his qualms about parliamentary democracy, so widespread in Europe among both leftist and rightist in the 1920s and 1930s.[73]

Bataille's anti-authoritarian traits are also expressed in his indifference towards money. Throughout the development of the general economy, he thus discusses – sometimes in great detail – resources, things and commodities and deals with sacrifices, gifts, labour, trade, growth, savings, accumulation and wealth; however, when it comes to money he states, simply and almost in passing, that money is a form of energy.[74] This means that Bataille ignores a basic piece of knowledge gained by classical political economy, namely that money, as Locke notes, has the special quality of allowing an almost unlimited accumulation of wealth when recognized as value. This is not the case with produced goods, and even less so with living and thereby perishable resources.[75] It is the very social recognition of the value of money that makes it a specific social resource: the energy depends precisely on the actual recognition. Bataille's disregard of money can therefore be interpreted as a disregard of what is specifically capitalist about modern society, since capital in particular could never come into existence without money in this sense.[76]

Bataille clearly sees that desire can be directed towards something perishable, just as it can be directed towards something immaterial like value, but apparently he has not noticed the societal mediation that bestows almost magical value upon money – what Marx calls the fetish character of money.[77] In the natural scientific energy perspective of the general economy, this is of course a recognition of a fictional resource, but as Locke clearly sees, the acceptance of this fiction is crucial for the development of social inequality as distinct from the naturally given inequality.[78] Dead matter is socially recognized as valuable, in the form of houses, money, jewelry and consumer goods such as washing machines, and social inequality is primarily expressed through the social adaptation, organization and distribution of dead matter. However, in the general perspective, dead matter is not as perishable or explosive as living matter, and

---

73   See Sørensen, "At tage ved lære af fascismen", pp. 251 ff (or Sørensen, *I Lyset af Bataille*, pp. 153 ff).

74   See Bataille, "L'Économie á la mesure de l'univers", p. 13.

75   See John Locke, *Two Treatises of Government* (1698) (Cambridge University Press, 1988), p. 162.

76   See Marx, *Das Kapital*, vol. 1 (1867), MEW 23 (Berlin: Dietz Verlag, 1974), pp. 85–98.

77   See Marx, *ibid.*, pp. 107–08.

78   See Locke, *Two Treatises of Government*, pp. 301–02; see also Sørensen, "Value, Business and Globalization", p. 162 (Ch. 1 above, Sect. A).

there are therefore no urgent practical reasons, nor any ontological necessities with respect to energy, that call upon the one in possession of such an excess to expend it without retribution.

In the perspective of societal economy, the accumulation of wealth can be a problem, since it can be a sign of surplus production and lack of purchasing power. This problem was solved politically by Keynesian economics through continuous redistribution of the socially recognized dead values, primarily money. It is, however, not the energy movement of life that necessitates this redistribution; it is the social misery that makes the exploited masses boil over in rage against the reigning injustice. Social pressure can thus be experienced from these parts of society, despite the exploitation that strips them of their natural living energy. Nevertheless, Bataille does not distinguish between use-value and exchange-value; he has no specific concept of surplus-value and no systematic concept of capital either. Since he does not share the objectively orientated theory of labour-value in the classical political economy of Locke, Smith and Marx, instead siding with the neo-classical conception of value as subjectively constituted by desire, it becomes difficult for his general economy to criticize economic inequality at the societal level. As mentioned above, for Bataille accumulation is not primarily a problem in relation to the societal distribution of economic goods; it is mainly a problem because of the pressure generated by the surplus energy. Bataille is not really interested in the distribution of goods at a societal level, nor in the form of government in a society, and I therefore find it fair to characterize the general economy as apolitical in the same sense that liberalism can be considered apolitical.[79]

iii   *Post-modern Capitalism and Communism*

Bataille considers his general economy a political economy, and even though it can be thought of as apolitical, one can detect a more or less implicit preference for a certain kind of economic principle, as I have argued. The problem is that the kind of economic thinking that may find some legitimacy in Bataille's general economy is precisely a kind of economic thinking that is normally considered very questionable from a left-wing perspective. According to Jean-Joseph Goux, the general economy can be considered a precursor of the post-modern way to legitimize capitalism found in the work of the modern neo-conservative ideologist George Gilder. With reference to Mauss, Gilder thinks of modern capitalism as an economy of excess that provides objects of

---

79   See e.g Vincent Valentin, "Libéralisme, anarchie et démocratie: perspectives contemporaines", in *Le liberalisme au miroir du droit. L'État, la personne, la propriété*, ed. Blaise Bachofen (Lyons: ENS Editions, 2008), p. 230.

desire before they are in demand. Desire as such is undetermined and can be formed according to the possibilities offered for satisfaction. This means that it is supply that determines demand, not the other way around.[80] According to Gilder, capitalism as a system is irrational, and it is precisely its nucleus of play and gambling that has secured its ideological success, confronted with the rationality of socialism. In post-modern capitalism, you do not know which object your desire will be directed towards, and all kinds of satisfaction of desire can be developed into a profit-making industrial production of objects. In such an economic system, however, it is not possible to distinguish at a fundamental level between necessity and luxury – that is, between needs and desire – the way it has traditionally been the case in political economy. In consumer capitalism, objective utility is finally reduced to a contingent choice,[81] a preference, which at the same time expresses subjective needs and desire.

Employing this way of thinking in developing a post-modern ideology for post-bourgeois hedonist consumer capitalism thus brings Bataille, who thinks of himself as a radical leftist, in "bad company".[82] The general economy does not seem, as Bataille had hoped, to offer a clear alternative to an, in principle, always restricted capitalist economy; on the contrary, it actually seems that the principles of his general economy are precisely what capitalism needed to expand beyond its own ideological contradictions and limitations, in particular the conflict between neo-classical economy as a mechanical system objectifying the ideal of *homo economicus*, and the idea of value as defined by subjective preferences, demand and desire. Economy in Bataille's general sense thus seems to be realized as part of the neo-liberal world order, which in fact is not an order at all, and the general economy can therefore be considered the ideological foundation for post-modern desire-capitalism run amok.

Today, however, being a communist like Antonio Negri and Michael Hardt,[83] implies thinking that we must go through precisely this kind of capitalism in order to achieve the final liberation of humankind. In this case, however, the liberation is not thought to be the result of the efforts of the proletariat. For the post-modern communist, liberation is brought into being by the class that post-modernity made the subject of history, i.e. the most recently chosen people: the so-called 'multitude'. The modern welfare society is a disciplinary

---

80 See Jean-Joseph Goux, "General Economics and Postmodern Capitalism", *Yale French Studies* 78 (1990), pp. 210 ff.

81 See Goux, ibid., pp. 220–21.

82 See Goux, ibid., pp. 223–24.

83 See Hardt and Negri, *Empire*, p. 350.

society in the sense Gilles Deleuze attributes to Michel Foucault,[84] i.e. a form of bodily control that facilitates both modern government and production.[85]

Disciplinary society is a factory society, whereas post-modern society is characterized by the aspiration to avoid factory work.[86] Right now we are experiencing the transition from disciplinary society to control society, i.e. a transition from discipline as something transcendent to discipline as something immanent.[87] In this process, discipline is internalized as self-discipline and self-management.

The requirement of post-modern capitalism for an ever-increasing demand, however, causes desire to be liberated. The result is, according to Hardt and Negri, the creation of a new, generalized desire. This desire is not directed towards simple satisfaction of needs but can direct itself towards pleasures in various forms – luxury, play, game, art, etc. – and it is this generalized desire that, according to Hardt and Negri, is transformed into the multitude's desire for liberation.[88] Such a desire does not recognize any limitations; it is the desire for life as such, including the desire simply to exist and reproduce.[89] It is with this desire for liberation that the multitude creates the social spaces where new forms of life and cooperation are developed,[90] and it is this general desire for liberation that gives reason to and motivates the modern slogans demanding global citizenship, basic income and reappropriation of the means to producing and reproducing life.

Gilder emphasizes the constitutive significance of the undetermined desire for post-modern capitalism, while Hardt and Negri express great confidence in the political possibilities of a generalized desire towards a future beyond capitalism. For Bataille, however, it cannot be desire that holds the key to a future just society. Bataille would think it quite right to characterize generalized desire as a desire for liberation, but he does not believe in the possibility of a final reconciliation of a multitude constituted by an infinity of individual desires. Bataille emphasizes that desire is directed towards something that is in reality unachievable, namely sovereignty. Sovereignty is the exact opposite of the servitude and rationality implied by productive labour,[91] and it is therefore

84   See Hardt and Negri, *ibid.*, pp. 419–20.
85   See *ibid.*, pp. 243–44.
86   See *ibid.*, pp. 261 ff, 274 ff.
87   See *ibid.*, pp. 330–31.
88   See *ibid.*, pp. 250 ff.
89   See *ibid.*, p. 349.
90   See *ibid.*, p. 397.
91   See Bataille, *La Souveraineté*, pp. 324–25.

only possible as an exception,[92] a subjective rupture in the objective logic of production and reproduction: as Bataille clearly underlines in his analysis of Stalin's idea of communism, sovereignty can never be the goal of history.[93]

Sovereignty is the manifestation of desire as inner experience, and both are irreducibly subjective. Nevertheless, the general economy emphasizes – as science and ontology, philosophical anthropology and thus metaphysics – the real ontological necessity of subjective desire for the specifically human way of being. The subjective desire for individual sovereignty cannot be sublated, as puritan idealists have often hoped. Bataille maintains the contradiction between needs and desire, and the irreducible reality of both. However, he does not give ontological primacy to the subjective desire; it is still the satisfaction of needs through the negation of nature by work and morality that civilizes, and in contrast to Gilder, Hardt and Negri, Bataille can therefore not condone post-modern consumer capitalism ideologically, neither as a goal in itself nor as a necessary step towards the coming of a communist society.

iv   *In the End: Theoretical Aporias, but also Practical Hope*

It should be clear by now that in my opinion, Bataille's general economy entails some serious aporias when considered as a political economy. Goux believes that this might be caused by Bataille's historical situation, living in a period when capitalism was only about to develop into its post-modern consumer form.[94] Such an explanation, however, would only make the insufficiency of Bataille's general economy a historical problem that supposedly we should have overcome by now; this is clearly not the case. As I hope to have shown beyond any reasonable doubt, there is definitely no academic consensus about the understanding of economy today – in fact, quite the contrary after the emergence of the contemporary financial crises.

To sum up Bataille's aporias, one can say that at the ontological level he clearly oscillates between the universal economy of energy and the individual experience of desire, and that in his normative recommendations he oscillates between moral appeals to the individual and a wish for a world government to control the flow of energy on and in the earth as a whole. In terms of economy, Bataille maintains a macro-perspective on a universal scale so comprehensive that one cannot distinguish clearly between energy and matter, while in his micro-perspective he turns the very rationality of planning and

---

92   See Sørensen, "At tage fat om ondets rod", pp. 191 ff (or Sørensen, *I Lyset af Bataille*, pp. 73 ff).

93   See Bataille, *La Souveraineté*, p. 322.

94   See, e.g., Goux, "General Economics and Postmodern Capitalism", p. 224.

organization suspicious in itself. Whereas in the micro-perspective he fights against the reductionism and objectification of desire in neo-classical economy, in the macro-perspective he himself reduces everything to energy.

In a practical perspective, the natural foundation of society can be considered as consisting of energy in different forms, some of which make energy accessible to human exploitation. Therefore, in spite of the theory of relativity and our knowledge of the world as one coherent ecosystem, in a practical perspective it makes good sense to distinguish between dead and living matter and between matter and energy.[95] These distinctions illustrate the conflict between, on the one hand, the circulation of money and commodities understood mechanically as dead matter, and, on the other hand, living organisms that are transformed quantitatively and qualitatively because of the accumulated energy inside living matter. The traditional models of economic thought are clearly hostile to the self-organizing life of nature,[96] and with good reason. Economy in the ordinary sense aims at the optimal management of resources, and management is only possible when assuming an appropriate degree of standstill and unchangeability; if everything moves and emerges by itself, conscious management is impossible.

Bataille's theoretical struggle to assimilate the unreduced desire and the flow of energy in nature into economy leaves an impression of economy as totally unmanageable and uncontrollable in a practical sense. The anti-authoritarian, theoretical perspective means that the general economy loses its character of political economy, instead transforming itself into a scientistic ontology, the alleged necessity of which contributes to legitimize ideologically a total liberation of desire and consumption which, in turn, can legitimize a capitalist development without any restrictions. As mentioned, this was clearly not Bataille's intention, but the conceptual logic in this branch of his thinking does not leave him much choice. However, in this account of the objective basis for the general economy, as it is presented in the first part of *The Accursed Share*, there are not many signs of the dialectical thinking that is the foundation of the other two parts;[97] this tension makes the project as a whole vulnerable to criticism due to inconsistency. In fact, Bataille himself became aware of the problem with reconciling the wish for political results – which was connected with the account of the objectively given – and the in-depth

---

95   See, e.g., Hoffmeyer, *Samfundets naturhistorie*, p. 14.

96   See Brodbeck, *Grundlagen*, pp. 125 ff.

97   See, e.g., Sørensen, "The Inner Experience", pp. 597 ff (Ch. 4 below).

reflections concerning the inner, subjectively given experiences;[98] he actually ended up declaring that it was deeply problematic to attempt to create a connection between the subjective experiences of eroticism and sovereignty and what is objectively given through use of resources.[99]

Thus, the general economy turns out to have its greatest limitations as political economy. The basic problem is that with Bataille's extended sense of economy, it becomes very difficult to recommend a definite economic strategy at the ordinary political level. His main concern is the material conflict between the human being and life as such, between the human expression of desire that liberates energy for loss, and the accumulation of energy on earth and in nature in general. Over the course of the historical development of civilization, the human being has developed an ever-greater consumption of energy; hence, it is not just capitalism that is self-destructive, but the very human way of being. What Bataille has pointed out at the individual and historical level is in fact an ontological problem. The full actualization of the potential of human desire in sovereignty can lead only to exhaustion of all disposable energy resources on earth, and that will mean the end, if not of life as such then at least of the human way of living. The complete realization of the human potential of civilization liberates the energy accumulated in and on earth only to recommence the interrupted flow that destines energy to be lost for good in the tepidness of the universe.

Theoretically, the human being is a negation of nature, i.e. negation is our specific human way of being. This negation, however, we handle in practice every day. With the kind of ecological awareness that has become common today, we can see quite clearly that it is the human destiny to destroy its own collective natural habitat much more irrevocably than any other species in the history of the earth; nevertheless, it will probably still be a while before we have completed this self-defeating project, and hopefully – with the right way of organizing politically the streams of energy and matter – we can postpone it for some generations. We might even – if we are politically wise and very lucky – end up realizing Bataille's hopes of reconciling ourselves as cosmopolitans with nature and life in general, and thus, through the right kind of

---

98   See Georges Bataille, "[Ebauche pour une Introduction générale]" ('1954'), in OC$_B$ VIII, p. 595. This sketch was meant to be the general introduction to the 1954 edition of the whole of *The Accursed Share*. See also above, notes 23 and 56.

99   See Georges Bataille, "[Corrections et notes pour une réédition de *La Consumation*]" ('1954'), in OC$_B$ VII, p. 482. These were corrections for the never realized 1954 edition. See also above, notes 23 and 43.

world governance, fulfil the dreams of contemporary utopian ecologists. There is still a lot left to fight for, politically and economically, in theory as well as in practice, and Bataille's general economy reminds us that, in contrast to the restricted model of neo-classical economy, developing a political economy today means that we must include the ecology of earth, the household of society and the business of individual enterprises. Sometime in a hopefully distant future it might simply be over with, if not the specifically human way of being as such then at least the very modern way of living that we know from contemporary western societies; precisely therefore, we must use the time until then in a reasonable way.

PART TWO

Dialectics

∵

CHAPTER 3

On the Contribution of Dialectics: Plato *et al.*

Alan Singer makes a case for the relevance of dialectical reasoning and under-standing in business strategy, politics and especially in ecology.[1] He argues that dialectics is the optimal way to handle conceptually tensions, paradoxes, dilem-mas and contradictions, and that dialectics has been ignored mainly as a result of "guilt by association", i.e., because of its linkages to totalitarianism and anti-capitalism. He also makes a case for philosophy informing strategy, and this is what I will attempt to do in the following comments, first, by focusing on the concept of dialectics as seen from a philosophical point of view, second, by trying to show some of the tensions in the concept as employed by Singer, and finally by sketching some implications in relation to politics and strategy. In doing this, I will distinguish between various types of dialectics, which differ in relation to method and theory, epistemology and ontology, nature and culture, and theory and practice.

A   From the History of Dialectics

As Singer points out, Plato's dialectics was concerned with ideas. Ideas, how-ever, had a special status in platonic thinking. Plato thought of dialectics as the reasonable way to achieve true knowledge (which for Plato was a pleonasm, knowledge being by definition true as opposed to mere opinion) through the method of sceptical questions and increasingly precise answers, forcing those involved in the dialogue to make their proposals both consistent and true in a universal way. To Plato, this method was closely linked to both theory of knowl-edge and ontology. Gaining true knowledge was equivalent to gaining access to and participating in eternal ideas, which were thought to exist as a special, unchangeable and true realm of reality in opposition to our part of reality, dominated by mere change and opinion.[2]

---

1 See Alan Singer, "Global business and the dialectic", *Human Systems Management* 21, no. 4 (2002), pp. 249–65.

2 See Plato, *Phaedo*, trans. R. Hackforth (Cambridge: Cambridge University Press, 1955/1980), *Phaedo* 80 B and Plato, *The Republic*, trans. Desmond Lee (Hammonsworth: Penguin, 1974), *Rep.* 476–78; see also Asger Sørensen, "Sansning og erkendelse hos Platon", *Semikolon* 2, no. 4 (2002), pp. 44–56.

Plato's goal was not simply to describe or understand dualities and contradictions but to solve them, letting reason and argument reveal and overcome inherent contradictions. Strict logical reasoning facilitates intuitive knowledge of reality, a reality that is inherently reasonable.[3] Employing the dialectics of Plato to approach modern day ambiguities, dilemmas, paradoxes, etc. would simply mean recognizing them as the mere starting point of a process of reasoning, which would eventually do away with all such things. Hence, for Plato, dialectics is first and foremost a method to get rid of all kinds of tensions rather than simply a scheme for understanding them as either ontologically real or epistemologically true.

The latter is far more the case in the writings of Aristotle, who distinguishes dialectics from apodictic demonstration. Dialectics is a way of arguing that analyses concepts on a pragmatic base, i.e. what is believed about them.[4] It is concerned with testing arguments as they are used in practice, e.g., in ethics, politics and law, i.e., human affairs, which could be otherwise.[5] Dialectics employs the logic of deduction; however, it steps forward through questions and does not, like demonstrations, proceed directly to universal truth.[6] The break between ideas and reality in British empiricism is reinforced by Kant, who – as Singer notes – confines dialectics within the realm of ideas as distinguished from the things in themselves, reality as such, of which we have no immediate knowledge (knowledge still being true by definition). Dialectics is thought of as a process of reason, driven forward by the negative force of contradictions appearing; however, since knowledge of reality is problematic, we cannot say anything certain about the reason of reality. Reason becomes a human faculty, and dialectics is confined to the mind and the human process of thinking.

Nevertheless, this concept of dialectics makes it possible to distinguish between natural and cultural reality. In general, we cannot know anything about reality, but in human reality – i.e. culture – we can assume that reason and dialectics play a part. In that sense, the Kantian concept of dialectics is supported by, and itself supporting, two distinctions; one within reality between nature and culture, and another between unspecified reality, on the one hand, and knowledge, mind, reason and dialectics on the other hand. It is these dualizing

---

3   See Plato, *Rep.* 511.

4   See Karsten Friis Johansen, *A History of Ancient Philosophy*, trans. Henrik Rosenmeier (London & New York: Routledge, 1998), pp. 311–15.

5   See Aristotle, *Nicomachean Ethics*, trans. W.D. Ross and revised by J.O. Urmson, in *The Complete Works of Aristotle*, ed. Jonathan Barnes (Princeton NJ: Princeton University Press, 1984/1995), vol. 2, *Eth.Nic.* 1139a.

6   See Aristotle, *Sophistical Refutations*, in *The Complete Works*, vol. 1, *Soph.el.* 172 a–b.

distinctions that Hegel – combining Plato and Aristotle – tries to overcome through his development of dialectics – not by denying the conceptual distinctions, but by dialectically showing them to be self-contradictory when realized as positions, yet solvable through a transformation of the premises.

It is important to emphasize that contradiction, as it is thought in Hegel's dialectics, is neither a tension, nor an ambiguity, nor two diametrically opposed polarities; it is a contradiction,[7] as between p and non-p. It is also important to note that for Hegel, the contradiction arises from within the position itself when realized,[8] i.e. during the attempt to transform ideas of the mind to realities of the world, or in the process transforming theory to praxis; it is not an anti-thesis coming from somewhere outside of the position itself.

Hegel does away with the destructive scepticism of Kant and the empiricists through a very subtle analysis. Scepticism is universality employed in a negative way, meaning that a sceptic argument always aims at showing that a proposition cannot claim universal validity. However, if the truth of a proposition is denied by a sceptic, it is precisely that specific proposition which is claimed to be false, and this claim itself is supposed to be true. By showing something determinate to be false, we know that something is not the case, and in this way that which is denied is at the same time affirmed and kept as part of the new stage in the development of knowledge. This is Hegel's famous idea of the determinate negation, showing that critique is not just something negative; it also has a positive outcome, namely that we have gained new ground when proposing a new proposition. Through dialectics, we have had an experience, i.e. we have learned something.[9]

Expressed in this way, Hegel's line of thought resembles the method of falsification as described by Popper. What makes Hegel different, however, is that he does not acknowledge the universal validity of the above-mentioned dualities, which means that ontological figurations, natural as well as cultural, obey the same logic as propositional knowledge. The experience does not only change knowledge; it also changes 'the knower', whether thought of as an individual or a collective entity (Spirit), as well as the object of knowledge, all of the latter being changed by the experience thus gained.[10] As Hegel is often

---

7   See, e.g., G.W.F. Hegel, *Phänomenologie des Geistes* (1807), in Hegel, *Hauptwerke in sechs Bänden* (Darmstadt: Wissenschaftliche Buchgesellschaft, 1999), vol. 2, p. 58 (page numbers of this edition are equal to those of GW_{II} 9; TWA 3, 76).

8   See Hegel, *ibid.*, p. 56 (TWA 3, 72).

9   See *ibid.*, pp. 56–57, 60–61 (TWA 3, 73–74, 78–80).

10   See *ibid.*, p. 61 (TWA 3, 79).

quoted, "[w]hat is reasonable is real, and what is real, is reasonable",[11] which implies that contradictions and thus dialectics apply to both logic and ontology. Ideas become true when realized, but in this process contradictions can be experienced that invalidate both the idea and reality formed by the idea. Since reality must be reasonable, being is inherently structured by logic, and since we are also real and reasonable, it is possible to achieve knowledge about reality – in the end absolute knowledge. But that is not all. Being part of reality, we regain access to reality ourselves and can actually change not only reality, but also theory and practice as they are all part of the same reasonable reality.

Marx criticized the idea that reality is reasonable for being an ideology that legitimized current injustice. Still, he held on to the idea of the unity of reality, of ontology and logic, and of theory and practice, and Engels developed a dialectical materialism that specified developmental laws of both society and nature. This way of understanding dialectics was developed by the Bolsheviks, whereas Western Marxists who were influenced by neo-Kantian philosophy, such as Lukács, Horkheimer and Adorno, confined dialectics to the truth about human reality,[12] even though that very same Kantianism prevented them from obtaining knowledge about it.

B   Empiricist Displacements

In this split in the dialectical tradition, Singer wants to side with those thinkers who find dialectics to be applicable to both nature and culture, i.e. Hegel and Engels. He convincingly argues that the fate of dialectical reasoning has been determined by its association with Marxism. I find the case he makes for the relevance of dialectical reasoning in business strategy and politics as well as in ecology – by pointing out the isomorphism of the logic of self-reference and the ontology of self-replication – a stimulating challenge to our habitual thoughts about the way nature is structured.

Singer, however, employing the style of a cautious modern academic, refrains from total commitment to dialectics, proposing it instead as a scheme of thought that *can* and *should* be used, but not out of necessity. Since Singer

---

11   G.W.F. Hegel, *Grundlinien der Philosophie des Rechts* (1820), in Hegel, *Hauptwerke in sechs Bänden* (Darmstadt: Wissenschaftliche Buchgesellschaft, 1999), vol. 5, p. 14 (TWA 7, 24).

12   The same applies to a non-Marxist, left-wing dialectician like the young Bataille (see Georges Bataille and Raymond Queneau, "La critique des fondements de la dialectique hègélienne" (1932), in Bataille, *Œuvres complètes*, vol. I, ed. Denis Hollier (Paris: Gallimard, 1970); see the following chapter for a more detailed discussion.

is apparently unaware of the Aristotelian conception of dialectics, this implies an epistemological voluntarism that reinstalls the empiricist – or positivist – split between knowledge and reality, and between theory and practice, making it difficult to use dialectical reasoning as guidance in political action. Singer's empiricist leanings also become apparent from the fact that he thinks of dialectics not only in terms of full-scale contradictions but also as a means to understand ambiguities, contrasts, paradoxes, dilemmas and value-differences. In doing so, he accepts as real what is perceived, whereas most of the dialecticians mentioned above would think of such phenomena precisely as perceived, i.e. unreal, and in principle solvable through the logic already described – i.e. the determinate negation – which simultaneously does away with the perceived contradiction and preserves the conflicting elements as inherent in the experience obtained.

C   A Reflection on Business

Finally, since dialectics aims at the truth of reality as a whole, it is – in most of its forms – hostile to the idea of basing politics only on the perceived wants of single individuals, as modern capitalism does in its purest form. Just like the moral philosopher Adam Smith, as a philosopher of law, Hegel recognized the idea of the invisible hand as the cunning of reason, i.e. reason regulating social reality behind our individual backs to the benefit of the totality. Dialectics is certainly more suitable in formulating the needs of the nation as a whole than the desire of the individual, and given this anti-liberal implication, introducing dialectics into business strategy might signal a shift in focus from market to organization, i.e. from coping with universal competition outside the company to handling internal affairs, just as it is relevant in an economy dominated by the monopolies of multi-national corporations.

CHAPTER 4

Totalizing Negativity and Change: Bataille, Hegel *et al.*

Like many left-wing intellectuals in the 20th century, Georges Bataille made Hegel the main point of reference for discussions of dialectics, citing in particular his *Phenomenology of Spirit*. Following a quite normal path from political-theoretical discussions within various left-wing groups to discussions of Hegelian dialectics, Bataille, however, is distinguished by belonging to a small and very privileged group of French thinkers. Not only did he attend the famous lectures by Alexandre Kojève in the 1930s and followed his extensive commentaries on the *Phenomenology*, he was also able to discuss the issues raised there with Kojève himself, since he very soon became part of the inner circle together with, among others, Jacques Lacan and Raymond Queneau. Bataille remained in contact with Kojève while writing extensively on Hegel, and their philosophical discussions went on until the very end of Bataille's life.

Despite this, today Bataille is most often associated with the kind of thinking that rejects the idea of dialectics as such. This impression is primarily created by Michel Foucault and Jacques Derrida who both praised Bataille in the 1960s, the former for giving voice to a non-dialectical philosophical language and, the latter, for presenting an alternative to Hegel's dialectics, which had allegedly reduced thinking to labour and closure. Since then, very few philosophers have discussed dialectics and the relationship between Hegel and Bataille in any detail. This article is a contribution to filling this gap and thereby adding to the understanding of both dialectics as such and the thinking of Bataille.

First, Foucault's and Derrida's employment of Bataille in the critique of dialectics is presented as based on a conception of dialectics that is not shared by Bataille (A). Instead, Bataille's dialectics must be understood in conjunction with his peculiar epistemological position (B) and his materialist ontology, which extends the scope of dialectics beyond conscious being and history (C). Bataille's dialectical ontology also extends the concept of desire, which results in a different constitutional logic for self-conscious being (D). The conclusion is that Bataille's dialectics is related to that of Hegel in a way that distinguishes it from most modern dialectics by totalizing dialectics even more than Hegel, admitting both nature and the original human consciousness to have a history on par with humanity, but without the idea of one determinate end of history. Bataille's dialectics can be said to be the result of a determinate negation of Hegel, which makes him one of the few non-Marxists in the 20th century to have maintained and positively endorsed a totalizing metaphysical concept of dialectics. However, including reality *per se* within the scope of dialectics, and in an even wider sense than Hegel, makes it very difficult for Bataille to positively endorse a specific course of political action (E).

A   Critique of Dialectics

To the young Foucault, criticizing Hegel was not just a matter of denying the widely accepted conception of history as collective human progress, nor of negating Kojève's idea of communism as "the end of history"; like the classical positivists, he wanted to do away with all varieties of dialectics, metaphysics and speculative philosophy, and it was with this aim he employed Bataille. In the now seminal article about Bataille from 1963, "A Preface to Transgression", Foucault claims that the language of philosophy is linked "beyond all memory (or nearly so) to dialectics",[1] and a critique of dialectics is therefore a critique of philosophy as such.

Foucault construes "dialectical thought" as "the experience of the contradiction",[2] and what he praises in Bataille's thinking is what he conceives of as the attempt to break with "the sovereignty of the philosophizing subject" to insert a "fracture" that can develop "the form of a non-dialectic philosophical language",[3] "a language that speaks and of which he is not the master".[4] To such a "mad philosopher" "the philosophical language proceeds as if through a labyrinth" in the middle of "the transgression of his being as philosopher".[5] A transgression takes place through inner experience and cannot as such be accessed by transcendental analysis or "dialectical movement"; is best described as a "non-positive affirmation",[6] and, like Nietzsche's, Bataille's thought is "a critique and an ontology" that "understands both finitude and being".[7] According

---

1 Michel Foucault, "Préface à la transgression", *Critique* xix (195–96) (1963), p. 759 (hereafter: "Préface"; Foucault, "A Preface to Transgression", in *Aesthetics, Method, and Epistomology*, trans. Robert Hurley *et al.* (London: Allan Lane, 1994), p. 78 (hereafter: "A Preface")). All translations have been translated from the original texts by the present author, but have been compared with authoritative translations when available.

2 Foucault, "Préface", p. 754 ("A Preface", p. 72).

3 "Préface", p. 766 ("A Preface", p. 84).

4 "Préface", p. 760 ("A Preface", p. 79).

5 "Préface", p. 762 ("A Preface", p. 80).

6 "Préface", p. 756 ("A Preface", p. 74).

7 "Préface", p. 757 ("A Preface", p. 75).

to Foucault, Bataille introduces a "philosophy of being speaking" in the place of a "dialectics of production", i.e. "a philosophy of the working man".[8]

In spite of these radical claims about Bataille as contesting dialectics, and thus philosophy as such, Foucault never went into detail about the concept of dialectics or the relationship between Bataille and Hegel. Also, even though Foucault's perspective is often recognized as being determined by Bataille,[9] Foucault only published one more text on Bataille, namely the very short presentation of Bataille's *Complete Works*, and it does not contain anything of philosophical substance.[10]

Derrida's reading of Bataille, on the other hand, focuses precisely on the relationship to Hegel and dialectics. In his very influential article, "From Restricted to General Economy: a Hegelianism without reserve", Derrida delivers a detailed, well-argued and well-substantiated analysis of Bataille, which has become the final word for many thinkers on these matters. In Derrida's interpretation, Bataille also stages a radical critique of metaphysics, which aims to do away not only with the idea of history, but with the ontological conception of dialectics as such. However, as Derrida correctly emphasizes, "all of Bataille's concepts are Hegelian",[11] and the negation of Hegel could therefore easily be called determinate or immanent, and thus dialectical.

Derrida, however, prefers to interpret Bataille's thinking as "displacing" Hegel's. According to Derrida, Bataille displaces the very conception of reality as a conscious being whose experience can be understood dialectically as an *Aufhebung*: "the speculative concept *par excellence*, says Hegel, the concept whose untranslatable privilege is wielded by the German language".[12]

---

8   "Préface", pp. 766–67 ("A Preface", pp. 84–85).

9   See, e.g., Sverre Raffnsøe, "Grænsens uomgængelige uomgængelighed. Grænsens problematik hos Bataille og Foucault", in *Excesser – af og om Georges Bataille*, ed. René Rasmussen and Asger Sørensen (Århus: Modtryk, 1994), p. 91; see also Jürgen Habermas, *Der philosophische Diskurs der Moderne* (Frankfurt a. M.: Suhrkamp, 1985), pp. 279–80 (Habermas, *The Philosophical Discourse of Modernity*, trans. Frederick Lawrence (Cambridge: Polity Press, 1987), pp. 238–39).

10   See Michel Foucault, "Présentation", in Bataille, *Œuvres Complètes*, vol. I, ed. Denis Hollier (Paris: Gallimard, 1970), pp. 5–6. References to a volume in Bataille's *Œuvres complètes* will be indicated as OC_B nn.

11   Jacques Derrida, "Un hégélianisme sans réserve", *L'arc* 32 (1967), p. 26 (Derrida, "From Restricted to General Economy: a Hegelianism without Reserve (1967)", in *Writing and Difference*, trans. Alan Bass (London: Routledge, 1978), p. 320, (hereafter: "From Restricted to General Economy")).

12   Derrida, "Un hégélianisme sans réserve", p. 29 ("From Restricted to General Economy", p. 324).

"The *Aufhebung* is included within the circle of absolute knowledge, never exceeds its closure, never suspends the totality of discourse, work, meaning, the law, etc."[13] Hence, to Derrida, it is the same ontological logic that structures Hegel's conceptions of both history and experience, and Derrida identifies the dialectical logic with the totality of the ontological movement towards a determined end, i.e. the accomplished movement of conscious being which, through the experience of determinate negation, has sublated itself to a (pre-) determined result.

In doing this, Derrida makes use of Hegel's remarks, that the dialectical movement cannot find rest until the ultimate end, and that the goal is as necessary for knowledge as is the progression for understanding dialectics.[14] In this sense, he can denounce dialectics as a "closure"; however, it is an interpretation of dialectics that is not universally shared. Max Horkheimer, for example, reads the same remarks as an expression of the non-dialectical, dogmatic aspect of Hegel's philosophy rather than a statement about dialectics.[15]

Like Foucault, Derrida makes Bataille his ally in a critique of dialectics as such, claiming that Bataille has "displaced" "the Hegelian logos".[16] However, obviously Derrida's reading also displaces Bataille, and towards the end he admits that this actually amounts to interpreting "Bataille against Bataille".[17] The reason why this becomes necessary is simply that Bataille did not want to contest Hegelian dialectics in the same radical sense as Foucault and Derrida, because Bataille thought of dialectics in a different sense, closely related to that of Horkheimer. In this sense, dialectics is a method that, as it has been put by Hans-Georg Gadamer, aims at grasping conceptually reality in motion,

---

13   "Un hégélianisme sans réserve", p. 43 ("From Restricted to General Economy", p. 348).

14   See G.W.F. Hegel, *Phänomenologie des Geistes* (1807), ed. Johannes Hoffmeister (Hamburg: Felix Meiner Verlag, 1952), p. 69 (PHG$_{TWA}$, 74; Hegel, *Phenomenology of Spirit*, trans. A.V. Miller (Oxford: University Press, 1977), p. 51). In the present chapter, the following page references are indicated in brackets in the text as PHG$_H$, nn (PHG$_{TWA}$, nn; PHS, nn). Unfortunately, the English translator of the *Phenomenology* has chosen to depart from a "rigid consistency in rendering Hegelian locutions" (Miller, "Translator's Foreword", in Hegel, PHS, xxxi). It has therefore been necessary to correct the wording in most of the quotations used here.

15   See Max Horkheimer, "Zum Problem der Wahrheit", *Zeitschrift für Sozialforschung* IV, no. 3 (1935), pp. 330–32 (GS$_H$ 3, 287 ff) (or Horkheimer, "On the Problem of Truth", in Horkheimer, *Between Philosophy and Social Science*, trans. G. Frederick Hunter, Matthew S. Kramer, and John Torpey (Cambridge, MA: MIT Press, 1993), pp. 185–87).

16   Derrida, "Un hégélianisme sans réserve", p. 29 ("From Restricted to General Economy", p. 325).

17   Derrida, "Un hégélianisme sans réserve", p. 43 ("From Restricted to General Economy", p. 348).

reality in change.[18] Thus, whereas Foucault and Derrida had a concept of dialectics that implies system, totality, identity, end of history and thus closure, Bataille's concept of dialectics is inherently open-ended.

For Bataille, it is therefore possible to criticize Hegel and Kojève very strongly and still (or perhaps precisely therefore) consider his own thinking dialectical in the same sense as those criticized, i.e. negated. Like Marx, Bataille states that his thought is the "opposite" of Hegel's,[19] but immediately after he adds: "I only found myself there dialectically, if I may say so, Hegelically". As in the case with Marx, Bataille's opposition to Hegel must be understood dialectically, as a determinate negation, and Bataille can therefore, in the words of Queneau, be said to develop "a kind of anti-Hegelian dialectics".[20]

This may come as a surprise to those familiar with the post-structuralist discourse and rhetoric that often surrounds Bataille. What may be even more surprising is that despite initially arguing for the now common position reserving dialectics only for the *praxis* of the changeable human world, Bataille keeps the possibility open for reintroducing nature into the realm of dialectics,[21] and, as we shall see, in his later work he actually revives and uses Hegel's and the traditional Marxists's totalizing concept of dialectics as a basis for his understanding of reality *per se*. Bataille can thus be employed to negate various forms of closure, but this is not the same as claiming he denounced dialectics – quite the contrary.

B   Experience and Scientific Knowledge

Nevertheless, today the majority of recognized 20th century readers of Hegel's *Phenomenology* conceive of dialectics as the proper way to think of human reality in contrast to nature. By acknowledging the epistemological importance of this ontological distinction, they implicitly adopt the traditional Aristotelian, non-empiricist way of understanding the relation between epistemology and ontology, i.e. that it is the structure of the being in question that determines

---

18   See Hans-Georg Gadamer, "Hegel und die antike Dialektik" (1961), in Gadamer, *Gesammelte Werke,* vol. 3 (Tübingen: Mohr Siebeck, 1986–99), pp. 10–11.

19   See Karl Marx, *Das Kapital,* vol. 1 (1867), in Marx & Engels, *Werke* (MEW), vols. 23 (Berlin: Dietz Verlag, 1974), p. 27 and Georges Bataille, "Notice autobiographique" (1958), in OC_B VII, ed. Thadèe Klossowski (Paris: Gallimard, 1976), p. 615.

20   Raymond Queneau, "Premières confrontations avec Hegel", *Critique* XIX (195–96) (1963), p. 696.

21   See Queneau, ibid., p. 698.

the right way to understand that being, and, given that human reality is structured differently from natural reality, intellectually we should relate differently to these two spheres.

This was also the case for the young Bataille and Queneau, who criticized Friedrich Engels's totalizing and reductive concept of dialectics by understanding dialectical development as part of the "real existence" of "every human being", namely as the "lived experience [*expérience vécue*]" of "negativity", i.e. something very close to Foucault's conception of dialectics as the experience of contradiction mentioned above. Such an experience structures dialectics as a specific "method of thought", thus making it "risky" to conceive of it as the "intelligence of nature".[22] However, for Bataille, to accept the metaphysical implications of such a restricted conception of dialectics is complicated by, first, his concept of 'inner experience' and, second, his unconditional materialism. It is probably the gradual realization of these complications in his later work that makes the idea of a dialectics of nature reappear, although in another form than the one conceived of by Engels.

Inner experience is a development of the idea of lived experience, which for Bataille was something similar to the German *Erlebnis*.[23] In *The Inner*

---

22   Georges Bataille and Raymond Queneau, "La critique des fondements de la dialectique hègélienne" (1932), in OC$_B$ I, pp. 288–89 (Bataille and Queneau, "The Critique of the Foundations of Hegelian Dialectic", in *Visions of Excess: Selected Writings 1927–1939*, ed. Allan Stoekl, trans. A. Stoekl, with Carl R. Lovitt, and Donald M. Leslie (Minneapolis: University of Minnesota Press, 1985), p. 113.) Although making claims about Hegelian dialectics, in 1932 Bataille had not studied Hegel as such (see Bataille, "Notice autobiographique", p. 615). It was only after following Koyré's and especially Kojève's lectures from 1933 to 1939 that Bataille can be said to know the 'right' Hegel (see Queneau, "Premières confrontations avec Hegel", p. 700). From then on, when Bataille refers to Hegel, he is normally careful to specify that he is discussing "the fundamentally Hegelian thought of Alexandre Kojève" (Georges Bataille, "Hegel, la mort et le sacrifice" (1955), in OC$_B$ XII, ed. Francis Marmande and Sibylle Monod (Paris: Gallimard, 1988), p. 326). And by this he means Kojève's thought as it is expressed in the translations and notes from the lectures, i.e. Alexandre Kojève, *Introduction à la lecture de Hegel*, ed. Raymond Queneau (Paris: Gallimard, 1947). However, as Derrida notes, when referring to the *Phenomenology*, Bataille is not consistent in his use of Kojève's translation, and this indicates that Bataille was familiar with Jean Hyppolite's translation of the *Phenomenology* from 1941 (see Derrida, "Un hégélianisme sans réserve", p. 27 ("From Restricted to General Economy", p. 436)).

23   The conceptual connection between these three terms, i.e. 'inner experience', 'lived experience' and '*Erlebnis*', is made explicit by Paul Ludwig Landsberg, who was a close friend of Bataille in the 1930s (see Paul Ludwig Landsberg, *Einführung in die philosophische Anthropologie* (Frankfurt a. M.: Vittorio Klostermann, 1960), pp. 178–79, and Georges Bataille, "Les Présages" (1935), in OC$_B$ II, ed. Denis Hollier (Paris: Gallimard, 1970), pp. 266–70).

Experience from 1943, he concentrates on the more dramatic aspects of inner experience, like anxiety, ecstasy and meditation, attempting through the textual form to communicate the inner experience in a way that "corresponds to its movement", thus avoiding "a dry verbal translation".[24] This becomes a kind of textual communication comprising aphorisms, poetry and prose, which Bataille takes as constitutive of a larger textual project called *The Atheological Sum* that was only conceived of after the end of ww II.

The analysis of laughter, however, reveals to Bataille "a field of co-incidences between the facts [*données*] of a common and rigorous emotional knowledge [*connaissance*] and the facts of a discursive knowledge",[25] i.e. some objects of experience common to both scientific cognition and lived, inner experience. In *Eroticism* from 1957, Bataille can therefore attempt a more traditional discursive characterization of the objects of inner experience and of inner experience itself. Inner experience is taken to comprise all those experiences that are not scientifically objectifying, i.e. the experience of art, eroticism, laughter, etc. Science aims to describe reality as objects "from without", whereas Bataille wants to investigate reality experienced "from within", in the case of religion, for instance, not like the historian or sociologist but as a theologian or as Brahman himself. Inner experience can thus be communicated discursively, and Bataille also emphasizes that "the inner experience is not given independently of objective views".[26] Such a discursive communication of inner experience and its relation to scientific knowledge constitutes Bataille's other big project, *The Accursed Share*, of which *Eroticism* was planned to be volume two.

Like Hegel's concept of experience, Bataille's inner experience is the experience of a consciousness. Bataille, however, makes a distinction between two different ways of experiencing reality, which do not depend on the object aspect of experience but on the subject aspect. Though still within an ontological framework, these epistemological distinctions imply that the link between conscious being and reality as such becomes less definite for Bataille than for Hegel. It is therefore possible for Bataille to conceive of the experience of reality, both human and natural, in two ways that are parallel yet each in themselves unique: scientific cognition and inner experience. It is within the latter that dialectics finds its place as the discursive translation of lived experiences

---

24   Georges Bataille, *L'Expérience intérieure* (1943/54), in OC$_B$ V (Paris: Gallimard, 1973), p. 18.

25   Bataille, *ibid.*, p. 11.

26   Georges Bataille, *L'Érotisme* ('1954', 1957), in OC$_B$ X, ed. Francis Marmande and Yves Thévenieau (Paris: Gallimard, 1987), p. 35 (Bataille, *Eroticism*, trans. Mary Dalwood (London: Penguin, 2001), p. 31). In the present chapter, the following page references are indicated in brackets in the text as ER, nn (ER$_E$, nn).

of real negations, similarly to what was already the case in Bataille's early discussion of dialectics mentioned above.

However, just as it is the case for Hegel in the *Phenomenology*, for Bataille dialectics includes the ontological movement of experience, which conscious being must go through in order to realize it-self as self-conscious. Still, there are crucial differences: one is that Bataille's concept of experience is more comprehensive than Hegel's; another is that Bataille thinks of experiences as communicable in more than one way; yet another is that when Bataille speaks of science, it is in a modern sense as empirically based natural science, rather than the classical philosophical sense used by Hegel.

To Aristotle, scientific knowledge (*epistemé*) is knowledge of that which necessarily is, and this knowledge gains its validity from being structured by syllogistic logic.[27] The idea of knowledge as of that which necessarily is – and that being is eternal, unchangeable and structured by logic, whereas that which changes, becomes, or disappears simply is not being, neither in the ontological nor in the logical sense – goes back at least as far as Plato.[28] Hegel, however, modifies the antique conception of knowledge and being by accepting change as inherent in what is, conceiving of life as the infinite movement-by-it-self.

For Hegel, the dialectics of life is fundamental to the dialectics of being: it is life that, sublated through experience, becomes absolute knowledge. Being to Hegel is always already in-it-self conscious being, and as such being is only fully realized as sublated to the conceptual movement-by-it-self of pure self-conscious being and spirit, *Selbst-bewußt-sein* and *Geist*, when the dialectical process of experience reaches its end in absolute knowledge. Reconstructing this movement conceptually as Hegel does in the *Phenomenology* is, as the original subtitle says, the *Science of the Experience of Conscious-being*, and this science leads to the *Science of Logic*. To Hegel, ultimately science is philosophy,[29] which produces wisdom in the Aristotelian sense, i.e. intuitive insight into the principles of reality, which becomes scientific knowledge through being well-founded in reason.[30]

---

27 See Aristotle, *Nicomachean Ethics*, trans. W.D. Ross and revised by J.O. Urmson, in *The Complete Works of Aristotle*, ed. Jonathan Barnes (Princeton NJ: Princeton University Press, 1984/1995), vol. 2, *Eth. Nic.* 1139b–40b.

28 See Plato, *Republic*, trans. Paul Shorey, in Plato, *Collected Dialogues*, ed. Edith Hamilton and Huntington Cairns (Princeton NJ: Princeton University Press, 1961), *Rep.* 521d.

29 See Carl-Göran Heidegren, *Hegels Fenomenologi. En analys och kommentar* (Stockholm and Stehag: Brutus Östling, 1995), p. 345.

30 See Aristotle, *Eth. Nic.* 1141a.

As mentioned above, for Bataille science produces objective knowledge from without; that is, objectifying knowledge rather than knowledge about what necessarily – or objectively – is. Science is not philosophy and does not deliver the only possible or the whole truth about reality. Bataille's concept of science is therefore very different from Hegel's, and, as Lyotard pointed out, the conflict between the two concepts is that with a Hegelian conception of scientific knowledge, modern empirical science cannot be said to produce knowledge as such.[31] It is, however, only with such a modern positivist conception of science that Bataille can legitimately divide what to Hegel is ultimately only one. To sum up: first, experience is more than (scientific) knowledge in both the senses mentioned, and as such it can have other kinds of validity; second, with the modern idea of empirical science, one can distinguish between an experience from without, which is objectifying, and an experience from within, which is not; third, such inner experiences can be communicated in various ways: discursively (or dialectically), simply verbally or even without words, and they all have their peculiar validity as forms of communication.

C   Matter and Life

This complex epistemological position is, as mentioned above, coupled with a materialism that Bataille in his formative period declared to be "excluding all idealism".[32] What is important is that the matter in question must not be understood as physical matter in the sense often employed by empiricists, i.e. as something that is fundamentally unchangeable but can be moved in bulks and thus be understood primarily in terms of mechanics. Neither must matter be understood in the sense often employed by Marxists. Bataille distances himself from "giving matter the role that thought had" in Hegelian idealism, which would make matter "a source of contradiction",[33] determining the direction and end of the general history of man.

Bataille's ideals of scientific knowledge are not taken from classical philosophy, nor from Newtonian physics or classical economy, but from 20th-century

---

31   See Jean-François Lyotard, *La condition postmoderne* (Paris: Minuit, 1979), pp. 63–4 (Lyotard, *The Postmodern Condition: A Report on Knowledge*, trans. Geoff Bennington and Brian Massumi (Manchester: Manchester University Press, 1984), pp. 37–38).

32   Georges Bataille, "Matérialisme" (1929), in OC_B I, p. 180 ("Materialism", in *Visions of Excess*, ed. Stoekl, p. 16).

33   Georges Bataille, "Le bas matérialisme et la gnose" (1930), in OC_B I, p. 221 ("Base Materialism and Gnosticism", in *Visions of Excess*, ed. Stoekl, p. 52).

scientific theories. Bataille's epistemology is developed on the basis of the new experiences of physics, biology, psychology and sociology, i.e. sciences investigating and trying to grasp reality in change. Accordingly, Bataille's ontological materialism is inspired by thinkers such as Nietzsche, Freud and Mauss. Matter to Bataille is first of all living matter in natural and human beings, and excluding all idealism means that it "can only be defined as the non-logical difference that represents in relation to the economy of the universe what the crime represents in relation to the law",[34] i.e. the difference involved in a violation or transgression. Matter signifies for Bataille the insubordination of nature in relation to culture, the continuous rebellion of life against all boundaries; in short: growth.[35]

Absolute knowledge about, and in, being is the only desirable goal for the kind of ideal self-conscious being that Hegel brings to the experience of it-self, but not necessarily for other kinds of conscious being. From the very beginning of Hegel's *Phenomenology*, consciousness is defined by the desire to become scientific knowledge of reality in the ancient sense. However, to a living conscious being who, like Bataille, is having inner experiences of both the negation of its own material life and the material transgression of the result of this negation, this goal can only be realized in death. Bataille recognizes the essential link between ontology and epistemology, but conceives of both being and experience as essentially changing and constantly in motion.

Bataille's materialist dialectics of nature within the perspective of inner experience thus attempts to offer something that neither the ancient nor the Hegelian conception of dialectics could offer, namely a comprehension of the material *flux* of life as a historical process, i.e. grasping it with concepts that do not degrade it to, at best, a deficient mode of being that must be negated in order to make consciousness appear. However, Bataille thinks of his dialectics

---

34   Georges Bataille, "La notion de dépense" (1933), in OC_B I, p. 319 ("The Notion of Expenditure", in *Visions of Excess*, ed. Stoekl, p. 129).

35   To many liberal and left-wing rationalists such an organic way of understanding reality in its totality is assumed to be irrational and as such in itself leading to fascism. Whatever can be said of this general line of reasoning, when it comes to Bataille, the charge is up against not only his explicit statements, personal sympathies and organizational practice, but also the standard definition of fascism employed by political science (see, e.g., Asger Sørensen, "Georges Bataille: At tage ved lære af fascismen: Mellem modstand og analyse", in *Tradition og fornyelse i sociologien*, ed. Michael Hviid Jacobsen, Mikael Carleheden, and Søren Kristiansen (Ålborg: Ålborg Universitetsforlag, 2001), pp. 241–60 (or Asger Sørensen, *I lyset af Bataille – politisk filosofiske studier* (København: Politisk Revy, 2012, Ch. 6)).

as the result of a determinate negation of Hegel's, which of course preserves the Hegelian dialectic in the dialectics of Bataille as *Moment*.

In *Eroticism*, Bataille is mainly concerned with inner experiences, but he also describes "the physical condition" (ER, 95 (ER_E, 94)) of the objects of inner experience as "established by objective science" (ER, 19 (ER_E, 13)); this description is dialectical in the sense already mentioned, i.e. as the attempt to grasp change conceptually. According to Bataille, non-sexual reproduction, which is the most primitive kind of reproduction, is the division of one cell into two. In the reproductive movement there is, as Bataille emphasizes, a "passage" where the first cell dies as a discontinuous being; however, "as it dies, there is this moment of fundamental continuity between the two new beings" (ER, 20 (ER_E, 14)), and on this level, reproduction cannot be distinguished from growth (see ER, 96 (ER_E, 95)).

Being cannot, of course, be considered conscious on this level, but when Bataille lets himself be guided by "our human inner experience" (ER, 104 (ER_E, 103)), the cell must also have an "experience from within" (ER, 100 (ER_E, 99)), which in the moment of change is an experience of a "crisis" (ER, 97 (ER_E, 96)). Within a traditional ontology, this moment is best described as contradictory in the Hegelian sense: being at one and the same time neither one nor many, but exactly in the process of both disappearing and becoming, giving birth and dying, growing and reproducing, being continuous and discontinuous. However, such a moment is part of a real material process, and for Bataille such a process is evolution with a direction. The new continuity is the result of a determinate negation, which both annihilates and preserves the old continuity as *Moment*. The resulting continuity is both the same as the old continuity and different from it, both itself and not itself. Hence, it remains conceptually contradictory while also being the result of an *Aufhebung* in the Hegelian sense.

In sexual reproduction, the initial production of sexed cells is a reproductive division, but now distinguished ontologically from growth, and therefore not contradictory on the same level. On another level, however, this kind of division means that the same becomes even more different, i.e. that the ontological and logical contradiction within life becomes even more pronounced. The sexed cells of life are produced in different beings, and even when produced in the same particular being they are not the same. For the reproduction to be complete, however, it is necessary that what is only living as differences again becomes one and the same, i.e. that two cells of different sex melt together and become one, thus that the fission is followed by a fusion and what was discontinuous becomes continuous. As Bataille expresses it, "a continuity establishes itself between the two beings to form a new being, originating from the death, i.e. the disappearance of the two separate beings"

(ER, 20 (ER$_E$, 14)). The continuity of life is established by the death of discontinuous beings, and this movement shows that "the lost continuity can be found again" (ER, 99 (ER$_E$, 98)).

This scientific knowledge about asexual versus sexual reproduction was of course not known to Hegel. Nevertheless, Hegel's speculative account of life also focuses on the contradictions of the fundamental movement of life. He describes life as essentially determined by an event, namely as when that which does not rely on anything else, or is same-to-itself, *das Sichselbstgleiche*, divides itself: "The differences between dividing [*Entzweiung*] and becoming-same-to-itself [*Sichselbstgleichwerden*] are in themselves precisely only this movement of sublating itself [*sich Aufhebens*]" (PHG$_H$, 126 (PHG$_{TWA}$, 133; PHS, 100 f)). What is self-reliant as same-to-it-self is then in opposition to the division, and as such not same-to-it-self but in-it-self relying on something else, and thus divided. The result is to Hegel "the infinity or this absolute unrest of pure movement-by-it-self [*Sich-selbst-bewegens*]" (PHG$_H$, 126 (PHG$_{TWA}$, 133; PHS, 101)).

> This simple infinity, or the absolute concept, is to be called the simple essence [*Wesen*] of life, the soul of the world, the universal blood, which as omnipresent is not blurred and will not be interrupted by any difference, rather itself being all differences, as well as its sublated being [*Aufgenhobensein*], pulsating within itself without moving, vibrating in itself, without being restless. It is equal to itself [*sichselbstgleich*], for the differences are tautological; it is differences that are not (PHG$_H$, 125 (PHG$_{TWA}$, 132; PHS, 100)).

This movement must be considered so fundamental and objective that in an ontological sense it necessarily exists. According to Hegel, life simply is, but its way of being is simultaneous disappearance and appearance, death and birth, one and many, etc. This way of being is best described as the ontologically necessary and constantly changing material identity of that which is different and formally contradictory; in short, simply as material *flux*. To Hegel, life is in-it-self a "general fluidity", where the different "parts" become "independent" by negating "the universal substance", "the fluidity and continuity with it" (PHG$_H$, 136 f (PHG$_{TWA}$, 140–41; PHS, 107)). Negating is first "consuming", and this maintains the independence of the being in question. This "immediate unity", however, passes from a stage of "immediate continuity" to become a "reflected unity", which is the "pure" or "simple I" (PHG$_H$, 138 f (PHG$_{TWA}$, 142–43; PHS, 108 f)).

Whereas Bataille focuses on the reproduction of life as a material development with a result that can be thought of as an *Aufhebung*, and therefore within the sphere of history, what is at stake for Hegel is only the initial constitution of conscious being by the negation of life as such. Hegel does not make any distinction here between the reproductive structure of a complex sexual being in relation to life and that of primitive asexual cells; both move in the reproductive act between being one and two, continuous and discontinuous. Higher as well as lower forms of life proceed through the process of fission and fusion, continuity and discontinuity. Apparently, the only difference between primitive life and higher forms is the number of necessary elements in the process of reproduction and the complexity of the ordering.

D   Desire and Conscious Being

To understand what is at stake here, and how Bataille can be said to develop Hegel's dialectics beyond Hegel, it is necessary to be more detailed in the account of life and the initial constitution of the self. One can say that in Hegel's dialectics of life, the ontologically necessary correlate of division and discontinuity must be attraction, and within the consciousness of one of the two resulting parties such an attraction is experienced as a desire directed towards that which is different, i.e. the other or another. The human being is as self-conscious being constituted by the negation of life, which means that "self-consciousness is certain of itself only by the *Aufheben* of this other that presents itself to self-consciousness as independent life" (PHG_H, 139 (PHG_{TWA}, 143; PHS, 109)). If this desire is experienced as hunger, it is consciousness's desire to annihilate another independent living being, "consuming" (PHG_H, 137 (PHG_{TWA}, 141; PHS, 107)) the other; Hegel calls such an annihilation of another being "natural" or "abstract negation" (PHG_H, 145 (PHG_{TWA}, 149–50; PHS, 114)). This is precisely the primary movement of self-conscious being, still only in-it-self and not yet for-it-self, namely the desire for an opposite, which is "a living thing" (PHG_H, 135 (PHG_{TWA}, 139; PHS, 106)). Desire in this sense can therefore be considered a contradiction of life within the experience of consciousness: life giving birth to death. What in reality is one, self-conscious being-alive, develops into a contradictory opposition.

For Hegel, the problem for desire as consciousness is that satisfaction in itself makes the object of desire disappear, which leaves desire to look for a new object. However, regardless of whether desire is experienced from without or from within in the reproduction of life, it is not only directed towards nourishment but also towards the other sex. The development of life towards higher forms is precisely expressed in this duality of desire. Whereas Hegel focuses on hunger, Bataille interprets desire primarily as the inner experience of sexual attraction. As such, desire naturally presupposes a difference; however, more importantly, it presupposes an opening-up towards communication with another: "the passage from the normal state to that of erotic desire presupposes in us the relative dissolution of the being constituted in the discontinuous order" (ER, 23 (ER$_E$, 17)). It should also be pointed out in this context that satisfaction is not an abstract negation in the case of erotic desire, but an event that leaves the object capable of being negated and thus of satisfying desire again.

For Bataille, as for Hegel, desire must be considered the desire to become continuous with the other by negating its independency: to annihilate the other as (an)other. In relation to life, independent continuous beings are discontinuous. Sexual activity must in this perspective be seen as the "critical moment of the isolation" (ER, 101 (ER$_E$, 100)), and this crisis is solved by the real continuity of the moments of sexual union. In a Bataillian perspective, however, this only makes desire even more contradictory. The desire of a being is directed towards a momentary union with another being that both annihilates and preserves the difference by sublating it to a "momentary continuity" (ER, 103 (ER$_E$, 103)). Such a momentary *Aufhebung* of independence and isolation gives, objectively speaking, birth to more life, i.e., it makes life as such grow, although the more we enjoy the act in itself the less we worry about the possible outcome, i.e. the children (see ER, 103 (ER$_E$, 102)).

Desire is necessary for the fusion of sexual reproduction and therefore for the growth of life once it has become sexualized, but desire is also a negation of life, creating contradictions within life on various levels. The discontinuity of life as experienced in desire forces every being to make distinctions and chose what to annihilate by consumption, and what to treat as attractive in the sexual sense. The necessity of choosing between the objects of desire introduces a pause, a temporal discontinuity that inhibits the continuous process of life, and a choice like this must be termed conscious in some rudimentary sense.

Conscious life is thus in itself a contradiction, and in an even more radical way than the contradictions on the unconscious level. As a contradiction, conscious life appears within life itself, not as something antithetic coming from outside life but exactly as the determinate negation of life by life itself. Such a consciousness of distinction and choice, however, requires justification, first in the simple form of reasons to make one distinction rather than another, one choice instead of another, and later as full-blown subjective rationality, which claims to be in accordance with objective reason. This is the logic in "the passage of existence in-it-self [*en soi*] to existence for-it-self [*pour soi*]", where the animal's "sentiment of it-self" becomes a "self-consciousness" (ER, 100 (ER$_E$, 99)).

In Hegel's account of life in the *Phenomenology*, there is only movement and change, no development and no direction; history begins with the negation of life by conscious being and comes to an end when consciousness is realized as self-conscious being. With his concept of desire, Bataille opposes Hegel's un-differentiated and ahistorical concept of life, introducing a development, both within the process of life's reproduction of it-self and in the evolution from asexual to sexual reproduction. This also transforms Hegel's idea of history that is restricted to the progression of the human spirit through experience to become absolute knowledge, being thus initiated by the birth of human con-sciousness in the fundamental negation of nature. As Queneau notes, Bataille conceives of the dialectics of nature as constituting "a sort of natural history" already in his early writings.[36] Bataille can be said to extend history back to the development of consciousness in nature; he can therefore also think of history as continuing beyond the disappearance of man. In contrast to Hegel, Bataille thinks of life as historical, although this history has neither beginning nor end. This contrast reappears, when Bataille turns to the development of human consciousness.

Hegel's dialectics of being is objective in-it-self, as it is obvious in his con-ception of life, but the dialectical movement of conscious being only gains its validity for-it-self through conscious being's experience of its own devel-opment. This experience leads self-conscious being to *Geist* and absolute knowledge: being comes to know itself in-and-for-it-self. To both Hegel and Bataille, self-consciousness is specifically human, but whereas Hegel thinks of its constitution as an undifferentiated negation of life as such, Bataille in his perspective speaks of the passage from animal to man as a "dialectical process of development",[37] i.e. a material movement experienced as an inner experi-ence of negation by being becoming human. Bataille notes that no one can know how this really happened in the natural history of human beings; what can be said with certainty is only how conscious life relates to reality as such, namely by negating it, i.e. by being moral and rational, by working and by an-nihilating something else.

To Bataille, this development is not merely a matter of one negation and thus one *Aufhebung* of life. It is a complex sequence of real material and his-torical negations that together, through real inner experiences, finally sublates being to become human. These negations are first of all the universal taboos in

---

36   See Queneau, "Premières confrontations avec Hegel", p. 698.

37   Georges Bataille, *L'Histoire de l'érotisme* ('1951'), in OC$_B$ VIII, ed. Thadée Klosowski (Paris. Gallimard, 1976), p. 36 (Bataille, *The History of Eroticism*, in Bataille, *The Accursed Share*, vols. II–III, trans. Robert Hurley (New York: Zone Books, 1993), p. 43).

relation to death and reproduction, which anthropological studies have called to our attention. As Bataille says, "man is an animal which remains suspended [*interdit*] before death and sexual union" (ER, 53 (ER$_E$, 50)). It is not just a matter of the prohibition against incest, for instance, which to Bataille is just one particular "aspect" of "the totality of religious prohibitions" (ER, 54 (ER$_E$, 51)). The point is that the confrontation with whatever is prohibited in this sense produces an inner experience that cannot be caused only by what is experienced in itself. In a modern scientific perspective, such a prohibition is "not justified" and therefore termed "pathological" as a "neurosis", but, as Bataille stresses, this objective knowledge "from without" does not make the experience disappear, and seen "from within" such a prohibition can be both "global" and "justifiable" (ER, 40 (ER$_E$, 37)).

To Bataille, what is prohibited in the taboo is the "violence" of nature, and the human attitude is precisely the "refusal" of such violence (see ER, 64 (ER$_E$, 61)). Prohibitions are thus negations of nature as experienced from consciousness. Without such prohibition, human beings would never attain "the clear and distinct consciousness [...] on which science is founded" (ER, 41 (ER$_E$, 38)). The human 'no' to natural violence, however, is never definitive. According to Bataille, it is only a pause, "a momentary suspension, not a final standstill" (ER, 65 (ER$_E$, 62)). The basic non-logical difference does not disappear, it just reaches a temporary unity that makes life's activity human, i.e. makes activity conscious and reasonable as *poiesis* and *praxis*. The resulting unity is not stable but rather what Bataille would call a necessary impossibility. As such an impossibility, human life will break down again and again – not because of outer pressure but because of the basic inner difference that cannot be annihilated; it just keeps returning in new forms. It is not desire as such that breaks mechanically through civilization, but desire interpreted and thus transformed into a *Moment* of conscious being. In this form, desire negates the basis of civilization, and it is in such acts of sovereignty that man transgresses the boundaries set by civilization.

E   Conclusion

If the conflict between the reasonable order of civilization and the subversive, violent pleasure of nature is understood theoretically as a logical contradiction, it must be resolved. Hence, what was described above as the ontologically necessary contradiction in life as self-conscious being must be explained away. A non-conflicting, i.e. non-dialectical, solution can only consist in siding with one or the other, idealizing either a self-defeating critique of civilization as such, or a pure and therefore senseless negation of nature as a whole. Hegel chose the latter solution, idealizing ultimately only being sublated to reason, spirit and absolute knowledge.

This is what Horkheimer termed the dogmatic aspect of Hegel's philosophy. However, if dialectics is understood in the sense proposed by both Horkheimer and Gadamer, i.e. as the method employed in Hegel's *Phenomenology* to grasp change, one can oppose, both theoretically and practically, almost any given social organization to be, as Herbert Marcuse expresses it, "in contradiction with its own truth".[38] Of course, these reasons must be specific, and the result of the negation will not be something entirely new *ex nihilo*, since truth, as Marcuse says, is "a real process that cannot be put into a proposition".[39]

However, Hegel's dialectics makes it possible to conceive of politics as a matter of reason and truth, i.e. as society's reflective and autonomous organization of itself, rather than merely a matter of how the ruling classes organize the distribution of power and wealth.

Hegel's dialectics makes it possible to claim that a real existing society has not realized itself as a society, if it is not a just society, because the very concept of society implies justice. The practical opposition of a conscious being against such an insufficiently realized (and thus untrue) society can be said to be a determined negation, and the dialectical movement that it provokes becomes a real experience to conscious being. The theoretical aspect of such an opposition occurs within the existing consciousness and can as such be labelled immanent critique, both in the logical and the ontological sense.

The existing solution, i.e. self-conscious being as we know it, is the result of an infinity of real negations and *Aufhebungen*, but it can itself always be negated by practical scepticism, i.e. by consciousness demanding a reason why the existing solution is worth choosing. As Hegel has demonstrated, it is possible to criticize and oppose any particular way of organizing our social being politically, just as it is possible to change that organization quite radically, if only we can give reasons that are acceptable to those affected by the change, i.e. reasons that are tenable in relation to the yardstick of the social being in question. Scepticism requires an acceptable reason for the determinate negation, and the critique will therefore always be immanent.

However, even without the dogmatic aspect of Hegel's philosophy, dialectics understood in terms of theoretical reasoning, i.e. logic and ontology, might be considered inhuman. Instead, inspired by Bataille's dialectics, one could

---

38   Herbert Marcuse, *Reason and Revolution* (1941), 2nd ed. (London and New York: Routledge, 2000), p. 51 (s$_M$ 4, 56).

39   Marcuse, *ibid.*, p. 100 (s$_M$ 4, 96). See further below, Ch. 7.

understand the basic contradiction in and of human life as a conflict, a tension inherent in human and social being, and as such an ontological condition that is dealt with – and solved – practically every day. The point to discuss politically is therefore not whether we can dissolve what the dialectical tradition would call the contradictions of the existing solution and reach the truth of the social being in question; the contradictions are always already solved practically, and the question is only how to make these practical solutions better.

No society is completely homogeneous, since any human being takes part in more than one social being, e.g., families, classes, subcultures, associations, etc. The social being is in constant motion and change, and man, as a self-conscious being, is constantly in himself in conflict, negating nature and culture in himself and outside, obeying the norms and transgressing them, working and enjoying life, alone and together, thinking and acting. The only thing that does not make sense in such a dialectical materialist perspective is to hope for, and attempt once and for all to realize, a fixed ideal of conscious social being, i.e. a final and eternally valid solution.

Perhaps the problem is that Bataille's dialectics is so thoroughly atheist and materialist that it does not lend any ontological credit or epistemological validity to those pure ideals and values that we normally let ourselves be motivated by in politics, morality and religion. Bataille's dialectics allows for critique and improvement, but there is nothing in his materialism that attributes ideal meaning and validity to some individual actions and not to others; there is nothing unconditional and absolute worth dying for, since such ideal values are just death in a symbolic form, i.e. fixed solutions that negate life. Reality changes, but since it is difficult to give reasons for choosing between various lines of closure and action, the postponement and the pauses keep growing longer. Politics demand a negation of change in the form of a disciplined effort over time, as well as a disciplined organization powerful enough to exercise authority, again over time. Revolts are always possible, but revolutions and reforms, i.e. real political action, require fixed goals and sometimes inhuman discipline, treating human beings almost like things. In relation to such demands, Bataille's materialist dialectics, his recognition of the validity of inner experience as such and his radical critique of authority risk constituting a mystifying ideology for a world organized only by the market, since no long-term political action, no persistent use of force, seems legitimate in Bataille's perspective.

To sum up, contrary to Foucault's and Derrida's views, Bataille is one of the few 20th-century philosophers who have actually taken Hegel's totalizing concept of dialectics seriously, acknowledging the importance of consciousness for the process and developing it in a consistently materialist way. Bataille describes the processes of nature and human culture dialectically, without comforting himself with dreams and hopes of ideals of a harmony that history or experience will realize in the end. As such, Bataille's dialectics makes it possible to criticize not only any given society, but any attempt to give social being a determinate form, any vision about the perfect society, and it is this anti-idealism that Foucault and Derrida perceive as a critique of dialectics.

This anti-idealism, however, is also a source of a great vagueness in Bataille's work, when it comes to saying positively how society should be. For Bataille to believe in an ideal for humanity that could demand sacrifice would mean negating dialectics undialectically, i.e. willingly renouncing change, changing change into rest, forming ultimately the identity of identity and difference, i.e. the unity in rest incorporating motion and change as *Moments*, consciously accepting the unacceptable, and believing the unbelievable, in spite of knowing all beliefs to be futile. Needless to say, this is not easy.

In short, with an epistemology and ontology like Bataille's, it is very difficult to believe in anything worth dying for – and that is a shame. The world is in need of political action that can confront the fundamentalist belief in the blessings of market economy with equally strong beliefs in human solidarity and the possibility of practicing politics with respect for human reason. Hence, we may have to reject Bataille's material dialectics, not in order to be able to criticize but in order to believe in the possibilities of practical politics.

CHAPTER 5

From Ontology to Epistemology: Tong, Mao and Hegel

One of China's finest contemporary philosophers, Tong Shijun, keynote speaker at the World Congress of Philosophy in Seoul, Korea 2008,[1] has been so daring as to employ the idea of dialectics in the titles of two of his early books, *Chinese Philosophy: Practical Reason and Dialectical Logic* from 1989 and *The Dialectics of Modernization. Habermas and the Chinese Discourse of Modernization* from 2000, the latter being his PhD thesis from Bergen, Norway 1994. One could think of this as just a result of youthful enthusiasm for catchy book titles, but Tong does in fact use the word dialectics frequently and discusses dialectics in various contexts in the books. Given that dialectics ranks among the most important ideas in philosophy, the matter thus warrants further investigation.

Hence, the word dialectics is very much present, when reading Tong. However, what seems a bit puzzling is that his actual way of thinking and discussing does not, to me at least, appear very dialectical. In other words: if Tong's way of analysing and discussing is dialectical, then it is dialectical in a different sense than the one I have become accustomed to. Already at this stage I must therefore indicate, wherefrom I get my idea of dialectics, since this of course conditions my verdict. Hence, to me, dialectics first of all appears in Hegel's *Phenomenology of Spirit* and in work inspired by Hegel, i.e. in Horkheimer and Adorno's writings, in Marcuse's, in Gadamer's, and in the writings of Kojève and Bataille.[2]

Of course, one's notion of dialectics can be based on many sources, and this is not the first time I encounter conflicting concepts of dialectics.[3] Hence, the

1 Tong Shijun, "Overlapping Consensus on Overlapping Consensus", in Tong, *Theoretical Dialogues in Practice* (NSU Summertalks, vol. 4) (Malmö: NSU Press, 2009).

2 See, e.g., Asger Sørensen, "Dialectics – a commentary to Singer: 'Global Business and the Dialectic'", *Human Systems Management* 21 (2003; above Ch. 3); Sørensen, "The Inner Experience of Living Matter: Bataille and Dialectics", *Philosophy & Social Criticism* 33, no. 5 (2007; above Ch. 4); Sørensen, *Om videnskabelig viden. Gier, ikker og ismer*, (Frederiksberg: Samfundslitteratur, 2010), pp. 138–40, 308–10; Sørensen, "Kritisk teori", in *Videnskabsteori*, ed. Michael Hviid Jacobsen, Kasper Lippert-Rasmussen, and Peter Nedergaard (København: Hans Reitzel, 2012), pp. 261–68; see also the Interlude above and below, Ch. 7.

3 I have discussed the conflict between a French and a German understanding of dialectics in Sørensen, "The Inner Experience" (Ch. 4 above).

© KONINKLIJKE BRILL NV, LEIDEN, 2019 | DOI 10.1163/9789004362420_009

roots of my puzzlement may just be that there are two different concepts of dialectics at play, i.e. that Tong simply means something different by the word 'dialectics' than I do. Whereas I was formed philosophically by Critical Theory and analytical philosophy in a Danish philosophy department in the 1980s, Tong was formed intellectually during the Cultural Revolution in China in the 1970s, i.e. through the thoughts of Mao Zedong, whose concept of dialectics was based on yet other sources. Naturally, this has given Tong an idea of dialectics that is quite different from mine.

Furthermore, another more general thing also struck me as curious. In both of the books mentioned, Tong claims that classical Chinese philosophy did not develop logic in the same formal sense as Aristotle and subsequent Greek thinkers. I have been educated to think that the universalist criteria of logic are crucial for Hegel's dialectics, so when Tong mentions that Chinese dialectical thinking sometimes degenerates into "romantic nonsense" or "sophistry",[4] I therefore immediately associated this with the alleged negligence in Chinese traditional thought concerning the development of formal logic.

This leads to one further point, namely that I suspect that this is the reason why Tong has an ambivalent relationship to dialectics in the sense that he himself understands it. Even though Tong apparently uses the word dialectics approvingly in his book titles, he is very sceptical about dialectics as the ideal of philosophical thinking. To Tong, some of the so-called dialectical thinkers have simply degenerated into "mysticism or sophism" (CP, 10). Nevertheless, Tong obviously appreciates dialectics, even in his own understanding. He thus recognizes that dialectics plays a major role in the Chinese tradition of thought, i.e. not just in Mao but also in Dao. At the same time, however, he seems to be sceptical towards the philosophical fruitfulness of dialectics as it has developed in Chinese thinking.

I suspect that this ambivalence is precisely the reason why Tong is so preoccupied with analysing dialectics in Chinese thought as well as in Chinese social reality. I further suspect – and this is my hypothesis – that his ambivalence must be linked to the understanding of dialectics he has inherited from his philosophical predecessors.

If this is the case, it is with good reason that Tong has drifted towards a kind of transcendentalism inspired by neo-Kantians like some of the logical

---

4 Tong Shijun, *Chinese Philosophy: Practical Reason and Dialectical Logic* (Bergen: Filosofisk Institutt, Universitetet, 1989), pp. 85–87. In the present chapter, the following page references are indicated in brackets in the text as CP, nn.

positivists, Popper (see CP, 142) and, especially, the late Habermas.[5] Neverthe-less, in light of this reconstruction, a challenge to Tong could be to argue that his concept of dialectics is shaped by Mao, Lenin and classical Chinese think-ing, that their concept of dialectics is not the only one available to philosophy, and that Tong therefore does not need to be so sceptical about dialectics as such.

My point is thus that I think Tong as a critical theorist would be better off with a concept of dialectics like the one I have adopted through my philosoph-ical education. This paternalist analysis is offered as a gift to Tong in the most classical sense, i.e. as a donation of something that the recipient may not know that he needs, and therefore it is a gift that he may not actually want when he discovers what it contains. As such, the donation is an expression of both generosity and antagonism.[6]

In short, I will argue the following:

(a) Mao's conception of dialectics is mainly practical and therefore suscep-tible to theoretical critique.

(b) The Chinese concept of dialectics from Dao to Mao is mainly causal and material, i.e. not logical or epistemological in the sense in which these words are most commonly understood by mainstream academic philosophy.

(c) Tong accepts such a practical, causal and material conception of dialec-tics when he criticizes dialectics, and he is sceptical about dialectics in this sense as an ideal of philosophical thinking.

(d) Tong, however, draws the wrong conclusions about dialectics, since in Hegel's *Phenomenology*, classical Critical Theory and Gadamer's philosophical hermeneutics we have a much stronger concept of dialec-tics, which does not succumb as easily to theoretical critique as the prac-tical and materialist concept of dialectics that Tong both criticizes and uses.

---

5 See Tong Shijun, *The Dialectics of Modernization. Habermas and the Chinese Discourse of Modernization* (The University of Sydney East Asian Series, Number 13) (Sydney: Wild Peony, 2000).

6 For a presentation of the classical concept of the gift offered by Marcel Mauss, see, e.g., my analysis in Asger Sørensen, "Marcel Mauss. Kvinder, høfligheder og talismaner: Gaven som fuldstændig social kendsgerning", in *Tradition og fornyelse i sociologien*, ed. Michael Hviid Jacobsen, Mikael Carleheden, and Søren Kristiansen (Ålborg: Ålborg Universitetsforlag, 2001) (included in Asger Sørensen, *I lyset af Bataille – politisk filosofiske studier* (København: Poli-tisk Revy, 2012) as Ch. 5).

My conclusion is that we both can and should maintain dialectics as the ideal of philosophical thinking, and maybe even of scientific thinking, and that Tong as a critical theorist would be wise to accept this. To substantiate these points, I will focus on one of the primary sources of Tong's philosophy: Mao Zedong's dialectical materialism (A). Then, I will analyse Tong's ontological conception of dialectics, present an epistemological alternative and claim that Tong with his norms for science should take up the latter (B). Finally, I will argue that this discussion is less about East versus West and more about politics. The problem is that dialectical materialism is much more reconcilable with the dynamics of desire and greed than the dialectics of absolute knowledge (C).

A   Mao's Idea of Dialectical Materialism is Mainly Practical

I must admit that I am by no means a Mao scholar; I may therefore have misunderstood a lot. Nevertheless, let me introduce a concept of dialectics that arises from my reading of some of Mao's key texts. To gain easy access to the core of Mao's thinking, I have consulted a Danish friend who was a dedicated Maoist in his youth. According to my friend, two texts were considered essential in the heyday of European Maoism: "On practice" and "On contradiction". Therefore, I will focus on these texts in the next two sub-sections (i and ii). Both texts date from 1937 and are manuscripts for speeches given to students from the Communist party at the military and political college in the city of Yan'an, which was the capital of Red China after the long march and until the revolution finally succeeded in 1949.

i   *The Perspective of a Military Commander Must be Practical*
in a Pragmatic Sense
Mao is addressing young party members who are about to go to war, not professional philosophers. Nevertheless, the subjects addressed include what they as party members should know about essential philosophical matters such as practice, contradictions and dialectics. Given the context, it is understandable that Mao issues a general warning against developing into classical book worshippers.[7] Mao recognizes that knowledge is important, but he shows no sign of wanting to discuss epistemology proper. According to Tong, this was also the general attitude in traditional Chinese culture (see CP, 165), and, as Tong notes, it is "extremely difficult, even impossible" to abandon one's cultural basis (see

---

7   See Mao Tse-Tung, "Oppose Book Worship" (1930), in Mao, *On Practice and Contradiction*, ed. Slavoj Žižek (London: Verso, 2007), pp. 44–45.

CP, 77). Tong emphasizes that after the death of Mao, Deng Xiaoping said: "Practice is the only criterion of testing truth", and in general his idea was to learn "everything useful" "from capitalism" (CP, 166).

Hence, knowledge in the classical philosophical and scientific sense does not appear to be very important in China, neither for Mao nor his predecessors or successors. Thus, recognizing the importance of knowledge does not lead Mao to claim or search for criteria for the validity of knowledge in the sense that Plato, Hume, Kant or Popper would want them, and there is no mention of principled scepticism either. For Mao, "man's knowledge is verified only when he achieves the anticipated results in the process of social practice (material production, class struggle or scientific experiment)".[8] Expressing himself in this manner, Mao's concept of knowledge is practical in a pragmatic sense and similar to the one we know from Dewey;[9] in fact, according to Tong, Dewey was widely read in China in Mao's formative years (see CP, 117). Tong also emphasizes the similarity between pragmatism and the traditional Chinese emphasis on "practical rationality" (CP, 130); hence, the practical bias of Mao's thinking could be rooted both in his own cultural basis and Dewey's pragmatism. Regardless of whether this was the case or not, Mao's perspective appears to be practical in the Deweyan sense, and as Tong rightly mentions, Dewey cannot distinguish between technical and practical problems.[10]

One could even say that Mao's concept of knowledge is pre-critical, since he simply talks about things, essence and causal processes of cognition.[11] Some of this resembles what Aristotle might say, and apparently Hsun Tzu, who is often called China's Aristotle, seems to be saying something similar on the subject of things (see CP, 90 f). Mao does not appear to distinguish between the ontological and epistemological aspects of experience and knowledge. He does, however, distinguish between perceptual and rational – i.e. "logical' – knowledge, albeit not so much in terms of validity as in terms of scope and as two stages in the "movement of knowledge".[12] Further, whereas Aristotle opposes the practical and poetic types of knowledge with a strong theoretical sense of knowledge,[13] for Mao they all basically belong to the same type. As he

---

8   Mao Tse-Tung, "On Practice" (1937), in Mao, *On Practice and Contradiction*, pp. 54–55.

9   See, e.g., John Dewey, *The Pattern of Inquiry* (1938) – (Ch. VI of *Logic*), in *Pragmatism*, ed. H.S. Thayer (New York & Toronto: New American Library, 1970).

10   See Tong, *The Dialectics of Modernization*, p. 245.

11   See Mao, "On Practice", p. 55–56.

12   Mao, ibid., p. 61.

13   See Aristotle, *Nicomachean Ethics*, trans. W.D. Ross and revised by J.O. Urmson, in *The Complete Works of Aristotle*, ed. Jonathan Barnes (Princeton NJ: Princeton University Press, 1984/1995), vol. 2, *Eth. Nic.* 1139b.

expresses it: "Theoretical knowledge is acquired through practice and must then return to practice".[14]

For Mao, what is important is realizing goals or objectives, and such a teleological process sometimes requires changing the plan along the way.[15] Mao clearly wants his listeners to become practical in the pragmatic sense and avoid being theoretical in the Aristotelian sense. Whereas Aristotle considers useless theoretical knowledge to be the finest,[16] the important goal for Mao is practical, and 'practical' should probably not even be understood in the Aristotelian sense. In these speeches, at least, it does not seem as if Mao wants the party students to become political or ethical in the Aristotelian sense. An Aristotelian understanding of 'practice' would imply recommending a mixed constitution,[17] which is close to the ideal of modern parliamentary democracy. In contrast to this, Mao, at least in this context, apparently holds a much more instrumental conception of democracy.[18] Tong mentions that Mao argued for an idea of a "new democracy", but the overall criterion was that it should be "useful" for "the practice of the Chinese revolution" (CP, 122 f).[19]

Sociologist and China scholar J.W. Freiberg notes that in general, Mao is more of a military commander than a professional philosopher.[20] This must hold true especially in the context of the speeches analysed here, since they are directed precisely to an audience that has to participate in civil war, class struggle and revolution. So, what we have from Mao is a causal account of how to acquire knowledge as impressions and ideas, and how to practically apply knowledge in the revolutionary struggle. Apparently, he has no wish for an epistemological criterion for truth or falsity by which we can evaluate the knowledge acquired, to see if it really is knowledge or only an illusion. The truth is already decided. As Mao puts it: "[D]ialectical materialism is universally true, because it is impossible for anyone to escape from its domain in his

---

14   Mao, "On Practice", p. 61.

15   See Mao, ibid., p. 63.

16   See Aristotle, *Metaphysics*, trans. W.D. Ross, in *The Complete Works of Aristotle*, vol. 2, *Met.* 983a.

17   See Aristotle, *Politics*, trans. B. Jowett, in *The Complete Works of Aristotle*, vol. 2, *Pol.* 1296.

18   See Mao, "Oppose Book Worship", p. 48.

19   For a more extended discussion of Mao's relation to democracy, see, e.g., the work by Lin Zhang, "The Border Areas' Transient Practices of Democracy and the Limitations in Mao Zedong's Notion of Democracy", in *Multible Democracies in Theory and History*, ed. Simen Andersen Øyen and Rasmus T. Slaattelid (Bergen: University of Bergen: SVT Press, 2009).

20   See J.W. Freiberg, "The Dialectic in China: Maoist and Daoist", *Bulletin of Concerned Asian Scholars*, no. 9 (1977), p. 14.

practice".[21] In this practical perspective, in terms of metaphysics, Mao is thus clearly a materialist. However, in terms of epistemology he is just as clearly a naïve realist. This also seems to be the case when we take a closer look at Mao's idea of dialectics.

ii   *The Idea of Contradiction is Universal, Material and Causal*

Mao is indeed very practical in the speech "On practice". More interesting from a philosophical perspective is the speech "On contradiction". Mao's conceptual framework is dialectical materialism, and it is this perspective that gives contradictions their importance. To Mao, being occupied with material dialectics means that one must study the internal contradictions of things; further, this means that material dialectics is seen as opposed to "metaphysics", which is concerned with the exterior influence on things and the interaction between things. It is the internal contradictions that set things in motion, just as growth in nature also comes from such contradictions.[22] As an example, Mao states that the history of China is formed by changes within Chinese society, not changes in climate or geography (see ONC, 70).

Mao emphasizes the "universality or absoluteness of contradiction", namely that "contradiction exists in the process of development of all things" (ONC, 72). Mao also distinguishes between, on the one hand, temporary and historical contradictions and, on the other hand, stable contradictions such as those between forces and relations of production, theory and practice, and base and superstructure (see ONC, 91 f). The main point for Mao, however, still seems to be practical, namely that it is important to study the particularity of every contradiction in order to find the right method to resolve it, whether it is stable or not. Mao is still talking to party members; the aim of the analysis of the "movement of opposites in different things" is to find "methods for resolving contradictions" (ONC, 71).

To Mao, dialectics is thus characterized by contradictions. In contradictions, both aspects are always in unity, just as they are or become identical, and one of the aspects can or will be transformed into the other (see ONC, 93). Mao refers to Lenin with regard to this conception of dialectics and contradiction; he also quotes Lenin with regard to the absoluteness and universality of motion as opposed to the temporality of unity (see ONC, 97). There "is nothing in the world except matter in motion and this motion must assume certain

---

21   Mao, "On Practice", p. 62.

22   See Mao Tse-Tung, "On Contradiction" (1937), in Mao, *On Practice and Contradiction*, p. 69. In the present chapter, the following page references are indicated in brackets in the text as ONC, nn.

forms" (ONC, 75–76). Furthermore, Mao approvingly quotes Lenin when it comes to the juxtaposition of various types of opposed terms as examples of contradictions: in mathematics between integral and differential summation, in mechanics between action and reaction, in physics between positive and negative electricity, in chemistry between the association and dissociation of atoms, and finally in the social sciences the class struggle (see ONC, 73). Mao deftly summarizes the idea, namely that it is not a matter of whether there are contradictions in reality but merely what kind they are (see ONC, 74).

In the practical spirit of resolving contradictions, Mao urges his audience to be objective, specific and concrete as opposed to being one-sided, subjective and superficial. In order to understand the whole, it is crucial to understand the parts. It is necessary to understand both sides of the contradiction; it is not enough to understand just one (see ONC, 79). Mao's point is that dialectics is clearly about contradictions within or between things already existing in reality. Mao qualifies some of these contradictions as sometimes "temporary" and more or less "intense" (ONC, 81); examples of such contradictions include military conflicts between warlords and between the Kunmintang and the people (see ONC, 82, 84). Mao does focus a lot on war in these speeches (see ONC, 87, 95), which is quite understandable given the context. In fact, Freiberg has argued that Mao's dialectics is first of all an expression of the dialectics found in the Daoist Sun Zi classic *Art of war*,[23] and that looks like a promising strategy of interpretation.

Mao thus thinks of dialectics as anti-metaphysical. According to Mao, metaphysical thinking is determined by the idea that the qualitative principles of reality are unchangeable and that only quantitative change is possible. When we have discovered these principles, then we will know what reality is, and also how it will change in the future, since it cannot but change quantitatively (see ONC, 68–70). This, however, appears to be a very narrow concept of metaphysics. In the mainstream philosophical understanding of metaphysics, a dialectical materialism such as Mao's would qualify as indeed very metaphysical. Tong mentions that Leibniz's metaphysics is comparable to those of some of the classical Chinese philosophers, and I think it is obvious that Mao's idea of dialectical materialism is metaphysical in the same sense.

Hence, Mao develops the principles of reality on a speculative basis of pure reflection, and only with reference to philosophical and political authorities such as Lenin. Rather than being principles of quantitative change only, they are also qualitative; nevertheless, they are speculative principles. Moreover, Mao apparently totalizes these principles in the most classical philosophical

---

23   See Freiberg, "The Dialectic in China", pp. 12–18.

way, saying for instance that "all processes transform themselves into their opposites," and that constancy is only relative, whereas "the transformation of one process into the other is absolute" (ONC, 98).

At the end, Mao quotes without hesitation, what I would consider the sophistry of Lenin, stating that "there is an absolute in the relative" (ONC, 99). However, sophistry or not, as it will become obvious below, in his understanding of dialectics Mao is in fact on par with the tradition of dialectical materialism, and consequentially so is Tong.

B   Tong Could Make Good Use of a Different Idea of Dialectics

By my philosophical standards, Mao demonstrates in his metaphysics an extremely broad conception of contradiction, apparently including all kinds of oppositions. Normally, I would take the point of reference for the term 'contradiction' to be the principle of contradiction which, according to a standard textbook like Wilfrid Hodges's, states that p and non-p cannot both be true, no matter the time and place.[24] The principle of contradiction is a formal principle of normative logic telling us how to think clearly about matters in general, namely that we should avoid contradicting ourselves, at least in scientific discourses. One normally expresses the point by saying that literally everything can be deduced logically from contradictions, and since we cannot distinguish truth from falsity, we cannot know anything in the strong sense of the word. The idea is thus that stating something contradictory amounts to stating nothing at all, since no truth condition or value is implied by such an utterance.

In the account of dialectics given by Mao, contradictions are supposed to exist in and between all kinds of real things that oppose each other. Mao's dialectics can be said to be both ontological and empirical in a very broad sense, as well as normative in a pragmatic sense. He thus provides a general conceptual account of the causality of change and opposition, while also calling for practical solutions to empirical problems caused by the contradictions. What is missing in Mao's conception of dialectics, however, is precisely the acknowledgement of the importance of validity. There is no recognition of the role played by truth in epistemology or formal logic, and apparently Mao does not distinguish causal or material oppositions from logical contradictions in the sense just mentioned. As mentioned above, according to Tong the lack of interest in formal logic is characteristic of Chinese thought (see CP, 106, 181),

---

24   See Wilfrid Hodges, *Logic* (1977) (Hammondsworth: Penguin, 1986), p. 16.

so in this respect Mao demonstrates himself to be very loyal to the Chinese tradition.

In view of this, I argue that an idea of dialectical logic can be traced from Dao to Mao, that Tong's conception of dialectics and logic seems to reflect this, and that he therefore has good reason to be ambivalent about dialectics (i). As an alternative, I introduce the dialectics of Hegel's *Phenomenology*, emphasising the importance for Hegel of epistemology and formal logic, which also implies taking seriously the distinction between contradiction and opposition (ii). Finally, I argue that in dialectics theory must be prior to practice. To substantiate this, I explain what I take to be the core of this conception of dialectics, namely scepticism, determinate negation and the idea of *Aufheben*, which constitute the epistemological basis of Hegel's dialectics as well as the idea of *Bildung* (iii).

i   *Tong is Critical of How the Material Dialectics of Practice Ignores Validity and Formal Logic*

First, Tong emphasizes the principled distinction between validity and usefulness.[25] This means that he, in contrast to Mao, can discuss matters of epistemology beyond those of technology and political strategy. Second, he proposes a strong criterion of knowledge: the idea of cognitive rationality and truth found in the traditional understanding of scientific knowledge,[26] like the one we know from Plato and Aristotle. Together, this means that Tong does not restrict his philosophical reflections to the pragmatist perspective of, for instance, Dewey or Mao, but can occupy himself with theory of knowledge and science in the tradition from Kant. Finally, he follows Popper in emphasizing that philosophy of science must be occupied with "problems in the context of justification" (CP, 149).

In such an almost classical 20th-century philosophical perspective, dialectics in the sense described above is not the most attractive option for philosophical thinking, and this is precisely the point. Even though Tong says that dialectical thinking is the most important contribution made by Chinese philosophy, immediately afterwards he says that dialectical logic cannot replace formal logic and that we – i.e. Chinese philosophers – should pay more attention to formal logic (see CP, 101). To Tong, apparently the implication is that Chinese philosophy, at least for a while, should leave behind dialectics and focus on formal logic in the Aristotelian or modern western sense. Nevertheless, Tong appears somehow ambivalent about these matters. According to Mao,

25   See Tong, *The Dialectics of Modernization*, pp. 63–64.
26   See Tong, *ibid.*, pp. 61–62.

one must not be one-sided (see ONC, 79), and in spite of Tong's emphasis on the importance of formal logic and epistemology in philosophy, he apparently also wants to give credit to the intellectual achievements of traditional Chinese thought (see CP, 14).

What is interesting is that apparently the conceptions of dialectics are very similar in the sources that are constitutive of Tong's philosophical conception of dialectics, namely the Chinese classics, especially Daoist and neo-Confucian, and Mao's thinking. In fact, Freiberg argues that a rather consistent conception of "dialectical logic" can be traced from Dao to Mao.[27] However, in light of Tong's discussion there is good reason to be sceptical, even critical, towards this way of thinking and the conception of logic it implies. Roughly speaking, one may claim that in the classical academic philosophical perspective adopted by Tong, this way of thinking does not appear to be about logic at all, or only in a very limited or general sense.

However – and this is the important point – even though Tong may have good reason to be sceptical or even critical towards dialectics in the sense mentioned above, I will claim that he still accepts a general understanding of dialectics in precisely this sense. Tong thus credits Liu Yu-Hai as the first to have developed the idea of contradiction from two statements contradicting each other to "two real forces, which oppose each other" (CP, 97), just as he states that *The Book of Changes – I Ching* in Chinese – contains important ideas of "dialectical logic" (CP, 90), and many other references could be mentioned. Tong also has a broad conception of ontology (see CP, 147), which supports conceptually his rather causal conception of dialectics. Furthermore, he refers approvingly to his teacher, Feng Qi, who claimed that dialectical logic is distinguished from formal logic by being part of philosophy proper (see CP, 157).

Tong seems to be caught up in a classic argumentative trap. As an active part of an intellectual tradition, Tong has unwittingly accepted a particular understanding of a concept. Accepting an understanding of a concept, however, does not mean agreeing with the content and implications of it. Still, the acceptance means that Tong criticizes a particular understanding of dialectics, even though there are other and more promising interpretations available.

Using some Hegelian terms to be explained below, my point is as follows: instead of following the neo-Kantians and simply abandon the ideal of dialectics as a result of abstract sceptical critique, hence relegating dialectics to the past, the causal and materialist concept of dialectics should be negated in a determinate and very concrete way in order precisely to demonstrate the limitations of the understanding at hand. This is what I intend to do with

---

27   See Freiberg, "The Dialectic in China", p. 11.

my critique in this article. Or, put differently, instead of ending up praising formal logic or venturing into transcendentalism, Tong could take a look at different ways of conceiving of dialectical thinking, which I think are much more promising than the conception of dialectical materialism developed from Dao over Lenin to Mao.

ii   *I Emphasize the Distinction within Dialectical Metaphysics between Logic and Causality*

The main point is – as Jørgen Huggler has argued in detail in his *Habilitation* on Hegel's *Phenomenology*[28] – that without the universalist criteria of knowledge and logic, i.e. without scepticism, there would be no determinate negation and thus no dialectics in Hegel's *Phenomenology* at all.[29] This point seems to be overlooked by Lenin if he, as Freiberg claims, believes that negation is not sceptical.[30] As Carl-Göran Heidegren has stated in his commentaries on the *Phenomenology*, indeed Hegel does want to unite theory and praxis.[31] Whereas 'theory' should clearly be understood in the classical sense of Plato and Aristotle, it is in Hegel's writings we find the roots of the unified concept of 'practice' used by Dewey and Mao. However, in contrast to their respective ways of thinking, in Hegel's dialectics it is the strong theoretical criterion of knowledge, and the accompanying scepticism, that is made the criterion of practice, not the other way around. What is often called formal logic is therefore a necessary condition for Hegel's dialectics.

Without a formal and very strict logic, there is no dialectics in the Hegelian sense. As Huggler argues, it is scepticism and thus the above-mentioned logical principle of contradiction, as well as the law of the excluded middle, that propel Hegelian dialectics.[32] Hegel's dialectics should thus be thought of as an ontology in the most literal sense, i.e. a logical conceptual reconstruction of being. Therefore, in Hegel's dialectics the causality is also by necessity logical

---

28   See Jørgen Huggler, "English summary", in Huggler, *Hegels skeptiske vej til den absolutte viden* (København: Museum Tusculanum, 1999), pp. 339–49.

29   See Jørgen Huggler, "Hegel's Phenomenology of Rationality", in *Dialectics, Self-consciousness, and Recognition. The Hegelian Legacy*, ed. Asger Sørensen, Arne Grøn, and Morten Raffnsøe-Møller (Malmö: NSU Press, 2009), pp. 34–35. For an informative discussion of scepticism and dialectics in relation to Hegel's earlier Jena writings, see Hartmut Buchner, "Skeptizismus und Dialektik", in *Hegel und die antike Dialektik*, ed. M. Riedel (Frankfurt a. M.: Suhrkamp, 1990).

30   See Freiberg, "The Dialectic in China", p. 5.

31   See Carl-Göran Heidegren, *Hegels Fenomenologi. En analys och kommentar* (Stockholm and Stehag: Brutus Östling, 1995), p. 15.

32   See Huggler, "English summary"; see also Huggler, "Hegel's Phenomenology of Rationality".

in the strong formal sense. As Gadamer has argued, dialectics is about grasping motion conceptually.[33] Since both 'motion' and 'concept' are to be understood in their most literal sense, most philosophers in this Hegelian tradition have considered dialectics to be a forever unfinished story of the impossibility of synthesis or reconciliation. Dialectics in this sense is thus about the theoretical understanding of the principles of reality, not about resolving contradictions practically for pragmatic purposes.

The important point here, however, is that this does not seem to be the case when it comes to Mao's and Tong's dialectics. One way to express the nature of their conception of dialectics is to do like Freiberg and make a distinction between formal or positive logic and dialectical logic.[34] Whereas the former is thought of as primarily constituted by the principle of identity, the latter is constituted by the idea of the unity of contradictions and change.[35] Such a conception of dialectics can first of all be used to describe classical Chinese philosophy, as it is employed by Tong and others. However, by referring to the works of Lenin, Freiberg can also argue that such a conception constitutes the core of dialectical materialism, and thus that it is the Marxist conception of dialectics.[36]

If this is the case, it is not at all surprising that it is this conception of dialectics that is found in Mao's thinking. What we see, both in the Mao's writings and in the Chinese classics, is precisely the idea of unity in contradictions at all levels of reality. We even find a classification of contradictions distinguishing between universals and particulars, just as we are told that the particular is only a contradiction because universality is "residing" (ONC, 85) in particularity. However, this formulation, it must be noted, appears very metaphysical, even in Mao's own rather narrow sense. In a classical philosophical perspective, dialectical materialism must thus be considered a kind of metaphysics.

Even so, Mao's conception of dialectics is very different from the one inherent in Hegel's dialectical metaphysics. As Wolfgang Röd emphasizes, Hegel's ambition was to distinguish at the same time as uniting the logical justification and causal explanation into a strict ontology of change.[37] Such an idea of dialectics would enable us to distinguish real, necessary logical and dialectical

---

33 See Hans-Georg Gadamer, "Hegel und die antike Dialektik", (1961), in Gadamer, *Gesammelte Werke* (Tübingen: Mohr Siebeck, 1986–99), vol. 3, pp. 10–11.

34 See Freiberg, "The Dialectic in China", pp. 2–4.

35 See Freiberg, ibid., pp. 4–7.

36 See ibid., pp. 4–6.

37 See Wolfgang Röd, *Dialektische Philosophie der Neuzeit* (München: C.H. Beck, 1974), vol. 2, pp. 210–11.

contradictions from merely apparent, particular and causal oppositions or conflicts. Apparently, Mao does not see that only a strictly logical reconstruction of the causal dynamics of society and history, such as Hegel and Marx attempted, can legitimate calling, for instance, class struggle a contradiction. Particular historical military conflicts, like the ones mentioned by Mao, would not qualify as contradictions in this sense. Mao states that the opposites are identical because they are conditions of each other. However, in the examples mentioned it seems to be a matter of empirical reality and being, rather than of logic, since it is said in the same context that a "thing transforms itself into its opposite" (ONC, 94).

To Hegel, dialectics is not primarily causal, organic or material; it is primarily epistemological and thus logical in the formal or positive sense mentioned above. Since reality is changing, dialectics becomes 'onto-logical' in the strong sense of both parts of the word. Therefore, dialectics is also metaphysical, but this is actually something we should be happy about. It is only because it is metaphysical that it can give us hope of getting to know – and thus changing – reality. If dialectics was only a causal drive, we would merely be things that were pushed around at the mercy of a matter beyond our understanding and influence.

Hence, ontologically speaking, Hegel's dialectics is realistic, and so it should be. As the young Habermas is believed to have said when criticising positivism, it is only realism that allows us to change anything through conscious action, i.e. *praxis* in the Aristotelian sense mentioned above. As critical thinkers within the dialectical tradition from Hegel, we should be realists, although not naïve. In fact, Hegel already discusses the challenges of empiricism and positivism in the introduction and the first few chapters of the *Phenomenology*.[38] So, already from Hegel himself we have a reflective basis for a kind of dialectics that is ontologically constituted by strict logic and thus different from the one employed by Mao and Tong.

iii   *And I argue for a Conception of Dialectics in which Theory*
        Predominates over Practice

Clearly, as argued above, it is the unified practical and pragmatic perspective that is the key to understanding Mao's position, and apparently it is in the spirit of Hegel that Mao explicitly aims at uniting theory and practice. I would

---

38   See G.W.F. Hegel, *Phänomenologie des Geistes* (1807), in Hegel, *Hauptwerke in sechs Bänden* (Darmstadt: Wissenschaftliche Buchgesellschaft, 1999), vol. 2, 53–81 (TWA 3, 68–107). In the present chapter, the following page references are indicated in brackets in the text as PHG$_{HW}$, nn (page numbers of this edition are equal to those of GW$_H$ 9).

claim, however, that in Hegel's synthesis theory gains the upper hand, since it is the theoretical criterion of validity that rules rather than the practical criterion of success. In Mao's and Sun Zi's dialectics, the exact opposite seems to be the case, namely that practice gains the upper hand and, even more so, that the two military commanders understand 'practical' exclusively in the pragmatic sense, i.e. not in the Aristotelian sense encompassing ethics.

Furthermore, I would claim that the two alternatives are not of equal philosophical importance. Without uncompromised theoretical commitment, there is no reason to scrutinize conceptual distinctions, no reason to idealize the rational will to precision, no logic and, I would say, no reason to will a professional philosophical development. As it has been forcefully argued *In Defence of Philosophy*, pragmatism can be said to express *The American Evasion of Philosophy* or even an *Eclipse of Reason*.[39] As a fellow professional philosopher, I therefore understand that Tong had a need to discuss the tradition, he grew up with and especially the pragmatic and materialist concept of dialectics that is shared by the classical Chinese tradition and Mao's thinking.

Add to this a fact that Tong has also called attention to, namely that until recently the very idea of a scholar in China was someone who explained the already accepted canon of classical texts (see CP, 165). Combining this fact with the lack of training in formal logic in the Chinese philosophical tradition enables us to understand why there is a risk of superficial and imprecise common-place sophistry, for example about the so-called unity of contradictions, which does not have much to offer philosophical dialectics in the strong sense.

Still, dialectics can be better than this. Even though an appreciative and serious exponent like Röd reaches the point of accusing Hegel of sophistry,[40] he also demonstrates that Hegelian dialectics rests on a solid epistemological principle: the principle of the determinate negation. Here, the basic point is that denying something implies affirming something else. A negation is thus determinate, since it negates something specific and leaves the rest of the totality as a basis for the negation in question.

Hegel extends this logical argument to scepticism and doubt in general. Scepticism cannot be maintained if it ends up in "the abstraction of nothingness or emptiness". To Hegel, scepticism must therefore also be determinate in

---

39 See, respectively, Maurice Cornforth, *In Defence of Philosophy* (London: Lawrence & Wishart, 1950); Cornell West, *The American Evasion of Philosophy: A Genealogy of Pragmatism* (Madison: University of Wisconsin Press, 1989) and Max Horkheimer, *Eclipse of Reason* (New York: Oxford University Press, 1947).

40 See Röd, *Dialektische Philosophie der Neuzeit*, vol. 1, p. 198.

terms of being directed towards something (see PHG$_{HW}$, 56–57; TWA 3, 73–74). When confronting, doubting and negating truth claims, scepticism has to be specific in order to be justified. For Hegel, being sceptical means employing a determinate negation in relation to what is proposed. This constitutes a demand for universal validity, although in the negative form, and it should never be done without a reason. If there is no reason to be sceptical, it is unreasonable and irrational. Scepticism must always be concrete and specific, otherwise it is abstract and thus, according to Hegel, empty. In other words, scepticism must be intentional if it is to be rational. You can only have doubts about something if you accept other things. Accepting the truth of some propositions gives you a basis for questioning the validity of other propositions. You cannot doubt everything at once, but you must always be ready to doubt something particular. Just as reasons must be given for thinking positively and making affirmative propositions about real matters, reasons must also be given for being sceptical and doubtful. Both affirmation and negation are truth claims, and in order to be rational they must be based on reasons given.

The epistemological concept of dialectics developed by Hegel enables us to deal with contradictions, albeit in a different sense than Mao's. The contradiction has to be shown to be a logical contradiction. Only then might we be able to circumvent or deconstruct the contradiction by the rational reconstructions of the constituting conditions, either demonstrating them to be reconcilable or arguing against assuming the conditions in question. To Hegel, the result is a metaphysical process driven by principled scepticism and the demand for absolute knowledge. The unconditional demand for universal truth means that each particular determination of the truth becomes the object of a dialectical "*Aufheben*" (PHG$_{HW}$, 80; TWA 3, 106), i.e. a sublation, where what is negated is sublated into a new form of the same object (see PHG$_{HW}$, 60; TWA 3, 78–79). Even though Tong does mention *Aufhebung* and is quite aware of the importance of the displacement from logical contradiction to causal opposition, he fails to emphasize that for Hegel, dialectics is not about two opposing and real entities. In fact – and this is where Tong's and my interpretation of Hegel's dialectics differ – for Tong this displacement is what constitutes the idea of contradiction "in a dialectical sense" (CP, 97).

In the *Phenomenology*, Hegel develops an idea of dialectics that departs from the basic epistemic model of a consciousness confronted with an object. As Röd emphasizes, 'object' should be understood in a very broad sense, since the German word "*Gegenstand*" literally means "what is opposite to".[41] Hegel's claim is that any concept or idea must be realized ontologically in order to

---

41   Röd, *ibid.*, vol. 1, p. 167.

be completely true; only by *becoming* true can a concept *be* true. The point is that only in the realization of the concept, i.e. in the process of becoming real, it becomes manifest, either conceptually or by material resistance, that the concept contains an inherent logical contradiction. As Röd makes clear, even though Hegel uses the word 'movement', it must be understood in a logical rather than an ontological sense.[42] We are not dealing with an opposition between real beings but with a logical contradiction, namely the one between the assumed completeness of the concept, theory or idea and the specific limitations that come to the fore, when it has to legitimize itself by realization, either theoretically or practically.

For Hegel, this is the basic contradiction that drives the logical development. It is therefore always the same, and there is no special "dialectical sense" turning contradiction into opposition, as assumed by Tong. One might even claim that there is only one contradiction in Hegel's dialectics: the one between the universal validity claimed by a position (concept, idea, proposition, theory) and the particularity of the position as realized (see PHG$_{HW}$, 58–59; TWA 3, 75–77). Hegel emphasizes that the experience of this contradiction is a negation of the position, and that this experience results in an "*Aufheben*" (PHG$_{HW}$, 72; TWA 3, 94). In that sense, an *Aufheben* is something that only happens for good reasons, namely when we have learned something about what we claimed. What we learned was that the claimed position was not, after all, the whole truth. It might have been true in some sense, but not true *per se*.

For Hegel, such a successful *Aufheben* constitutes the dialectical process of experience, or maturation, and the determinate negation therefore has a "result" (PHG$_{HW}$, 57; TWA 3, 74). For a successfully experiencing consciousness, the outcome will be the kind of intellectual formation the Germans call "*Bildung*" (PHG$_{HW}$, 56; TWA 3, 73), which to Hegel ultimately means the freedom achieved through alienation.[43]

Of course, all kinds of complexities need to be dealt with to understand Hegel's dialectics in depth. Sometimes, for instance, the striving for truth and knowledge is not just a rational scientific enterprise, but also a sign of insecurity, and the link between doubt and despair is acknowledged by Hegel in his dialectical reconstruction of experience (see PHG$_{HW}$, 56; TWA 3, 72).[44]

---

42 See *ibid.*, p. 158.

43 See Asger Sørensen, "Alienation, Language and Freedom. A Note on *Bildung* in Hegels Writings", *Nordicum-Mediterraneu* 7, no. 2 (2012), (4 p. HTML); for a more extensive analysis, see next chapter.

44 It is Nietzsche, however, who deconstructs science as simply an expression of existential longing for security and safety (see Friedrich Nietzsche, "Die fröhliche Wissenschaft"

The point is simply that with a conception of dialectics like the one just presented, Tong would be able to maintain a positive concept of dialectics, appreciating the importance of validity, formal logic and strong epistemological concepts of knowledge and truth. In other words, with such an understanding of dialectics there is no contradiction or principled opposition between dialectical logic and logic as such, i.e. no opposition between dialectical thinking and the way of thinking that has appealed to professional philosophers since Plato. Chinese philosophers do not have to renounce dialectics to practice logic, quite the contrary. In this sense, Tong is already practicing dialectics, and if he accepts what I am offering him, he can even take pride in doing so.

C   This Discussion about Dialectics is Not Primarily about East vs. West – It is about Politics

This concludes my presentation of the conception of dialectics I would like to offer Tong instead of the one he has inherited from Mao and Dao. To wrap up the story, let me just add a few comments to explain the perspective that for me makes such an argument interesting, and to avoid possible misunderstandings.

An important point is to avoid the East-West stereotype. The materialist conception of dialectics, which I have attributed to Mao and Dao, can easily be found west of China. Röd has traced the history of dialectics from Kant up until to the Frankfurt School and Sartre, and already in Hegel's natural philosophy can be found some of the basic roots of dialectical materialism. Apparently, it is here that Hegel most obviously blurs the difference between contradiction and opposition,[45] i.e. between validity and causality. For Röd, this is clearly an important point, no doubt due to his epistemological point of departure. Röd emphasizes that Hegel's dialectical method has its roots in the "analytical theory of experience", as it is developed in the *Phenomenology*.[46] The fundamental structure of dialectics is found in the "descriptive metaphysics of experience",[47] and – just to root out any possible misunderstandings – for Röd, the "dialectics of experience" provides the "model for the relations" that can

---

(1886), in Nietzsche, *Werke* (1955), ed. Karl Schlechta (Darmstadt: Wissenschaftliche Buchgesellschaft, 1997), vol. II, p. 222), and taking up this lead, Heidegger can take Descartes as the prime example of this pathology (see Martin Heidegger, *Nietzsche* (1961) (Pfullingen: Günther Neske, 1989), vol. II, p. 190).

45   See Röd, *Dialektische Philosophie der Neuzeit*, vol. 1, pp. 215–16.

46   See Röd, *ibid.*, p. 152.

47   *Ibid.*, p. 178.

be found within Hegel's "system". The "theory of experience" is thus the "key to understanding" "dialectics in its objective figure".[48]

A clear contrast to this position can be found in the collection of essays on dialectics by Evald Vassilievich Ilyenkov, published in the same period. Like Mao, Ilyenkov simply equates contradiction and opposition,[49] just as episte-mology has clearly given way to ontology. According to Ilyenkov, Hegel's dia-lectics is to be found in the *Science of Logic*, whereas the *Phenomenology* is only mentioned in passing.[50] Like logic in general, Hegel's logic is taken to be about thought. For Ilyenkov, the important point is how Hegel extends the scope of logic from merely considering thought to considering reality *per se*, including practice.[51] According to Ilyenkov, Hegel sees quite clearly that logic as the sci-ence of thought transcends language. Thinking is part of reality, just as reality is the result of thought via man's actions.[52] In this practical and materialist perspective, however, scepticism is something that is only mentioned in rela-tion to Kant as his "negative dialectic". To Ilyenkov, being sceptical means that thought is "feeling bewildered" and "powerless to choose and prefer".[53]

This might call to mind yet another East-West stereotype, namely the Cold War. In order to avoid any cultural geographical prejudices, let me just mention that dialectical materialism is also constitutive of the philosophy of, for instance, Maurice Cornforth, where we find statements that are very similar to Mao's. Cornforth thus confirms the "necessary truth" of dialectical materialism,[54] just as he equates contradiction and opposition;[55] in his expla-nation of the unity of opposites he even mentions the similarity to the Mao's thinking.[56]

The circle thus closed, Mao's dialectical materialism can be located well within the boundaries of mainstream university philosophy. The discussion of dialectics presented here can be considered part of the ideological struggle

---

48   *Ibid.*, p. 212.

49   See Evald Vassilievich Ilyenkov, *Dialectical Logic. Essays on Its History and Theory* (1974) (Moscow: Progress Publishers, 1977), p. 194.

50   See Ilyenkov, *ibid.*, p. 207.

51   See *ibid.*, p. 210.

52   See *ibid.*, p. 175.

53   *Ibid.*, p. 192. Just like Nietzsche and Heidegger, Ilyenkov thus interprets scepticism rather as a psychological pathology than as the principled starting point of epistemology.

54   See Maurice Cornforth, *The Open Philosophy and The Open Society* (New York: Interna-tional Publishers, 1968), p. 111.

55   See Cornforth, *ibid.*, p. 109.

56   See *ibid.*, p. 101.

among left-wing Hegelians, i.e. the discussion between the Leninist bolshe-vism of various communist parties and what is sometimes considered the less dogmatic strands of left-wing intellectual thought. This might seem like an old, obsolete story from the bygones of both politics and philosophy. My problem is that I do not believe that to be the case. First of all, Tong has obviously carried the practical and materialist conception of dialectics with him into contempo-rary philosophy. Even more important, however, is what I take to be a general tendency in current intellectual debates: hence, my impression is that today, though often unconsciously and by proxy, the pragmatic materialist concep-tion of dialectics is much more widely accepted than the conception of dialec-tics I have proposed above.

The point is that to me, the predominance of causal relations in dialectical materialism makes it a kind of vitalist metaphysics, i.e. a general way of think-ing about reality inspired by living reality, organic matter and biology. Such a metaphysical vitalism can be attributed to various influential philosophers of the 19th century. One prominent example in this context is Dewey. Another is Henri Bergson, and, according to Tong, besides Dewey, Bergson was one of the western philosophers most extensively translated into Chinese in the first decades of the 20th century (see CP, 130).

I will assume that a vitalist way of thinking is somehow congruent with much Chinese thinking in the Daoist tradition. What is interesting in this context, however, is that in China this way of thinking has been believed to contribute to dialectical thinking, whereas in France, for instance, it has been thought to contribute to a way of thinking that, according to Alain Badiou, must be considered "essentially anti-dialectical",[57] namely the philosophy of Gilles Deleuze, in which Bergson plays an crucial role.[58] What is even more interesting is that a closer look at the vitalist metaphysics of Deleuze in *Dif-ference et Repetition*, reveals that much of it is very similar to the dialectical materialism discussed in relation to Mao, Lenin and Chinese philosophy.[59]

To stretch the associationist logic a bit further, what could be considered alarming in a political perspective is something that Slavoj Žižek calls atten-tion to in his recent introduction to the texts by Mao referred to above. Many post-modern thinkers argue that the thinking of Deleuze represents some-thing subversive to capitalism, but Žižek – as a self-proclaimed Leninist – would argue that the contrary is the case. Deleuze's thinking has thus been

---

57   Alain Badiou, *Deleuze: la clameur de l'être* (Paris: Hachette, 1997), p. 51.

58   See Badiou, *ibid.*, pp. 62–63, 79.

59   See Gilles Deleuze, *Différence et Repetition* (1968) (Paris: Presses Universitaires de France, 2008).

used by the Israeli defence to conceptualize military tactics and operations in counter-insurgency against the Palestinians.[60] Moreover, the ideal of fluidity is also an ideologically flexible structure in relation to the mechanisms of market dynamics, namely the general economic equilibrium that is assumed to be the result if we do not interfere politically but only mind our own particular interests. Vitalist metaphysics do not call for political or ethical interference, because the basic fluidity of living reality leaves us no primary conceptual ideal to refer to.

This is what we find in Deleuze: being is one,[61] "everything is the same"[62] and it is all about chance. For Deleuze, ontology "is a throw of dice",[63] but still the "necessary liberation"[64] will occur. As Badiou emphasizes, for Deleuze there is no primary and secondary, no original and copy.[65] In short, for Deleuze there is no ideal beyond anything else.[66] In his ontology of multiple fluent singulars, interferences are functional operations on an equal footing. Interventions can only be valued pragmatically and instrumentally, i.e. only in relation to their intended consequences. Construed in this, admittedly hasty and sketchy, manner I think it is obvious that Deleuze's vitalist pragmatism is only too well-suited as an ideological support for the neo-liberal conception of global, stateless free market capitalism.

Just like dialectical materialism, Deleuze's vitalism is all about the movement and unity of opposites, which is the reason why I think of it as a proxy to dialectical materialism. After all, it is a matter of filling out the same functional and ideological role. However, in contrast to dialectics, the basic principles of vitalism are not logic, laws and necessity but rather incidents, play and chance. According to Deleuze *et al.*, living matter moves like it is supposed to do according to Hegelian dialectics, but in a less predictable manner. The post-modern version of vitalism is even more radical in its fluidity than both dialectical materialism and the interpretation of dialectics I have argued for. My point is that only in the latter case can dialectics be made to accept the logic of universal validity and reasonable scepticism, and therefore it is only in the latter case that dialectics can function as the ontological counter-weight to the dynamics of desire, greed and the free market. In contrast to a Leninist like Žižek, I find

---

60   See Slavoj Žižek, "Introduction", in Mao, *On Practice and Contradiction*, p. 26.

61   See Deleuze, *Difference et Repetition*, pp. 52–3.

62   Deleuze, *ibid.*, p. 388.

63   *Ibid.*, p. 257.

64   *Ibid.*, p. 385.

65   See Badiou, *Deleuze: la clameur de l'être*, p. 67.

66   See Deleuze, *Difference et Repetition*, p. 385.

the pragmatics of dialectical materialism all too lenient in relation to a capitalism that is backed up by a vitalist ontology of chance.[67]

My argument thus employs guilt by association, slippery slopes and probably also a few other questionable moves. Let me therefore conclude the argument by suggesting an even more radical claim, which is a version of the famous Hegelian idea of reason unfolding history behind our backs. Hence, it is a historical irony that the vitalist and pragmatic implications of Mao's dialectical materialism may have prepared the ideological ground for the "necessary liberation" of exploitative capitalist playfulness in contemporary China.

From a traditional left-wing perspective it might therefore be with good reason that Tong is sceptical about dialectics in the materialist and vitalist sense he knows so well. Nevertheless, and this is the main point in my remarks to Tong, there is a sense in which dialectical thinking is constitutive of Critical Theory from Horkheimer to Habermas, and this is the sense worth maintaining as the ideal of philosophy. I therefore sincerely hope that Tong will accept my gift and use it well in continuing the development of undogmatic left-wing thinking.

---

67   For further reflections on the ideological implications of dialectical metaphysics, see my analysis of Bataille's dialectics (Sørensen, "The Inner Experience") and of his general economy (Sørensen, "On a Universal Scale. Economy in Bataille's General Economy", *Philosophy of Social Criticism* 38, no. 2 (2012)), in the present compilation, respectively, Chs. 4 and 2.

CHAPTER 6

Critique Presupposes Alienation: Hegel

The idea of formation – in German '*Bildung*' – traditionally occupies a central place in northern European discussions about science, education and culture. As a term, however, '*Bildung*' is notoriously difficult to translate adequately into English.[1] *Bildung* can be said to be a specific kind of cultural formation, and as such the word can signify both the process of what in the US would be called liberal education, and the normative aim of such an education, namely to acquire *Bildung* or to end up as an educated person. This is the spectrum of meaning I will move within, acknowledging the suggestions by Gadamer of the importance of the core meaning of "*Bild*",[2] i.e. 'picture,' and the associations to "*Nachbild*" and "*Vorbild*", respectively 'copy' and 'ideal.' Specifically in the case of Hegel, however, some have chosen to translate '*Bildung*' to 'culture,'[3]

---

1 The problems of translating '*Bildung*' into English are widely recognized (see, e.g., Hans Friedrich Fulda, "Einleitung", in *Gestalten des Bewußtseins. Hegel-Studien. Beiheft 52*, ed. Birgit Sandkaulen, Volker Gerhardt, and Walter Jaeschke (Hamburg: Felix Meiner, 2009), p. 181; Frederick C. Beiser, "Romanticism", in *A Companion to Philosophy of Education*, ed. Randall Curren (Oxford: Blackwell Publishing, 2003), p. 131; and G. Felicitas Munzel, "Kant, Hegel, and the Rise of Pedagogical Science", in *A Companion to the Philosophy of Education*, p. 116). I have dealt with it briefly in another context (see Asger Sørensen, "From Critique of Ideology to Politics. Habermas on Bildung", *Ethics and Education* 10, no. 2 (2015), pp. 253–55), but in the present work I have refrained from going into too much detail. First, even though German speakers might think that the connotations of *Bildung* are exclusively German (see, e.g., Fulda, "Einleitung", p. 181), as a Danish speaker I have a more or less equivalent to '*Bildung*', namely the word '*dannelse*', and the basic research on these matters was carried out for a chapter in Danish for a Norwegian philosophical history of *dannelse* (Asger Sørensen, "Hegel. Bevidsthed, fremmedgørelse og sprog", in *Danningens Filosofihistorie*, ed. Ingerid Straume (Oslo: Gyldendal Norsk, 2013)). Second, readers of Hegel are likely to be somehow familiar with the German language. I have therefore restricted myself to a simple technical solution of the translation problem. In the following, I have, like for instance Wolfgang Mann, simply used the original German term whenever there was any possibility of misunderstandings (see Wolfgang Mann, "The Past as Future? Hellenism, the Gymnasium, and Altertumswissenschaft", in *A Companion to the Philosophy of Education*, pp. 144; 50–51; 55; 57).

2 Hans-Georg Gadamer, *Wahrheit und Methode* (1960), in Gadamer, *Gesammelte Werke* (Tübingen: Mohr Siebeck, 1986), vol. I, pp. 16–17.

3 See, e.g., Robert Stern, *Routledge Philosohy Guide Book to Hegel and the Phenomenology of Spirit* (London Routledge, 2002), p. 148; Dag Petersson, *The Art of Reconciliation* (Basingstoke et al.: Palgrave Macmillan, 2013), pp. 164–66; Jørgen Huggler, "Hegel's Phenomenology of

probably in order to emphasize the collective aspect of the process as well as the individual. However, such a translation tends to make the processual aspect of *Bildung* less notable, and, as Gadamer argues, ignores the crucial transition from the Kantian idea of culture to the idea of *Bildung* as it was conceived of by Herder, Humboldt and Hegel. Adorno expresses it aptly when arguing that *Bildung* in its original sense is the subjective aspect of culture, namely its "acquisition [Zueignung]".[4]

Habermas has explained how the idea of *Bildung* was crucial for the educational ideology of the progressive bourgeois class,[5] and recently Michael Winkler has emphasized how *Bildung* is closely linked to the ideal of *Mündigkeit* (authority or maturity) synthesizing promises of reason, freedom, autonomy and authority.[6] Yet, in the 20th century the idea of *Bildung* took a conservative turn, allegedly proving to be compatible even with the authoritarianism of a national socialist state.[7] As such, the ideal of *Bildung* became an object of suspicion and critique, and as Winkler sees it, this is still the case in relation to modern society as we know it today.[8] Nevertheless, in spite of suspicion and critique, both Habermas and Winkler recognize an element of truth in the original idea,[9] and it is to support this recognition with further conceptual substantiation that I suggest a return to Hegel's original conception of *Bildung*.

Attempts have already been made to revive Hegel's social and political thinking, combining *Bildung* with freedom, and focusing on developing an

---

Rationality", in *Dialectics, Self-consciousness, and Recognition. The Hegelian Legacy*, ed. Asger Sørensen, Arne Grøn, and Morten Raffnsøe-Møller (Malmö: NSU Press, 2009), pp. 26–27; Jean Hyppolite, *Genèse et structure de la Phénoménologie de l'ésprit de Hegel* (Paris: Aubier, 1946), p. 365 (hereafter: *Genèse et structure*) (Hyppolite, *Genesis and Structure of Hegel's Phenomenology of Spirit*, trans. Samuel Cherniak and John Heckman (Evanston: Northwestern University Press, 1974), p. 377 (hereafter: *Genesis and Structure*)), the latter also suggesting "civilization" as yet another possibility.

4   Theodor W. Adorno, "Theorie der Halbbildung" (1959), in Adorno, *Gesammelte Schriften* (GS$_A$) (Frankfurt a. M.: Suhrkamp, 1972), vol. 8, p. 94.

5   See Jürgen Habermas, *Strukturwandel der Öffentlichkeit* (1962), 8th ed. (Neuwied: Luchterhand, 1976), p. 115.

6   See Michael Winkler, "Bildung als Entmündigung? Die Negation des neuzeitlichen Freiheitsversprechen in den aktuellen Bildungsdiskursen", in *Bildung und Freiheit*, ed. Klaus Vieweg and Michael Winkler (Paderborn: Ferdinand Schöningh, 2012), pp. 20–21.

7   See Jürgen Habermas, "Heinrich Heine und die Rolle des Intellektuellen in Deutschland", in Habermas, *Eine Art Schadensabwicklung* (Frankfurt a. M.: Suhrkamp, 1987), p. 46.

8   See Winkler, "Bildung als Entmündigung?" pp. 26–27.

9   See Winkler, ibid., pp. 27–28; Habermas, *Strukturwandel der Öffentlichkeit*, p. 193.

idea of *Bildung* appropriate for the 21st century.[10] Hegel's *Philosophy of Right* has been chosen as the main reference in many of the discussions of *Bildung* in this context.[11] This makes perfect sense, when the concept of freedom is the point of departure, given that the *Philosophy of Right* is where Hegel gives his famous definitions of freedom, allegedly claiming that it "is the absolute goal of reason that freedom becomes real [ist absoluter Zweck der Vernunft daß die Freiheit wirklich sei]", and that the state is the "realization of freedom [Verwirklichung der Freiheit]".[12] Obviously, starting the discussion of *Bildung* with freedom in this perspective points to certain ideological and conceptual implication and not to others. Especially those with a traditional liberal concept of freedom, but also the young Marx himself as well as many Marxists, have often experienced Hegel's republican conception of freedom as totalitarian and thus very provoking in this context.

Choosing *Bildung* as the explicit point of departure, however, makes a notable difference in this respect. Consulting Helmut Reinicke's index of Hegel's works thus reveals the *Phenomenology of Spirit* to be the most extensive reference concerning *Bildung*,[13] and even a quick glance at the table of contents of the *Phenomenology* indicates that for Hegel, *Bildung* plays an important role as a general philosophical concept, independently of freedom. Precisely therefore, it is strange, as Birgit Sandkaulen has commented, that there are no ongoing research discussions about it, not even in German-speaking circles.[14] Apparently, for Hegel the concept of *Bildung* is closely intertwined with alienation – i.e. *Entfremdung* – and in such a perspective freedom might not

---

10 See Klaus Vieweg and Michael Winkler, "Vorbemerkung", in *Bildung und Freiheit*, ed. Vieweg and Winkler, p. 9.

11 This is for instance the case in Klaus Vieweg, "Das Recht der Besonderheit des Subjekts und die 'Reiche der Besonderheit'. Zur Modernität von Hegels Begriff der Freiheit"; Francesca Menegoni, "Recht des Einzelnen und Recht der Gemeinschaft. Hegel und die Idee einer Spekulativen Bildung zur Gemeinschaft"; Folko Zander, "Anerkennung als Moment von Hegels Freiheitsbegriff", and most of the other contributions in *Bildung und Freiheit*, ed. Vieweg and Winkler.

12 G.W.F. Hegel, "Vorlesungen über die Philosophie des Rechts. Nachschriften zu den Kollegien der Jahre 1824/25 und 1831", in Hegel, *Gesammelte Werke* (GW$_H$), vol. 26,3, ed. Klaus Grotsch (Hamburg: Felix Meiner, 2015), p. 1405; Hegel, "Grundlinien der Philosophie des Rechts" (1820), in Hegel, *Werke in 20 Bänden* (TWA), ed. Eva Moldenhauer and Karl Markus Michel (Frankfurt a.M.: Suhrkamp, 1970), vol. 7, § 258 Zusatz, p. 403.

13 See Helmut Reinicke, *Register* (Frankfurt a. M.: Suhrkamp, 1979), pp. 86–87.

14 See Birgit Sandkaulen, "Bildung bei Hegel – Entfremdung oder Versöhnung?" in *Hegel gegen Hegel. Hegel-Jahrbuch*, ed. Andreas Arndt, Jure Zovko, and Myriam Gerhard (Berlin: de Gruyter, 2014), p. 430.

reconcile itself that easily, neither with reason, nor with the state, nor even with society. In other words, in the *Phenomenology* Hegel offers a philosophical perspective much less offensive and therefore much more appealing to traditional liberals and Marxists, as Marx himself recognized in the *Economic and Philosophical Manuscripts*. Referring to these manuscripts, Herbert Marcuse argues that the *Phenomenology* contains critique in the "concrete-revolutionary sense [bestimmt-revolutionären Sinne]",[15] and as Sandkaulen affirms, there might still be a political potential in the Hegelian idea of *Bildung*.[16]

The point is that there seems to be a difference, at least in emphasis, between the reconciliatory mood of the mature professor Hegel publishing his philosophy of law in Berlin in 1821, and the alienation experienced and expressed by the young Hegel completing his almost desperate writings about the spirit in Jena 1807.

Therefore, when taking the latter work as point of departure, not only the connection between *Bildung* and freedom, but also the idea of *Bildung* itself, comes out differently. Since it is Hegel's concept of *Bildung* I will pursue in this article, I have chosen to orientate my analysis mainly around studies in the *Phenomenology* rather than *Philosophy of Right*. As a result, I will point to conceptual possibilities for social philosophy and philosophy of education rather than philosophy of law or political philosophy. One of the constitutive ideas in social philosophy is the acknowledgement of the troublesome, sometimes even pathological, relation between man and society in modernity. This is most often expressed through the concept of alienation and as Honneth has stressed, classical references to such an approach are Rousseau and Marx.[17] However, as Carl-Göran Heidegren emphasizes,[18] precisely in relation to the German conception of alienation as *Entfremdung*, Hegel can be recognized as having renewed and developed the philosophical vocabulary, being inspired by Goethe and his translation of Diderot's novel *Rameau's Nephew*. As we already know now, in the *Phenomenology* Hegel thus lets alienation draw its main conceptual content from its relationship to *Bildung*. This is affirmed by

15   Herbert Marcuse, "Neue Quellen zur Grundlegung des Historischen Materialismus" (1932), in Marcuse, *Schriften* (s_M) (Springe: zu Klampen Verlag, 2004), vol. 1, p. 554.

16   See Sandkaulen, "Bildung bei Hegel – Entfremdung oder Versöhnung?" p. 438. I will return to this discussion in DDD III, *Justice, Peace and Formation*.

17   See Axel Honneth, "Pathologien des Sozialen. Tradition und Aktualität der Sozialphilosophie" (1994), in Honneth, *Das Andere der Gerechtigkeit* (Frankfurt a.M.: Suhrkamp, 2000), pp. 16 ff. See also my analysis of Honneth's transformation of contemporary critical theory into social philosophy above in the Interlude, Sect. E.

18   See Carl-Göran Heidegren, *Hegels Fenomenologi. En analys och kommentar* (Stockholm and Stehag: Brutus Östling, 1995), p. 226.

Sandkaulen, for whom it has implications for the interpretation of the *Philoso-phy of Right*.[19] I will return to this in the last section.

In relation to a concept like *Bildung*, however, it seems fair to make one further displacement, namely to put some emphasis on education. This fo-cus I believe will reveal further layers of the general philosophical meaning of *Bildung* and thus transcend what is merely educational. In a philosophy that focuses on the development of consciousness as well as that of spirit and his-tory, *Bildung* is naturally a philosophical core concept.[20] As Willy Moog has noted, for Hegel *Bildung* is a dialectical process of unfolding that can be recog-nized not only in the development of an individual consciousness but also in the spirit and the absolute, i.e. reality as such. Hegel's thinking is an example of how the educational concept of formation can become so important to the philosophical concept that they become virtually indistinguishable from each other.[21]

The emphasis on education makes it noteworthy that soon after the pub-lication of the *Phenomenology* in Jena, Hegel became rector of the new hu-manistic *Gymnasium* in Nürnberg, a position he remained in until 1816. Some less known writings from this period explicitly discuss *Bildung* and relate it to educational matters. Some of these writings are speeches that Hegel gave in the years 1809–11 as part of his work as rector at the *Gymnasium*. These speech-es were written and published at the peak of Hegel's philosophical maturity, when he was working on *The Science of Logic* and the *Encyclopaedia*, and they therefore deserve serious attention, especially when focusing on the concept of *Bildung*.

In these texts, Hegel acknowledges the importance of alienation for second-ary education but also notes that education can somehow contribute to recon-ciliation; in both cases, *Bildung* is essential. For education to become *Bildung*, the appropriation of classical, yet alienating, culture is required. *Bildung* thus seems to be reserved for the upper strata of society, which in turn sheds light on the conservative leaning mentioned above. When the *Phenomenology* and the Nürnberg writings are brought together, not only should the connection

---

19   See Sandkaulen, "Bildung bei Hegel – Entfremdung oder Versöhnung?" p. 431.

20   The main passages in Hegel's works in relation to *Bildung* and transcripts of a number of classical comments are collected in *Hegels Theorie der Bildung. Vol. I: Materialien zu ihrer Interpretation & Vol. II: Kommentare*, ed. Jürgen-Eckhardt Pleines (Hildesheim: Georg Olms, 1983 & 1986).

21   See Willy Moog, "Der Bildungsbegriff Hegels", in *Verhandlungen des dritten Hegelkongress-es vom 19. bis 23. April 1933 in Rom*, ed. B. Wigersma (Tübingen: Mohr, 1934); here cited after *Hegels Theorie der Bildung*, ed. Pleines, Vol. II, p. 72.

between *Bildung* and freedom be interpreted differently, so should a notion of *Bildung* associated with Hegel for a long time, namely that *Bildung* is the result of productive – or even manual – labour.

This being my frame of reference, in the present article I first provide a brief account of my general argument concerning Hegel's concept of *Bildung* (A), then add some details from the *Phenomenology* to support the argument (B) and some further details from the Nürnberg writings (C). Finally, I conclude with some general remarks related to other interpretations of *Bildung* in the *Phenomenology* (D).

A   The General Argument

Hegel's concept of *Bildung* in the *Phenomenology of Spirit* is widely explained and discussed with reference to the Preface,[22] two propositions in the In-troduction (PHG$_{GW \& TWA}$, 56 & 73), a passage in the famous dialectics of the master and the slave in Chapter 4 (see PHG$_{GW \& TWA}$, 114 ff & 153 ff), or a combi-nation of these. Following some frequently cited and therefore almost classi-cal passages, it is generally concluded that for Hegel experience, negation and productive work are the determining elements in the *Bildung* of consciousness as self-conscious being, in German *Selbst-bewußt-sein*.

In contrast to this, I argue that for Hegel *Bildung* cannot be achieved through the negation implied by productive labour. In his thinking, *Bildung* requires alienation – *Entfremdung* – in a much wider sense than simply work-ing to produce something, and reconciliation can only be hoped for through the acquisition of classical culture. These claims are based on close readings of not only the passages mentioned above but also the most elaborate discussion of *Bildung* in the *Phenomenology*, which is found in Chapter 6 on *Der Geist*, i.e. the spirit. Here, it becomes clear that it is the acute alienation experienced in the laceration [Zerrissenheit], i.e. the devastating tearing apart of the self, rather than merely the trembling fear of death experienced by the slave, that provides the constitutive condition for *Bildung*.

Further, for Hegel *Bildung* presupposes not only the experience of alien-ation but also the expression of it. Hence, language is a necessary condition for

---

22   See G.W.F. Hegel, *Phänomenologie des Geistes* (1807), ed. Wolfgang Bonsiepen and Reinhard Heede, in Hegel, GW 9 (Hamburg: Felix Meiner, 1980), pp. 24–25; Hegel, *Phäno-menologie des Geistes*, in Hegel, TWA 3, pp. 13–14 and 31–33. In the present chapter, the work itself is referred to as PHG, and the page references to the two editions are indicated by, respectively, GW and TWA. In the text the references to the work will thus appear in brackets as PHG$_{GW \& TWA}$, nn & nn.

Bildung. What also becomes clear in the chapter on spirit is that Hegel thinks of *Bildung* not as a phenomenon primarily linked to the consciousness of an individual human subject, but as something which is basically part of a collective development. Spirit is first of all realized as a people and a family, and as such spirit has social and political importance. For Hegel, wealth, power and law can thus be represented as figures of the spirit that change their interrelationship in the historical development. This dialectical process drives alienation until the peak of devastating fragmentation and revolution. *Bildung* takes place in relation to the spirit in this collective sense. It is not primarily something happening to an individual consciousness working with some material; rather, *Bildung* is inherently cultural, social and political.

This interpretation of *Bildung* will be elaborated further in the next section (B.). In the rest of the present section (A.), I will stick to completing the general philosophical argument, sketching thus one further aspect of *Bildung*, namely education, which will be discussed in more detail in the third section below (C.).

Changing focus to Hegel's educational work at the *Gymnasium* in Nürnberg,[23] it becomes clear that Hegel put a lot of emphasis on the link between alienation and *Bildung*. In his speeches as rector he thus paid homage to the traditional idea of *Bildung*, but he also argued for opening the minds of the students for new developments. For Hegel, the point was that both concerns required confronting the students with classical works in their original form, i.e. in Greek and Latin. Learning a foreign language requires discipline, and since the classical languages are very strange in being different to the students's everyday language, they also break with everyday conformity. Therefore, the result of learning these unfamiliar languages is alienation, but at the same time the content of the classical works provides the instruments to reconcile oneself with human reality once again. As is to be expected from his reputation as spokesman for the state, Hegel emphasizes discipline in general, while at the same time being very careful to stress that the youth needs time for themselves to be able to develop the character necessary for granting them freedom and liberty.

These texts thus support my reading of the *Phenomenology*: Rather than working with a physical material only, *Bildung* clearly requires alienation and higher education in the humanist tradition. At the most, material work can create what today would be called 'tacit knowledge,' whereas *Bildung* in the full sense presupposes language and high culture. A close reading of the account of *Bildung* in Hegel's writings thus negates many interpretations of Hegelian

---

23   See Hegel, *Nürnberger Gymnasialkurse und Gymnasialreden (1808–1816)*, in Hegel, GW$_{H}$
      10,1, ed. Klaus Grotsch (Hamburg: Felix Meiner, 2006); or Hegel, *Nürnberger und Heidel-*
      berger Schriften 1808–1817, in TWA 4.

dialectics and philosophy of history in the slipstream of 20th century Marxism. For Hegel, the historical subject can never be the working class. The historical subject must have studied Greek and Latin in the *Gymnasium*, but that does not mean that *Bildung*, as it is conceived of in the *Phenomenology*, will lead to the universal realization of freedom in the state.

B   Some Details from the *Phenomenology* Supporting the Argument

The above being the general argument, I will emphasize some details from the *Phenomenology* to further substantiate the argument: first negatively, by showing that a close reading of the first part of the book in itself demonstrates that Hegel does not credit productive labour with the capacity for *Bildung*, and that the idea of *Bildung* we are left with is apparently incoherent (i); second positively, by sketching how Hegel actually develops the idea of *Bildung* conceptually through the dialectics of the chapter on the spirit (ii).

i   *Formation is Spirit – and It Does Not Work*
In the *Phenomenology of Spirit*, the point of departure is *Bewußt-sein*, conscious being, which in English is normally translated into 'consciousness.' Conscious being is human being, as distinct from the being of plants and animals. The *Phenomenology* is thus about human consciousness, and more specifically how consciousness becomes conscious of itself, or perhaps even better, how man as conscious being becomes conscious of him or herself as conscious. For Hegel, consciousness only becomes real as spirit, and here it might be helpful to think of spirit in the sense we use when talking about, for instance, the 'spirit of 1968.' The title of the book can thus be interpreted as referring to a doctrine of a spirit which, as a phenomenon, appears before itself. For Hegel, however, the necessity of this development means that "this road to science itself is already science [dieser Weg zur Wissenschaft selbst schon Wissenschaft [ist]]." For Hegel, the *Phenomenology* is therefore the "science of the experience of consciousness [Wissenschaft der Erfahrung des Bewußtseyns]" (PHG GW & TWA, 61 & 80), which, as Eva Moldenhauer and Karl Markus Michel note, was also the original subtitle.[24]

In the introduction to the *Phenomenology*, Hegel explicitly links the concept of *Bildung* to the development that leads consciousness through a sequence of figures. Consciousness must be formed in this way due to the fact that again and again in its investigation of a given bid for the truth of reality, consciousness

---

24   See Eva Moldenhauer and Karl Markus Michel, "Anmerkung", in TWA 3, p. 596.

must experience the particular figure in question as untrue, as it turns out that it cannot be universalized. For Hegel, it is a "determinate negation [bestimmte Negation]" (PHG$_{GW\&TWA}$, 57 & 74) when consciousness in this way experiences the falseness of a specific figure. This experience immediately becomes an active element – in German '*Moment*' – in a new bid for the truth about man's conscious being, and consciousness now explores the content of the new bid. Each new bid thus contains the positive "result [Resultat]" (PHG$_{GW\&TWA}$, 61 & 80) of the preceding experience that has already been made, namely the knowledge of the negated figure's falsehood.[25]

This is where Hegel employs the concept of *Bildung*: "The series of figures, which consciousness moves through on this road, is rather the detailed story of the formation of consciousness into science. [Die Reihe seiner Gestaltungen, welche das Bewußtseyn auf diesem Wege durchläufft, ist vielmehr die ausführliche Geschichte der Bildung des Bewußtseyns selbst zur Wissenschaft.]" (PHG$_{GW\&TWA}$, 56 & 73). For Hegel, each step is thus conditioned by the previous formation achieved. Consciousness's experience of the truth about itself requires formation, the steps of which are analyzed in detail in the first seven chapters of the *Phenomenology*. The truth, however, can only be known in what Hegel calls the "science of the spirit [Wissenschafft des Geistes]," or in the "absolute knowledge [absoluten Wissen]" (PHG$_{GW\&TWA}$, 62 & 81), which is also the title of the eighth and final chapter. Consciousness is only truly conscious being as spirit, and without *Bildung* there would be no realization of conscious being as *Geist*. As Sandkaulen has argued, *Geist* and *Bildung* mutually condition each other.[26] Nevertheless, consciousness is only truly spirit when its formation has brought it to the absolute knowledge. It is the road thereto, or as Jørgen Huggler puts it, the "exposition of spirit's coming to itself",[27] that is reconstructed in the *Phenomenology of Spirit*.

An important step in this development is when consciousness is brought from being conscious of something different from itself to also being conscious of it-self or being self-conscious. This is what happens in Chapter 4, which is accordingly titled "self-consciousness [Selbstbewußtseyn]," where Hegel addresses the situation in which one consciousness is facing another. One consciousness thus has the other consciousness as its object and *vice versa*.

---

25   See Asger Sørensen, *Om videnskabelig viden. Gier, ikker og ismer* (Frederiksberg: Samfundslitteratur, 2010), pp. 135–47 for further analysis and discussion of the Hegelian conception of experience.

26   See Birgit Sandkaulen, "Hegels Konzept(e) der Bildung", in *Grundbegriffe des Praktischen*, ed. Thomas Sören Hoffmann (Freiburg: Alber, 2014), p. 15.

27   Huggler, "Hegel's Phenomenology of Rationality", p. 33.

Inspired by Spinoza, Hegel states that all determination is negation,[28] but consciousness is not only a subject perceiving or experiencing: in the previous sections, Hegel has emphasized that consciousness is also a living and desiring entity. For Hegel, consciousness is conscious being, and as such it is alive. This means that consciousness also negates by destroying or devouring its surroundings. Consciousness thus maintains its independence as a living creature through the material negation of its surroundings, and therefore a real conflict must arise when one consciousness is facing another.

Hegel believes that this conflict is realized in a necessary battle of life and death, which can only be solved by one consciousness abandoning the attempt to negate the other, which entails giving up its independence and strive for sovereignty. This is where we encounter the dialectic of master and slave.[29] The decisive moment – also '*Moment*' in German! – is experiencing the fear of the "pure [reine]," "abstract [abstracte]" and "absolute negation [absolute Negation]" (PHG$_{GW\&TWA}$, 111–12 & 148 ff), i.e. the fear of destruction and death, anxiety in itself. The fear of death, "the absolute master [des absoluten Herrn]" (PHG$_{GW\&TWA}$, 114 & 153) shakes consciousness, and the necessary result is, for Hegel, that one of the consciousnesses shattered by anxiety chooses life, giving up sovereignty and thereby accepting the role of a servant or a slave, a "serving [dienende[s]]" and "working consciousness [arbeitende[s] Bewußtseyn]" that "forms [bildet]" (PHG$_{GW\&TWA}$, 114–15 & 153–54).[30] The service of a servant consists in working for another, i.e. in servitude accepted in anxiety. What is essential for the servant is the master, his wishes and desires. A slave is a servant forming something for a master, and as mentioned above, it is in this productive labour that *Bildung* is supposed to take place.

Desiring implies the "pure negation of an object [reine Negiren des Gegenstandes]," which thus disappears. Work is for Hegel "inhibited desire, postponed disappearance [gehemmte Begierde, aufgehaltenes Verschwinden]"

---

28   See Hegel, G.W.F. Hegel, *Vorlesungen über die Geschichte der Philosophie* (1805–1831), vol. III, in TWA 20, pp. 164–65. See also Hegel, *Wissenschaft der Logik. Erster Band. Die Lehre vom Sein* (1832), in GW$_{II}$ 21, ed. Friedrich Hogemann and Walter Jaeschke (Hamburg: Felix Meiner, 1984), p. 101; or Hegel, *Wissenschaft der Logik. Erster Teil. Die objektive Logik. Erstes Buch* (1832), in TWA 5, p. 121.

29   See Asger Sørensen, *I lyset af Bataille – politisk filosofiske studier*, ed. Johannes Sohlmann, Rævens sorte bibliotek (København: Politisk Revy, 2012), pp. 69–73 for more conceptual details on this part of Hegel's dialectics.

30   For classical reconstruction of the logic in this process, see Herbert Marcuse, *Hegels Ontologie und die Theorie der Geschichtlichkeit* (1932), in s$_M$ 2, pp. 290–98. For an illustration of the significance attributed to work in Marx's reading of Hegel, see Marcuse, "Neue Quellen zur Grundlegung des Historischen Materialismus", in s$_M$ 1, pp. 509–55.

that "forms" – i.e. *bildet* – "the object-side" (PHG$_{GW\&TWA}$, 114–15 & 153). The object will then have '*Form*,' and for Hegel it is important to emphasize that all the "moments, the fear and the service as such, as well as the forming [Momente, der Furcht und des Dienstes überhaupt, so wie des Bildens]" (PHG$_{GW\&TWA}$, 115 & 154) are necessary:

> Without the discipline of service and obedience, the fear remains merely formal and does not expand itself to the conscious reality of being. Without the forming, fear remains internal and dumb, and the consciousness does not become for-it-self (PHG$_{GW\&TWA}$, 115 & 154).[31]

Crucial to Hegel is that the slave in this forming of a thing "comes to himself [kömmt [...] zu sich selbst]." The working consciousness achieves an "view of its own independent being as itself [Anschauung des selbstständigen Seyns, als seiner selbst]" (PHG$_{GW\&TWA}$, 114–15 & 153–54); without such forming, human being cannot become conscious of itself.

It has been common to highlight how Hegel links the working on an object conceptually to formation – i.e. *Bildung* – as such. Among the most striking examples are the famous lectures by Alexandre Kojève, where it is work that "educates (bildet) the consciousness of the slave, forming it ['éduque' (bildet) la conscience de l'Esclave, il la 'forme']".[32] Work "liberates" and "creates a real world," which is "non-natural," "cultural," "historical" and "human." For Kojève, it is simply "work alone" that "'forms-or-educates' man ['forme-ou-éduque' l'homme]".[33] As Charles Taylor puts it, "in transforming things we change ourselves".[34] One is assumed to form oneself through work, i.e. through the forming of an object according to one's own idea. In the forming of the thing, one exteriorates oneself – in German '*entäußert sich*' – but afterwards, one can recognize oneself and "the power to remake things according to concepts"[35] in what has been formed.

Following this reading, it is assumed that when Hegel in this figure lets the truth of consciousness be in the slave, and consciousness through work

---

31   Ohne die Zucht des Dienstes und Gehorsams bleibt die Furcht beym formellen stehen, und verbreitet sich nicht über die bewußte Wirklichkeit des Daseyns. Ohne das Bilden bleibt die Furcht innerlich und stumm, und das Bewußtseyn wird nicht für es selbst.

32   Alexandre Kojève, *Introduction à la lecture de Hegel* (1947), ed. Raymond Queneau (Paris: Gallimard, 1994), p. 121.

33   Kojève, *ibid.*, pp. 30–31.

34   Charles Taylor, *Hegel* (Cambridge: Cambridge University Press, 1975), p. 156.

35   Kojève, *Introduction à la lecture de Hegel*, p. 157.

is formed to self-consciousness, then formation – *Bildung* – must also be the result. Ludwig Siep thus confirms that Hegel calls this "function of work [Funktion der Arbeit]" *Bildung*,[36] whereas Paul Cobben emphasizes the "formative effect of work [bildende Wirkung der Arbeit]" and the resulting "*Bildung*"[37] of work.[38] With Moog it can thus be concluded that "work as a whole is the formation of intelligence [Arbeit als Totalität ist Bildung der Intelligenz]".[39]

It is common to support such a reading of the *Phenomenology* with a further reference to the *Philosophy of Right*, where Hegel explicitly characterizes *Bildung* as the "hard work [harte Arbeit]" that leads to liberation from desire and enables the subjective will to achieve the objectivity that makes it possible for it to become the "reality of the idea [Wirklichkeit der Idee]".[40]

Nevertheless, I will argue that this is not the concept of *Bildung* that Hegel develops in the *Phenomenology*. As Sandkaulen emphasizes, the two projects cannot simply be juxtaposed.[41] Furthermore, closer scrutiny reveals that Hegel, apparently consistently, avoids to use the word '*Bildung*' in this context. Instead, as already indicated, he uses '*Bilden*' when he writes about the forming of things, and neither of the two words appears in connection with his reconstruction of the development of consciousness in this passage.[42] It is certainly the case for Hegel that the thing is formed according to the labourer's idea, that consciousness is formed through work, and even, as Gadamer emphasizes, that the truth of self-consciousness at this stage is to be found in the

---

36   Ludwig Siep, *Der Weg der Phänomenologie des Geistes* (Frankfurt a. M.: Suhrkamp, 2000), p. 106.

37   Paul Cobben, "Arbeit", in *Hegel-Lexikon*, ed. Cobben (Darmstadt: Wissenschaftliche Buchgesellschaft, 2006), p. 135.

38   However, in the entry on "Bildung" in the same *Hegel-Lexikon*, Koen Boey does not relate *Bildung* to work at all (see Koen Boey, "Bildung", *Hegel-Lexikon*, ed. Cobben, pp. 167–69).

39   Moog, "Der Bildungsbegriff Hegels", p. 73. Similar interpretations can be found in Nicolai Hartmann, "Phänomenologie des wahren Geistes" (1931), in *Hegels Theorie der Bildung*, ed. Pleines, vol. II, pp. 36–37; Friedhelm Nicolin, "Hegel im Blickfeld der Pädagogik", in *Geist und Erziehung*, ed. Josef Derbolav and Friedhelm Nicolin (Bonn: Bouvier, 1955), pp. 97–98, just as it is mentioned in a footnote in Heidegren, *Hegels Fenomenologi*, p. 464.

40   G.W.F. Hegel, "Grundlinien der Philosophie des Rechts" (1820), in GW 14,1, ed. Klaus Grotsch and Elisabeth Weiser-Lohmann (Hamburg: Felix Meiner, 2009), § 187, p. 163; Hegel, "Grundlinien der Philosophie des Rechts", in TWA 7, § 187, p. 345.

41   See Sandkaulen, "Bildung bei Hegel – Entfremdung oder Versöhnung?" p. 433.

42   Linking closely the forming of the thing with the formation of consciousness is so common that in Reinicke's index of Hegel's *Werke*, reference to this particular passage in the *Phenomenology* can be found under the heading '*Bildung*' (Reinicke, *Register*, p. 86). However, in the entry in question the word '*Bilden*' is indicated in full instead of the abbreviation 'B' referring to *Bildung*.

consciousness of the slave.[43] However, that does not mean that consciousness achieves *Bildung* through manual labour, and neither, as Taylor puts it, that "the slave becomes universal consciousness through his work".[44]

For the young Hegel there is a crucial difference between, on the one hand, the forming as an occupational shaping or processing of things and, on the other, the formation of conscious being as *Bildung*. It is misleading to blur this distinction, and even worse to conflate it with a conception of *Bildung* formulated much later as part of Hegel's mature philosophy of law. To maintain the awareness of this distinction, I have therefore tried to distinguish consistently – in English as well as German – between the 'forming' (*Bilden*) of a thing as productive manual labour, and the 'formation' that conscious being, according to Hegel, must go through and achieve as *Geist*, i.e. '*Bildung*' in the stricter sense. Insisting on this distinction might seem a bit forced; therefore I will return to the question in the concluding remarks, both to further address the implications of this misreading, which has been quite widespread – at least in my generation of Hegel-scholars – and to indicate a possible alternative interpretation of the remarks on *Bildung* in the *Philosophy of Right*.

Apparently, that leaves *Bildung* to be determined mainly by the remarks from the Introduction, which determines *Bildung* as an all-inclusive reconciliation of the different steps of the development of spirit, consistent with the conservative understanding of *Bildung*. However, as Sandkaulen has pointed out, some of the remarks in the Preface suggest a more radical interpretation.[45] Whereas the Introduction talks about a development completed through "accomplishing scepticism [vollbringende[m] Skepticismus]" ($PHG_{GW \& TWA}$, 56 & 72), in the Preface we are told that the spirit only finds itself in the "absolute laceration [absolute[n] Zerissenheit]" ($PHG_{GW \& TWA}$, 27 & 36); and this difference is analyzed by Sandkaulen.

Following Fichte, for Hegel *Bildung* was from the outset understood as a result of the scientific work of the intellect [*Verstand*] and as such it was Enlightenment. However, where Hegel in his early writings completely dismisses the value of *Bildung*,[46] in the *Phenomenology* he employs it affirmatively, albeit suggesting that the "intellectuality [Verständigkeit]" as it becomes itself is

---

43   See Hans-Georg Gadamer, "Hegels Dialektik des Selbstbewußtseins", in *Materialien zu Hegels Phänomenologie des Geistes*, ed. Hans Friedrich Fulda and Dieter Henrich (Frankfurt a. M.: Suhrkamp, 1973), p. 234.

44   Taylor, *Hegel*, p. 157.

45   See Birgit Sandkaulen, "Wissenschaft und Bildung", in *Gestalten des Bewußtseins*, ed. Sandkaulen, Gerhard, and Jaeschke, p. 199.

46   See Sandkaulen, "Wissenschaft und Bildung", pp. 190–91.

realized by "reasonableness [Vernünftigkeit]" (PHG_{GW & TWA}, 40 & 54). However, *Bildung* is only completed beyond the "elevation to universality [Erhebung zur Allgemeinheit]" (PHG_{GW & TWA}, 28 & 36); in this sense, complete *Bildung* means the enligtenment of the Enligtenment, sublating the "rigid determinating thought [festen bestimmten Gedanken]," dissolving the categories of the intellect, and realizing *Bildung* as spirit through the "fluidity [Flüssigkeit]" (PHG_{GW & TWA}, 28 & 37) of thought – a motive that was also brought forward in the aesthetics of Friedrich Schiller. According to Sandkaulen, this concept of *Bildung*, although proposed in the Preface, should be regarded as the result of the analysis conducted later in the *Phenomenology*, i.e. in the chapter on the *Geist*.[47] I will now turn to that.

ii   *Alienation and Formation are Inescapably Intertwined*

From the Introduction in the *Phenomenology* it becomes clear that *Geist* is realized through *Bildung*. Therefore, it is hardly surprising that the most comprehensive philosophical reflections on formation are to be found in Chapter 6, "The Spirit [Der Geist]." What is new, however, is the importance attributed to linking *Bildung* and alienation, which can be noticed at first glance. The combination of both of these elements constitutes the title of the chapter's Section VI.B., "The Spirit Alienated from Itself. The *Bildung* [Der sich entfremdete Geist; Die Bildung]". Furthermore, Sub-section VI.B.I., titled "The World of the Spirits Alienated from Themselves [Die Welt des sich entfremdeten Geistes]," includes a sub-sub-section, VI.B.I.a., with the title "The *Bildung* and its Realm of Reality [Die Bildung und ihr Reich der Wirklichkeit]". As Siep remarks, these sections and sub-sections are notable for being among the most extensive in the book: depending on the layout of the edition, Section VI.B covers between 80 and 120 pages, or almost 14% of the entire book.[48]

Again, one can point to a striking lack of interest among scholars; in this case when it comes to commenting on this specific section.[49] This, Sandkaulen suspects, may be due to the discomfort of realizing that the Hegelian idea of

---

47   See Sandkaulen, ibid., pp. 200–02.

48   See Siep, *Der Weg der Phänomenologie des Geistes*, p. 189.

49   Siep devotes only nine pages to this section (see Siep, *ibid.*, pp. 189–97), and Taylor even fewer, "leaving out a great deal of interesting detail in the dialectic" (Taylor, *Hegel*, p. 179). Kojève addresses this section relatively extensively (see Kojève, *Introduction à la lecture de Hegel*, pp. 113–44) but as indicated above, even though he recognizes the importance of alienation (see Kojève, *ibid.*, p. 121.), his interpretation of *Bildung* is basically defined by the idea of work in the dialectics of the master and slave (see, e.g., Kojève, *ibid.*, pp. 119 ff and 24–25.).

Bildung differs from the one normally assumed.[50] One notable exception to this pattern is Jean Hyppolite's classical commentary that is very detailed regarding the dialectics of this section, and especially when it comes to Sub-sub-section VI.B.I.a.[51] Among the modern commentaries, however, the only really helpful one in relation to this section is Heidegren's.[52] Since Sandkaulen's comments on the chapter are also rather brief,[53] in the following I propose a modest interpretation based primarily on Heidegren's and Hyppolite's comments.

Hegel emphasizes, as mentioned, that man's conscious being only becomes real as spirit: "Spirit is [...] the in-it-self-sustaining, absolute real essence. [Der Geist ist [...] das sich selbsttragende absolute reale Wesen.]" (PHG$_{GW \& TWA}$, 239 & 325) This means, for Hegel, that all previous figures can be considered as abstractions, in which only the conditions for realization of the spirit are analyzed. "The spirit is thus consciousness as such [Der Geist ist also Bewußtseyn überhaupt]" (PHG$_{GW \& TWA}$, 239 & 326). As Heidegren emphasizes, Hegel now moves on to analyze "historical epochs," reconstructing the history of "culturally conditioned conceptual schemes",[54] and, as Siep adds, then it is no longer possible to abstract from the factual order of the historical development.[55] It is only in such a concrete spiritual and historical reality, i.e. in "the real ethical essence [das wirkliche sittliche Wesen]," "the living ethical world [[d]ie lebendige sittliche Welt]," or "the real self-consciousness of the absolute spirit [das wirkliche Selbstbewußtseyn des absoluten Geistes]" (PHG$_{GW \& TWA}$, 239–40 & 326), that Hegel will talk about *Bildung* in the strict sense. It then becomes important to examine which factors Hegel takes into account in this allegedly real movement of conscious being, since it is these factors that determine how formation is being realized, and thus what *Bildung* really is according to Hegel.

The point of departure in Hegel's analysis of the real world of *Geist* is clearly political, and, as Sandkaulen argues, so is the aim.[56] He begins with an analysis of the simple *sittliche Welt* of the people: "As the real substance it is a people, as real consciousness, citizen of the people [Als die wirkliche Substanz ist er

---

50   See Sandkaulen, "Bildung bei Hegel – Entfremdung oder Versöhnung?" pp. 430–31; Sandkaulen, "Hegels Konzept(e) der Bildung", p. 15.

51   See Hyppolite, *Genèse et structure*, pp. 364–449 (*Genesis and Structure*, pp. 376–464).

52   See Heidegren, *Hegels Fenomenologi*, pp. 226–61.

53   See Sandkaulen, "Wissenschaft und Bildung", pp. 202–05; Sandkaulen, "Bildung bei Hegel – Entfremdung oder Versöhnung?" pp. 432–33; Sandkaulen, "Hegels Konzept(e) der Bildung", pp. 22–24.

54   Heidegren, *Hegels Fenomenologi*, pp. 208–09.

55   See Siep, *Der Weg der Phänomenologie des Geistes*, p. 175.

56   See Sandkaulen, "Hegels Konzept(e) der Bildung", p. 21.

ein Volk, als wirkliches Bewußtseyn, Bürger des Volkes]" (PHG$_{GW\&TWA}$, 242 & 329). As Heidegren notes, this is obviously a reference to the antique Greek city state, i.e. the *polis*.[57] For Hegel, however, the immediate coherence is confronted with another equally immediate and even "natural ethical common essence [natürliches sittliches Gemeinwesen]" (PHG$_{GW\&TWA}$, 243 & 330), i.e. the family. This is analyzed through the example of the classical tragedy of Antigone; and in the *Geist* chapter, this is one of the most commented passages. For Hegel, the point is that "the absolute law of the ethical self-consciousness comes into conflict with the divine law of the essence [das absolute Recht des sittlichen Selbstbewußtseyns kommt mit dem göttlichen Rechte des Wesens in Streit]" (PHG$_{GW\&TWA}$, 253 & 344), and the result becomes the formalization of law, i.e. the "state of law [Rechtszustand]" as it is realized by the Romans. Here, the ethical whole is atomized into individuals, realizing an "equality [Gleichheit]," where everyone counts as "Personen" (PHG$_{GW\&TWA}$, 260 & 355). As Heidegren comments, this figure nevertheless goes down in "a tumultuous orgy of excess, amusement and destruction".[58]

Initially, for Hegel the importance of *Bildung* consists in the fact that it represents the opposite of the "spiritless universality of law [geistlose Allgemeinheit des Rechts]". Only a universality that has come into being is real. That is why, in order to be science, the *Phenomenology* must reconstruct the dialectical logic of the entire genesis of science. For the same reason, the individual human being only has reality and validity through formation; as Hegel puts it, "to the extent it has formation, to such a degree it has reality and power [soviel sie Bildung hat, soviel Wirklichkeit und Macht]" (PHG$_{GW\&TWA}$, 267 & 364). The individual's *Bildung* and "its own reality is therefore the realization of the substance itself [seine eigne Wirklichkeit ist daher die Verwirklichung der Substanz selbst]" (PHG$_{GW\&TWA}$, 268 & 365), 'substance' thus for Hegel referring to the essential, or the universal, which is the truth of conscious being. The entry of consciousness into the realm of reality thus indicates the aim of the *Phenomenology*, i.e. the absolute knowledge, but this does not mean that the contradictions become less pronounced.

In the "Land" (PHG$_{GW\&TWA}$, 266 & 362) of *Bildung*, formation becomes associated with a specific form or figure of conscious being, in which consciousness has not only become exterior to itself, but also alien to itself. As noticed by Heidegren, the figure shares some structural resemblance with the unhappy consciousness of Chapter 4 in the *Phenomenology*;[59] however, since the alienation

---

57   See Heidegren, *Hegels Fenomenologi*, p. 210.

58   Heidegren, *ibid.*, p. 225.; see also PHG$_{GW\&TWA}$, pp. 263 & 358.

59   See *ibid.*, pp. 225, 466.

of the spirit is also in itself a real figure of the spirit, Hegel now goes as far as to claim that the "alienation will alienate itself [Entfremdung wird sich selbst entfremden]" (PHG$_{GW\&TWA}$, 269 & 366). For Hegel, consciousness is here confronted with conflicts, contradictions and divisions, which are developed in relation to objects, consciousness itself, and even the very contradictions. Parallel to the beginning of the formation of consciousness, the basic contradiction is between the universal, which consciousness aims to propose, and the individual or particular, which manifests itself in the specific figure of consciousness. Consciousness believes each figure to possess the truth about itself, but again and again the assumed figure proves not to be of universal applicability, and thus for Hegel of no reality at all in the strict sense.

As Siep notes, also the figure of the spirit encompasses those contradictions, which have so far driven consciousness from one figure to the next.[60] Apart from the general logic, however, in the land of *Bildung* and its realm of reality, for Hegel there is one crucial, real and material contradiction, namely the one between "*Staatsmacht*" and "*Reichthum*", i.e. state power and wealth. Initially, consciousness considers state power as good and wealth as evil (see PHG$_{GW\&}$ $_{TWA}$, 269–70 & 367), but after a great deal of upheaval – i.e. unfolding of internal contradictions, change of perspective and various reconciliations – consciousness is brought to consider the matter in the completely opposite manner. At first, Hegel lets consciousness perceive the state as the universal, therefore devoting itself to an "elevated obedience" through which the idea of the state becomes real as action. Such real state power, however, comes into conflict with the individual, for whom power is experienced as "the oppressive substance and the evil [das unterdrückende Wesen, und das Schlechte]" (PHG$_{GW\&TWA}$, 272 & 370); therefore, wealth replaces it as the good. As Heidegren has pointed out, historically it is this reversal that can be seen in the transition from the feudal world to the dawn of modern capitalism.[61]

For Hegel, however, the dialectical process is brought forward by further differentiation. The result is two other figures, the first figure considering both wealth and power as good, the second considering both as bad. The first figure is the "noble mind [edelmüthige Bewußtseyn]," in which consciousness is at the service of both state and wealth. The noble consciousness is characterized by its "heroism of service [Heroismus des Dienstes]," which is the "virtue, where the individual human being sacrifices itself for the general good [Tugend,

---

60 See Ludwig Siep, "Moralischer und sittlicher Geist in Hegels Phänomenologie", in *Hegels Phänomenologie des Geistes*, ed. Klaus Vieweg and Wolfgang Welsch (Frankfurt a. M.: Suhrkamp, 2008), p. 420.

61 See Heidegren, *Hegels Fenomenologi*, p. 232.

welche das einzelne Seyn dem Allgemeinen aufopfert]" (PHG$_{GW\,\&\,TWA}$, 274 & 373). This is the "proud vassal [stolze Vasall]," serving the public with "honour [Ehre]" (PHG$_{GW\,\&\,TWA}$, 275 & 374). In the second figure, consciousness is "vile [niederträchtig]", insisting that there is "inequality [Ungleichheit]" in both fields, just as the idea of "domination [Herrschergewalt]" always implies "shackles and oppression [Fessel und Unterdrückung]". In this figure, consciousness is therefore "always poised to revolt [immer auf dem Sprunge zum Aufruhr]" (PHG$_{GW\,\&\,TWA}$, 273 & 372).

It is not until this stage that Hegel introduces language, thus relying on the results of the linguistic turn achieved by Herder and Humboldt. In reconstructing the logic of this "dizzying dialectic [dialectique vertigineuse]",[62] Hyppolite's comments are very useful. In terms of formation, it is thus crucial that conscious being, in its noble servitude, expresses itself linguistically, in what Hegel calls the "council [Rath]." Here, "different opinions about the common good [verschiedene Meynungen über das allgemeine Beste]" are presented, even though a council, according to Hegel, is "still not a Government and therefore not a true state power [noch nicht Regierung, und somit noch nicht in Wahrheit wirkliche Staatsmacht]" (PHG$_{GW\,\&\,TWA}$, 275 & 374 f). As Amelia Valcárcel explains, the problem is one of conflicting interests and mutual suspicion between the state and the council, the former demanding the will of the latter and the latter demanding the power of the former.[63]

For Hegel, the important point is that 'only' language really makes alienation and formation possible. Language is "the pure being of the self as self [das Daseyn des reinen Selbsts, als Selbsts]"; only language "expresses I [spricht Ich aus]" (PHG$_{GW\,\&\,TWA}$, 276 & 376). Language thus enables the "the individuality of self-consciousness [Einzelnheit des Selbstbewußtseyns]", on the one side allowing the dumb noblesse to transform heroic servitude into "heroic flattery [Heroismus der Schmeicheley]", and on the other raising power to the "to spirit refined life [zum Geiste geläuterten Daseyn]", the purified "equality to itself: The monarch [Sichselbstgleichheit; – Monarch]" (PHG$_{GW\,\&\,TWA}$, 278 & 378). Language thus facilitates the absolute monarchy aggravating the alienation experienced even more. Language allows the monarch to proclaim himself as the only name – "the state, it's me [L'État c'est Moi],"[64] as Louis the XIV famously phrased it – and for the noble consciousness, the sacrificial alienation is therefore pushed to the extreme.

62   Hyppolite, *Genèse et structure*, p. 378 (*Genesis and Structure*, p. 390).

63   See Amelia Valcárcel, *Hegel y la ética*, (Barcelona: Anthropos, 1988), p. 211.

64   Hyppolite, *Genèse et structure*, p. 392 (*Genesis and Structure*, p. 405).

The result is a "laceration [Zerrissenheit]" where everything that is universal, everything "that is called law, good and right [was Gesetz, gut und recht heißt]," falls apart and perishes; "everything equal is dissolved [alles gleiche ist aufgelöst]" into "the purest inequality [reinste Ungleichheit]" (PHG$_{GW \&}$ $_{TWA}$, 280 & 382). According to Hegel, however, it is precisely in this acute and absolute alienation that the truth of *Bildung* must be found: "The language of laceration is [...] the perfect language and the true existing spirit of this whole world of formation [Die Sprache der Zerrissenheit [...] ist die volkommne Sprache und der wahre existirende Geist dieser ganzen Welt der Bildung]" (PHG$_{GW \& TWA}$, 282 & 384). Self-consciousness is elevated, in its rejection, to "the absolute equality-with-itself in the absolute laceration [die absolute Sichselbstgleichheit in der absoluten Zerrissenheit]". The "pure formation [reine Bildung]" is the "absolute and universal distortion and alienation of reality and thought [absolute und allgemeine Verkehrung und Entfremdung der Wirklichkeit und des Gedankens]" (PHG$_{GW \& TWA}$, 282 & 385). Being thus alienated in the *Bildung* and its realm of reality, consciousness transcends both the noble loyalty of the servant and the vile meanness of the rebel.

In this complete and "pure laceration [reine Zerissenheit]" (PHG$_{GW \& TWA}$, 281 & 384), being thus divided, torn apart and fragmented, consciousness has its existence as "universal speech and lacerated judging [allgemeine[s] Sprechen und zerreissende[s] Urtheilen]," which, however, expresses "what is true and irrepressible [das Wahre und Unbezwingbare]." As Sandkaulen explains, the truth of the enlightened world of *Bildung*, being determined by speech, judgement and decision, breaks radically with the validity of tradition, and although this happens consciously and knowingly through the intellect, the result is an unstable order.[65] The "consciousness torn to pieces [zerrissene Bewußtseyn]" is a "distorted consciousness [Bewußtseyn der Verkehrung]" (PHG$_{GW \&}$ $_{TWA}$, 283 & 386), since it distorts "all concepts and realities [alle Begriffe und Realitäten]". The point is, however, that the "shamelessness to utter this deception [Schamlosigkeit, diesen Betrug zu sagen]", "alternately furious and soothing, tender and mocking [wechselsweise rasend, besänftigt, gebieterisch und spöttich]" is "the greatest truth [die größte Wahrheit]" (PHG$_{GW \& TWA}$, 283–84 & 387). For Hegel, this "devastation of conscious being that is aware of itself and pronounces itself [ihrer selbstbewußte und sich aussprechende Zerrissenheit des Bewußtseyns]", is a "scornful laughter at existence as well as at the confusion of the whole and at itself [Hohngelächter über das Daseyn so wie über die Verwirrung des Ganzen und über sich selbst]" (PHG$_{GW \& TWA}$, 285 & 389); nevertheless, this is the truth of *Bildung*.

---

65   See Sandkaulen, "Hegels Konzept(e) der Bildung", pp. 23–24.

With this, Hegel has said what he wanted to say about formation in the *Phenomenology*. The spirit of alienation has its "life [Daseyn]" in the "world of formation [Welt der Bildung]" (PHG GW & TWA, 286 & 391). Only once does he return to the question of formation, namely in the end of Section VI.B. where he analyzes the French Revolution. Here, the point is to remind the reader that the world of *Bildung* was "the most elevated and the last [die erhabenste und letzte]" step. In this world, the "negation is the fulfilled [Negation ist die erfüllte]," either as wealth, honour, or the "insight that the lacerated consciousness obtains [Einsicht, die das zerrissene Bewußtseyn erlangt]". Thus, the negation does not assume the form of "pure abstraction [reine[r] Abstraction]". Formation achieves its essence in the "interaction [Wechselwirkung]," as opposed to the absolute freedom of the revolution, where "negation is the meaningless death [Negation ist der bedeutungslose Tod]" (PHG GW & TWA, 321–22 & 439).

In the *Phenomenology*, formation is clearly conditional on a culturally developed, modern society, where it is possible through a refined language to relate both to oneself, one's surroundings, and the contradictions encountered by both in relation to themselves and each other. Formation reaches its peak in the conscious recognition of the contradictory nature of existence in modernity. *Bildung* is only self-consciousness as truly alienated – that is, as a consciousness that is not only alienated from itself and its surroundings but also from its very alienation. Educated is especially the one who has allowed him or herself to be formed by exteriorization and alienation. Such a self-conscious human being can utter the truth about the world of *Bildung*, i.e. the truth about the contradictions on which it itself is based.

These material contradictions are most evident in the elevated, noble consciousness that considers both state power and wealth as goods, but also the low and vile consciousness becomes involved in contradictions. The vile consciousness may very well be allowed to utter the contradictions through the devastation as a *bohemian*. However, when it comes to rebellious activity in absolute freedom, i.e. the revolution, the result is mere abstract negation, namely death, and such annihilation can, for Hegel, not be a bid for the truth about man's conscious being. On the other hand, neither can the true alienated formation – *Bildung* – be conscious being in its truth.

In spite of the contradictory nature of the figure of *Bildung*, for Hegel it marks the highest possible aspiration of the spirit in the political process of trying to balance the ideals of politics and economy. Or, to put it differently: modern society is basically divided, fragmented and contradictory, and it does not allow for any political and societal reconciliation beyond the *Bildung* achieved on the conditions of modernity. From the Introduction, however, we know that spirit and formation can be mutually interdependent in another way than assumed in the present analysis, and that the realization of *Geist* as such is conceived of as a process of *Bildung*. This is confirmed by Sub-section VI.B.I., i.e. the world of the *Geist* alienated from itself, where Hegel adds that *Bildung* is completed by "the self that grasps itself [das sich selbst erfassende Selbst]" (PHG GW & TWA, 266 & 362).

The ultimate truth of conscious being is therefore to be found through a process of *Bildung* beyond the world of *Bildung*, and therefore also beyond the real political realizations of the spirit. The world of *Bildung* is part of the process of "enlightenment [Aufklärung]" and as such, it "confuses and revolutionizes [verwirrt und revolutionirt]" (PHG GW & TWA, 240 & 327). It is a particularly privileged moment of self-conscious, albeit impotent, insight in the contradictions of modernity, but it is not scientific knowledge about reality in the strongest possible sense of the word. More can be said about the self-consciousness of the spirit. The *Phenomenology of Spirit* has to continue its progression, and thus also the *Bildung* of consciousness beyond the figure of pure *Bildung*, i.e. from spirit as morality through religion to absolute knowledge. In the last section, I will return to the implications of this in relation to the political question.

C   Further Details from Nürnberg

It is with this complex concept of formation, Hegel takes up the position as rector of the upper secondary school in Nürnberg, thus becoming subject to the Bavarian regulations for the new humanistic *Gymnasium*. These regulations required that high school students during their four years of education were to carry out "exercises in speculative thinking" in relation to logic, cosmology, theology, psychology, ethics and law. The aim was that the high school students at the end of their education would be able to understand a juxtaposition of subject areas previously treated only speculatively and in isolation. The juxtaposition was to take on the form of a "philosophical encyclopedia [philosophische Enzyklopädie]",[66] and, as mentioned by Moldenhauer and Michel, Hegel was finally able to publish such an encyclopedia in 1817,[67] i.e. just after leaving Nürnberg.

As a rector, Hegel develops the concept of formation to be more practical and specifically educational in nature. *Bildung* is thus much more oriented

---

66   As specified in the *Allgemeine Normativ* for the Bavarian Gymnasium from 1808, quoted in Moldenhauer and Michel's "Anmerkung" in TWA 4, pp. 598–99.
67   See Moldenhauer and Michel's "Anmerkung" in Hegel, *Enzyklopädie der philosophischen Wissenschaften III* (1817), in TWA 10, pp. 421–23.

towards the education of the individual and accommodating in relation to traditional societal virtues. The educational formation of conscious human being towards spirit and science is now a practical institutional task, which is reflected in speeches and curricula. Therefore, from time to time in this section I have felt obliged to simply translate '*Bildung*' into 'education.'

According to Hegel higher education must contribute to distinguishing dream from reality, and the ability to do this, he believes, is strengthened by ancient wisdom. As early as Antiquity, the educated human being could be said to differ as much from the uneducated as "human beings altogether from stones [des Menchen überhaupt vom Steine]". Hegel therefore pays tribute to the teacher as the someone who is entrusted with maintaining and passing on the "treasure of education, knowledge and truth [Schatz der Bildung, der Kenntnisse und Wahrheiten]"[68] to the next generation. The particular aim of the *Gymnasium* is for Hegel preparation for learned studies, built on the ground laid by the Greeks and the Romans. Although art and science have grown to become independent, neither has broken free from the "older formation [ältern Bildung]." And so it should be. For Hegel, every revival of "science and education [Wissenschaft und Bildung]" ($N_{GW \& TWA}$, 456 & 314) must always return to Antiquity.

For Hegel, the new humanist *Gymnasium* differed from the Latin school by bringing "the old into a new relationship with the whole," whereby that which is essential "is preserved just as much as it is changed and renewed." In the Latin school, language teaching was considered "the only higher means of education [das einzige höhere Bildungsmittel]" ($N_{GW \& TWA}$, 457 & 314–15), and the art of mastering languages therefore achieved the status of more or less the only end. That was not the case anymore, since the *Gymnasium* had been given a "sister institution [Schwesteranstalt]," i.e. the "*Real*'-institution," where "the study of science and acquisition of higher spiritual and useful skills [das Studium der Wissenschaften und die Erwerbung höherer geistiger und nützlicher Fertigkeiten]" takes place independently of the "old literature [alten Literatur]" ($N_{GW \& TWA}$, 458 & 316). This, however, also means for Hegel that the new *Gymnasium* can afford to continue cultivating classic formation – i.e. *Bildung* – and classical languages without being accused of being biased.

---

68   Hegel, *Nürnberger Gymnasialkurse und Gymnasialreden (1808–1816)*, p. 450; Hegel, *Nürnberger und Heidelberger Schriften 1808–1817*, p. 307. In the present chapter, hereafter the Nürnberger texts are referred to collectively as N, and the page references to the two editions are indicated by, respectively, GW_H and TWA. In the rest of the present chapter the references to these texts will thus appear in brackets as $N_{GW \& TWA}$, nn & nn. It should be noted that, due to different editiorial principles, the volume referred to in the former edition (GW_H 10.1) only contains few of the texts included in that of the latter (TWA 4).

The fact thus remains that, as Hegel puts it, the "noblest nutrient in the noblest form, the golden apples in silver bowls [edelste[r] Nahrungs-Stoff [...] in der edelsten Form, die goldnen Apfel in silbernen Schaalen]" are the ancient works in Greek and Latin. No education is more "excellent, admirable, original, versatile and instructive [Vortreffliches, Bewundernwürdiges, Originelles, Vielseitiges und Lehrreiches]" than the one that takes the student through the classical works, and according to Hegel this "wealth is [...] tied to the language [Reichthum [...] ist an die Sprache gebunden]" ($N_{GW \& TWA}$, 460 & 319):

> Language is the musical element, the element of fervor that disappears in translation – the delicate fragrance through which the sympathy of the soul indulges in pleasure, without which a work of the ancients only tastes like a Rhine wine that has evaporated ($N_{GW \& TWA}$, 460 & 320).[69]

To gain access to these experiences, it is necessary to take on the hard work of learning the ancient languages. Only then is it possible to approach the "substances [Stoffe]" ($N_{GW \& TWA}$, 460 & 320) of *Bildung*. Formation requires "substance and subject matter [Stoff und Gegenstand]," which it can process, change and form. To become "Gegenstand" – which rather than 'object' in German is 'something that faces' – nature and spirit must appear in the figure of something "alien [Fremdartigem]," and this means that the ties that bind "the disposition and the thoughts [das Gemüth und den Gedanken]" to life, i.e. "faith, love and confidence [Glauben, Liebe und Vertrauen]," are "torn apart [zerrissen]" ($N_{GW \& TWA}$, 461 & 321). In other words: *Bildung* presupposes objectification.

For Hegel, formation is thus not a "quiet progress [ruhige[s] Fortsetzen]" ($N_{GW \& TWA}$, 461 & 320). There is a "demand of separation [Forderung der Trennung]," and it is "necessary [nothwendig]." Only the "alien [Fremdartige]" and "distant [Ferne]" are able to attract young people and make them take upon themselves the necessary toil: "[W]hat is worthy of desire is inversely proportional to what is nearby [[D]as Begehrenswerthe steht im umgekehrten Verhältnisse mit der Nähe]" ($N_{GW \& TWA}$, 461 & 321). As Lars Løvlie accurately puts it, "the relationship between the student and the learning material" is "determined by absence rather than presence".[70] It is this desire that is thought to drive a man both into and out of the experienced fragmentation, making it

---

69   Die Sprache ist das musikalische Element, das Element der Innigkeit, das in der Uebertragung verschwindet; der feine Duft, durch den die Sympathie der Seele sich zu genießen giebt, aber ohne den ein Werk der Alten nur schmeckt, wie Rheinwein, der verduftet ist.

70   Lars Løvlie, "Hegels dannelsesbegrep – Noen synspunkter", in *Dannelse – Humanitas – Paideia*, ed. Øivind Andersen (Oslo: Sypress Forlag, 1999), p. 58.

possible, through learning alien languages, to gain access to the spiritual wealth that allows him the "retrieval of his self [Wiederfinden seiner selbst]" ($N_{GW\&}$ $_{TWA}$, 462 & 322). As is the case in the *Phenomenology*, Hegel thus emphasizes the close connection between classical languages, alienation and *Bildung*.

For Hegel, however, also the merely mechanical learning is important, because it gives the learner an understanding of relating to lifeless reality. Related to this idea, and even more important, is the grammatical study. Grammatical abstractions are "quite simple [ganz Einfache]" and thus something "comprehensible for the youth [faßliches für die Jugend]," but studying them also represents the beginning of the "logical formation [logische Bildung]," and as such the study of the grammatical terminology is a study of "elementary philosophy [elementarische Philosophie]" ($N_{GW\ \&\ TWA}$, 462 & 322). It is therefore not only a means but also an end in itself. Studying grammar implies both perpetual subsuming of the particular under the universal, and particularization of the universal. For Hegel, strict grammar study therefore becomes the "most universal and precious means of formation [allgemeinste und edelste Bildungsmittel]" ($N_{GW\&TWA}$, 462–63 & 323). Accordingly, the core of secondary education continues to be the study of the ancients in their own language and the grammatical study, although Hegel emphasizes that these subjects in the new *Gymnasium* take up relatively less time than in the old Latin school (see $N_{GW\&TWA}$, 464 & 324).

There is no doubt that Hegel also in a practical educational perspective makes *Bildung* dependent on alienation, laceration of natural ties and the pains of mechanical learning. Discipline and castigation are considered necessary to the formation of morality, and Hegel also emphasizes the necessity of peace and quiet, sustained attention and "respect and obedience to the teacher [Respect und Gehorsam gegen die Lehrer]" ($N_{GW\&TWA}$, 472 & 334), as well as to the other students. Hegel presupposes that "ethical castigation [Zucht der Sitten]" ($N_{GW\&TWA}$, 473 & 335) has taken place before high school, but if this is not the case it must be rectified in the *Gymnasium*, since formation requires discipline. That, however, does not mean that Hegel recommends authoritarian measures or corporal punishment.

Hegel emphasizes the need to create a free sphere where the young people can learn how to act responsibly. Hegel notes how school discipline has changed, so that "upbringing [Erziehung]" is now more about "support than suppression of the growing self-esteem [Unterstützung als Niederdrückung des erwachenden Selbstgefühls]," since the aim is "education to independency [Bildung zur Selbstständigkeit]". The aim is no longer to give the youth a "feeling of submission and servitude [Gefühl der Unterwürfigkeit und der Unfreiheit]," just as there is a move away from "empty obedience [leere[m]

Gehorsam]" (N$_{GW \& TWA}$, 485 & 350). Peace, quiet, and obedience, are still required, but only to achieve the aim of the studies.

> Bringing up to independence requires that the youth at a very early stage can get used to drawing on their own sense of decency and their own intelligence to advise, and that one lets them have a free sphere for themselves and free from older people, where they themselves can decide about their behavior (N$_{GW \& TWA}$, 486 & 351).[71]

Only in this way can the high school meet its objective: imparting to each single individual the *Bildung* that is necessary for living in the "real world [wirkliche[n] Welt]" and participating in "public life [öffentlichen Leben]" (N$_{GW \& TWA}$, 486–87 & 352). Hegel stresses, however, that even when the school has finished its training, this is only a preparation that by no means completes the education, i.e. *Bildung*. In principle, a student in school is in a permanent state of striving, but as a good educator Hegel knows that there is always the possibility that a given student "just has not found his true interest yet, or has not yet reached that point, where this interest breaks through [sein eigentliches Interesse, nur noch nicht gefunden, oder auch nur den Zeitmoment noch nicht erreicht hat, in welchem es mit ihm durchbricht]" (N$_{GW \& TWA}$, 487 & 353). *Bildung* cannot be forced upon students if they are not ready and receptive, and Hegel therefore allows the whims of nature and individuality to play a considerable role in education and formation.

D Concluding Remarks: Formation Requires Education; Critique Requires Alienation

According to Hegel's idea of education, there has to be truth and knowledge in formation. The content is certainly not chosen at random, and philosophy obviously plays an important role. It is clear that formation as *Bildung* is not possible without formal higher education. Therefore, it is somewhat imprecise when Robert Pippin simply describes *Bildung* as a "learning process".[72]

---

71 Die Erziehung zur Selbstständigkeit erfordert, daß die Jugend frühe gewöhnt werde, das eigene Gefühl von Schicklichkeit und den eignen Verstand zu Rathe zu ziehen, und daß ihr eine Sphäre freigelassen sey, unter sich und im Verhältnisse zu ältern Personen, worin sie ihr Betragen selbst bestimme.

72 Robert B. Pippin, *Hegel's Practical Philosophy. Rational Agency as Ethical Life* (Cambridge: Cambridge University Press, 2008), p. 122.

In the way this expression is often understood, that would imply that it does not matter what you learn, and that there is – *pace* Dewey – something inherently experimental in the process. As I have argued, neither is that the case for Hegel. Formation requires both discipline and authority, as well as alienation and freedom, and the substance of *Bildung* is to a great extent already given by the content of the great works of classical Antiquity.

Still, Pippin's Kantian characterization of formation as "collective self-cultivation"[73] is also somehow misleading. Even in the most general sense, formation is not cultivation. The latter is the process of bringing up a plant or an animal with nutrition and care. In contrast, *Bildung* as human formation both requires and is the enabling condition of alienation, fragmentation and freedom; brought to a head, alienation can be said to be the necessary condition for formation and thus education. Formation is therefore not a conscious teleological activity aimed at an end, which can be determined in advance. As Gadamer stresses, *Bildung* is not a means to shape dispositions that are already given.[74] In formation, man must break with what is merely natural and rise to universality through negation. It was only in this sense that, for an entire epoch, *Bildung* could become the "*Zauberwort*", i.e. the magic word, as Sandkaulen puts it.[75]

The complex understanding of *Bildung* developed so far is assumed to apply to both the general philosophical concept of formation, as described in the *Phenomenology*, and the pedagogical concept of formation, as developed by Hegel in his Nürnberg speeches. Pedagogically speaking, for Hegel there must then be a conflict in the conception of *Bildung* between being educated and having completed an education. It thus seems that formation is so closely intertwined with alienation and laceration that formation as a process can never be brought to a close. As Sandkaulen concludes, *Bildung* does not lead to absolute science.[76]

Nevertheless, I would argue for some kind of closure. Humboldt thus thinks of *Bildung* as the transformation of the "unrestful strive [unruhige Streben]" towards "wholeness [Allheit]" into determinate "wise action [weise Thätigkeit]".[77] In Hegel's case, firstly, it can also be said that *Bildung* means achieving a state

---

73   Pippin, *ibid.*, p. 126.

74   See Gadamer, *Wahrheit und Methode*, p. 17.

75   See Sandkaulen, "Bildung bei Hegel – Entfremdung oder Versöhnung?" p. 432.

76   See Sandkaulen, "Wissenschaft und Bildung", p. 206.

77   Wilhelm von Humboldt, "Theorie der Bildung des Menschen" (1792/93), in Humboldt, *Werke* (1960), ed. Andreas Flitner und Klaus Giel (Darmstadt: Wissenschaftliche Buchgesellschaft, 1981), vol. 1, p. 238.

of mind where consciousness, i.e. human conscious being, can still be moved by impressions that are worth being moved by. With formation – i.e. being educated – what is developed is an ever better capacity for judging correctly, but not a set of final judgements.

Secondly, we also know from Hegel that conscious being has to go through a process of formation to reach the final goal, absolute knowledge, and absolute knowledge must – as science – be assumed to include final judgements of some kind. Nevertheless, there is a genuine sense of indeterminateness in the idea of formation as it is expounded in the *Phenomenology*, and with such an open concept of *Bildung*, it may be possible to develop even stronger conceptual ties between freedom and formation in a contemporary perspective than by using the *Philosophy of Right*.

It is common to distinguish between a humanist and a political concept of formation, i.e. between the formation of the human being and the education of the citizen. For Hegel, however, the point seems to be that you can only be formed as a human being through the formation to become a citizen and *vice versa*. The very concept of *Bildung* is determined in relation to the actual historical development of culture and politics, as well as formal education. As a special kind of spiritual formation and education, *Bildung* requires experiences of both freedom and alienation, as recommended by Hegel in his speeches as rector. Such education is clearly relevant for the citizens of a self-governing republic, and, as Lukács has argued, for the young Hegel the free republics of Antiquity were the political ideal.[78]

Alienating formation means that a citizen does not experience a case as having a predefined conclusion, nor that the answer to a question is already given. This constitutes a certain degree of freedom in decision-making, and *Bildung* in the Hegelian sense can thus be considered a precondition for autonomy – individual as well as collective. For Hegel, the idea of *Bildung* is thus to develop the human capacity of republican citizens in terms of legislation and making the right judgements about specific cases in the very complex and contradictory reality of a modern society.

Sandkaulen emphasizes that Hegel in the *Philosophy of Right* reaffirms the "absolute worth [absolute[n] Werth]"[79] of *Bildung*. However, contrary to the analysis of the spirit alienated from itself, he does not speak of "reine," i.e. *pure Bildung* (see PHG$_{GW \& TWA}$, 282 & 385).[80] Sandkaulen interprets this as a

---

78   See Georg Lukács, *Der junge Hegel* (1944) (Frankfurt a. M. : Suhrkamp, 1973), vol. 1, pp. 92–111.

79   Hegel, GW 14,1, § 20, p. 41; TWA 7, p. 71.

80   See also Sandkaulen, "Bildung bei Hegel – Entfremdung oder Versöhnung?" p. 433.

hint that something has changed, even though Hegel might still hold on to the original analysis. In the *Philosophy of Right*, Hegel thus limits the achievement in bourgeois society to the mere "formal [formelle]"[81] freedom and the universality of knowing and willing,[82] i.e. to what can be expressed by Kant. I can add that in this passage, Hegel only talks about the forming of subjectivity, not of formation as such. There are hence no traces of alienation or laceration,[83] and the conclusion must be that an affirmative turn has taken place in Hegel's *Bildung* program. Apparently pure *Bildung* is no longer considered a necessary step in the formation of spirit. Be that as it may, in no way does manual work provide formation. Sandkaulen thus points to the fact that what is hard work [*harte Arbeit*] in relation to *Bildung* is the liberation from subjectivity and the "immediacy of desire [Unmittelbarkeit der Begierde]",[84] not production as such.

Sandkaulen's point is that there is a critical potential in the idea of pure formation that Hegel expounded in the world of *Bildung* in the *Phenomenology*. It is precisely this potential that was recognized by Marcuse in the young Marx's studies of Hegel. For Marx, the entire *Phenomenology* remains within the figure of alienation,[85] but that also means that the critical elements are said to remain only in an alienated form.[86] Still, in *One-Dimensional Man*, Marcuse introduces his critique of the immediate, automatic identification with society in high industrial civilization as follows, clearly continuing the Hegelian-Marxist line of thought:

> This identification is not illusion but reality. However, the reality constitutes a more progressive stage of alienation. The latter has become entirely objective; the subject which is alienated is swallowed up by its alienated existence. There is only one dimension, and it is everywhere and in all forms.[87]

---

81   Hegel, GW 14,1, § 187, p. 62; TWA 7, p. 343.

82   See Sandkaulen, "Bildung bei Hegel – Entfremdung oder Versöhnung?" p. 433.

83   See Sandkaulen, ibid., p. 435.

84   Hegel, GW 14,1, § 187, p. 63; TWA 7, p. 345; see also Sandkaulen, "Hegels Konzept(e) der Bildung", pp. 24–25.

85   See Marcuse, "Neue Quellen zur Grundlegung des Historischen Materialismus", in S_M 1, p. 550.

86   See Marcuse, ibid., p. 555.

87   See Marcuse, *One-Dimensional Man. Studies in the Ideology of Advanced Industrial Society* (1964) (Boston: Beacon Press, 1968), p. 11. On the current relevance of Marcuse's critique of capitalism, see Ch. 7 in the present book.

According to Sandkaulen, this critical political potential is suppressed and erased in the *Philosophy of Right*. In its place can be found an impure figure of reconciliation,[88] which somehow reflects the comprehensive reconciliatory idea of *Bildung* presented in the Introduction to the *Phenomenology*. As Honneth remarks, Hegel was never a democrat,[89] and as a meritocratic republican he could be open to reconciling himself with an aristocratic rule. This is the slippery slope leading to what Sandkaulen calls the "domestication of *Bildung*"[90] and the acceptance of German society as it was.

Thus, the human qualities appropriate for a republican citizen are also relevant for those high-ranking officials of the authoritarian German *Rechtstaat* that the *Gymnasium* of that time was mainly to educate. Positions as officers, judges, doctors, priests, professors etc. require people who are not only obedient but also able to take responsibility for the final decision, even surrounded by total chaos. The point is that in the alienating fragmentation of modernity, a human being with official responsibilities must be able to decide freely and with authority according to law in each individual case. This is simply what can be expected of a *Beamter*.

In the gender and class perspective of standpoint theory, i.e. conducting a critique of ideology, it can therefore be said that the sons of the upper-class in the neo-humanist *Gymnasium* are trained for the conditional freedom, responsibility and sovereignty required to hold office in the authoritarian bourgeois state of law. In this perspective, it is also relevant that *Bildung* requires an education that is only possible for the upper strata of society, i.e. a time-consuming cultural formation that takes place at the expense of those others being forced to provide the material livelihood. This was also pointed out by the young Habermas.[91]

Maintaining the critical perspective, as argued at length above it has been common to emphasize the close relationship in the philosophy of Hegel between the forced forming of things and formation of consciousness. Hyppolite claims that Hegel, by playing on the word *Bildung*,[92] lets the slave become "master of the master".[93] The slave is supposed to carry with him the future

---

88   See Sandkaulen, "Bildung bei Hegel – Entfremdung oder Versöhnung?" pp. 433, 38; Sandkaulen, "Hegels Konzept(e) der Bildung", p. 25.

89   See Axel Honneth, *Leiden an Unbestimmtheit* (Stuttgart: Reclam, 2001), p. 127.

90   Sandkaulen, "Hegels Konzept(e) der Bildung", p. 25.

91   See Sørensen, "From Critique of Ideology to Politics. Habermas on Bildung", for further details and references. This article will be included in DDD III.

92   See Jean Hyppolite, *Studies on Marx and Hegel* (1955) (New York: Harper & Row, 1969), p. 21.

93   Hyppolite, *ibid.*, p. 17.

of humankind, and for Taylor this line of thought shows "how much Hegel's philosophy of history anticipates historical materialism".[94] With such an understanding of formation and education, Marxist readers of Hegel have been able to argue that raising the class consciousness of the workers would lead to a revolution that would realize conscious being as *Geist* in the strong Hegelian sense. Productive work thus caused the crucial increase in human consciousness, and therefore the working class could be said to be the subject of history, i.e. the figure that brings the story of humanity to the final sublation of all contradictions.

With such strong links between Hegel and Marx, the eclipse of Marx's idealization of work is therefore also an eclipse of Hegel's philosophy and what is supposed to unite them, i.e. dialectics and philosophy of history. The young Michel Foucault therefore distances himself from dialectics, denouncing it as "the working man's philosophy",[95] and the same goes for the young Jacques Derrida: "the independence of self-consciousness becomes ridiculous at the moment it frees itself by serving, that is, when it enters into work, that is, into dialectics".[96]

As I have argued above, however, not much in Hegel gives credit to attributing such historical importance to the productive labour of the servant. Negation is clearly a necessary element in the formation of consciousness, but the forming of productive work is not the only kind of negation, and actually it is a rather primitive one, since it is non-linguistic. In the real formation, it is experience through education of the strangeness of classical Antiquity that provides the negative breaks with the given reality. It is through the hard work of studying the classics in Greek and Latin that one can develop the necessary alienation and divisionary fragmentation, and it is precisely through the very same works, in the midst of lacerated despair, that one can find oneself again. It is alienation that provides the necessary negative component, and this can be provoked to happen in the experience of learning alien languages. It is hard

---

94   Taylor, *Hegel*, p. 157.

95   Michel Foucault, "Préface à la transgression", *Critique* XIX (195–96) (1963), p. 767.

96   Jacques Derrida, "De l'économie restreinte à l'économie générale. Un hégélianisme sans réserve", *L'arc* 32 (1967), p. 28. See also my analysis of Hegelian dialectics in relation to Foucault, Derrida and Georges Bataille, Asger Sørensen, "The Inner Experience of Living Matter: Bataille and Dialectics", *Philosophy & Social Criticism* 33, no. 5 (2007); Ch. 4 above). A classic introduction to Hegel's importance for French philosophy in the 20th century is provided by Descombes (Vincent Descombes, *Le Même et l'autre. Quarante-cinq ans de philosophie française (1933–1978)* (Paris: Minuit, 1979)); see also Bruce Baugh, *French Hegel: From Surrealism to Postmodernism* (New York *et al.*: Routledge, 2003) for a recent and an even clearer statement of this point.

work to overcome the alienating distance to Antiquity, but it is not productive and, even less, manual labour. For Hegel, forming of consciousness certainly happens through productive labour, but it does not in itself provide consciousness with formation – i.e. *Bildung* – in the proper sense of the word.

Hegel's subject of history has obviously studied in the *Gymnasium*, while the worker, who in distress and anxiety is forming material things for his master, only achieves conscious being at a very rudimentary level, namely what today could be labelled 'tacit knowledge.' It might represent a necessary step in raising consciousness, but it can never be sufficient. For Hegel, in order to achieve the *Bildung* necessary for living in freedom and taking responsibility, the worker has to take classes in high school or, even better, university. Hegel's dialectics cannot be taken to support the Marxist idea of the proletarian revolution, and there is therefore no reason to blame Hegel for the shortcomings of this latter idea. It would be much better to blame him for holding less stringently to the republican ideals of his youth.

CHAPTER 7

On the Way to Liberation: Marcuse

Contemporary Critical Theory has been keen to distance itself from elements that were considered crucial by the first generation of critical theorists, i.e. Herbert Marcuse, Max Horkheimer and Theodor W. Adorno. Critical Theory still insists on theory's relevance to practice, but the ideas of theory and practice implied by this figure of thought seem less radical today. Of the leading contemporary proponents, Jürgen Habermas's stance has shifted from a radical critique of the system to an affirmative reconstruction of the legitimacy of law and democratic thought as developed within capitalist modernity.[1] Axel Honneth, meanwhile, remains critical by focusing on the concrete suffering and violations of modern life, but does not emphasize how the affronts of human beings are conditioned materially by the capitalist economy. For Habermas it has for decades been important to criticize the philosophy of consciousness inherent in the Marxist focus on production alongside a general emphasis on the post-metaphysical character of his own interactional thinking. Mining a similar vein, Honneth has been concerned with negating the philosophy of history inherent in classical Critical Theory, considering the latter primarily as social philosophy and critique of ideology.[2]

From the very beginning, a core element in Critical Theory was the idea of dialectics as it was understood by Hegel and Marx, especially for Marcuse and Horkheimer. It was only later that the optimism connected to dialectics as a positive possibility gave way to the negative versions developed in Horkheimer and Adorno's *Dialectic of Enlightenment* and Adorno's *Negative Dialectics*. For both Habermas and Honneth, critical engagement with these ideas of dialectics has constituted an important part of their intellectual development, but today it seems that the idea of dialectics in itself, whether positive or negative, has fallen into disrepute and become obsolete. Whatever the philosophical details of this process may be – apart from the conceptual work of Habermas and Honneth, one can also point to the criticisms of dialectics by Adorno, Michel Foucault and Jacques Derrida – one can ask how many of such core elements can be discarded before Critical Theory loses its self-proclaimed identity as a 'critical theory of society'.

---

1 To this question, I will return in DDD III, *Justice, Peace and Formation.*
2 For a discussion of this development, see above in the Interlude, especially Sect. D and E.

In this chapter I will argue that precisely the idea of dialectics is indispensable to Critical Theory, since it implies ways of thinking that are crucial in order to remain critical in the classical sense. To substantiate my present argument for dialectics as a condition of radical critique, I will narrow in my focus to Marcuse's investigation of the connection between dialectics and critique as it is outlined in *One-Dimensional Man* published in 1964,[3] only supplementing it with his other writings, when it comes to some specific aspects of the idea of dialectics.

The most important conclusion is that radical dialectical critique enables us to imagine a viable future for humanity. In *ODM* we thus get a presentation of thinking that is two-dimensional, negative and positive, critical and liberating, and it is this kind of thought that Marcuse considers dialectical.

First, however, I will make three introductory remarks about dialectics, Marcuse and Critical Theory (A). Next, I provide an outline of the critique of one-dimensionality and empiricism in ODM (B), followed by an explanation of how Marcuse connects dialectics, negativity and history (C). Finally, I offer an account of how dialectical thinking also entails the possibility of imagining liberation and an alternative way of being human (D).

A   Marcuse, Dialectics and Critical Theory

Before going into the conceptual details, it might be appropriate to indicate why one should, if at all, find dialectics so interesting (i), what is so special about *ODM* and Marcuse in relation to Critical Theory (ii), and finally what makes Marcuse particularly interesting in relation to dialectics (iii).

i   *Dialectics as a Phenomenon*
For many of us whose intellectual horizons were formed in the wake of what after Marcuse was termed the "great refusal" of the 1960s and 70s, dialectics seemed to be a natural part of the agenda referred to in conversations among educated intellectuals. This is evident in the work of one of Marcuse's personal acquaintances, Arthur Koestler. His tragi-comedy *The Call-Girls* from 1972 introduces us to the world of the leading lights of the professional intelligentsia

---

3   See Herbert Marcuse, *One-Dimensional Man. Studies in the Ideology of Advanced Industrial Society* (1964) (Boston: Beacon Press, 1968) (or Marcuse, *Der eindimensionale Mench* (1967), trans. Alfred Schmidt, in Marcuse, *Schriften* (s_M) (1978–89) (Springe: zu Klampen Verlag, 2004), vol. 7). In the present chapter, hereafter *One-Dimensional Man* will be referred to in the text as *ODM*, and the page references will appear in brackets as (ODM, nn (s_M 7, nn)).

at a time when traveling around the world to present papers was a privilege granted only to the chosen few. The setting is a fictional conference on "the Origins of Violence, the Ethics of Science and the Concept of Democracy, the Responsibilities of Scientists in a Free Society",[4] and at one of the dinner parties, a professor remarks casually:

> [A]s regards Cartesian lucidity you are even more out of date. Cartesian dualism has long been replaced by Hegelian trinity of thesis-antithesis-synthesis, reflected in Marxist-Leninist dialectics. This in turn has been re-interpreted in the philosophy of Chairman Mao, but also amalgamated with the existentialism of Sartre and the structural anthropology of Levi-Strauss.[5]

This prompts a light conversation around the table about goulash – we are in the Alps – during which a third participant, a British poet, denounces Levi-Strauss as "pure jabberwocky" and adds some depreciative remarks about the

> dialectics of boiled, roast and smoked food – the contrast between honey and tobacco – the parallel between honey and menstrual blood – hundreds of pages of insane verbal jugglery – the biggest hoax since the Piltdown skull.[6]

Back then dialectics was thus an intellectual commonplace, considered by some to be of the utmost importance, while merely prone to ridicule by others. When I enrolled as a philosophy student at the University of Copenhagen in 1980, the idea of dialectics could thus be experienced as something very prominent, held in high esteem both inside and outside of the university. It was treated with great respect among radical students, and the most damaging critique one could wage against an opponent was that his or – less often – her way of thinking was undialectical. Outside the university, in left-wing circles, labelling something, or somebody, as undialectical also functioned as a valid and very strong self-sustained argument. The problem was that most of us had only a very vague idea of what dialectics was supposed to be.

Marx was, of course, the key reference regarding dialectics, but it was also well-known that he had actually said very little on the subject, since he regarded it as a complicated issue. Dialectics was supposed to have been the

---

4 Arthur Koestler, *The Call-Girls* (London: Hutchinson & co., 1972), p. 1.

5 Koestler, *ibid.*, p. 73.

6 *Ibid.*, p. 74.

method employed by Marx when he succeeded in criticizing the capitalist logic of political economy; however, in some very famous remarks, he postponed the study of dialectics until after the critique of political economy.[7] Outside the university, leftists would often turn to Engels or Lenin, since it was known in such circles that they had written on these matters. However, to radical students outside the various communist parties, this was not considered to be of any great philosophical or theoretical importance. As a philosophy student one would thus be taught that Plato and especially Hegel provided the key contributions to the idea of dialectics, although their ideas did little to reduce the complexity surrounding dialectics.

Marx supposedly learned the dialectical method from Hegel and, since even Marx himself never reached the point where he was able to formulate his understanding of dialectics, doing so was understood to be an overwhelming task. The only real and respectable source regarding dialectics was therefore considered to be Hegel himself. Although getting to grips with Hegel's dialectics was considered of the utmost importance, his ideas were seen as very difficult, maybe even obscure or mysterious. Hegel's philosophy was considered one of the biggest challenges for philosophy students and, out of awe, only very few of us actually allowed ourselves to study Hegelian dialectics.

One possible reaction to such discursive commonalities and structures is suspicion, the result often being a certain hostility towards dialectics. This was the reaction of thinkers as different as Popper, Foucault and Deleuze, thus following the traditional critique of dialectics as just a form of mystifying rhetoric. However, one could also accept the basic intuition regarding the fecundity of the philosophical idea of dialectics and try to figure out how it should be explained in detail to convince. This latter approach was quite respectable for most of the 20th century, both for various schools of self-declared Marxists and for hermeneutical philosophers such as Hans-Georg Gadamer. In the early 1970s, this strategy became almost hegemonic, and arguments about dialectics therefore became a serious matter.

Especially among Marxists, one issue assumed great importance; namely whether or not dialectics as the preferred scientific method *per se* could also be applied in relation to nature, and if so how. One side would claim that dialectics is a comprehensive idea applicable to both historical and natural reality, arguing that this conception was employed not just by Engels and Lenin, but

---

7 See Karl Marx, letter to "[...] Engels um den 16. Januar 1858", in Marx & Engels, *Werke* (MEW), vol. 29 (Berlin: Dietz Verlag, 1978), p. 260, and Marx, letter to "[...] Joseph Dietzgen 9. Mai 1868", in MEW 32 (Berlin: Dietz Verlag, 1978), p. 547.

also by Marx himself.[8] As I have shown elsewhere, also Mao Zedong would naturally fall into this category,[9] and so too would a French philosopher such as Georges Bataille.[10] The other side, meanwhile, would take care to stress that dialectics can only be applied to societal reality, not to nature,[11] and this is the concept of dialectics which Marcuse defends, for instance in an article "On the History of Dialectics" published a few years after ODM.[12] This was no coincidence; Marcuse consistently and continuously reflected philosophically on dialectics for more than half a century, from the failed German revolution of 1918 to the student rebellions of 1968 and beyond. For an investigation into the relationship between critique and dialectics in Critical Theory, Marcuse therefore seems a good place to start.

ii   *Marcuse's Position within Critical Theory*
Contemporary Critical Theory is a global network of intellectuals: a worldwide research community with preferred topics, journals, book series, institutions, conferences etc., and whose members all over the world interconnect, interact, and discuss with each other. Within this multitude there are various ways to demarcate Critical Theory as a field, and even though it is impossible to arrive at a definitive judgement of its aims and scope, one can nevertheless decipher certain patterns.

Traditionally, Critical Theory has been recognized as having a special affiliation with the city of Frankfurt am Main in Germany, and this has made it common to talk about a Frankfurt School,[13] related at the same time to the *Institut für Sozialforschung*, i.e. the Institute for Social Research, and the university. In this approach to Critical Theory, Marcuse is normally considered one of the founding fathers, the natural third mentioned after Horkheimer and Adorno,

---

8   See, e.g., Robert Steigerwald, "[Diskussionsbeitrag]", in *Die 'Frankfurter Schule' im Lichte des Marxismus*, ed. Johannes Heinrich von Heiseler *et al.* (Frankfurt a. M.: Verlag Marxist-ischer Blätter, 1974), pp. 155–58.

9   See, e.g., Asger Sørensen, "Contradictions are Theoretical, neither Material nor Practical. On Dialectics in Tong, Mao and Hegel", *Danish Yearbook of Philosophy* 46 (2011); Ch. 5 above.

10   See, e.g., Sørensen, "The Inner Experience of Living Matter: Bataille and Dialectics", *Philosophy & Social Criticism* 33, no. 5 (2007); Ch. 4 above.

11   See, e.g., Gunnar Skirbek, *Nymarxisme og kritisk dialektikk*, (Oslo: Pax, 1970), p. 41.

12   See Marcuse, "On the History of Dialectics" in s_M 8, p. 225. In the present chapter, the following page references to s_M will be indicated in brackets in the text.

13   See, e.g., Rolf Wiggerhaus, *Die Frankfurter Schule* (1986) (München: dtv Wissenschaft, 1993), pp. 9–17; Helmut Dubiel, *Kritische Theorie der Gesellschaft* (Weinheim & München: Juventa, 1992), pp. 11–16; Stefan Gandler, *Fragmentos de Frankfurt* (México: Siglo xxi, 2009), pp. 9–16.

the former being the director of the institute, the founder of its journal *Zeitschrift für Sozialforschung*, i.e. the Journal for Social Research, and the first professor in social philosophy at the Frankfurt university. However, among the intellectual achievements of the first generation of Critical Theory, Marcuse's ODM is recognized as something extraordinary, being the first, and probably only, major philosophical work from the Frankfurt School to be translated into a vast range of languages within just a few years of its original publication and to sell hundreds of thousands of copies all over the world.[14]

Although Critical Theory in general directs its critique towards late capitalism and its ideological representations, ODM is the only evidence of an attempt to present the particular Frankfurt form of critique of capitalism in a comprehensive, systematic and theoretical form. Since Critical Theory as a specifically critical theory of society aimed, according to Horkheimer, to be a "theory of the contemporary society as a whole",[15] this makes ODM a prime example of Critical Theory. This was noticed already a few years after its publication by the young Habermas,[16] and today, with fifty years of hindsight, one can recognize ODM as an impressive monument to the conceptual potentials of classical Critical Theory. Hence, when Peter Lind considers ODM "Marcuse's worst book and in many ways quite unrepresentative of his other writings",[17] I must disagree.

The Frankfurt approach to Critical Theory is quite common,[18] but there are those who prefer a broader definition emphasizing the Marxist roots, including, for instance, Marx himself and British Cultural Studies.[19] Others include various forms of Deweyan pragmatism, or discussions of justice within mainstream political philosophy such as the work of Rawls, Dworkin, Sen, etc.[20]

---

14   See Barry Kätz, *Herbert Marcuse and the Art of Liberation. An Intellectual Biography* (London: Verso, 1982), p. 168.

15   Horkheimer in Douglas Kellner, *Herbert Marcuse and the Crisis of Marxism* (Berkeley: University of California Press, 1984), p. 95.

16   See Jürgen Habermas, "Zum Geleit", in *Antworten auf Herbert Marcuse*, ed. J. Habermas (Frankfurt a. M.: Suhrkamp, 1968), p. 12.

17   Peter Lind, *Marcuse and Freedom* (London & Sydney: Croom Helm, 1988), p. 6.

18   See *Critical Theory*, ed. David Rasmussen and James Swindal (London: Sage, 2004), vol. I, pp. v–xi.

19   See Douglas Kellner, "Critical Theory", in *A Companion to Philosophy of Education*, ed. Randall Curren (Oxford: Blackwell Publishing 1996), 167–70.

20   See, e.g., Gustavo Pereira, *Las voces de la igualidad. Bases para una teoría critica de la justicia* (Cànoves y Samalús: Proteus, 2010), pp. 25–7, 139–54; Rainer Forst, "Die Rechtfertigung der Gerechtigkeit", in Forst, *Das Recht auf Rechtfertigung* (Frankfurt a. M.: Suhrkamp, 2007), p. 127.

Others again include Foucault, or, at least, social critique inspired by him,[21] while among literary critics, Critical Theory might even include phenomenology, semiotics, post-structuralism, post-colonialism, and feminism.[22]

Among those loyal to the Frankfurt approach, different parts of the movement still express different theoretical sympathies. There is thus a perceptible conflict between those who prefer the classical dialectical formulations of the first generation of Critical Theory, i.e. Horkheimer, Adorno, Marcuse *et al.*, and those who prefer to discuss using categories and concepts obtained from Habermas and Honneth – such as communicative rationality or recognition – or other more recently emerged contemporary thinkers. From the perspective of the former, the latter are often denounced as reformists, revisionists, or even traitors. From the perspective of the latter, the former seem lost in fundamentalist, outdated, metaphysical, or just irrelevant categories. As Helmut Dubiel, director of the Frankfurt institute from 1989 to 1997, put it already years ago: "Today the children of Critical Theory are fighting each other."[23]

Within the Frankfurt approach it is common to focus on the royal lineage of Frankfurt professors and directors since the 1930s. Most prominent are the chairs in social philosophy and sociology, and everybody thus relates to the holders of these chairs: firstly, Horkheimer and Adorno, and then their successors Habermas and Honneth. Still, even accepting this lineage approach, there are disagreements about who to acknowledge as worthy of reverence. One such Frankfurt professor is thus often ignored, namely Alfred Schmidt, who was the main translator of most of Marcuse's seminal works from English into German, including *ODM*. He held the chair after Habermas for almost thirty years, from 1972 to 2001, and was the author of several philosophical works, e.g. *The Concept of Nature in Marx* from 1962,[24] but still he is largely neglected. As

21   See, e.g., Nigel Blake and Jan Maschelein, "Critical Theory and Critical Pedagogy", in *The Blackwell Guide to the Philosophy of Education*, ed. Nigel Blake *et al.* (Oxford: Blackwell Publishing, 2003), p. 55; Martin Saar, "Macht und Kritik", in *Sozialphilosophie und Kritik*, ed. Rainer Forst *et al.* (Frankfurt a. M. : Suhrkamp, 2009), 282–85.

22   See, e.g., David Masey, *Dictionary of Critical Theory* (London: Penguin, 2000); David Lodge, *Nice Work* (1988), in Lodge, *A David Lodge Trilogy* (London: Penguin, 1993), pp. 837, 858; Robert Dale Parker (ed.), *Critical Theory: A Reader for Literary and Cultural Studies* (New York: Oxford University Press, 2012).

23   Dubiel, *Kritische Theorie der Gesellschaft*, p. 123.

24   See Alfred Schmidt, *Der Begriff der Natur in der Lehre von Marx* (Frankfurt a.M.: Europäische Verlagsanstalt, 1962) (or Schmidt, *The Concept of Nature in Marx* (1971), trans. Ben Fowkes (London: Verso, 2013)).

Stefan Gandler points out, this is for instance the case in the history of Critical Theory written by Dubiel.[25]

For Marcuse, adding a generational specification to the Frankfurt approach tends to favour him as a member of the first generation and thus one of the classics. Adding lineage to the generational and locational approach, however, means rendering him negligible. Marcuse never held a professorship in Frankfurt, and his rise to intellectual fame in the late 1960s was rather sudden and short-lived. As remarked by Habermas,[26] for a long time Marcuse was left standing in the shadows of Horkheimer and Adorno, and today, after Marcuse's fame somehow has waned away, this is more true than ever. Douglas Kellner, a long-time scholar of Marcuse and the editor of a series of his posthumous papers, states that Marcuse stood for "a dialectical imagination that has fallen out of favor in an era that rejects totalizing thought and grand visions of liberation and social reconstruction".[27] I will nevertheless side with Marcuse as a fine example of the contemporary potential of classical Critical Theory and one who, among the first generation of the Frankfurt School, stands out as particularly emphasizing the conceptual link between dialectics, critique, and liberation; a link which I still consider essential.

iii   The Dialectics of Marcuse

As already indicated, exploring the connection between critique and dialectics in ODM was not just a passing whim for Marcuse. Already in 1928, he quoted Marx, claiming that the dialectical method "in accordance with its nature is critical and revolutionary" (s_M 1, 367). As a revolutionary Marxist even prior to becoming a philosopher,[28] dialectics was at the center of his attention from the very beginning. Marcuse's first philosophical project was a "dialectical phenomenology", where he added historical materialism to Heidegger's idea of man's being as historical. Referring to Karl Liebknecht, Rosa Luxemburg's companion, Marcuse could thus claim that "Dasein as being-in-the-world is always already 'material' and 'spiritual', 'economic' and 'ideological'" (s_M 1, 375).

In 1930–31, this project was followed up in two articles on "The Problem of Dialectics". Here Marcuse's basic idea is that, from Plato to Hegel, "dialectics is only a [...] method for knowledge, because being itself, i.e. true reality, is

---

25   See Gandler, *Fragmentos de Frankfurt*, pp. 114–15.

26   See Habermas, "Zum Geleit", pp. 11–2.

27   Douglas Kellner, "Marcuse", in *A Companion to Continental Philosophy*, ed. Simon Critchley and William R. Schroeder (Oxford: Blackwell Publishing, 2003), p. 393.

28   See Wiggerhaus, *Die Frankfurter Schule*, pp. 113–14; Kellner, *Herbert Marcuse and the Crisis of Marxism*, pp. 13–8.

intrinsically dialectical" (s_M 1, 413). As a philosophical method it is the "pronouncement and presentation of the necessary movement, the necessary becoming of reality itself" (s_M 1, 414). This brings forward the idea of being as historical, but for Marcuse it is only "human *Dasein*", i.e. the human life in its "full being", including "all of its works and creation" (s_M 1, 418), which can be historical. The point for Marcuse is that dialectical thinking demonstrates "the ambiguity, originality and limit of historical ways and forms of *Dasein*". As far as "historical reality as reality claims constancy, clarity and validity" (s_M 1, 420), dialectics must imply a critical position in theory as well as in practice. Following the young Marx, for Marcuse the Hegelian idea of conscious being comprises "the basic relation of life". In dialectical phenomenology this becomes the "concrete way of *Dasein*", which again means a "concrete way of relating" that is "practical as well as theoretical [...], thinking as well as acting" (s_M 1, 427). In this early project of an "'existential' Marxism",[29] Marcuse distinguishes himself from his Frankfurt compatriots by his "anthropological emphasis",[30] and, as is obvious, already in these early reflections on dialectical issues, he only thought of dialectics as applicable in relation to human beings, i.e. social and historical reality.

In 1932 Marcuse refrained from submitting his completed habilitation thesis on Hegel's ontology and the theory of historicity, supervised by Heidegger, and he instead started working at the Frankfurt Institute. Still in exile, Hegel and dialectics remained at the centre of his attention. Hence, when Marcuse in 1941, as Lind has pointed out, provided the first major exposition of Critical Theory in English, i.e. *Reason and Revolution*,[31] it was a work on Hegel where dialectics was being discussed extensively, and when the work was republished in 1960, it was with the important addition of "A Note on Dialectics". As Kellner has noticed, one can trace the very idea of dimensionality back to Marcuse's reading of Hegel,[32] and in a lecture in 1966, two years after the publication of *ODM*, Marcuse is still occupied with "the task for dialectics today". Confronted with late capitalist modernity, he thus wants to "work through this basically new situation theoretically, without simply enforcing upon it inherited concepts" (s_M 8, 198), and, for Marcuse, such flexibility of thought requires dialectics.

---

29   Kellner, *Herbert Marcuse and the Crisis of Marxism*, p. 38.

30   Alfred Schmidt, "Herbert Marcuse – Versuch einer Vergegenwärtigung seiner sozialphilosophischen und politischen Ideen", in *Kritik und Utopie im Werk von Herbert Marcuse*, ed. Institut für Sozialforschung (Frankfurt a. M. : Suhrkamp, 1992), p. 15.

31   See Lind, *Marcuse and Freedom*, p. 23.

32   See Kellner, *Herbert Marcuse and the Crisis of Marxism*, p. 76.

Dialectics was also the focus of attention for Horkheimer and Adorno, as already evident in their early work as critical theorists.[33] In a recent analysis of the discussions about dialectics between Horkheimer and Adorno, Pierre-François Noppen has argued that, for both of them, the object of dialectics was "the processes of critical thought".[34] However, whereas the former argued for an "open dialectics", accepting the Hegelian idea of truth as a totality, the latter considered the whole idea of a totality as simply false, implying both "idealism" and "bourgeois ideology",[35] and he refused to accept the "thought-concept of truth".[36] At that stage of the discussion, Horkheimer's reply was that Adorno's idea of dialectics was "not realizable",[37] but that did not stop Adorno from pursuing the matter, leading him to become even more critical of the Hegelian idea of dialectics.

Marcuse stuck to the classical idea of dialectics as aimed at uncovering the truth. In his 1966 article "On the History of Dialectics", he emphasizes that dialectical thinking, from its very conception in pre-Socratic Greek thought, was conceived of as the "path to the truth". Marcuse nevertheless stresses the inherent negativity of dialectics. Dialectical thinking thus implies a "negation", breaking with "the immediacy" of experiencing reality as given. Even in its most superficial and rhetorical versions, dialectics maintains its "critical power in the destruction of the 'ideology'" which protects the establishment, and this quality is also manifest in the dialectical dialogues of Plato. What people in general think is just is not justice. As Marcuse puts it: "People live in ignorance, in untruth – and they do not know" (s_M 8, 200–201). What one refers to conceptually in ordinary speech and action is not what is expressed in such speech and action. It is therefore untrue. The truth of justice is beyond ordinary speech and action, to be reached only through the critique implied by dialectics.

As Wolfgang Röd has noticed, Marcuse places considerable "emphasis on the normative components of dialectics".[38] For Marcuse, dialectical thinking was thus to be employed both in philosophy and in the revolutionary struggle of the oppressed. Marcuse was in this sense preoccupied with the question of dialectics – theoretically and practically – for more than four decades, and,

---

33   See Wiggerhaus, *Die Frankfurter Schule*, pp. 202–17.

34   Pierre-François Noppen, "L'objet de la thèorie dialectique. Le dèbat entre Max Horkheimer et Theodor W. Adorno", *Archives de Philosophie* 75, no. 3 (2012), p. 469.

35   Noppen, ibid., p. 459.

36   Ibid., p. 461.

37   Ibid., p. 467.

38   Wolfgang Röd, *Dialektische Philosophie der Neuzeit* (München: C.H. Beck, 1974), vol. 2, p. 123.

seen as a whole, his work offers us the most detailed and comprehensive scholarly account of dialectics, from Plato over Hegel to Marx, within the perspective of Critical Theory. As Habermas mentions, among the first generation of the Frankfurt School, Marcuse was the one closest to "scholarly philosophy".[39] And as Honneth adds, in contrast to the dialectical work of Horkheimer and Adorno, Marcuse expresses himself in a language that is quite straightforward and "not tortuous".[40] Or, to quote Habermas again: "He says aloud what others leave hanging in the air".[41] To answer the question of the role of dialectics in Critical Theory, a reflection on Marcuse's work is thus indispensable. In the following sections, I will therefore go into some detail about how Marcuse conceptualizes these issues and argues his case.

B   One-dimensional Thought

As suggested by the title, the key object of critique in ODM is the alleged one-dimensionality of late modern society. Central to this critique is the claim that thought becomes one-dimensional by becoming operational, and Marcuse backs up this claim with a series of detailed "Studies in the Ideology of Advanced Industrial Society", which is also the book's subtitle. Of the three parts, "One-Dimensional Society", "One-Dimensional Thought", and "The Chance of the Alternatives", the first part reconstructs the logic of everyday thought and social science as the dominant ideology of modern society. The point is, however, that part of this ideology also presents itself as philosophical thought, and the critique of one-dimensionality within philosophy is therefore the central concern, especially in the second part. To approach the explanation of how dialectics is connected to critique, I will sketch Marcuse's critique of one-dimensional thinking as the typical ideology encountered in late modernity (i), focusing in particular on empiricism as a crucial element of that ideology (ii).

i   *Operationalism in Political Science*
For Marcuse, the task of philosophy is to grasp reality in order to tell the truth, but the problem is that reality constantly changes. This makes it impossible to state what reality really is, since the minute after this has been stated, what is

---

39   Habermas, "Zum Geleit", p. 11.
40   Axel Honneth, "Herbert Marcuse und die Frankfurter Schule", *Leviathan* 31, no. 4 (2003),
       p. 497.
41   Habermas, "Zum Geleit", p. 12.

real has already become unreal; reality has changed into something different and is thereby both unreal and real, although in a new way. This is what makes dialectics necessary for philosophy. For Marcuse, however, dialectics is not only about change; it is also about tension, antagonism and contradiction. It is to cope with all of these challenges that thinking must be dialectical, maintaining the necessary two-dimensionality in spite of the dominant ideology.

The basic point is that reality has more dimensions than "the factual state of affairs" (ODM, 115 (s_M 7, 134)). For Marcuse, one-dimensionality consists in denying this multi-dimensionality and condemning "the excess of meaning" as "'unrealistic'" (ODM, 114 (s_M 7, 132–33)). To illustrate the point with an example, Marcuse takes a look at the social science of his contemporaries, i.e. the behaviourism and positivism prevalent in social science in the 1950s and 60s. Denying the excess of meaning in this case implies that an "investigation [becomes] locked within the vast confine in which the established society validates and invalidates propositions" (ODM, 114 (s_M 7, 133)). The claim is then that investigations carried out in this manner assume an "ideological character". To substantiate his point, Marcuse analyses how democracy is treated as a subject by political science in a specific "study of political activity in the United States" (ODM, 114 (s_M 7, 133)).

As Marcuse explains, one can take an election as the empirical point of departure. A research question could then be whether this election is democratic or not, and such a study requires a definition of democracy. Marcuse then analyses the criteria offered by the political scientists in question, and what he sees is that "the criteria for judging a given state of affairs are those offered by [...] the given state of affairs" (ODM, 115 (s_M 7, 134)). It is in this sense that an analysis can become "locked" (ODM, 115 (s_M 7, 134)). Limiting reality to the most immediate factual state of affairs means that one cannot judge "the context in which the facts are made, man-made, and in which their meaning, function, and development are determined" (ODM, 116 (s_M 7, 134)). To make the point even more concrete, Marcuse adds that if the term "democratic" is defined in the so-called "realistic" terms of the "actual process of election, then this process is judged as democratic prior to the results of the investigation." Put in unequivocal terms: such an "investigation becomes circular and self-validating" (ODM, 116 (s_M 7, 135–36)).

For Marcuse, this is a prime example of how one-dimensional thought manifests itself in the social sciences. This kind of research thinks of itself as "operational", and, for Marcuse, this term becomes the overall term for a pragmatic empiricist outlook expressing instrumental rationality. Instead Marcuse argues that, to be able to answer the original research question, one has to go beyond the "operational framework" (ODM, 116 (s_M 7, 135)) to reach a "non-operational concept" of democracy. Within the operational framework, such a concept is typically rejected as "unrealistic" (ODM, 116 (s_M 7, 135)), but as Marcuse emphasizes, even a non-operational concept can be very useful.

By being beyond the demands of short-term technical rationality, such a concept can thus be made very precise in its definition, and Marcuse's suspicion is that this may actually be the real reason why it is rejected. The point is that, as a non-operational, universal concept, democracy would be defined as "the clear-cut control of representation by the electorate – popular control by popular sovereignty" (ODM, 116 (s_M 7, 135)). This would make it clear that the "historical intent of democracy, the conditions for which the struggle for democracy was fought [...] are still to be fulfilled" (ODM, 117 (s_M 7, 135)), and this is precisely thanks to a definition of democracy which, as Marcuse puts it, is "impeccable in its semantic exactness because it means exactly what it says" (ODM, 117 (s_M 7, 135–36)). Such a philosophical and normative understanding of democracy would thus imply radical changes in the established ways of doing politics, and the insufficiency of the operational framework therefore functions an ideological cover-up for sticking to democracy as it is already established and institutionalized in various capitalist societies today.

Marcuse's point is thus that operational concepts are insufficient to grasp the meaning of what a concept really is, that they therefore are ideological and ultimately false, being only particular in their validity and not universal as they pretend to be. Moreover, as he emphasizes, this is not just the case, if the task is to comprehend facts for "what they 'mean' for those who have been given them as facts and who have to live with them" (ODM, 118 (s_M 7, 137)). Operational concepts are also insufficient as purely descriptive. The problem is that the "determining, constitutive facts remain outside the reach of the operational concept". The "descriptive analysis of the facts blocks the apprehension of facts and becomes an element of the ideology that sustains the facts" (ODM, 119 (s_M 7, 138)).

ii   *Empiricism as Ideology*

According to Marcuse, the basic problem is the "ideological empiricism" (ODM, 120 (s_M 7, 138)) inherent in one-dimensional operationalism. For the logical positivist philosophy of science, empiricism means that they suspend "judgment on what reality itself may be" (ODM, 151 (s_M 7, 166)), and for Marcuse this means facilitating the transition from questions about what things are to functional questions about how to do things. Logical positivism thus facilitates pragmatic operationalism which approaches reality as "a (hypothetical) system of instrumentalities" (ODM, 152 (s_M 7, 166)), and for Marcuse empiricism thus means that the "science of nature develops under the technological *a priori* which projects nature as potential instrumentality, stuff of control and organization" (ODM, 153 (s_M 7, 168)).

In general for Marcuse the definitions of "truth and objectivity [...] remain related to the human agents of theory and practice, and to their ability to comprehend and change the world" (ODM, 166 (s_M 7, 180)). Reality, however, is not just natural; it is also societal and historical. Change can thus be technological as well as political, but this fact is blurred by the technological *a priori* of empiricist philosophy of science, which thus also functions as an ideology. Moreover, at a more general level, Marcuse points to what he calls "total empiricism" as an ideology that creates barriers for "coming to grips with reality" (ODM, 169 (s_M 7, 183)). Marcuse attempts to demonstrate this with his critique of the "linguistic analysis" of his contemporaries as "one-dimensional philosophy" (ODM, 170 (s_M 7, 184)); and since this latter kind of philosophy, today known as analytical philosophy of language, like the positivist philosophy of science, still remains very influential, sometimes even hegemonic, at universities all over the world, this critique merits further consideration.

The declared goal of linguistic analysis is to expose the mystifying character of "transcendent terms, vague notions, metaphysical universals, and the like" (ODM, 191 (s_M 7, 205)). As Marcuse argues, however, the result is a "new mystification", where "magic, witchcraft, and ecstatic surrender are practiced in the daily routine of the home, the shop, and the office, and the rational accomplishments conceal the irrationality of the whole" (ODM, 190 (s_M 7, 204)). When we calculate the quantitative and technical aspects of various forms of human annihilation, for instance war, climate change, or business strategy, we thus rationally deal with things that we should fight politically, or simply refuse to take part in. Analytical philosophy of language mystifies precisely by leaving the terms of ordinary language "in the repressive context of the established universe of discourse" (ODM, 191 (s_M 7, 205)). As Marcuse emphasizes, "the real context in which the particular subjects obtain their real significance is definable only within a *theory* of society" (ODM, 190 (s_M 7, 205)), i.e. the Critical Theory of society. Critical Theory is precisely characterized by not leaving everything as it is, since it criticizes the ideology of advanced industrial society and encourages the development of theory into praxis.

Marcuse calls attention to a particular trait of modern empiricist philosophy, namely the "tremendous" effort to "reduce the scope and the truth of philosophy", which is supported by the philosophers proclaiming "the modesty and inefficacy of philosophy". For the late Wittgenstein it is thus important to assure us that in his *Philosophical Investigations*, philosophy "leaves everything as it is". For Marcuse, however, this becomes an example of "academic sadomasochism, self-humiliation, and self-denunciation of the intellectual whose labor does not issue in scientific, technical or like achievements" (ODM, 173 (s_M 7, 187)). The only ideals this kind of thinking can recognize are thus ordinary, accepted language, the common man on the street and his trivial daily experiences, another fine example thus being Gilbert Ryle's *The Concept of Mind*.[42]

The problem with empiricist philosophy is that it relates to a very "restricted empirical universe" and does not take seriously the "real empirical world". The object of analysis is typically "withdrawn from the larger and denser context, in which the speaker speaks and lives" (ODM, 180 (s_M 7, 194–95)), i.e. the world of human joy and suffering, exploitation, war, *haute couture* and sports cars. The analysis takes great pain in clarifying a restricted everyday discourse in relation to a restricted and reified universe. It officially aims to clarify ambiguities and obscurities, but it makes no attempts to deal with "the established reality in its repressive and irrational structure" (ODM, 183 (s_M 7, 197)). The point for Marcuse is that, even if this kind of philosophy is very clear in its analysis of the chosen objects, it implies a reduction of human speech, thinking and being. This "poverty of philosophy [...] distrusts the possibility of a new experience" (ODM, 178 (s_M 7, 192)), and for Marcuse there is a sad ideological consequence of this poverty: "The world remains, as it were, unfulfilled" (ODM, 179 (s_M 7, 193)).

It is in this sense that empiricist philosophy is also positivist, thus maintaining an affirmative attitude in relation to the world as it is. Ever since John Locke, empiricism has not said anything about the things in themselves, only about perceptual ideas, and this is not changed by linguistic analysis. By barring philosophy from leaving the very restricted field of linguistic analysis, i.e. by "enclosing thought in the mutilated universe of ordinary discourse", analytical philosophy of ordinary language creates barriers for conceiving a world of "unmutilated reality" (ODM, 199 (s_M 7, 213)), and thus for real political change. By translating universal concepts into operational concepts, empiricism affirms reality as it is, and through this positivist approach it excludes itself from the major tool of rational critique, i.e. "the concepts of negative thinking" (ODM, 183 (s_M 7, 197)). As Manfred Gangl has emphasized, the ideology of "one-dimensional society" is a result of the abandonment of "a dialectical conception of society and reason".[43]

42	See Gilbert Ryle, *The Concept of Mind* (1949) (Harmondsworth: Penguin, 1966), Ch. 1.

43	Manfred Gangl, "Quelques implications sociales de la technologie moderne. Herbert Marcuse dans le contexte de la Théorie critique in Faut-il oublier Marcuse", *Archives de Philosophie* 52, no. 3 (1989), p. 410.

C   Two-dimensional Thought

So much for the basic critique of the one-dimensionality of operational and positive thinking. The example of how to handle the idea of democracy in the social sciences has already given a quite clear indication that critique presupposes a concept of reality beyond the factual state of affairs, and this is precisely why Marcuse wants to stress the importance of two-dimensional dialectical thinking in ODM. Marcuse argues that dialectics is negative, and it is this negativity that is presupposed in the critique of Critical Theory. The next three sub-sections present the dialectical logic of two-dimensional thinking, (i.) its negativity and potentials for critique (ii.), and the historical dimension, as it is conceived of in Marcuse's Marxist perspective (iii.).

i   *Essence and Normativity*
As already indicated, Marcuse endorsed the classical philosophical idea of dialectics, thus attributing to philosophical thinking the task of grasping reality in its truth. Philosophical thought is conceptual, and is therefore not limited to what is immediately experienced. Thought necessarily transcends empirical reality, and this means that idealism is inherent in philosophy. What is more, for Marcuse it is precisely this idealism that makes philosophy critical, since philosophical thought finds itself "blocked by the reality from which it dissociates itself" (ODM, 135 (S_M 7, 151)). When empirical reality, i.e. reality as it is immediately experienced, appears not to have achieved its truth – for example, when society is still not just, life still not good, and human beings still not human – then it is important that empirical reality does not present an insurmountable obstacle for realizing true reality.

For Marcuse the point is thus that linguistic analysis cannot be upheld as a philosophical project. To fulfil its task, philosophy cannot leave reality as it is; doing so would be an expression of the ideological empiricism of one-dimensional thought, and against this Marcuse asserts the right of the contradiction, giving as an example a statement by his friend Ernst Bloch saying "that which is cannot be true" (ODM, 120 (S_M 7, 138)). Marcuse's intention is to defend Bloch's "ridiculous" and "outrageous" statements as reasonable, and the idea is to do this by developing the understanding of the concept of dialectics. Marcuse thus argues that, to attain the truth of reality, reason has to become dialectical, being thus realized both in theory and praxis.

To reach this point, Marcuse first had to establish the facts of the "closed operational universe of advanced industrial civilization", and that was the object of the first part of ODM. Marcuse's second point is then to argue that this societal reality is already in itself a contradiction, "with its terrifying harmony of freedom and oppression, productivity and destruction, growth and regression" (ODM, 124 (s_M 7, 140)). Considered as a whole, the real world *is* both contradictory and antagonistic, i.e. positively given, but afflicted with want and negativity, constantly threatened by destruction, and at the same time structured as a cosmos. Philosophy is doing its thinking within "a universe which is broken in itself", at the same time being both "appearance and reality, untruth and truth", "unfreedom and freedom" (ODM, 125 (s_M 7, 141)), "is and ought" (ODM, 133 (s_M 7, 149)). In reality, "stabilizing tendencies" alternate with "subversive elements", and the "power of the positive" with "negative thinking" (ODM, 124 (s_M 7, 140)). It is in order to be able to cut through the harmonizing ideology of positive one-dimensionality which impedes the true conception of reality, that reason must be dialectical, and that dialectics must be negative. This is the condition of critique as a reasonable enterprise.

For Marcuse, the tension between appearance and reality, as well as that between 'is' and 'ought', is ontological, i.e. they are both real. It is this "living contradiction" between essence and appearance that Marcuse calls "inner negativity" (ODM, 141 (s_M 7, 156)), with reference to Hegel. The ambition to deal with this negativity thus prompts reason to become dialectical. In contrast to formal logic, for which the content does not matter, Marcuse emphasizes that dialectical logic is "determined by the real which is concrete" (ODM, 140 (s_M 7, 156)), i.e. antagonistic and constantly changing. That the two-dimensionality of philosophy is reduced to one-dimensionality by the operationalism of modern scientific thought and technology is critical, since the lack of dialectical thinking in modern philosophy makes it unable to fulfil its task as philosophy. The task of philosophy is to grasp reality in its truth, and in order to grasp an antagonistic, changing reality, philosophy itself must be dialectical.

ii   *Negativity and Critique*
In the article "On the History of Dialectics", Marcuse emphasizes that stressing the function of the negative is something "qualitatively new in Hegelian dialectics" (s_M 8, 217). To explain how dialectics and negativity are linked by necessity, in *Reason and Revolution* Marcuse thus refers to Hegel who emphasizes "over and over that dialectics has this negative character." As Hegel puts it in the *Science of Logic*, "the negative 'constitutes the genuine dialectical procedure.'" The basic idea is twofold: Dialectical thought thus implies a negation of "the fixed and static categories of common sense", and as such it is critical in relation to what is immediately experienced. At the same time, however, negativity can be said to be inherent in reality, since "nothing that exists is true in its given form. Every single thing has to evolve new conditions and forms, if it is to fulfil its potentialities." Marcuse can therefore also quote Hegel, stating

that "the first step 'towards the true concept of Reason' is a 'negative step'",[44] namely critique.

In *ODM*, Marcuse returns to classical Greek philosophy and its concept of reason. Reason is the cognitive faculty by which we relate to reality in terms of truth and falsity. Reality is, and truth therefore primarily refers to that which is, i.e. being, rather than to propositions. Plato's idea is that if one gets to see the world as it "really is" (ODM, 125 (S_M 7, 142)), then one will act in accordance with the truth. Reality is more than just one-dimensional, and according to Marcuse, the Greeks, and especially Plato, were able to unite epistemology and ethics, is and ought, into one dialectical way of thinking. Moreover, to the Plato of the later dialogues, being is subject to change. Finite being is, as given, thus unrealized being. Being changes from potentiality and actuality until it is realized as true, complete and independent in itself, and for Marcuse that means that being, and especially human and social being, is ultimately realized as "free" (ODM, 127 (S_M 7, 143)).

For the Greeks, the point is that philosophy, by affirming conceptually how reality is and can be, at the same time denies that which is the case empirically. In the Platonic dialectics of the dialogues, dialectical thought thus transforms reality into truth by subverting the immediate experience, and for Marcuse this ontological scheme of the Ancient Greeks remains valid. The idea of a fundamentally divided and antagonistic reality is what makes reasonable the allegedly ridiculous and outrageous statement of Bloch, i.e. "that which is cannot be true". True human being is still a potential to be realized; that which is, factual being, is only apparently true and thus in reality false. To be even more specific: "Seen in the light of a truth which appears [...] falsified or denied, the given facts themselves appear false and negative" (ODM, 133 (S_M 7, 149)).

This is where the negativity of dialectics comes in. The conceptualization and, even more, the realization of the essential potentiality implies a "subversion of the established order", and the subversive character of truth in turn has "an imperative quality" (ODM, 132 (S_M 7, 148)). 'Is' thus implies 'ought', and this is not limited to just the form of dialectical logic. This holds true for all philosophy that wants to come to grips with reality. As Marcuse puts it:

> The propositions which define reality affirm something that is not (immediately) the case; thus they contradict that which is the case, and they deny its truth. The affirmative judgment contains a negation which disappears in the propositional form (S is p) (ODM, 132 (S_M 7, 148)).

---

44 Herbert Marcuse, *Reason and Revolution* (1941/55), 2nd ed. (London and New York: Routledge, 2000), p. 123 (S_M 4, 115).

Thus, when we as philosophers argue that man *is* free, that he *has* inalienable rights, that he *is* a political animal, or that he *is* reasonable, then we "do not state a fact but the necessity to bring about a fact". The copula 'is' states an 'ought', the "categorical statement thus turns into a categorical imperative" (ODM, 133 (s_M 7, 148–49)), and the verification becomes a practical process of realizing what ought to be. The dialectical movement of philosophical thought therefore "has political content". Socrates's search for definitions of justice, virtue and knowledge becomes subversive, because "the concept intends a new polis" (ODM, 134 (s_M 7, 149)). It is in this sense that dialectical thinking for Marcuse implies both critique and liberation in relation to any given social reality. As he puts it in the 1960 preface to *Reason and Revolution*: "The liberating function of negation in philosophical thought depends upon the recognition that the negation is a positive act".[45] Nevertheless, the Hegel scholar Pierre-Jean Labarrière concludes that by "the author" of ODM we find no "true dialectical negativity";[46] a conclusion which I find completely incomprehensible.

iii   *History as a Real Possibility*

As Gangl has noted, already in 1936, Marcuse "mobilizes the essence against the facts", using the "dialectical concepts" to transcend social reality in order to "achieve the real possibilities contained in the essence itself".[47] This points to another important aspect of reality obscured by the one-dimensionality of late modernity; namely the "historical dimension". In ODM, Marcuse stresses that the negative thinking of dialectics entails the possibility to recognize the historical character of the contradictions of reality. Dialectical thinking thus reveals the temporal dimension of real social contradictions; that is, both their past and their future, both their origin in a particular form of society and the possibility of "their mediation", i.e., of overcoming the antagonism by actualizing "the potentiality as historical possibility", by realizing thought "as historical event" (ODM, 97 (s_M 7, 116)). And for Marcuse it is important to emphasize it as a potential or a possibility. There is no guarantee that history will ever realize true reality. As he puts it: "As historical process, the dialectical process involves consciousness"; therefore

---

45   Herbert Marcuse, "A Note on Dialectics" (1960), in Marcuse, *Reason and Revolution*, 3rd ed. (Boston: Beacon Press, 1969), p. x.

46   Pierre-Jean Labarrière, "De la Raison comme histoire. Un confrontation avec Hegel", *Archives de Philosophie* 52, no. 3 (1989), p. 402.

47   Gangl, "Quelques implications sociales de la technologie moderne", p. 414.

the determinate negation of capitalism occurs *if* and *when* the proletariat has become conscious of itself and of the conditions and processes which make up its society. This consciousness is prerequisite as well as an element of the negating practice (ODM, 222 (S_M 7, 234)).

According to Marcuse, for Marx negation is also inherent in reality, in an even more concrete sense than was the case for Hegel. *Reason and Revolution* thus argues that the general idea of Marxian dialectics is that negation is "the moving and creative principle" of historical and social reality.

> Every fact is more than a mere fact; it is a negation and restriction of real possibilities. Wage labor is a fact, but at the same time it is a restraint on free work that might satisfy human needs. Private property is a fact, but at the same time it is a negation of man's collective appropriation of nature.[48]

But negation is not just a restriction. Negation is also the principle for overcoming the negativity of reality: "The negativity of capitalist society lies in its alienation of labor; the negation of this negativity will come with the abolition of alienated labor." For Marx, negation is contestation and critique, and Marcuse can therefore quote Marx affirmatively, when he concludes that dialectic can only be understood as the "dialectic of negativity".[49] In the social world, the negativity manifests itself in the "contradictions of class society", working as the "motor of social progress",[50] and "the negativity of reality" therefore "becomes a historical condition". This means that, for Marx, the "dialectical method" has become a "historical method".[51]

For Marcuse, the historical character of the "Marxian dialectic" embraces both the negativity of reality as immediately experienced and the negation of this reality, which can be understood as "two different phases of the same historical process". As he says: "The negative state as well as its negation is a concrete event within the same totality." Still, Marcuse emphasizes that this process does not happen automatically. The "truth" of the old situation can only be "set free" "by an autonomous act on the part of men".[52] A negation is always an act of a consciousness, and historical progress therefore is the result

---

48   Marcuse, *Reason and Revolution*, 2nd ed., p. 282 (S_M 4, 249).
49   Marcuse, *ibid.* (S_M 4, 249).
50   *Ibid.*, p. 312 (S_M 4, 274).
51   *Ibid.*, p. 314 (S_M 4, 275–76).
52   *Ibid.*, p. 315 (S_M 4, 276).

of human action, i.e. praxis. As he makes it clear in the 1966 article "On the History of Dialectics", "thinking", and thus "subjectivity", continues, also in Marxian dialectics, to be "a crucial factor of the dialectical process: The function of class consciousness bears witness to this" (S_M 8, 224).

D   Imagining Liberation

In *ODM*, Marcuse makes it clear that the "obstacles that stand in the way of materialization are definable political obstacles" (ODM, 232 (S_M 7, 243)), and again he emphasizes that historical progress always has an element of freedom and chance; if not it is just nature, and: "History is the negation of Nature" (ODM, 236 (S_M 7, 247)). That, however, also means that the "critical theory of society" cannot make any promises or predictions regarding the actual chances for realizing a reasonable society. In the final chapter of ODM, Marcuse does not leave much ground for optimism: "Confronted with the omnipresent efficiency of the given system of life, its alternatives have always appeared utopian" (ODM, 254 (S_M 7, 264)). That does not mean that Critical Theory or, as he says here, "dialectical theory" is refuted by the current malaise, "but it cannot offer the remedy". Originally Critical Theory could understand itself as part of a historical practice responding to that theory, defining historical possibilities and human necessities, but "at present", i.e. fifty years ago, "the practice gives no such response" (ODM, 253 (S_M 7, 264)).

In the critical perspective of classical Critical Theory, all this could seem true in 1964. A few years later, however, Marcuse himself had good reason to be much more optimistic, and even in the 1980s, his diagnosis in *ODM* of the "stability of capitalism" could seem "exaggerated".[53] Moreover, from a European perspective, the alleged pessimism of *ODM* could be seen as an expression of the specific conditions in the USA during the 1950s, and one could express hopes of the New Left of the late 1960s and 1970s breaking the closure of one-dimensional discourse.[54] In such a perspective, one could further argue that the one-dimensionality experienced by "any traveller" in the US – "highways all the same, supermarkets all the same, middleclass suburbs all the same, anywhere you find restaurant chains and motels decorated in the same way" – was a sign of capitalist expansion having reached "monopoly capitalism"

---

53   Douglas Kellner, "Herbert Marcuse's Reconstruction of Marxism", in *Critical Theory*, ed. Rasmussen and Swindal, vol. I, p. 382.

54   See José E. Rodríguez- Ibáñez, *El sueño de la razón* (Madrid: Taurus, 1982), p. 109.

and thus turned "dysfunctional".[55] This diagnosis made it reasonable to conceive of a future beyond capitalism. In contrast to this alienating system, the constructive Critical Theory of Habermas thus provided the idea of the life-world where human beings could realize the possibility of undistorted symbolic interaction.

However, as the contemporary social critique of Honneth indicates, it is still relevant to criticize specific affronts of human beings as victims of various forms of marginalization. Taking the critical argument of ODM seriously, it is obvious that today the one-dimensionality experienced in the daily life of a consumer in the Western world has expanded even more. This is one of the main characteristics of what we now call globalization, and one might therefore be tempted to simply update Marcuse's diagnosis to the global level and conclude that, in spite of his Critical Theory, he in fact – as many revolutionary Marxists – underestimated the innovative potentials and the strength of capitalism. We might be in the phase of late monopoly capitalism, but somehow it seems that this phase can last indefinitely, or at least until the globe cannot sustain our very costly form of human life any more. As Horkheimer would phrase it during WW II, we have in fact reached the *Eclipse of Reason*.

Still, in the spirit of Marcuse, there are also other ways to think of a practice informed by theory. One can thus remind oneself of 1968, 1989 or, more recently, the Arab Spring in 2011. Nobody seems to be able to predict when protests become revolutions, and even though the results are not always that impressive, they at least confirm that the basic human intuition of justice, and especially of injustice, is somehow intact and has been transmitted successfully from generation to generation. In the spirit of Habermas, who argues that people can achieve undistorted symbolic interaction in the public realm and the life-world when not troubled by the system, i.e. the economy and the state, one can also point to the millions of people involved in obtaining peaceful solutions to all kinds of conflicts all over the world every day. It is thus not totally unreasonable, or without empirical justification, to insist on the possibilities of progress and even the survival of human civilization.

As Schmidt has noticed,[56] an important point for Marcuse is that Freud was wrong in regarding culture as burdensome in itself. In a small book on *Psychoanalysis and Politics* from 1968, Marcuse thus argues that human beings work because they experience it as a pleasurable activity. Employing the optimism

---

55   Rodríguez-Ibañez, *ibid.*, 235.
56   See Schmidt, "Herbert Marcuse – Versuch einer Vergegenwärtigung seiner sozialphiloso-
       phischen und politischen Ideen", pp. 37–38.

of the original existential Marxism, and of Schiller's letters *On the Aesthetic Education of Man*, work is conceived of as a "play" which supplies the needs for living, "not a means for living, but life itself". The Freudian conflict between the principles of pleasure and reality is not an ontological necessity, and neither is the idea of culture as conditioned by the traumatic change of human being into "an instrument of alienated labor". For Marcuse, culture as domination is only "one specific form of culture".[57] It is therefore possible to think of "the free society as a real possibility for everybody", namely a society where "growing mechanization"[58] means that progress does not imply more alienation, prohibition, and renunciation, but a real liberation from all such restrictions; in short: "a better world, in which the *Dasein* fulfills itself".[59]

Hence, in ODM Marcuse ultimately argues that advanced technological development can be seen as enabling the realization of hitherto metaphysical ideas such as "the Good Life, the Good Society, Permanent Peace" (ODM, 230 (s_M 7, 241)). New technology thus opens a possibility for a "new human reality – namely, existence in free time on the basis of fulfilled vital needs", realizing "the art of living beyond the necessities and luxuries of domination", "transcending the technological rationality" (ODM, 231 (s_M 7, 242)). Through history, nature becomes part of the human world, and in this transformation nature is realized as "non-natural" (ODM, 236 (s_M 7, 247)). As he puts it: "Civilization produces the means for freeing nature from its own brutality, its own insufficiency, its own blindness by virtue of the cognitive and transformative power of Reason" (ODM, 238 (s_M 7, 249)).

Reason is for Marcuse to be understood as "post-technological rationality" (ODM, 238 (s_M 7, 249)), which he identifies as the rationality in arts. The "artistic", or "aesthetic", transformation of nature, linking "mastery and liberation", thus becomes a model for political liberation. The "conquest of nature" does not always involve "ferocity". As he puts it: "Cultivation of the soil is qualitatively different from destruction of the soil, [as is] extraction of natural resources from wasteful exploitation" (ODM, 240 (s_M 7, 251)).

Liberation in the advanced industrial society is for Marcuse a "reduction of overdevelopment"; a liberation from the "affluent society". The modern capitalist society during the Cold War Marcuse described as a "prosperous warfare and welfare state" with a "permanent mobilization" (ODM, 242 (s_M 7, 253)) against real or imagined enemies, and today, in the middle of the War against

---

57   Herbert Marcuse, *Psychoanalyse und Politik* (Frankfurt a.M.: Europäische Verlagsanstalt, 1968), p. 27.

58   *Ibid.*, p. 48.

59   *Ibid.*, p. 51.

Terror, this is even more the case, even though the enemy has changed. Liberation from such a society would therefore mean a "pacification of existence" (ODM, 243 (s_M 7, 254)), which for Marcuse means both living peacefully with nature and with each other. Marcuse's project thus aims at realizing a "technology of pacification" (ODM, 240 (s_M 7, 251)), which is qualitatively different from technology as we know it. Pacification presupposes mastery of nature, but the point is that mastery can be both repressive and liberating.

For the young Habermas, however, this idea of relating to nature in a non-dominating way is just religious "mystique" about resurrecting the "fallen nature",[60] characteristic of not just Marcuse, but also of Marx and of the first generation of Critical Theory in general. Claus Offe has in the same spirit denounced the project as vulnerable to charges of "obscurantism",[61] whereas Robert Steigerwald argues against the whole idea of a negative dialectics and of something qualitatively new that we cannot recognize as of yet. According to him, Marcuse simply speaks the language of "negative theology",[62] and this might actually be an adequate characterization. As Per Jepsen has brought to our attention, the late Horkheimer explicitly argued that "Negative theology is also valid in politics".[63] For Steigerwald the point is that when Marcuse argues that socialism demands human nature to be changed, i.e. when the ambition is to realize the idea of a new human being, then he reduces socialism to just a "beautiful dream". When he furthermore criticizes the idea of the "organization in itself", he robs the working class of its only real weapon, namely its organization of itself, and the result is the "disarmament of the revolutionary forces". Marcuse's revolutionary radicality can therefore be accused of being "defeatist and positivist in disguise".[64]

As we have seen, Marcuse took great pains in rebutting those who would accuse Marxism of historical determinism, i.e. of believing the progress of civilization to be caused automatically by the superhuman dialectics between the forces and the relations of production. Still, among other Marxists, this effort to define dialectics as both human and open-ended only earned him accusations

---

60   Jürgen Habermas, "Technik und Wissenschaft als >Ideologie<", in Habermas, *Technik und Wissenschaft als >Ideologie<* (Frankfurt a.M. : Suhrkamp, 1968), p. 54.

61   Claus Offe, "Technik und Eindimensionalität", in *Antworten auf Herbert Marcuse*, ed. Jürgen Habermas (Frankfurt a. M.: Suhrkamp, 1968), p. 76.

62   Robert Steigerwald, "Wie kritisch ist Marcuses 'kritische Theorie'?" in *Die 'Frankfurter Schule' im Lichte des Marxismus*, ed. Heiseler *et al.*, p. 100.

63   Per Jepsen, "Aporien negativer Politik? Gesellschaftsutopie und Askese der politischen Theorie im Spätwerk Horkheimers und Adornos", in *Staat und Politik bei Horkheimer und Adorno*, ed. Ulrich Ruschig and Hans-Ernst Schiller (Baden- Baden: Nomos, 2014), p. 210.

64   Steigerwald, "Wie kritisch ist Marcuses 'kritische Theorie'?" p. 98.

of subjectivism, idealism and, as Steigerwald puts it, "petit-bourgeois radicalism".[65] The charge is that Marcuse, by the radical negation of historical continuity, equates the Marxist determinate negation with an "unmediated jump",[66] a "wonder" that does not require "preparation",[67] and this again reduces the legitimacy of organizing and disciplining the anti-capitalist forces.

The critique is thus that Marcuse's project is itself ideological, i.e. that his endorsement of the New Left is false, because it weakened the Old Left and thus the left as such. However, as Kellner notes, Marcuse's project "is surely revolutionary, but not irrational or logically impossible".[68] Marcuse may be more radical and speculative than most of his contemporaries, but the charge of mysticism or radicality does not in itself provide an *a priori* or conceptual reason to discard attractive ideas as merely ideological. In fact, confronted with today's global crises, i.e. military confrontations, capitalist economy and climate changes, it seems perfectly reasonable to try to conceive of technology in a qualitatively new way, as proposed by Marcuse. And confronted by the development of still more inhuman means of exploitation and weapon systems, the idea of an inherently peaceful kind of technology also seems more appealing than ever. This way of conceptualizing our future as humanity might seem far-fetched and unreal, expressing the utopian dreams of a revolutionary refusing to turn old and grey. But let's get real: What is the alternative?

---

65   Steigerwald, ibid., p. 102.

66   Ibid., p. 99.

67   Ibid., p. 100.

68   Kellner, *Herbert Marcuse and the Crisis of Marxism*, p. 332.

Postscript: Continuing the Critique of Capitalism and Political Economy

Within Critical Theory, Marx's critique of political economy occupies a very special place. When it comes to critique of ideology – i.e. demonstrating the ruling ideas that present themselves in the interest of all, and are maybe even believed to be so, yet in reality only serve the interests of the rulers[1] – the critique of political economy is simply the paradigmatic case, offering a conceptual demonstration of inherent contradictions of the ruling economic thought, supplemented with a critique of the real injustice and suffering caused by capitalist society having allowed itself to submit to such thought. The critique of liberal political economy is simply an essential part of the foundation on which classical Critical Theory rests.

Engaging in the critique of political economy is motivated by the immediate experience in modern capitalist society of alienation and social injustice. Nevertheless, in the work realized after WW II, Critical Theory has to a large extent neglected detailed discussions of economy. From the outset, political economy has been the attempt to understand and govern the economy of a society, and this is also the case with the critique of it. Neglecting this kind of economic thought can only contribute to the experience of mystification and impotence in relation to, not only the perceived dynamics of economy, but also the government of society. Hence, giving up on the critique of political economy can only strengthen what is already the most powerful ideology and ideological practice of the existing rulers of capitalist society, i.e. liberal economics.

As a modest contribution to revert this unfortunate tendency, this postscript offers a critical investigation into contemporary political economy. As an initial indication of the point of this work, let me quote the great British economist John Maynard Keynes: "The outstanding fault of the economic society in which we live is its failure to provide for full employment and its arbitrary and inequitable distribution of wealth and incomes".[2] This is the reason why we have criticized capitalism and the dominant political economy for more than two centuries; today, after decades of globalization, this seems an even more

---

1 See Karl Marx and Friedrich Engels, *Die deutsche Ideologie* (1845–46), in Marx & Engels, *Werke* (MEW), vol. 3 (Berlin: Dietz Verlag, 1969), pp. 46–47.
2 John Maynard Keynes, *The General Theory of Employment, Interest, and Money* (1935), Harbinger ed. (New York: Harcourt, Brace and World, 1964), p. 372.

urgent task than in my youth, when most people in the Western World were still working to realize some kind of social democratic welfare state.

I will try to give substance to these intuitive conclusions concerning capitalism by deconstructing the idea of political economy in order to reveal its ideological character. Hence, its categories pose as universally valid, but in reality, are they very particular, being especially beneficial for some rather than others (A). As an example, I analyse the theory of comparative advantage that has been recognized as crucial in economics for more than two centuries (B). I then argue that the neo-liberal offensive is indeed the result of a coordinated effort by certain protagonists, but that it is difficult to decide whether the project has been political or just the aggregated result of the individual efforts of a multitude of egoists (C). Whatever is the case, the neo-liberal critique of neo-classical economics provides ideological support for creating such entrepreneurs that take little, if any, interest in societal stability or other traditional aims of political economy (D). In such a world of radicalized capitalism, I finally return to the question of value that has somehow haunted me for decades, wondering if the critique of political economy can develop a broader concept of value recognizing both labour and utility (E).

A   Introductory Moves

It is arguable that before venturing into a specific empirical discipline such as political economy, first I should make my theoretical and methodological presuppositions clear. However, what I am doing here is not social science; it is philosophy, i.e. social and political philosophy, just as it has been the case in Critical Theory since Horkheimer became professor in social philosophy. What is at stake in the investigative reflection is conceptual clarification and an argument about normative issues. What is more, I have already committed myself to a particular way of relating to reality, arguing that classical Critical Theory still offers insights worth maintaining. Still, the philosophical argument in itself has to be strong enough to be self-sustained, at least within the philosophical community writ large, and that liberates us from social scientific commonplaces about theory and methodology as those just referred to.

The first problem, however, concerns what we want to criticize. Even taking economy as the object of enquiry, in many languages there is a fundamental ambiguity, namely that the word 'economy' is often used as referring to both to the real world object, i.e. the existing system of exchanges, and to the scientific discipline studying it, and that is the case even within that discipline, i.e. even among professional academic economists.[3] Although it is common to distinguish between 'economy' as referring to the subject matter and 'economics' as referring to the discipline studying it, still 'political economy' overlaps with 'economics', and I have made no attempt to change this wording in the following reflections.

In the 'critique of political economy' this ambiguity is even somehow constitutive, since the critique is directed at both the subject matter and the discipline. Hence, as critical theorists we most often want to criticize both, the basic intuition being that what must be criticized is both the actual economy as a functioning system, i.e. capitalism as reproducing social injustice, and the representation of this system, i.e. the liberal ideology telling us that private property rights and free market trade are to the benefit of all. This is also what will be the case in the present analysis. Therefore, in spite of – or maybe even because of – my soft spot concerning human suffering, and in spite my merely cultural Marxism, insisting on my continental European biases, I will strongly protest against being labelled a 'liberal'.[4]

Before being able to pursue my real agenda, I must however make some introductory moves. First, I have to make clear that the injustice of capitalism is presupposed and that no further analysis of justice will be undertaken in the present context (i).[5] Even though I have chosen to conduct my critique under Marx's classical title, there will be little reference to him; instead, I have chosen to focus on my contemporaries (ii). Still, some have to be selected at the expense of others, and I present some of the criteria used to avoid mere arbitrariness, thus introducing my idea of the disciplinary landscape of economics (iii).

i   *Injustice, Not Justice*
Hence, before going further into analysing and criticizing the material realities of social injustice under capitalism, one small thing has to be dealt with, namely the very idea of justice. As a philosopher writing in English, it would be natural first to discuss *A Theory of Justice* by Rawls, all the more since I have

---

3   See, e.g., Paul A. Samuelson, *Economics*, 10th ed. (Tokyo: McGraw-Hill Kogakusha, 1976), p. 3. In the present chapter the following page references are indicated in brackets in the text as EC, nn.

4   See also my recent critique of liberalism, Asger Sørensen, "Approaching Political Philosophy through the Critique of Liberalism", *Acta Politologica* 6, no. 3 (2014), which will appear as Ch. 1 in DDD III, *Justice, Peace and Formation.*

5   It will, however, be discussed in DDD III, especially in Part One.

written about it before.[6] In fact, being concerned about not only the inequality that we simply encounter, but being convinced *prima facie* that this inequality is unjust due to the exploitation of those deprived of property rights to the means of production, this would merit revisiting the critique of Rawls originally proposed by Robert Nozick. The existing injustice is not only a matter of natural or social contingency, as Rawls sometimes seems to believe. Capitalism is not a lottery, and the unequal distribution resulting from it is not arbitrary. Capitalism is a historical formation structurally and systematically organizing production in order to benefit the class with the ownership of production or controlling the means of production, i.e. the bourgeois class. The struggle between the various forms of liberals and critics from within a Marxist horizon is precisely related to the legitimacy of the transfer of value from workers to capitalists, i.e. those historical issues on which Nozick insists in opposition to Rawls.

Being a good libertarian, Nozick insists on a minimal state as the only just political order,[7] whereas social democrats *et al.* would typically endorse a more comprehensive state in order to be able to regulate the dynamics of the economy. But just like Nozick, the left is typically not only concerned about different end-states. Nozick argues that justice demands being concerned about historical principles and property rights;[8] and so do the classical leftists. They are also concerned about how the injustice in question came about and continues to be reproduced in capitalist society. Like Nozick, they – i.e. we – are not satisfied with Rawls's rational role modelling and abstract principles for hypothetical competitive situations, where ideal and instrumentally rational actors occupy themselves with the just distribution of all conceivable goods as if nobody were responsible for the factual injustice encountered.

As Vittorio Bufacchi has recently argued, whereas justice has received its fair share of philosophical attention, injustice has been "mysteriously"[9] neglected,

---

6   See, e.g., Mogens Chrom Jacobsen and Asger Sørensen, "Indledning" and "Efterskrift", in Rawls, *En teori om retfærdighed* (Frederiksberg: Det lille forlag, 2005), respectively pp. 9–15 and 551–68; Asger Sørensen, "Deontology – born and kept in Servitude by Utilitarianism", *Danish Yearbook of Philosophy* 43, 2008, pp. 69–96; Asger Sørensen, "Justice and Democracy. Some Preliminary Reflections", in *Bioética, neuroética, libertad y justicia*, ed. Francisco Javier López Frías *et al.* (Granada: Editorial Comares, 2013), pp. 494–508; and Sørensen, "Approaching Political Philosophy through the Critique of Liberalism". The piece on deontology will be included in DDD II, *Discourse, Value and Practice*, whereas the one on justice and democracy, as well as the critique of liberalism, will appear in DDD III.

7   See Robert Nozick, *Anarchy, State, and Utopia* (Oxford: Blackwell, 1999), p. ix.

8   See, e.g., Nozick, *ibid.*, pp. 153–55.

9   Vittorio Bufacchi, *Social Injustice*, 2nd ed. (London: Palgrave MacMillan, 2015), p. 1.

and it would be appropriate to "rebalance" things a bit. I agree, and I hope to be able to return to this, since I have a hunch that there may be some natural explanation to the mystery in terms of ideology; in this context, however, I will stick to an intuitive idea of injustice emphasizing lack of equality as well as of freedom, and let this idea guide me in my critique of capitalism and economics. In fact, this is where we all start, not only Bufacchi but also, for instance, Amartya Sen, who in his *The Idea of Justice* introduces the argument by referring to Charles Dickens's horrifying stories about child labour in 19th century Britain.[10]

As the eminent Spanish economist Pedro Montes remarks, it can be very difficult to define the good, but "it is easy to recognize the bad",[11] and even Rawls admits that for him political philosophy functions as a remedy for anger. Hence, as he puts it, "political philosophy may try to calm our frustration and rage against our society and its history".[12] However, as the historian Perry Anderson remarks: "Rage: who would have guessed Rawls capable of it – against his society or its history? But why should it be calmed?"[13] Like Anderson, I believe that it is precisely this rage that ultimately facilitates acquiring knowledge about the essential social realities of capitalism.

ii   *Choosing a Strategy for Criticizing*

Approaching the critique of political economy, we first have to get an idea of economy. In one sense, economy can be described as an auto-poetic and thus self-sustaining system, but since the causal drives of the system are basically more or less rational actors, the system becomes stronger, more stable and thus more resistant when the agents involved commit themselves to the kind of activities that uphold the system. Beliefs are thus important for economy, since they can affect economic activity within the economic system at all levels. However, beliefs are also important at the political level, where those in command are to take decisions about common issues, and further among those whose advice political decisions often rely on, i.e. academic economists. Important is thus the specific mediation between the individual causal drives and beliefs, namely that economics to a large extent is constituted by mathematical

---

10   See Amartya Sen, *The Idea of Justice* (Harvard: Harvard University Press, 2009), p. vii.

11   Pedro Montes, *El desorden neoliberal*, 3rd ed. (Madrid: Trotta, 1999), p. 19. In the present chapter the following page references are indicated in brackets in the text as DN, nn.

12   See John Rawls, *Justice as Fairness* (Cambridge, Mass.: Belknap Press of Harvard University Press, 2001), p. 3.

13   Perry Anderson, "Arms and Rights. Rawls, Habermas and Bobbio in an Age of War", *New Left Review*, no. 31 (2005), p. 39.

models that are produced by economists and implemented politically through legislation in order to regulate the economy of a society.

 Economics is the most directly effective ideology that exists in capitalist society. The economic policy chosen affects everybody, for good or for bad, and in practice it is always influenced by real life politics. A classic example is the situation in England during the 19th century, where the political compromise between mercantilism and liberalism brought the poor to the brink of starvation.[14] The nobility had an interest in protecting the prices on the crops they grew on their estates, and they succeeded in maintaining heavy duties on the import of corn. The bourgeois industrialists, on the other hand, referred to liberalism to determine the salary and workings conditions at the factories, and, workforce being plentiful, on the free labour market the salaries dropped. Hence, competition meant low salaries, but customs made food expensive; the result was a working class in dire misery, such as it was noticed by Dickens, Marx *et al.*

At all levels of society, the legitimacy of the economic and political system is at stake, and therefore it is important not just to refer to, describe and criticize actual existing injustice, but also to show how the established political economy functions as an ideology helping capitalism to appear, if not the ideal solution, then at least the only rational possibility of organizing our economic interactions. In modern times, this doctrine has been known as TINA: There Is No Alternative. This is where the question of liberalism becomes important. Liberalism is the ideology that makes capitalism appear not only necessary, but also attractive. Hence, a thorough critique of the injustice generated within capitalism must include a critique of liberalism as the ideology facilitating the legitimacy of the system.

Being a philosopher identifying with classical Critical Theory, and further with very strong Hegelian inclinations, this could be an argument for simply returning to Marx, following his line of thought from the critique of both authoritarian and liberal beliefs as ideologies to the critical in-depth reconstruction of the logic of capitalist economy. In fact, Marx is back on the intellectual agenda after years of neglect, and that is a good sign. It shows that concerned people, and especially the younger generation, now again attribute to economy the importance that it deserves. As Naomi Klein tells us, the American left allowed itself to be preoccupied with identity politics and representation exactly in the period when capitalism expanded to become truly global.[15]

---

14   See, e.g., Hartvig Frisch, *Europas kulturhistorie*, 2nd ed., ed. Svend Erik Stybe (København: Politikens forlag, 1962), vol. 4, p. 136.
15   See Naomi Klein, *No Logo*, 2nd ed. (London: Flamingo, 2001), pp. 212–24.

Nevertheless, as a spoiled bourgeois welfare child of the generation that received its intellectual formation in the post-modern and thus post-Marxist era, restricting myself to Marxian studies seems to me to be a little antiquated and dusty, and at risk of ultimately resulting in some quaint anachronistic dogmatism. Alternatively, I could have taken a closer look at what the most accomplished critical theorist have in fact been discussing in relation to political economy.[16] However, as far as I can see, the most important debate has been the discussion between Friedrich Pollock and Franz L. Neumann in the 1930s and 40s concerning whether capitalism can in fact survive its recurrent crises through the management of a state, be it democratic or totalitarian, or, as the latter would maintain, that its contradictions would persist and ultimately prove fatal, thus giving way to an emancipating and rational socialist organization of economy.[17]

Against orthodox Marxism, already in 1932–33 Pollock thus argued that in the "administered capitalism the depressions will be longer, the boom phases shorter and stronger, and the crises more destructive than in the times of 'free competition'";[18] hence, it was not capitalism "coming to an end but just its liberal phase".[19] Under such a "state capitalism", he concluded in 1941, "the profit motive is superseded by the power motive" and the "entrepreneurial and capitalist functions are [...] taken over by the Government".[20]

Interesting as these claims surely are, still more than a matter of economy, I take it that the said debate was primarily about the fundamentals of Marx's historical materialism, as it is argued persuasively by Moishe Postone.[21] For me, however, the critique of political economy is not tied to any particular philosophy of history. Capitalism is unjust, alienating and reifying, even if its fundamental contradictions do not create the historical dynamics conditioning the emergence of a societal order devoid of such life damaging consequences. Further, even though I insist on maintaining the main tenets of the classical version of Critical Theory, like Douglas Kellner I will insist that much

---

16   See, e.g., David Held, *Introduction to Critical Theory* (Berkeley and Los Angeles: University of California Press, 1980), pp. 40–76, and Douglas Kellner, *Critical Theory, Marxism and Modernity* (Cambridge: Polity Press, 1989), pp. 51–82.

17   See, e.g., David Ingram, *Critical Theory and Philosophy* (St. Paul, Minnesota: Paragon House, 1990), pp. 36–38, and Kellner, *Critical Theory, Marxism and Modernity*, pp. 52–64.

18   Pollock in Kellner, *Critical Theory, Marxism and Modernity*, p. 57.

19   Pollock in Kellner, *ibid.*, p. 59.

20   Pollock in Kellner, *ibid.*, p. 60.

21   See, e.g., Moishe Postone, "Critique, State, and Economy", in *The Cambridge Companion to Critical Theory*, ed. Fred Rush (Cambridge: Cambridge University Press, 2004), p. 169; see also the Interlude, Sect. C, where I give an account of parts of Postone's argument.

has indeed happened in capitalist societies since the 1940s and that therefore, in some aspects, Critical Theory "now requires development, revision and updating".[22] However, like Kellner I also insist that in capitalist society, for Critical Theory "economics plays a constitutive role in all social processes, so that it would be impossible to discuss politics concretely without discussing economics".[23]

I have therefore – in this postscript – taken the liberty to venture into another somehow both more and less ambitious project, in a way mimicking Marx himself, thus attempting to be even *plus royale que le roi*, while at the same time sidestepping the obligation to engage myself in the details of the economic writings of Marx or the classical Marxist discussions. Hence, I have set myself the task of understanding and criticizing, at least part of contemporary capitalist political economy, i.e. the present economic system and the ideology sustaining it, just as Marx, Pollock *et al.* studied their contemporaries.

iii   *Choosing Sources*

In light of the above, the most pertinent matter is therefore to decide to whom I should dedicate my attention among my many contemporaries. The main problem is that economy is a field so afflicted with vested interests and political aspirations that even if it poses, and is normally recognized, as a social science, it does not live up to any of the classical criteria that characterize science. We are dealing with a discipline with competing paradigms and research programmes, mutually hostile and maybe even incommensurable, where it is unclear whether even the most recognized theories and tools employed will allow reliable empirical predictions.[24] The challenge is therefore how to select my theoretical inspiration in a way that is not totally arbitrary, but actually with some probability will allow me to draw reasonable conclusions about the nature of economy, which will assist me in both aspects of the critical task: the critique of a economic system that in its practical functioning generates social injustice, and the critique of an ideological belief system that somehow succeeds in covering up what should be obvious. This means that I have to find an appropriate way of selecting to whom I should listen, apart of course from Marx himself.

Scanning the disciplinary landscape of political economy, mainstream economics appears to be well in tune with the dominating political inclinations of the north-western parts of the world, i.e. the rich countries dominating the world economy. Hence, for decades in mainstream economics it has been

---

22   Kellner, *Critical Theory, Marxism and Modernity*, p. 6.

23   Kellner, *ibid.*, p. 8.

24   See, e.g., the references in Ch. 2, mainly Sect. A.

difficult the see any alternatives to capitalism backed up ideologically by some kind of free market liberalism. Still, when it comes to specifying the names and characteristics supposed to be constitutive of the various programmes and categories, the task is not so easy. What I present here is therefore a very rough classification.

Within this broadly conceived approach to economics, the basic point of departure is the neo-classical economists, who were responsible for the so-called marginalist turn of political economy in the late 19th century, the main representatives being Stanley Jevons, Carl Menger and Léon Walras.[25] Neo-classical economics developed the idea about the general equilibrium being both the condition and the possible ideal outcome of a well-functioning economy. This idea was dominant up until Keynes, who in the 1930s questioned some of its basic elements. Today, one can distinguish between three main types of mainstream economics: Keynesian, monetarist and neo-liberal, all of them supported ideologically by increasingly rigid interpretations of liberal social and political philosophy. Of the three, Keynesian economics was dominant from the end of WW II until the 1970s, when monetarism became influential, whereas in the last three decades neo-liberalism has grown to become dominating in a lot of contexts.

Neo-liberalism has become a term with a very broad meaning. Nevertheless, I will try to restrict my use to a specific idea of political economy developed in the 20th century. Hence, the neo-liberals mainly include representatives of the so-called Austrian School, founded by Menger, such as Ludwig von Mises, Friedrich August Hayek and their followers. Where these are strongly critical of the neo-classical conception of economy, monetarists such as Milton Friedman can rather be considered radical successors to the pre-Keynesian neo-classicists. Today, variations of these non-Keynesian schools constitute mainstream economics taught at most universities and business schools. Even though they both tend to recommend the same economic measures, i.e. privatization, deregulation, marketization, etc., I will argue that their basic approaches to political economy are impossible to reconcile. Where monetarists appear to take seriously the interests of society as a whole, the neo-liberals only recognize one concern as legitimate, namely the freedom of the individual economic actor.

This is the basic problem. Political economy is supposed to guide us – i.e. our government – to the best political solutions for society at large, but when pressed, the neo-liberals have to admit that this is not what they do. Monetarist and, especially, neo-liberal approaches to political economy share this

---

fundamental shortcoming, and for me this means that liberalism and, especially, libertarianism is part of the problem rather than a possible solution, also when liberalism poses as political liberalism, as in the case of Rawls.[26] Hence, today a critique of political economy must primarily address the most libertarian variations of liberal economics, i.e. neo-liberalism and monetarism. However, as we shall see, even though they both share the liberal ideal of the free market, they disagree sharply on the idea of political economy, empirically as well as in terms of justice, i.e. descriptively as well as normatively.

Descriptively, the critique of mainstream economics gains added substance from the fact that some critics have concluded it to be either a species of applied mathematics or a formalization of liberal contract theory, or simply renounced it as mere rhetoric.[27] For me, however, the focus in the present context will be on the political and social shortcomings of these kinds of economics, i.e. the lack of a satisfying concern for what I take to be social justice. Even though alienation is sometimes recognized as an economic topic, being a consequence of the social division of labour (see, e.g., EC, 52–4), and even though this issue is of crucial importance when it comes to the perceived injustices of capitalism, in the present analysis I have nevertheless left it out of consideration, focusing instead on the distribution of wealth and power.

In the traditional spectrum of political economy, and assuming capitalism as inherently unjust, that leaves us with two approaches that merit acclaim, namely Keynesian and Marxian economics. Both of them of course presuppose and acknowledge various insights from both the classics of political economy and the contemporary schools just mentioned. Still, because of their concern for justice, Marx, Keynes and their followers are for me the main providers of legitimate approaches to political economy, and when it comes to the principled critique of capitalism, I consider Marxist inspiration to be especially relevant.

Still, one might argue that excluding from the very beginning the legitimacy of most of what is now considered the proper way to do economics by the majority of political and scientific authorities is simply not a serious way to handle an established and institutionally recognized scientific discipline. Instead of scholarly work, we will eventually end up with a badly conceived political tract determined by dogmatic preconception and prejudice. However, we only need to look back a few decades to find an establishment of economics that had for ages agreed to let itself be defined by Keynesian and Marxian

26   See, e.g., Sørensen, "Approaching Political Philosophy through the Critique of Liberalism".
27   See, e.g., William N. Butos, "Rhetoric and Rationality: A Review Essay of McCloskey's 'The Rhetoric of Economics'", *Eastern Economic Journal* 13, no. 3 (1987), pp. 295–304.

economics, i.e. precisely those approaches that I will refer to as authoritative (see, e.g., EC, 1). That may lead to claims that my reflections are outdated and thus not to be taken seriously; my answer is that contemporary economics is ideological and thus false.

As Bernat Riutort rightly observes, today the liberal preconditions have become hegemonic to such a degree that by proposing alternative approaches, one runs the risk of being labelled dogmatic or totalitarian.[28] This points to something important about political economy mentioned before, namely that it is so strongly linked to real life politics that it is difficult to uphold the cherished distinctions between values and facts, normativity and descriptivity, is and ought. Or, to put it in another way: in choosing to whom one ought to listen in economics, the 'ought' implied by the experiences of injustice and alienation gets mixed up with the 'ought' implied by the scientific ideal of truth.

So, this investigation is biased, but the claim is that it only takes into account the interest of the general public, thereby transcending mere partiality. Further, in order to balance the account that will result from this investigation, I have tried to let myself be inspired by a diversity of authorities, basically distinguishing between critique and affirmation, top and bottom, above and below. Hence, I take seriously, both the economics of the establishment in the Keynesian era, including their contemporary inheritors, as well as their Marxist critics, some of the latter being also institutionally recognized economists, while others are marginal figures, either scientifically or politically. Recognizing, however, the basic idea of marginality as a privileged standpoint when it comes to injustice and alienation,[29] relevant distinctions are furthermore man vs. woman, centre vs. periphery, black vs. white, North vs. South, the First vs. the Third world, etc. Finally, these social distinctions must be supplemented with a historical perspective. Hence, presupposing that capitalism is developing as a historical formation, the changes in the understanding of capitalist economy also seem to be linked to crucial historical events, foremost a series of crashes and crises. These ruptures have often made people reflect a little deeper on things that are normally taken for granted.

Referring to Hobsbawm, the Danish political economist Anders Lundkvist claims that the first global crisis of modern capitalism took place in 1857,[30] and

---

28   See Bernat Riutort, *La gran ofensiva. Crisis global y crisis de la Unión Europea* (Barcelona: Icaria editorial, 2014), p. 183.

29   See, e.g., Elizabeth Anderson, "Feminist Epistomology and Philosophy of Science", in *Stanford Encyclopedia of Philosophy* (2015).

30   See Anders Lundkvist, *Hoveder og Høveder. En demokratisk kritik af det private samfund. I. Privatejendom og markedsøkonomi* (København: Frydenlund, 2004), p. 306. In the present chapter the following page references are indicated in brackets in the text as POM, nn.

it was this crisis that prompted Marx to write his *Grundrisse*.[31] Hence, it was this first comprehensive crisis that gave rise to what is now commonly known as the critique of political economy, which, through the interpretations of Engels, Lenin, Trotsky, Stalin, Mao *et el.*, became the official doctrine behind the so-called realized socialism, which ruled more than half the world's population for decades in the 20th century. In the same vein, one can refer to the Wall Street crash in 1929 and the long crises of the 1930s as having set the agenda for Keynes and, together with the experiences of ww ii, defined the priorities of the economy in the western world in the post-war decades. This latter crisis was still mentioned on the first page of economics textbooks even in the 1970s (see, e.g., EC, 1).

A third crucial step was the big crisis provoked by the sudden increase in the price of petroleum in the 1970s in the wake of the Israeli attack on its Arabic neighbours. Part of this crisis was a new phenomenon, namely stagflation (see, e.g., EC, ix, 365), and the difficulties handling this brought the monetarist and neo-liberal agendas for economics into the game. Fourthly, there was the fall of the Berlin Wall in 1989, and in the wake of this, in the 1990s, the dissolution of the so-called realized socialism, or what was back then known as the Eastern Block. Without any political counter-weight this facilitated an accelerated implementation of monetarist and neo-liberal policies all over the globe, progressively dismantling social welfare and other defences against capitalist exploitation.

Fifth and finally, so far, is the series of crashes and crises that has circulated around the world since then, both defining and haunting the era of globalization, culminating in the 2008 Wall Street crash that has still not been overcome. Hence, at the time of writing, i.e. 2016, the predictions of the International Monetary Fund for the world economy are allegedly as depressing as in the 1970s,[32] and even though the central banks in the European Union (EU) and the USA have been pumping out enormous sums of money for years to stimulate the economy, the effects seem to be limited. Traditionally, increasing the amount of money would result in inflation, and combined with low interest rates this creates incentives for productive investments, but that has not happened this time. As it is recognized, the continued production of money in

---

31   See Das Marx-Engels-Lenin-Institut, "Vorwort", in Karl Marx, *Grundrisse der Kritik der politischen Ökonomie (Rohentwurf) 1857–1858* (1953), 2nd ed. (Berlin: Dietz Verlag, 1974), p. vii (later editions are included in MEW as vol. 42).

32   See Ed Conway, "Gloomy IMF hopes that something will turn up", *The Times*, April 15th 2016.

current years is a gigantic experiment,[33] and these recent developments have of course also produced a lot of critical reflections on economy. It is mainly from this literature that I draw my inspiration.

B   Approaching the Critique of Political Economy

Still, we need a better idea about what we are dealing with, i.e. what economy and economics are. Of course, we all have an idea about what economy is, and there is also an etymology worth consulting,[34] but it would be premature to stipulate a definition of what is to be discussed already at the outset of the process. Nevertheless, I will first delimit the idea of political economy that I will pursue, emphasizing its conflictual nature (i). Then I will present some of the various forms liberalism takes within political economy and economics (ii), illustrating the ideological assumptions by analysing two classical elements of political economy: first, the theory of comparative advantage (iii) and then Say's law (iv).

i   *From Economy to Economics*

As a first attempt to delimit the object in question, I will suggest that economy is about goods, i.e. production, distribution, circulation and consumption of goods. 'Goods' instead of resources, things, products or commodities, since the expression 'goods' indicates something we cherish, want or desire. So, we produce something that we want, we fabricate a good, or we may take something right away when we see it. As emphasized by Célestin Bouglé, one of Durkheim's students, this means that theft is the most economic way of acquiring something.[35]

We can, however, also be asked to give up the good in question, we can give it away to somebody else, or we can simply dispose of it. The good may continue its journey through other hands, it may be changed and be handled as another good, or it may also be consumed, used up or even deliberately destroyed. Hence, economy is this system of states and dynamics in the continuous exchange, transformation and movement of goods, and it is not unreasonable to

---

33   See, e.g., Philip Róin, "Når penge ikke er nok", *Information*, August 10th 2016, and Róin, "Hvor super er Mario Draghi?" *Information*, August 16th 2016.

34   See, e.g., *Intellectual History of Economic Normativities*, ed. Mikkel Thorup (New York: Palgrave MacMillan, 2016).

35   See Celestin Bouglé, *Leçon de sociologie sur l'évolution des valeurs* (Paris: Arman Collin, 1922), p. 103.

think of a general economy as an expansion of Marx's idea of work or production as "the metabolism between man and nature".[36]

Now, one can continue this line of thought in at least two directions, namely continuing and refining the description of the system of states and dynamics just presented, or one can already at this point introduce the basic conflict of interests that makes economy political. This first direction will bring one further towards the economic ontology of Bataille, or the sociology of Durkheim, which is a line of thought I have pursued before.[37] This time, however, I will pursue the second course, focusing directly on the political issues in a materialist perspective.

Taking as a point of departure the classical political economy, the most urgent matter is that goods may be scarce, or, more precisely, that a good may be in demand by more people than it can accommodate. Some goods can accommodate more than one person, but that does not mean that they can be used without limitations. For this reason, economists often emphasize a principle or law of scarcity (see, e.g., EC, 18).[38] This is not to say that the goods in question are not available at all. Goods may be plentiful, due to a generous nature or efficient industry, and a lot of goods in modern society may even be considered public. That was clearly what impressed Bataille, emphasizing how the surplus of life becomes manifest in so many instances.[39] When it comes to political thought, we can turn to Marcuse, who tried to envisage how human life would be beyond the exigencies put on us by scarcity,[40] and within the New Left of the 1960s there were various attempts to develop the idea of a post-scarcity society.[41] Still, it may be that at a particular time and location – defined by the specific needs and desires of some specific people – some goods are not available, be that because of distance, lack of technical means, other people's property rights or something else. The point is that concrete human beings have basic material needs, and some basic goods are necessary to sustain life, and if they are not available at a certain place within a certain period of time, then there is scarcity.

---

36   Karl Marx, *Das Kapital*, vol. 1 (1867), in MEW 23 (Berlin: Dietz Verlag, 1974), p. 57.

37   See above, Part One, i.e. Chs. 1 & 2.

38   See also, e.g., Poul Nyboe Andersen, Bjarke Fogh and Poul Winding, *Nationaløkonomi* (København: Einar Harcks forlag, 1952), p. 14.

39   See above, Ch. 2, Sect. B.

40   See, e.g., Barry Kãtz, *Herbert Marcuse and the Art of Liberation. An Intellectual Biography* (London: Verso, 1982), p. 144.

41   See, e.g., Murray Bookchin, *Post-Scarcity Anarchism* (1971) (London: Wildwood House 1974); for a critical analysis of Bookchin, see, e.g., Asger Sørensen, *I lyset af Bataille – politisk filosofiske studier* (København: Politisk Revy, 2012), pp. 442–48.

One may, in a bird's eye view, or in the long run, talk about scarcity as relative, since the goods in question could be delivered if the technology and the political will were there, or one may even believe that eventually there will be a general equilibrium between supply and demand. However, for those who do not have what they need here and now, this relative scarcity can ultimately become absolute, namely when they do not in time get enough nutrition to sustain their health or life. As Keynes is famously said to have replied to the free market optimists: "in the long run we are all dead!"[42] Life is fragile, people are precarious, and as the Danish professor of economics Hector Estrup has emphasized: basically, political economy is about survival.[43] So, political economy is dead serious. At a certain level, economy can be compared to war, where markets are battlefields with individual actors fighting for their own particular interests, each making strategies to win, conquer and eventually wipe out competitors in the field. As in sports, the means in economy are typically considered to be relatively peaceful; in economy, however, losing can be deadly.

This is why everybody is concerned with economy in some sense. There are those who insist that it is somewhat distasteful to be preoccupied with money, i.e. that money is not something one should talk about, but they are typically so well off that they can afford the luxury of ignoring the prospect of scarcity. For some, however, ignoring economics is a deliberate normative choice. Like Aristotle, they regard private business with contempt.[44] This stand is what makes high culture, fine arts, sports, etc. possible, i.e. a lot of what makes life worth living; therefore, ignoring how to earn money in order to spend one's time on something more worthwhile, should not be ridiculed. Moreover, ignorance is also a way of relating to the goods of economy. Spending your life on non-productive activities is the consumption made possible by the production and circulation of goods. However, in this case some have been in charge of the production, while others have been given the privilege to simply consume, and production is typically much more burdensome than consumption. This is in fact just another way of expressing the difference between those classes that, according to Marx, must necessarily be antagonistic and thus in conflict.

---

42   See, e.g., Paul Krugman, *The Return of Depression Economics*, 2nd ed. (London: Penguin, 2000), p. 156.

43   See Hector Estrup, *Nogle grundtræk af den økonomiske teoris udvikling* (1991), 2nd ed. (København: Jurist- og Økonomforbundets Forlag, 1998), p. 127.

44   See Aristotle, *Politics*, trans B. Jovett, in *The Complete Works of Aristotle*, ed. Jonathan Barnes (Princeton NJ: Princeton University Press, 1984/1995), vol. 2, *Pol.* 1257–58.

ii   *The Liberal Agenda of Political Economy*

Economy means potential, perceived and real conflicts. That some people have limited access to necessary goods is a real problem, as is the unequal distribution of the burdens that are necessary to uphold human life, and of the consummation that we all would like to take part in. There are various forms of scarcity in relation to needs and desires, and they are the basic challenges for classical political economy. Hence, the challenges are how to achieve the best possible allocation of the goods at hand, somehow balancing justice and efficiency, and the answer to such challenges is what divides people politically, according to their respective differences regarding beliefs, sensitivity, perspectives, interests, values etc.

Among some economists, this is known as the problem of "coordination", i.e. how the system of exchange is able to "coordinate the actions of the agents" (POM, 184). Traditionally, the two opposing poles within political economy are the belief in the self-regulating and harmonizing potentials of the economy as a system, and the scepticism about these potentials. Or, to put it differently, between those who are willing to let the free market system continue its chance to solve the said problem, in spite of strong indications of its shortcomings, and those who are outraged, repulsed or at least depressed by the social injustice produced, and the material suffering encountered, in globalized capitalism.

In between these poles, there are all kinds of trade-offs and compromises that we normally give headings such as 'social liberal' or 'social democratic'. However, even when leaning towards the latter of the two opposing poles just mentioned, i.e. the scepticism concerning self-regulation, further distinctions can be made between different ways of relating to the social reality encountered in a capitalist society. This is the reason why I have distinguished between 'dialectics' and 'democracy', the former departing from the idea of social reality as something out of reach and thus alienating, the latter assuming that political involvement is ready at hand and change for the better is possible. It is the former way of relating that I take for granted here, trying to reconstruct critically the ideological logic of the economy as an alien system and the societal ideology supporting such an economy, together producing experiences of alienation and injustice.[45]

Even though one could argue that Aristotle has provided the basics of political economy, distinguishing between the reasonable management of a household economy that he thinks worthy of philosophical attention and the pursuit of individual wealth, for which he has only contempt, let me nevertheless take the classical liberals as a point of departure, since they may still, thanks to both

---

45   Regarding the latter, i.e. democracy, I will postpone the reflections to DDD III.

neo-classicists and neo-liberals, be considered almost our contemporaries. In contrast to Aristotle, today it is common to appreciate business economy, thus endorsing Adam Smith's encouragement of pursuing individual business opportunities and his idea of God's invisible hand,[46] which has been secularized by neo-classical economics to become the general equilibrium theory.

It is sometimes thought that for Smith himself, the invisible hand was only of limited importance, being mainly employed in the discussion of foreign trade, where the possibilities of political regulation are more limited. However, as Joakim Kromann Rasmussen argues, the invisible hand does indeed play a crucial role for Smith, the roots of the liberal trust in the wonders of the free market economy being both metaphysical and religious.[47] Still, Smith's ideas about economy were political in the sense that he saw the coordination problem as a challenge and that he believed some government regulation of economy to be necessary.

Within the liberal tradition, however, there are also more radical examples of free market protagonists. One is Herbert Spencer, by now largely forgotten, but in his day in the 19th century the most important British philosopher. Spencer was a devout agnostic arguing for the rights of man against the dehumanizing power of the state, being also highly critical of the subjugation of other people under the British Empire. At the same time, however, he was a firm believer in natural selection, coining the famous expression 'survival of the fittest' after having read Darwin. The result was that at the time, whilst Dickens allowed himself to be outraged by the social consequences of primitive capital accumulation in England, Spencer argued against social welfare, referring to the natural order of things, and putting his faith in God's providence.[48]

Fundamental to this liberal relation to the world is thus one of wonder, puzzlement and awe, not knowing what God's intentions are, but trusting him, his hand and his foresight nevertheless, thereby being set free to pursue one's own private projects without having to care much about politics. This relation to God is sometimes, as in the case of Spencer, transposed into a similar trust in nature as God's creation, being also struck by the wonders of this creation uncreated by (wo)man. In this case, however, since nature is more ready at hand,

---

46   See, e.g., Adam Smith, *An Inquiry into the Nature and Causes of the Wealth of Nation* (1776) (Lausanne: MetaLibri Digital Library, 2007), p. 349 (IV.ii.9).

47   See Joakim Kromann Rasmussen, *The Invisible Hand: The Metaphysics in the Theory of Adam Smith Compared with Modern Economics* (Copenhagen Business School, 2011).

48   For a discussion of Spencer's metaphysics, see, e.g., Part Three of Asger Sørensen, *Den moralske virkelighed* (Malmö: NSU Press, 2012), and Sørensen, "Integreret integritet – idealet for integration", in *Pædagogiske værdier og politik*, ed. Kurt Nielsen and Anne-Marie Eggert Olsen (Århus: Danmarks Pædagogiske Universitets Forlag, 2007), pp. 23–40.

we have the possibility to investigate the regularities in a more systematic way, assuming God to have been reasonable in his or her creation after all, and one of the outcomes of such a scientific endeavour was the development in mathematics in the 18th and 19th centuries, bringing the inheritance from the Greeks beyond itself. Regardless of the details, from early on we see this strong alliance in economics between fundamentalist liberalism and advanced applied mathematics that is also characteristic of present-day neo-classical and monetarist economics. Among the first to pursue this strategy were Walras and Jevons, but as one of the leading Keynesian post-war economists, Paul Samuelson, tells the story, the decisive wave of mathematization of mainstream economics and the development of econometrics only took place in the 20th century after the 1930s (see EC, 844).

Characteristic of the liberal approach is a rather apolitical idea of political economy, leaving a high level of liberty to the individual civil society entrepreneur, but only little room for legitimate manoeuvring to whoever is in charge of the political decision making in the society in question. In other words, the liberal tradition provides the basic assumptions for the ideology of the 'nightwatchman' state, or the minimal state, that still haunts present-day politics and economics. Still, from classical political economy to monetarist economics, i.e. from Smith to Friedman, the coordination problem has been presupposed, thus making the harmony, the equilibrium and the stability of society legitimate concerns. The real radicals are only neo-liberal libertarians, such as Hayek, who do not idealize the free market by referring to the common good, but consider the market legitimate because it is the primary place for the realization of the legitimate self-interest of individual economic actors. In other words: the free market is the ideal social organization, simply because it sets the participants free to act as they see fit.

As mentioned already from the outset, I do not grant neo-liberal or monetarist economics much legitimacy, neither politically nor economically. As a contrast can be mentioned the conclusion by the French historian Fernand Braudel, claiming that capitalism is the exact opposite of a free market, i.e. it is not free at all, but based on force, and therefore it is dependent on the politics of the state. Capitalism will only triumph ultimately when it has taken over the state, "when it is the state".[49] As we shall see in the next section, even though free market liberalism is the official ideology of contemporary capitalism, the

---

49   Braudel in Domenico Moro, *Bilderberg. La elite del poder mundial*, trans. Juan Vivanco
       (España: El viejo topo, 2015), p. 208.

expansion of market economy is not a natural fact, but to a large extent the result of decisions taken by the global elite, i.e. those in power in politics, business and formation of opinion.

The liberal ideologies are the ruling ones, and even though their origin is dubious, in order to argue against their validity, I must take it upon myself to present some of their basic traits. Of course, I favour a certain critical left-wing perspective, but still the idea is to make my criticism live up to standards of immanence and objectivity. What I will eventually argue is that within contemporary liberal economics, there is a fundamental conflict between the neo-classicists and the neo-liberals. What is alarming, however, is that the critique of the former by the latter not only weakens monetarism, but also the Keynesianism that has been the foundation of the post-ww II social democratic welfare state. And, even more alarming, the neo-liberal critique of the neo-classicists can be seen as benefitting from criticism that understands itself as coming from the left-wing.

iii   *The Theory of Comparative Advantage is Ideological*

As an introduction to the logic of contemporary mainstream economics, I have chosen some classical elements, namely the theory of comparative advantage and Say's law. The former is based on an argument first presented by David Ricardo in 1817, arguing that comparative advantages for all nations can be achieved by developing the division of labour and free trade. Whereas Smith is said to have presented only some commonplace ideas to argue for the benefits of all by international free trade, Ricardo clarified the argument in such a strong way that even today it is considered a basic theoretical element in mainstream economics. As Montes shows, the theory of comparative advantage has been guiding economics in its understanding of international relations for decades (see DN, 53–56), thus being one of the constitutive elements of the economic politics enforced by the World Bank, the International Monetary Fund (IMF), the EU and the USA, i.e. the so-called Washington consensus, first specified in 1989, and in general advocating free trade, floating exchange rates, free markets and macro-economic stability.

Ricardo's claim is that it is to the advantage of all nations if international trade is conducted on a free market. The argument is elegant in its formal simplicity, even though it requires some attention to explain and understand. Taking his original example, assume thus that international trade only consists in the trade between, say, England and Portugal, which both produce two goods of identical quality, say cloth and wine. Of course, everyone can see that if England is more efficient in producing cloth than Portugal and the opposite is the case with wine, they should logically trade with each other. What Ricardo does, however, is to make a more difficult case, namely, as Samuelson recognizes (see EC, 671), arguing that trade will be mutually beneficial even if one nation is the most efficient in producing both goods.

Hence, in Portugal, the *a priori* more efficient country, it is possible to produce both wine and cloth with less labour than it would take to produce the same quantities in England. Apparently, Portugal thus has a clear competitive advantage in relation to England. However, there is a difference between the advantages in producing the two goods in the two countries. The hours of work necessary to produce one unit of cloth in England is thus 100, whereas in Portugal they only use 90 hours, but when it comes to producing wine, Portugal is even more efficient, using only 80 hours to produce one unit, while England has to use 120. As Montes sums up, this means that if the productivity of England is one, then Portugal, in relation to cloth, has a productivity of 1.11, but when it comes to wine it is 1.5, i.e. 50% more than in England (see DN, 54).

In this illustration, when England spends 100 hours of labour, it can produce either one unit of cloth, or only 100/120=5/6 units of wine. Meanwhile, in comparison, Portugal only has to spend 90 hours of labour to produce one unit of cloth or, alternatively, 90/80 units of wine, i.e. more than one unit. So, Portugal has an *absolute* advantage in relation to England when it comes to producing both cloth and wine, due to fewer labour hours needed in both cases, and intuitively England should protect its industry not to be wiped out of business. This, however, changes when the emphasis is put on the *relative* or comparative advantage.

In the absence of trade, England requires 100+120=220 hours of work to both produce one unit of cloth and one of wine, while Portugal requires 80+90=170 hours of work to produce the same quantities. England, however, is relatively more efficient at producing cloth than wine, and Portugal is relatively more efficient at producing wine than cloth. So, the claim is, first, that if each country specializes in the good in relation to which it has a comparative advantage, the global production of both goods increases. Hence, England can spend its 220 labour hours to produce 2.2 units of cloth, i.e. using the same time for production as when producing both wine and cloth, but now producing 0.2 units of cloth more than the two countries can separately. Similarly, the 170 hours that Portugal spends on production, when used exclusively on wine can produce 2.125 units, i.e. again more than was possible when producing in two countries, namely 0.125 units.

So, this proves the advantage for an economic system as a whole of the international division of labour when it comes to the total production of goods. This is not very surprising. More important is the second step, namely that if both nations specialize in this manner, and they start to trade their goods with each other, both nations will also benefit each by themselves. The idea is that the production surplus that stems from concentrating the available work hours on only one product becomes worth even more for the nation when traded with another nation having done the same thing in relation to the other indispensable product. Two assumptions are made: one is that the products bought abroad are not produced locally anymore; the other, as Montes notes in passing, is that for Ricardo the value of the goods, and thus the prices we trade in, are determined by the working hours spent (see DN, 54).

Hence, the increased productivity resulting from the English specializing in cloth means that one English work hour equals more cloth, i.e. that the price of cloth is lower in relation to a work hour. And the same thing goes for wine in Portugal. Now, buying wine in Portugal and cloth in England, for the work hours they have, i.e. respectively 170 and 220, both countries can therefore get more cloth and wine compared to the situation where both products were made in both England and Portugal. And this goes for both countries.

Put in another way: when England trades one unit of its cloth, instead of getting locally 5/6 units of wine, in Portugal it gets 9/8 units wine, i.e. 1.125; and for Portugal, instead of getting for one unit of its wine 8/9 unit local cloth, it can get 6/5 units of English cloth, i.e. 1.2. Hence, both countries can, with the same hours spent on production, consume at least the same as before, i.e. a unit each of cloth and wine, but more likely something more, since there remains a surplus of up to 0.2 units of cloth and up to 0.125 units of wine in each respective country to be consumed or exported. Consequently, both England and Portugal can consume more wine and cloth under free trade than by keeping all production within closed borders. The point is, as Montes explains, that ultimately when Portugal trades its wine in England, it is worth even more, namely $1.2*1.125=1.35$, assuming again that the prices depend on the work spent, and the curious thing is that the same goes for England selling its cloth in Portugal, i.e. $1.2*1.125=1.35$.

Ricardo can thus claim to have proved, i.e. not just argued, that it is to the comparative or relative advantage of both nations to trade, even though one of them has a clear absolute advantage, and this claim has since then received very strong backing in economics. Even a Keynesian, such as Samuelson, who is normally rather moderate in his wording, in the 1970s, i.e. before the emergence of the monetarist and neo-liberal revolution, characterizes the "theory of comparative advantage" as "unassailable" (EC, 668). It's "germ of truth [...] still remains" (EC, 670) and is "an unshakeable basis for international trade" (EC, 673). To leave no doubt about the advantage for all of free trade, he even translates the results at the national level directly to the individual level, ignoring differences of interest due to unequal distribution of private property, claiming that "workers everywhere get the imported goods for fewer hours of labour" (EC, 671). This belief in the benefits for all those involved, at all levels, in having a free international market has thus been one of main pillars in economics for almost two centuries.

Hence, the theory of comparative advantage is a real classic in the Gadamerian sense, i.e. being meaningful and even considered true in spite of the horizon having changed, transgressing its time but still being historical in its origin.[50] However, as both Estrup and Montes mention,[51] already one of Ricardo's contemporaries, the German national economist Friedrich List, was able to deduce the material implications of the theory, namely that when England due to its industry already had a strong competitive advantage regarding manufactured goods, this advantage would in fact increase, not just relatively, but also absolutely. Thus, on a free international market, some nations would have to remain producers of raw materials in order to retain the chance of having any comparative advantage at all, while others would be stimulated to develop the advantages of industrialized mass production that they had already obtained. This would of course fortify and increase the existing differences in development between the nations, since limitations on production in the primary sector are reached more readily than in the secondary and especially the tertiary sector, where services can be developed almost indefinitely. List therefore had good reason to defend German protectionism.

Moreover, Ricardo did not integrate at all in his economics the technological improvement of industrial production;[52] he endorsed the labour theory of value used by Smith,[53] which today is only advanced by few economists, most of them classical Marxists, and he took for granted that there was no mobility when it came to the productive factors (see. e.g., DN, 55). Hence, he explicitly made his argument dependent on the fact that money would not be flowing freely across borders,[54] since that would neutralize the comparative advantage in relation to the difference in absolute advantage.

All this should make the theory less attractive for contemporary economics, at least when considered in a scientific perspective, but, as mentioned, in fact

---

50   Hans-Georg Gadamer, *Wahrheit und Methode* (1960), in Gadamer, *Gesammelte Werke* (Tübingen: Mohr Siebeck, 1999), vol. 1, p. 295.

51   See Estrup, *Nogle grundtræk af den økonomiske teoris udvikling*, p. 169; DN, 32.

52   See, e.g., Estrup, *ibid.*, p. 170.

53   See *ibid.*, pp. 144–45.

54   See, e.g., David Ricardo, *Principper for den politiske økonomi og beskatningen* (1821), trans. Thorkild Jensen (København: Rhodos, 1978), pp. 117–19 (Ch. 7).

the opposite has been the case. Because of the present technological possibilities of managing the world economy, and due to the political forces expressed in the Washington consensus, Ricardo's theory has become more influential than ever. Whenever a nation, typically a poor one from the Third World, experiences serious economic difficulties, the demand from IMF *et al.* is to achieve macro-economic stability through free trade on free markets, i.e. deregulating and privatizing public goods, opening up markets, or constructing markets where there were none, removing so-called tax barriers and other measures considered to be 'protectionist', nationally as well as internationally.

iv   *Say's Law is Back, in Spite of the Great Crash*

In general, the political economy of neo-liberalism and monetarism demands more flexibility of the market, and when this is applied to the labour market, in real life this means that it should be easier to cut salaries, thus curtailing the power of the unions and the provisions of the welfare state. This is the famous 'politics of supply' (see, e.g., DN, 26), which today is haunting many countries in the EU in the words of the contemporary Keynesian economist Paul Krugman, "a crank doctrine" that only benefits "wealthy men".[55] It presupposes the validity of the other classical element of political economy, namely the Say's law, stating that whenever there is a supply, if the price is right, there will be a demand. This law dates back to 1803 and was a constituent part of economic orthodoxy for a long time, as Keynes tells the story.[56] The implication of the law is that there can never be surplus production, since there is always demand, just as there can never be too many people in the labour market. The only thing that matters is the price of the good offered on the market (see, e.g., EC, 348).

In contrast to the theory of the comparative advantage, which never went out of fashion, Say's law was greatly compromised by the crisis in the 1930s, when the price of labour just fell and fell for years without there being any real increase in demand. As Keynes puts it, Say's law is "equivalent to the proposition that there is no obstacle to full employment". If, however, "this is not the true law", then "there is a vitally important chapter of economic theory which remains to be written".[57] Hence, it was in relation to the politics of supply suggested by Say's law that Keynes developed the economics behind the seemingly successful 'politics of demand' that governed political economy for decades. Hence, to a Keynesian like Samuelson, Say's law can only be questionable,

---

55   Krugman, *The Return of Depression Economics*, p. 155.
56   See Keynes, *The General Theory of Employment, Interest, and Money*, pp. 18–20.
57   Keynes, *ibid.*, p. 26.

based on "rather vague arguments" and unable to account for "longer periods of considerable unemployment or of *underemployment*" (EC, 349).

The return to prominence of Say's law is thus one of the important signs of the current ideology of mainstream economics, in reality bringing us back to precisely the kind of politics that were deemed ineffective in the 1930s. However, this kind of political decision is not guided by empirical verification. When the economic consequence of the political measures chosen prove to be even more difficulties, the answer is ready at hand, namely that the structural reforms carried out have not been radical enough. Around the most recent turn of the century, Montes thus observed that for two decades the international tendency had been that the share of salaries in the national income had diminished, meaning that the real salary had increased less than the productivity per worker. Labour thus steadily became cheaper and cheaper, year after year, and although there was no tendency that employment went up in the same period, there was no change in policy (see DN, 69).

This was exactly the same situation that Keynes experienced in the 1930s. And similar to back then, the arguments are resistant to facts. The drive to lower the wages is not in any way affected by the fact that the demand for labour still does not grow when the price falls. Today, it can even be added that the most competitive countries are clearly not those with the lowest wages. Unaffected by the economic facts, the political pressure on the wages nevertheless continues and is also directed towards "indirect salaries" (DN, 117) such as public service, unemployment benefits, health insurance, etc., i.e. all the welfare provisions protecting ordinary people from the inhumane mechanics of the free market. However, this should not come as a surprise. As Montes puts it, the "economic depression is a weapon in class struggle and the neo-liberals are not neutral" (DN, 89).

C   Actors or Systems? What is behind the Neo-liberal Offensive?

What is indeed outrageous is that not only have the rich countries used their position to force the poor countries to open up their markets to the goods where the rich countries possess the absolute advantage; looking closer into the matter, it becomes clear that the competitive advantage due to the division of labour and free trade was obviously not enough for the rich countries. Hence, they have supplemented this official policy with all kinds of less principled policies and techniques to protect their own markets from the competition from the poor countries. What is obvious from the facts is that, being already privileged by the existing world order, the rich countries have little interest in advancing global justice. As Montes puts it, "this double language of the industrialized countries" reveals a "high level of cynicism" (DN, 33). The idea of free trade and the theory of comparative advantage can thus be said to serve as "weapon[s] in the ideological struggle" (DN, 43) to facilitate the exploitation of the Third World, although these official policies are obviously not considered sufficient to protect the interests of their protagonists.

For Montes, the economic policy of the western world since the 1970s is best described as a "neo-liberal counter-offensive" (DN, 36), and a similar expression is employed by Riutort.[58] Such a wording clearly makes one think in terms of intentional actions carried out by the coordinated effort of real actors. Just like in the case of double language, however, what is difficult to establish is not only whether this is indeed the case, but also what kind of faith is involved in these actions, i.e. whether the alleged offensive has been waged in bad faith, expressing simple greed, or is the result of coordinated efforts to promote the neo-liberal agenda as a sincere political project.

Hence, one question is whether the real actors involved in the political decision making – i.e. the economists in the Organization of Economic Co-operation and Development (OECD), the IMF and the World Bank, as well as the powerful politicians and business people in the western world – honestly believe that the economics they propose will really be advantageous for everybody, including the Third World, or whether they know all too well what List already pointed out, namely that it will secure the advantage of those already way ahead in economic development.

Apart from this question of individual honesty, there is the question of the coordinated efforts, i.e. whether these inconsistencies are openly admitted and even organized at the levels in society where most of us never come. If the latter is in fact the case, i.e. if those involved do not attempt to advance a cause that is right and moral, then we are faced with an example of such a "conspiracy to seize power" that president Eisenhower talked about more than half a century ago.

If we take the latter question first, i.e. whether the efforts are coordinated, then I have to make an initial clarification. As far as I can see, both Montes and Riutort use the term 'neo-liberal' in a rather broad sense, i.e. to signify both what I call neo-liberals and monetarists, and this usage is quite common.[59] Following my own more restricted use, however, we can indeed conclude that a political offensive of neo-liberals have been consistently pursued for decades.

---

58   See the title of Riutort, *La gran ofensiva*.

59   See also, e.g., Arne Johan Vetlesen, "Nyliberalisme – en revolusjon for å konsolidere kapitalismen", *Agora* 11, no. 1 (2011), pp. 6, 34.

As the journalist George Monbiot tells the story, the theory has been propagated since the 1930s, when the term was coined at a conference attended by two of the major neo-liberal ideologists, von Mises and Hayek. Later, Hayek founded a society for the advancement of neo-liberal ideas that was supported by various millionaires, and from this position he developed what has been called a "neo-liberal international", i.e. a network of politicians, academics and think tanks. "Among them were the American Enterprise Institute, the Heritage Foundation, the Cato Institute, the Institute of Economic Affairs, the Centre for Policy Studies and the Adam Smith Institute. They also financed academic positions and departments, particularly at the universities of Chicago and Virginia".[60] As Monbiot remarks, the "invisible doctrine of the invisible hand is promoted by invisible backers".[61]

Returning to the broad sense of neo-liberalism, a neo-liberal offensive has certainly taken place at least since the 1970s. First, Friedman helped to establish a monetarist economy during Pinochet's dictatorship in Chile, even though the regime already from day one was responsible for countless deaths. Later, in the 1980s, both Friedman and Hayek offered advice to the British prime minister Margaret Thatcher, from whom we have the memorable quotation: "There is no such thing as society. There are individual men and women and there are families". With this in mind, Thatcher crushed the power of organized labour in the UK through her handling of the striking miners, and brought families to the brink of starvation. From the same era, we have US president Ronald Reagan's equally catchy statement: "Government is not the solution to our problem; government is the problem". Reagan therefore chose to stimulate capitalist growth from early on by dismantling the anti-trust measures that had kept big businesses at bay since the 1930s.[62]

Heads of states are people, and the most powerful of them started meeting regularly at summits for the Group of Seven, i.e. G7, in 1975. That also happened at the celebration of the bicentenary of the French Revolution, July 1989 in Paris – and through the dark windows of the cortege of dark cars quickly passing by, heavily protected by security agents and across a barrier of uniformed policemen standing at attention along the whole route, I was myself able to see the shadowy glimpses of Thatcher, Kohl, Mitterrand and Bush Sr. As they did in fact meet, so did also their successors, the most important at the G7 and 8 summits, while some of them again met others at the meetings of Davos, Bilderberg and other closed meetings, where politicians meet business people

60   See, e.g., George Monbiot, "Neoliberalism – the ideology at the root of all our problems",
      The Guardian, April 15th 2016.

61   Monbiot, ibid.

62   See, e.g., Klein, *No Logo*, pp. 162–63.

out of reach for the press and the public. Finally, to back up these coordinated efforts between politics and business, there have been all kinds of agencies and organizations, such as the IMF, the World Bank and countless research institutions.

The Italian sociologist Domenico Moro has shown in great detail how the Bilderberg meetings and the less well-known Trilateral Commission are the places where the strategy of international capital is discussed and elaborated.[63] This is where finance meets politics, and both meet opinion formers from universities, media and think tanks.[64] According to Moro, the political economy of the Bilderberg group is neo-liberal, which in this case signifies the political and economic ideology accepted by contemporary mainstream politicians in the western world, i.e. from centre-left to centre-right.[65] Networks such as these reflect the transformation of capital, i.e. becoming multi- and trans-national. We are witnessing a *supra* national integration of capitalism, where finance is becoming increasingly independent of the limitations of the nation states. Capital is circulating freely around the globe, exchanged on markets with little or no public control, and it has placed its few nodal points offshore, i.e. out of reach of strong political powers.[66] In control of these processes is a global cosmopolitan elite, consisting in fact of only few families who know each other very well and are tied closely to each other by personal and economic bonds.[67] Those who meet at Bilderberg are members of this "trans-national bourgeoisie".[68]

Of course, there have been disagreements between various agents and segments in the neo-liberal network along the way, such as between opinion formers including Friedman and Hayek.[69] Whereas the former eventually became Reagan's favourite, the latter corresponded with Thatcher,[70] but the differences of opinion appear to have been minor compared to common interests and the consensus of backing up the ideological counter-offensive of free market capitalism.

Coordination must thus be considered a fact. However, from the outside one cannot see whether we are dealing with an idealist political movement coordinating its counter-offensive at the sessions just referred to, or it has in fact been a conspiracy all along to seize the power and the money. Indication of

---

63   See Moro, *Bilderberg. La elite del poder mundial*, p. 99.

64   See Moro, *ibid.*, pp. 108–09.

65   See *ibid.*, p. 133.

66   See, e.g., *ibid.*, pp. 193–94.

67   *Ibid.*, pp. 200–02.

68   *Ibid.*, p. 187.

69   See, e.g., Ryan Bourne, "Lady Thatcher's relationship with Friedrich Hayek and Milton Friedman", *www.Pieria.co.uk* (2013).

70   See, e.g., Vetlesen, "Nyliberalisme – en revolusjon for å konsolidere kapitalismen", p. 6.

the latter, however, is the documentary *The Inside Job*,[71] where some of the key figures behind the economic deregulation in the USA up until the 2008 crash are interviewed. They include former ministers, various professors of economy and people from Wall Street, and many of them really appear guilty. It is, of course, difficult to see whether they are experiencing remorse from knowing now what ultimately became the result of their deeds, or they were in fact in bad faith all along. They all seem to have profited quite well from their efforts, though, and an interesting testimony pointing in the same direction is a series of columns in the *New York Times* by Krugman. At first, he clearly considers his disagreements with the Bush administration, taking over office in 2001, as political. However, after trying to make sense of the political decisions through the first two years, the tone of his comments in the columns becomes more and more shrill, and ultimately he cannot explain the initiatives politically, i.e. as being in the interest of the nation. Instead, the facts suggest to him a conspiracy orchestrated by the very few extremely rich against the rest of the population.[72]

Since this question must be approached with reference to the individual honesty and integrity of the actors involved in the offensive, no clear-cut answer can be provided. Let me, however, suggest that reality is probably muddled as always, meaning that some probably believe in the wonders of monetarism, neo-liberalism or other kinds of radical libertarian economics, whereas others simply go along, hoping to benefit personally from the general deregulation, and some even consciously let their political ideals determine by the possibilities for profiting personally. The latter could simply be cynics, crooks or real criminals, all of them pursuing their personal interests by deceiving other people with open eyes. They could also, however, find themselves justified by various right-wing slogans liberating them from almost all responsibility for their surroundings, claiming, for instance, that 'Greed is good', insisting that one is always the best judge of one's own interests, or that one at least has the inalienable right to decide what these interests are.

There is, however, a strong tradition among Marxists and the like, advocating that one should not attribute the deeds on the market to particular selfish individuals, but rather think of the market economy as a system with a certain logic, thus relieving the single capitalist actor of any moral responsibility for the individual economic acts. Assisted by the term 'legitimate interests', in most of the 20th century it has thus been possible to have successful negotiations

---

71   See Charles H. Ferguson, *The Inside Job* (2010).

72   Paul Krugman, *The Great Unraveling: From Boom to Bust in Three Scandalous Years* (London: Allen Lane, 2003), pp. 215–17.

between capital, state and labour, not having to bear any moral grudges against the perpetrators, but being able to rationally weigh the interests in relation to each other. Still, when criticizing the system as inhuman because of its known consequences, the left-wing certainly exhibits a great deal of moral rage, and having nowhere to go with that rage, since according to this view nobody can be made responsible for the injustices committed, can only engender more frustration. Even if an anti-capitalist revolution were to be successful, there would be nobody to behead. And for the very same reason, trying to organize peacefully for peaceful political progress, there would be nowhere to go to change the system either, i.e. no reason to fight hard for a social democracy, since the system is supposed to have a logic that will be realized ontologically no matter who is in charge of the government. Thus disillusioned, it is very hard to make people believe in the rationality of organizing collectively to regulate and perhaps eventually even change the whole economy.

History, however, shows that it was possible for decades to keep capitalism under political control, and the hostile takeover of economics by neo-liberals and monetarists also strengthen the belief in the political possibilities of human beings committed to a cause. One could say that right-wing liberals have been much wiser in this regard than the left, who may be said to have weakened itself and the potentials of popular power by sustaining the structuralist ideology of the capitalist economy as a self-propelling system. This may be due to a kind of self-excusing, but then also self-fulfilling, rationalization of the weakness and despair often experienced in the fight for social justice. To those who rule capitalist society, however, there does not appear to have been much doubt that dedicated individuals can indeed make a great difference.

At least, this confidence in the significance of individual acts makes it understandable why, in so-called liberal democracies, we can still experience systematic surveillance of persons just moderately critical of establishment politics. Recently, it was discovered that the first British MP for the Green Party, Caroline Lucas, had been under police surveillance for years; and, as she commented: It "sends a chilling message to those who want to engage in peaceful political demonstrations".[73] It thus seems that there may be good reason to continue, not just critique of the type that I launch here, but also the traditional practice that it implies, i.e. organizing human beings politically to resist the degradation and exploitation that the capitalist economy as a historical formation, and its willing executioners, presently submits us to – if we dare, that is...

---

73   Lucas quoted in Bex Bastable, "Police spied on MP Lucas for eight years", *Brighton & Hove Independent*, April 29th 2016.

D   Struggling over the Definition of Political Economy

Whatever the inner private thoughts of the perpetrators, both in politics and academia there is an ongoing struggle about how to define political economy and economics, demonstrating a widespread awareness of the crucial implications of the power to define in this case. Most fundamental is the struggle about whether economics is inherently political or it can be regarded as a scientific or even technical discipline (i), and one important element of this discussion is about the mathematization of economics (ii) Before going into detail about the neo-liberal critique of neo-classical economics, we must consider these basic issues.

i   *Economics as both Political and Scientific*

As mentioned, Ricardo's theory of comparative advantage is a core element of contemporary mainstream economics. This, however – as Estrup remarks in passing, relating especially to this theory, and as I have reflected on a little earlier – points to a basic trait of political economy, namely that it is indeed political. Hence, a particular economic theory may be shown to imply, and even "mask",[74] benefits to some rather than others, providing the former with strong incentives to hold on to the theory in question, even though the theory on strictly scientific terms it is not really tenable. This is the kind of behaviour I mentioned in relation to the theory of comparative advantage and Say's law.

In such cases, Critical Theory talks about ideology. Not only is the scientific 'ought' often mixed up with the moral and political 'ought' ; the interests in economic theories are vested and mixed up with the values officially held. Still, some interests may be considered legitimate, acknowledging precisely that everyone may be admitted the right, not just to have what is basically necessary for a decent life, but also the right to pursue the goods that make life worth living, i.e. enjoyment, fulfilment, self-realization – in short, happiness. This brings us back to the problem of scarcity and the social conflicts it gives rise to, thus bringing to the fore two fundamental questions, namely: what is political economy and what, or maybe more precisely, *who* is it supposed to be good for.

For Smith and Ricardo, political economy was clearly political, i.e. offering advice to governments about how to make the best of the resources of a particular society, arguing that less regulation would liberate individual and selfish energies to the benefit of all. In that sense, political economy had a practical and even operational aim, officially being in the interest of all the citizens of a nation, as it is indicated by Smith's famous title, *An Inquiry into the Nature and*

---

74   Estrup, *Nogle grundtræk af den økonomiske teoris udvikling*, p. 169.

Causes of the Wealth of Nations. For Marx, the critique of political economy was still political, but in a way that somehow displaced, or even inversed, the focus. Instead of guiding those in command, he attempted to demonstrate scientifically, and argue philosophically, that the logic of capitalism, and the political economy backing it up, as a consequence would lead to exploitation, misery and eventually death for large parts of the population trying to make a living on the conditions offered. Hence, he provided with his analysis good reason to doubt what is today called 'trickle down economics', thus demonstrating how political economy can function as an ideology. Just like Dickens, it was to the people impoverished by capitalism that Marx directed his attention, i.e. not the government.

Even though Marx, in contrast to his predecessors, was clearly not interested in assisting the rulers in how to refine the developing capitalist economy,[75] his scientific and philosophical project was nevertheless also political in the sense that it had a practical and operational ambition, namely to facilitate enlightened political action by the population at large and especially the workers. Marx therefore participated in the initial attempts in the 19th century to organize workers to fight against capitalism, establishing what was later known as the First International. It was followed by the Second International that eventually identified itself as social democratic, and the Third International that was organized by Russian Bolsheviks after the 1917 revolution. This is the International that Monbiot refers to when he describes the current neo-liberal network as a neo-liberal International.

It is this lead that I presently follow, adding hopefully to the political consciousness of the injustices of a man-made system that could be different. However, from the beginning, political economy of course also took pride in its scientific and scholarly qualities. Still, there is serious disagreement about what characterizes science and scholarship in such a social and political context. Estrup, for instance, clearly thinks that it is Ricardo's analytics, i.e. his way of reasoning, using models and arithmetic calculation, which for the first time gave political economy a specific identity as a scientific discipline. He admits that the formalization of the models may be difficult to understand, and that meticulous descriptions and reasoning such as, for instance, Smith's may be more precise "than any mathematical formulation".[76] Nevertheless, in the perspective of contemporary political economy, Estrup can only consider Smith's reflections on political science and history to be mere "digressions".[77] As the

---

75   See, e.g., Paul Mattick, *Marx and Keynes. Blandingsøkonomiens grænser*, trans. Bodil Folke Frederiksen, Karen Helveg Petersen, and Preben Kaarsholm (Røde Hane, 1973), pp. 31–33.

76   Estrup, *Nogle grundtræk af den økonomiske teoris udvikling*, p. 106.

77   Estrup, *ibid.*, p. 130.

distinguished British economist Michael Lipton recalls, in the early 1960s it was still possible to attain the "highest honours" in economics "with or without" mathematical formalization; today, this is "unthinkable".[78]

I have already mentioned Keynes's depreciative remark to the market optimist exposing the insensitivity of this ideology. One answer to this challenge is the remark by the grand old man of monetarism, Friedman, upon the death in 2006 of John Kenneth Galbraith, who was his colleague at Harvard for many years. Even though Galbraith was a recognized Keynesian economist and a full professor of economy for decades, as Robert H. Frank reveals, to Friedman Galbraith was never a real economist, but rather a sociologist.[79] And Frank's mentioning in this context Galbraith's shortcoming in relation to game theory can only function as a confirmation that Friedman's categorization was in fact correct.[80]

Even Samuelson, who in the 1976 edition of his authoritative textbook recognizes Galbraith as one of "the titans of the present age" (EC, xi), ultimately only credits him for having provided criticism of "conventional wisdom", thus "softening the way" for more "professional radical economists" (EC, 849). No wonder: Samuelson considers himself part of the 20th century wave of mathematization (see EC, 844). And this perspective has further implications: Samuelson thus lumps together Friedman and Hayek with Ayn Rand under the sub-heading "Chicago School Libertarianism", but still it is obvious that he only takes one of them seriously as an economist, namely Friedman (see EC, 847–48).

These fundamental disagreements about the scientific status and legitimate content of economics may be interpreted politically, reflecting conflicts of interests and experiences between, say, somebody like Ricardo, an entrepreneur of independent means due to his speculative and analytical genius, i.e. a George Soros of the 19th century,[81] and Marx, a political refugee on the run from authoritarian regimes, struck by poverty as just another victim of the capitalist system. If anyone serves to confirm the basic idea of the standpoint theory, i.e. that a marginal position is beneficial for realizing the truth of injustice and alienation in a capitalist society,[82] it is Marx himself.

---

78   Michael Lipton, "Economics", in *Making the Future, A History of the University of Sussex*, ed. Fred Gray (Sussex: University of Sussex, 2011), p. 271.

79   Robert H. Frank, "Right for the Wrong Reasons: Why Galbraith Never Got the Prize", *New York Times*, May 11th 2016.

80   See Frank, ibid.

81   About Soros and his Quantum Fund, see, e.g., John Gapper and Nicholas Denton, *All that Glitters. The Fall of Barings*, 2nd ed. (Hammondsworth: Penguin, 1997), pp. 41–42, 212–13.

82   See, e.g., Anderson, "Feminist Epistomology and Philosophy of Science".

Thus, what Critical Theory has done in relation to science from the very start,[83] is interpreting science in social and political terms in order to reveal its ideological content, and in the process providing knowledge about the specific origins of a theory, and basically, this is also what I am trying to do here. In such an analysis, it helps to know about the field being criticized, i.e. the ruling economy and the political economy of the rulers. Revealing the ideological character of a set of ideas means revealing their origins as dubious or biased, and that of course implies, or presupposes, some knowledge about them. I will therefore look a little more into the essentials of contemporary economics.

ii   *The Mathematics of Economics*

A very important event in the history of political economy is the already mentioned marginalist turn in the second half of the 19th century, which paved the way for several important changes in the process of developing classical political economy into present-day scientific economics. A fundamental idea for the classicists was that of value being determined by what was needed in the production of a particular good. That was changed into the idea that what is of value may be what is useful, but basically what is considered valuable is what is in demand. So, Smith's famous puzzlement is not relevant anymore. Value means in demand; that is why diamonds, though not really useful, are more valuable than water (see, e.g., POM, 146). Still, why diamonds have exchange value, i.e. why they are in demand, is not explained.

Changing the fundamental perspective of political economy from production to consumption is a crucial element in the establishment of neo-classical economics. This change, however, means that the same thing can be considered of different value if the demand changes. This is what makes possible the basic marginalist idea, namely the fact that a specific market can be satisfied in relation to a certain good and this, so it is argued, means that the value of that particular good drops. When you have already eaten one ice cream, your appetites have changed, and the next one does not seem so valuable. Therefore, your readiness to pay diminishes, meaning that you are not willing to pay the same prices again for the next unit of the very same product. By this subjectivist logic, however, value becomes reduced to market price, and the result is that, even though an anachronistic relic such as the theory of comparative advantage still presupposes the labour theory of value, nowadays only few, mostly Marxists, would employ this theory of value; in fact, very few economists on the whole think much about value *per se*, and nobody thinks, as did Locke, Smith and Marx, in terms of a natural and just price depending on the value defined by the objective production costs.

---

83   See the above in the Interlude, Sect. A.

Understanding the market price as only depending on supply and demand opens up for the idea of the general equilibrium, namely the situation where all goods are allocated to those who want them, having been willing to pay a price that was satisfactory for those offering the goods in question. This is how the political side of the free market ideology can be presented, namely as a simple and desirable harmony of interest in a society where nobody is forced to do anything beyond their wishes and means. This not only confirms the basic liberal idea of leaving economic decisions to be taken by each individual; by allowing private business to grow and accumulate capital, it also stimulates the development of rational tools for the business economy of private enterprises such as bookkeeping, accounting, scientific management, etc.

Further, by thinking of the economy as a system basically constituted by individual desires and drives, only assisted by instrumental rationality – i.e. the kind of reason that can be in the service of the passions, as David Hume would put it – political economy can be further depoliticized and transformed in the direction of economics as a scientific, or even technological, discipline, since one can think of the whole economic system as a mechanical system of causal feedback loops which ensure that the system only oscillates around a certain predefined equilibrium, just like a central heating system controlled by thermostats. Hence, combining causal processes with the decisions of instrumentally rational actors we get a discipline called micro-economics, which is taught at business schools and directed to the managers of private businesses. Still, political economy is taught at universities in political science departments, but often it has become transformed into macro-economics defined in terms of micro-economics, using now as a model the needs of an organization rather than those of a complete and complex society, thus escaping the troubling aspect of social justice.

The techno-scientific approach to economics stimulates interest in the most important and powerful tool, namely mathematics. No reflection of economy can do without at least some arithmetic. Economy is mediated through money, the sum of which has to be calculated every time a transaction takes place. Selling, buying, saving, budgeting, accounting, investing, borrowing, lending, sharing, speculating, transferring, even stealing; all of such operations will eventually merit calculating the sums of money handled in the activity in question, as well as thinking in terms of fractions, percentage, etc. It is the goal-rationality of such calculative transactions that Max Weber analyses in relation to individual actions in *Economy and Society*.[84]

---

84   See Max Weber, *Wirtschaft und Gesellschaft* (1921–22) (Tübingen: J.B.C. Mohr, 1990).

What is important is that in economy, calculation and arithmetic are present all the time, and skipping the metaphysics of value in economy, i.e. both in political and business economy, mathematics can be employed both by the neo-classicists and the neo-liberals. Hence, mathematics can assist in understanding the economy as a mechanical system, establishing the regularities of relations through intricate numerical equations, ultimately establishing the general equilibrium. Also, mathematics can be useful for the entrepreneur seeking to optimize personal profit in the rational calculation of costs and benefits of individual strategic actions in relation to other rational actors, the latter resulting in what today is known as game theory, the most famous game being the so-called Prisoner's Dilemma.

In the Prisoner's Dilemma, two thieves have been caught, and isolated from each other they wonder whether to cooperate or not. The stakes are that if they both squeal and thus betray each other, each of them serves two years in prison. If only one of them informs against the other, who thus remains silent, the former will be set free while the latter will serve three years in prison. If, however, both of them remain silent, they will only serve one year each in prison because of the lesser charge.[85]

This setup has generated a wealth of discussions, refining all kinds of definitions, details and assumptions. One basic assumption is their mutual isolation and ignorance, i.e. that it is a so-called non-cooperative game.[86] Further, a perfectly rational individual economic man, i.e. the legendary *homo economicus*, is presupposed on both sides of a game, being guided only by maximizing the satisfaction of his or her individual preferences. Assuming that some kind of principled obligation could overrule this rationality, would, as Bruce Lyons emphasizes, "fundamentally undermine game theory".[87] Each player thus seeks his or her own advantage, and both threat each other strategically as opponents.[88] Relating this to the real world and softening this precondition, it may be comforting to know that good results for both actors can be achieved in a cooperative game, i.e. a game where both reveal their plans and options to the other. As Lyons emphasizes, if there is complete information and the players are perfectly rational, "there can never be a reason for a destructive fight".[89] This is the reason why the perfection of free market competition is believed to

85   See, e.g., Heap *et al.*, *The Theory of Choice*, p. 99.

86   See, e.g., Bruce Lyons, "Game Theory", in *The Theory of Choice*, ed. Heap *et al.*, p. 96.

87   Lyons, ibid., p. 120.

88   See, e.g., Albert Weale, "*Homo economicus. Homo sociologicus*", in *The Theory of Choice*, ed. Heap *et al.*, p. 62.

89   Bruce Lyons, "Bargaining", in *The Theory of Choice*, ed. Heap *et al.*, p. 138.

be explainable by a phenomenon such as the neo-classical general equilibrium theory.

Even the classical example of economic man, Robinson Crusoe, was able to develop his individualism when Friday arrived. Crusoe's selfish instrumental rationality can, although with some reluctance, imply opting for some kind of democracy, employing, as Albert Weale does it, the analogy between an economic and a "political market place".[90] Still, this is not the aspect of game theory most often emphasized, and when this interest in the common good is left out, as is often the case at business schools, the result may easily be a preoccupation with strictly individual and instrumentally rational strategic decision making in markets, thus mimicking the case of the isolated prisoner. That, however, must be considered unhealthy from an educational perspective, stimulating a formation of character only suitable for small scale crooks, not for citizens cooperating as equals in a democratic society.

The point here, however, is that the responsibility for the mathematization of economics can be ascribed both to the operational aims of micro-economics and macro-economics, and to the descriptive scientific ambition inherent in post-marginalist macro-economics (DN, 20–1). The mathematization is thus pervasive, functioning as a shield against possible critics unable to understand which of the allegedly simplifying assumptions made, as the arguments in economics evolve, are really just innocent attempts to achieve the kind of clarity necessary for the desired formalization, and which mask the kind of ideological implications found in the theory of comparative advantage and the supply politics recommended by Say's law. The pervasive mathematization of political economy is thus an almost ideal typical example of ideological mystification, i.e. a process which, by theoretical means, blurs the picture of a part of reality, making it impossible to pass judgement in relation to it for laypeople. In this case, it adds to the point that the part of reality in question can become a matter of life and death for those involved.

Scientific ambitions are also found in Marx's critique of political economy, as well as in the work of many later Marxist economists, and as mentioned, there is also an unfortunate tendency to consider the economy as a self-sustaining mechanical system. Economy, however, is a different kind of system, since it originates in conscious acts of individual human beings. It only becomes a system through objectification, thus being able to develop its own super human logic behind our backs, as Hegel famously phrased it. It becomes a system of actions without actors, which is also a system, but a system of a different kind, namely a functional system. It is not the causal mechanics of nature that

---

90   See, e.g., Albert Weale, "Democracy", in *The Theory of Choice*, ed. Heap *et al.*, p. 218.

maintains such a system, but an objectified fusion of conscious acts, which could be otherwise.

This is the reason why Marxism traditionally has been so preoccupied with raising the consciousness of the working class, namely in order to enable people to deconstruct the capitalist economic system and reconstruct the economy in a different way. Raising consciousness thus means giving back people collectively the freedom to decide their role in a new kind of society, giving back to the actors the power over their own acts.

However, I will not pursue this aspect of a political critique further here.[91] Instead, I want to look a little deeper into some of the differences within mainstream liberal economics, in particular the conflict already mentioned between neo-classical monetarists and the neo-liberal Austrians. This conflict reflects the radicalization of capitalism and liberalism that we are witnessing these years in the age of globalization, and because this conflict is not sufficiently understood, what is meant to be a left-wing social critique of economics can in fact benefit the individualist right-wing agenda. The ideological logic of this process is the theme of the following section.

E   The Neo-liberal Critique of the Neo-classicists

I have already mentioned that there is a fundamental ideological conflict between neo-classicists and neo-liberals, the former balancing various kinds of liberties with social harmony and stability, the latter almost exclusively emphasizing the freedom of the individual. Now, I will go a little further into the details in order to shed light on the possible complicity between right-wing and left-wing criticism of neo-classical economy. First, I will analyse the critique in terms of realism, bringing back to attention the fact that the market is for private property owners, not for people (i) and that market equilibrium presupposes many unrealistic assumptions (ii). After a short remark on the role of monetarism (iii), I direct my attention to the critique of neo-classical economics in terms of freedom (iv) that transforms the idea of economics from the governmental perspective to that of the individual entrepreneur (v). Finally, the realism demands that market instability and crisis can be conceptualized, and that money is recognized for its particular possibilities, namely storing value in times of uncertainty (vi).

---

91   The agenda of enlightenment, education and empowerment I will return to in DDD III.

i   *The Market is for Owners, Not for People*

The common point of departure for liberal political economy is the belief in the desirability and possibility of a free market economy. Hence, a good way to reconstruct the logic behind mainstream economics is to ask about the preconditions of the market as does Lundkvist. This way of inquiring makes clear, first, that the actors on the market are not human beings, they are private owners (POM, 232). If one has no property, one has nothing to bring to – and thus nothing to do on – the market. Further, this property is only marketable if it has use-value to somebody other than the producer, i.e. if it can pose as a good, and for the producer, the use-value of the product as market commodity depends on its having exchange-value (see POM, 22). The basic condition for a market is that there is something to exchange, i.e. that some property is in the possession of someone, that the property in question is offered for sale, that somebody else wants it as a good, and that it can be transferred legitimately. Market economy thus presupposes not only goods and actors, but also established rights to private property. If there are no property rights, there can be no legitimate private owners and thus nobody to offer and nothing to transfer to other owners.

Lundkvist makes it clear that the private property right to a market commodity is often confused with the origins of the good as a product. Locke thus intended to make the private possession of a good legitimate by the supposed added value of work to the original use-value of the good in question, an example at hand being agricultural products. This is the basic labour theory of value that all the classicists, including Marx, stuck to. For Locke, it gave the bourgeoisie, conceived of as a productive class, added legitimacy as property owners in relation to the nobility as leisurely inheritors of wealth; for Marx, it could similarly be used to argue for the rights of the real producers, i.e. the working class in relation to the real property owners, bourgeoisie as well as nobles (see, e.g., POM, 44).[92] Hence, when work was the main provider of value, namely as both use-value and exchange-value, and the workers furthermore produced more exchange-value than they received as salary, the difference was the surplus-value exploited from their work due to the bourgeoisie being in possession of the means of production.

Lundkvist's point, however, is that everything in principle can be sold on the market, also goods simply found (see POM, 24), be that water or air, or all kinds of cultural or social goods, or even immaterial goods such as conscience and honour. Simply by being brought to the market, a thing is converted into a

---

92   See also Ch. 1 above.

commodity and a potential good; hence, anything can become a commodity. Marx does not acknowledge this; he only considers produced commodities as real commodities. This error was already pointed out by in the 19th century by the Austrian economist Eugen Böhm von Bawerk (see POM, 23). Hence, the commodity form of market commodities *per se* only presupposes the right to private property, supply and demand, not labour.

In order to understand the basic logic of the market and formulate a contemporary critique of capitalism and political economy, one cannot just take for granted the objectivist labour theory of value presupposed by Marx. But Lundkvist also refuses to accept the universal validity of the subjectivist value theory of the neo-classicists, which makes the marginal utility of the good the foundation for economics. His argument is that accepting the subjectivist value theory as the general point of departure for political economy means focusing on economy in general, not on market economy as such (see POM, 22). Lundkvist therefore displaces the point of departure from the concept of value, be that labour value or use-value, to that of rights, namely private property rights.

The focus on private property rights brings to mind the young Marx's distinction between the citizen, the bourgeois and the human being. Traditionally, private property is supposed to provide freedom and independency to the owner, again the example being the man of independent means such as the farmer with land that can be cultivated. The freedom provided by the right to private property does not befall human beings in general, only those who in fact own some property, i.e. the landowner or the bourgeois. Formally, everybody is free, secured by the possibility of private property protected by rights, but precisely for the same reason, in reality there is little freedom for the proletariat in a free market economy thus conceived (see POM, 46). The free market is only free for property owners, not for those without means to barter.

ii   *Market Equilibrium is Unreal*

As Lundkvist argues, in fact not even the bourgeois property owners are as free in relation to the real market as was presupposed by the classical liberals. The point is that the classical approach to economy is modelled on the idea of Robinson Crusoe being a self-sufficient provider of all necessities for life. The market is thus an option, not a necessity; if the agent does not feel like selling, or if nobody wants to buy what is being offered for sale, the owner in question can simply do without the market. Hence, the agent has a substantial and real freedom, both *on* the market and *from* the market. According to Lundkvist, this pre-industrial presupposition is maintained in neo-classical economics, meaning that marketable goods are considered useful also for whoever possesses the goods in question.

This has important implications. First of all, there is always a demand for what is supplied; if nobody else wants it, at least the supplier does (see POM, 186). A transaction between two private owners is supposed only to take place if both parties perceive the marginal utility of the goods already possessed as lower than what is offered in exchange. This radicalizes Say's law, since supply now implies demand, because the supplier is always in demand of their own goods. However, this means that nobody has to sell anything. The sellers can do fine without, and for both seller and buyer, all the marketable goods can replace each other, as it is illustrated by the neo-classical examples of exchanged commodities. For Jevons, the exemplary goods exchanged are thus meat and grain, whereas for Menger they are horses and cows (see POM, 187). One can simply keep one's belongings without suffering any serious loss, maintaining, respectively, sufficient nutrition and work power.

Lundkvist shows how Walras incorporated the presupposition of self-demand in his marginalist equations. When an agent sells a commodity, their stock of that particular good is reduced. That, however, is supposed to simply increase its marginal utility for the agent in question. The agent will thus stop selling after some time, namely when the perceived marginal utility of the commodity already in possession reaches a particular equilibrium with that of the commodity offered in exchange. In reality, this would mean that the market does not function anymore, but by allowing for self-demand and thus self-exchange, one can say that the economic transactions do indeed continue, even though in fact no goods change hands. On the condition of such an eternal, uninterrupted market process, Walras can in his mathematical equilibrium theory show that unemployment and overproduction are impossible in a system where all prices and wages float freely. Eventually, as Samuelson puts it, there will be "prices and wages that will clear all markets" (EC, 828), and that was the conclusion criticized by Keynes in the 1930s.

Today, presupposing that an economic agent can act independently of the market is even more unreasonable. Hence, this may be true for a large household selling its agricultural products at a very small local village market, but when applied to a more general idea of the market as coordinating the global exchange of industrially mass-produced products, it cannot be maintained. However, in spite of almost all products on today's markets being produced only for mass consumption and profit, just as they are the result of an extensive social division of labour, according to Lundkvist, the basic idea of a self-sufficient Robinson Crusoe economy is still presupposed implicitly in the contemporary theory of general equilibrium that is supposed to capture the mechanics of the real world market.

Thus, modern adherents of the general equilibrium theory, such as Kenneth Arrow and Gerard Debreu, are said to assume that all consumers initially "possess stocks of every commodity and factor service" large enough to supply some of them "to the market".[93] As a consequence, one can avoid theoretically that households end up with zero income and that the demand also becomes zero for some commodities. Hence, one can avoid admitting the fact that markets can indeed break down and be unable to get working again, as we have experienced it during economic crises. Whatever are the detailed motives and reasons for this strange assumption, apart from the inconvenience caused by zeros in the denominator of fractions, the result is thus, as Lundkvist also affirms, that market economy can be represented by mathematical equations as a system exhibiting not only freedom, but also continuity and stability (see POM, 188).

Again we have an example of the ideological function of mainstream neo-classical economics. Nobody in a real modern world can choose freely whether to be part of that totality of social-economic relations that we call the market, neither as producer nor as workforce. Even if we presuppose that originally this could actually have been the case, for instance in the countryside in the days of Locke and Smith, the global division of labour developed since then means that today it can only be the case in very marginal, out-of-the-way places. And when it comes to economic theory and analysis, as Lundkvist emphasizes, the very idea of the market presupposes exchange (see POM, 189).

The market can be said to be subject to two existential conditions: first, that the market good is the private property of someone; second, that the good is of use-value to somebody else. This is what Lundkvist calls the "social character" of the market good, and together the two conditions imply that "the one with no interest in the good decides about it, whereas the one with interest in the good cannot take any decision about it" (POM, 250). This is the reason why self-sufficiency and self-demand should not be allowed as necessary presuppositions for the desired equilibrium. Without these assumptions, however, it is difficult for neo-classical economics to reconcile the freedom of the market and a stable economic system, the possibility of which has been a postulate of liberalism ever since Smith. Thus, in order to be able to argue for the stability of the general equilibrium, mainstream economics has to assume these questionable presuppositions.

The obvious inconsistencies of neo-classical economics have been pointed out by both Marxists and Keynesians for decades. An important element of this criticism has been the claim that the general equilibrium theory is ideological, and that successful handling of the economy would demand a more realistic approach, i.e., as the economist Jesper Jespersen puts it, being able to account

---

93   David Simpson, *General Equilibrium Analysis* (London, 1975), p. 51; here quoted from POM, 187.

for "macro-economic reality",[94] "explaining trends" and providing "a better understanding of the complex relationships between effective demand, supply
factors, employment and inflation".[95] Until the neo-liberal counter-offensive
this seemed like a successful strategy to counter the orthodox neo-classicists,
but somehow the latter were able to return in the guise of the monetarists.

That, however, has not silenced the demand for realism. In the spirit of
classical Keynesianism, Steven Lukes criticizes the real inequality of markets,
emphasizing that "real world markets exhibit asymmetrical information and
unequal power".[96] Today, however, after decades of free market hegemony,
clearly the most potent and successful critique of this kind comes from the
Austrian School. They have, so to speak, taken over the right to demand realism, but in the process the meaning of the central term has changed. For the
Keynesians, realism concerns the government of a modern society, whereas
the neo-liberal realism is closer to cynicism, i.e. presupposing that what is real
is only the selfish, greedy actor who simply follows his whims and inclinations.

I believe, it is this ideological realism of the neo-liberals that has given their
offensive momentum. What makes the Austrian critique so powerful is, I would
claim, its radical solidarity with the existential perspective of an isolated and
bewildered individual, i.e. abandoning the overwhelming burdens of collective responsibility implied by thinking of economics as real-world national or
political economy. Keynesian realism constitutes an idea of economy so complex that it is impossible for ordinary people to understand what is going on.
In contrast, the Austrians accept initial ignorance when engaging in economic
activity. Not only do they let go of economy as a totality, they are also favour-
able to what the neo-classicists regard as market failures, i.e. the real market as
it looks 99% of the time. In the Austrian perspective, such failures provide windows of opportunity, i.e. loopholes, and that is what an entrepreneurial agent
needs to prosper on the free market. Hayek may express complete confidence
in the spontaneous order created by the market, but this order is not one of

---

94   Jesper Jespersen, *Macroeconomic Methodology. A Post-Keynesian Perspective* (Chelten-
      ham, UK: Edward Elgar, 2009), p. 15. See also, e.g., Giorgio Baruchello, "The Unscientific
      Ground of Free-Market Liberalism", in *Ethics, Democracy, and Markets. Nordic Perspec-
      tives on World Problems*, ed. Giorgio Baruchello, Jacob Dahl Rendtorff, and Asger Sørensen
      (København: NSU Press, 2016), pp. 231–57.

95   Jesper Jespersen, *Introduction to Macroeconomic Theory*, trans. Niels Coley (København:
      Jurist- og Økonomforbundets forlag, 2005), p. 198.

96   Steven Lukes, "Invasions of the market", in *Worlds of Capitalism. Institutions, governance
      and economic change in the era of globalization*, ed. Max Miller (London: Routledge, 2005),
      p. 309.

social justice.[97] Further, for the more radical Austrians, ultimately there is no problem in dispensing with the overall stability and continuity of the economic system, as long as the freedom of the individual market agents is enhanced.

iii   *Remark: Monetarism*

Before looking further into the Austrian neo-liberalism, it is worth taking a brief look at the ideology which, I would say, paved the ideological way for the remarkable success of neo-liberalism, namely monetarism. The monetarist critique in the 1970s of the Keynesian consensus focused on the phenomenon of stagflation, i.e. at the same time inflation and stagnation. The problem was the experience already in the late 1960s that prices and wages went up, even before there was full employment and a complete use of the production capacity (see, e.g., EC, 824).

As Riutort explains, Samuelson represents the post-war fusion of Keynesian macro-economics with neo-classical micro-economics, i.e. the "canonical synthesis" of the "Golden age".[98] At the micro-level, Samuelson is thus already in line with the monetarists. As a Keynesian macro-economist, however, he faced a dilemma. The traditional means to fight the inflation of what is often called an over-heated economy would be to limit the supply of money in society by monetary and fiscal policy (see, e.g., EC, 823), i.e. raising the interest rates to stimulate private saving and limit public spending. This is supposed to weaken investment and the demand for labour, and thus in general lower the economic activity. However, what they were dealing with back then was apparently a new type of inflation that did not, as Samuelson likes to put it, wait for demand "to clear all markets" (EC, 837).

The first horn of the dilemma is given by the situation in which supply is still way above demand, a situation of under-consumption of both labour and money, i.e. unemployment and too little investment – in short, a situation of stagnation. In such a situation, there was already too little economic activity in society, and the traditional anti-inflationary measures would be likely to result in recession rather than recovery. The second horn of the dilemma, employing traditional Keynesian means to fight unemployment and underinvestment, i.e. increasing public spending, would mean risking increased inflation that could get completely out of hand and make the economy impossible to control. Samuelson thus reminds of the inflation in Germany in the 1920s, but this is not just a matter of history. At the time of writing, i.e. June 2016, Venezuela

---

97   See, e.g., Robert Sugden, "Social Justice", in *The Theory of Choice*, ed. Heap *et al.*, p. 282.
98   Riutort, *La gran ofensiva*, p. 198.

is struggling with a hyperinflation that makes it impossible for ordinary people to know if they have enough money to survive the next few months.

As regards this problem, Friedman *et al.* proposed a radical solution. Studying the history of money in the USA and many other countries, the Chicago economists became convinced that fiscal policy, i.e. the foremost Keynesian tool to stabilize a modern mixed economy against the recurring business cycles and crises, in fact did not have any effect on neither inflation nor employment (see, e.g., EC, 330–31). The only measure to be employed in the political governance of economy was stabilizing the growth of money in circulation, i.e. monetary policy; the "free market" could, in Samuelson's words, be trusted to "take care of the rest – interest rates, unemployment, price levels". Friedman wanted to put an end to all the "fine tuning" of "men or committees", but, as Samuelson argued, almost as a forewarning: although in principle one could as a monetarist employ this sole measure as a "stabilizing, counter-cyclical" policy, these "new dogmas" needed to be tested "before they harden into old orthodoxies" (EC, 332).

The monetarists can be said to have restored the general confidence of the ruling elites in the market as a self-regulating system, but still their argument was political. In other words, both the classicists and the neo-classicists, in particular Jevons and Walras, as well as the monetarists, all accept that economics has to provide a solution to the coordination problem, thus emphasizing that the reason why we should leave almost every economic decision to the individual participants on the free market is that it would in fact be in the interest of society as a whole. As Samuelson notes, intuitively it is strange that leaving most economic decisions up to a multiplicity of market agents does not produce complete chaos (see EC, 41–43). The possibility of a free and yet harmonious market economy was Smith's original claim, and this agenda has been maintained by neo-classical economics, taking pride in being able to show that freedom and stability could go hand in hand. As Lundkvist emphasizes, what Walras tried to prove with his mathematical equations was precisely that the market could provide a stable solution to the coordination problem. Walras developed the theory of general equilibrium before, and independently of, the theory of marginal utility, or 'rarity', as he himself called it (see POM, 193), and this neo-classical concern for stability was accepted by the monetarists.

However, it is precisely this concern for the stability of the totality that makes mainstream economics vulnerable to criticism from a neo-liberal Austrian such as Hayek. The point is that to formalize the stability of the economic system through mathematical equations into a general equilibrium, one has to presuppose rational agents making only rational choices under conditions of full information. However, apart from this condition being completely unrealistic, this way of thinking does not leave much room to the free choice of the agents, and one could in principle leave the equilibrium to be calculated by a powerful computer without any real agents being involved. Even though the neo-classical monetarists insist on disposing of men and committees, as long as they accept modelling economy as a whole in order to achieve a stable and continuous general equilibrium, there is not much freedom left on the allegedly free market. Hence, the neo-liberal critique of the neo-classical economics raises two issues: the lack of realism and the lack of freedom.

iv   *Equilibrium is Totalitarian; the Market Provides Freedom*
The basic point was already made by Walras's contemporaries, namely that maybe the impressing system of mathematical equations, and thus the general equilibrium theory as such, actually had validity beyond the market economy for which it was clearly intended. As Lundkvist explains, socialists thus saw in Walras's neo-classical economics a recipe for how to make priorities in a planned economy, and it can even be argued that his price theory did not presuppose money, but only the possibility of a kind of numerical comparison that could be taken care of by a central planning agency (see POM, 204–05). Thus, as the German economist Michael Wohlgemuth affirms, Walras's neo-classical theory was presented as "the proof that rational socialism was possible".[99]

What makes this important in the present context is that Hayek and the Austrians agree with this interpretation of the general equilibrium theory, i.e. that given its own presuppositions it would make the free market a waste of time. The possibility of the equilibrium thus presupposed that the economic system could be balanced by itself through complete information about all rational decisions before any market activity had actually taken place, making all the agents on the market passive recipients of prices already calculated by the system (see POM, 207–08). The point is that this is a rather strange reconstruction of what is supposed to be a free market, composed of market agents actively supplying and demanding.

The Austrian critique of the neo-classical mainstream has many dimensions, of which I will only mention a few. Particularly interesting, however, is the fact that this critique to a large extent has simply been ignored. As Lundkvist perceives it, the Austrians have thus been met with a "wall of silence" (POM, 237). To Wohlgemuth, the lack of communication is best regarded as an

99   Michael Wohlgemuth, "L'influence de l'économie authricienne sur le libéralisme allemand", in *Histoire du líberalisme en Europe*, ed. Philippe Nemo and Jean Petitot (Paris: Presses Universitaires de France, 2006), p. 996.

example of incommensurability in the Kuhnian sense,[100] and Lundkvist thinks they may have mutually considered each other as degenerative research programmes in Lakatos's sense.[101] Hence, the Austrians could think of mainstream general equilibrium theory as too preoccupied with unrealistic and totalizing formalizations, quantifications and equations, whereas the latter would claim that the former has not really contributed anything to quantitative price theory (see POM, 244). The Austrians therefore would not be recognized as real economists, and that would make whatever criticism they proposed irrelevant to economics, just like when Friedman categorized Galbraith as a sociologist.

What is interesting is that despite these very real conflicts, neo-classicists and neo-liberals have been able to live peacefully side by side, finding common ground in a lot of their criticism of Keynesians and Marxists, each in their own way stressing the general attractiveness of the idea of the free market. The monetarist neo-classicists have thus been very effective as professional economists collaborating with advocates of the welfare state, typically arguing for the possibility of generating increased social wealth by deregulation and privatization, thus claiming, as it is often heard in Northern Europe, that in a globalized economy such measures are simply necessary to save the welfare state. The Austrians, on the other hand, have as radical ideologists continued to insist on the value of freedom on the free market, thereby providing the political arguments for continuing to dismantle the welfare state altogether, simply because it is totalitarian. Hence, the monetarists could deal with the neo-classical and Keynesian establishment in economics, discrediting the core elements of the politics of demand and restoring the faith in neo-classical politics of supply,[102] whereas the Austrians could provide street credibility among business people fed up with regulation and bureaucracy.

This can be considered a very effective, although unequal, division of intellectual and ideological labour, where one part is creating the conditions for the other part. The monetarists thus insist that the free market can attain stability, which sets free the neo-liberal market agent to create and exploit opportunities, although little market stability in fact has been realized – rather the contrary. As Riutort explains, the north-western world very quickly turned its back on monetarist suggestions, realizing the stagnation and unemployment they produced. In Latin America, monetarism was maintained in a longer period

---

100   See Wohlgemuth, ibid., p. 997.
101   For my work on philosophy of science, see Asger Sørensen, *Om videnskabelig viden. Gier, ikker og ismer* (Frederiksberg: Samfundslitteratur, 2010), in relation to economy in particular Ch. 13, pp. 233–50.
102   See, e.g., Riutort, *La gran ofensiva*, p. 202.

in the 1970s and 1980s, and with even worse results, aggravating social and political problems. However, as Riutort argues, monetarism, and the shocks its
application caused in economy, can be said to have prepared the ground for
the neo-liberal offensive by disciplining the social agents.[103] Hence, together
these two economic ideologies have formed a tandem alliance so strong that
today it often seems that in fact, as Thatcher famously put it already in the
initial phases of the process: "There is no alternative", i.e. TINA. It is precisely
therefore it is important to specify some of the peculiarities of the Austrian
approach to economy. Without understanding its ideological logic, i.e. why it
is perceived as attractive, it is difficult to prevent it from becoming even more
influential than it already is.

Now, focusing on the Austrian critique, already from the very beginning it
took issues with the mathematization of economics. Hence, as the German
economist Jörg Guido Hülsmann shows, in a correspondence with Walras,
Menger took pride in reserving for his own method the term "exact". Menger
insisted that all the questions related to the exchange on the market were independent of human will, just as "the laws of chemistry" are independent of
the will of the "practical chemist".[104] Hence, the phenomena of economy are
supposed to "obey laws as strictly as those of nature".[105] The claim was that by
taking seriously the reconstruction of the "economic phenomena" into "true
constitutive factors (those that correspond to the real life)", one could arrive
at the "laws" of "political economy". Menger did little to conceal his contempt
for the "so-called rational" method, which would demonstrate perfect mastery
of "mathematics" yet still depart from "arbitrary axioms",[106] i.e. the method of
Walras to whom he was writing.

It is this real-life approach that leads Menger to the realization that the value
of commodities on real markets depends on the partial need of partial goods,
i.e. the idea of marginal utility.[107] The approach can be called methodological individualism, and, as Hülsmann brings testimony to, this methodological

---

103   See Riutort, *ibid.*, p. 207.

104   Carl Menger, *Principles of Economics* (New York: New York University Press, 1976), p. 48;
       here quoted from Jörg Guido Hülsmann, "L'École authricienne á la fin du XIXᵉ et au debut
       du XXᵉ siècle", in *Histoire du líberalisme en Europe*, ed. Nemo and Petitot, p. 1044.

105   Carl Menger, *Grundsätze der Volkswirtschaftslehre* (Wien, 1871), p. viii; here quoted from
       Karl-Heinz Brodbeck, *Die fragwürdigen Grundlagen der Ökonomie. Eine philosophische
       Kritik der modernen Wirtschaftswissenschaften*, 2nd ed. (Darmstadt: Wissenschaftlische
       Buchgesellschaft, 2000), p. 50.

106   Letter from Menger to Walras, Feb. 1884, quoted in Hülsmann, "L'École authricienne á la
       fin du XIXᵉ et au debut du XXᵉ siècle", p. 1041.

107   See, e.g., Hülsmann, *ibid.*, p. 1042.

stand went together with a radical liberalism, making a strong case for the capacity of civil society to generate institutions spontaneously, and thus for the idea that society can work "without state", providing "the most extreme formulations of the *laissez faire* principle" to be found in "the economic literature".[108] Characteristic of the 20th century Austrians is apparently that they maintained this basic approach, i.e. realism, individualism and liberalism, but to some extent gave up Menger's scientific ideals.

One implication of the realism and individualism is the insistence on the limitations as regards information available for the market. Presupposed in general equilibrium theory is, strange as it may seem to us non-economists, the idea of complete information. Whatever that may amount to in detail – and here I will skip the even more "extravagant fiction" of the "Walrasian auctioneer"[109] who allegedly plans equilibrium even before the market takes place (see, e.g., POM, 195–200, 209–12)[110] – for Hayek it is important to insist on the contrary, i.e. the limited knowledge of all the actual agents on the real market. This limitation has substantial consequences.

As Lundkvist makes clear, when the agents cannot know the prices on the market before the market takes place, one cannot claim that their decisions about the prices are rational as was also the assumption of the neo-classicists. And the best neo-classical answer he can find is that without the double assumption of both full information and rationality, economics becomes impossible as a science (see POM, 216–18). Or, as Riutort puts it, if reality cannot adjust to the models, "so much worse for reality".[111] Neo-classical economics cannot survive without these two questionable presuppositions; therefore, the conflict between Austrians and neo-classicists, even though they share the ideal of a free market, can be considered a matter of choosing paradigm or research programme.

Continuing this line of thought, the Austrians insist on the market as a dynamic process where real competition takes place, everybody looking for the cheapest buy and the most profitable sale. The critique of the equilibrium is not that it fails to take place, quite the contrary. To the Austrians, it is the equilibrium that would be a market failure. It is the lack of equilibrium that provides the business opportunities and thus makes real markets possible. Everybody goes there because of the possibility to get some kind of advantage, and equilibrium means that profits would approach zero, since supply

---

108   Hülsmann, ibid., pp. 1045–47.

109   Robert Sugden, "Anarchic Order", in *The Theory of Choice*, ed. Heap *et al.*, p. 188.

110   See also Sugden, ibid., pp. 187–90.

111   Riutort, *La gran ofensiva*, p. 190.

and demand outbalance each other. Even worse, politically the mere aiming at such an ideal can be considered dangerous, since it is almost an invitation to correct the alleged failures of the real market to reach such a desired harmony. If the real, existing market cannot but be considered imperfect, and we have a theory that can calculate the conditions for a perfect market, i.e. the general equilibrium theory, then it would be irresponsible not to intervene.

For the Austrians, the neo-classical ideal of general equilibrium can only be conceived of as totalitarian, legitimizing and encouraging state intervention as well as socialism (see POM, 220–21). What is important for the Austrians is the freedom of the individual human being in relation to the state, i.e. negative freedom. Interestingly, in the era of Hitler and Stalin we find similarities in the above-mentioned critique of state capitalism waged by Critical Theory.[112] Somehow the left and the right, or at least some versions of them, seem to converge in criticizing the state as inherently totalitarian; this is what is sometimes indicated by denouncing Critical Theory as anarchist, utopian, ultra-leftist or petit-bourgeois radical, i.e. as an ideology undermining the legitimacy of real socialist organization, social democracy and Keynesianism, thereby paving the way for the final victory of capitalism backed up ideologically by radical versions of liberalism.[113]

As it has been noticed by many good people, e.g., Arne Johan Vetlesen, there have also been remarkable similarities between left-wing criticism and right wing criticism of the welfare state, both emphasizing individual rights in confrontation with paternalism and bureaucracy,[114] just as one can point to the special role that post-modernism and, in particular, Michel Foucault played in the ideological offensive of neo-liberalism.[115] These similarities and convergences must of course be analysed and discussed further, but in the present context I will continue exploring the ideology of the Austrians.

v   *Economics Provides Tools for the Entrepreneur, Not the Politician*
Here, it is relevant to bring into play the famous Austrian idea of the entrepreneur, who is characterized by being alert to market opportunities. Opportunities occur when the market is in disequilibrium, i.e. precisely because of the real limitations in knowledge and rationality. Such markets can offer the opportunity of buying cheaply in one place and selling at inflated prices in another place. The entrepreneurs know very little when they enter the market,

---

112   See the Interlude, especially Sect. C.
113   See, e.g., Ch. 7, Sect. D.
114   See Vetlesen, "Nyliberalisme – en revolusjon for å konsolidere kapitalismen", pp. 17–19.
115   See Vetlesen, ibid., pp. 24–29.

but the market works as a discovery process in which the agents learn about the possibilities to become an economic success. As Lyons puts it, the important thing is to be "alert to new knowledge and act on it".[116] And this action also means changing the knowledge of others, for instance by advertising, "alerting people of their own tastes".[117] In the neo-classical perspective, advertising would typically be thought of as informing people about the commodities ready at hand on the market, and their prices, thus facilitating the economic coordination process in society to the desired equilibrium (see POM, 226). In contrast, for the Austrians, advertising means using all kinds of techniques to attract attention and alert consumers to their "unsuspected opportunities".[118]

As the young Hayek sees it, the interaction of the entrepreneurs, each involved in their own individual discovery process, will eventually tend to bring the market in equilibrium, thus proposing a solution to the coordination problem. He even considers this an "empirical proposition" about the "real world which ought, at least in principle, to be capable of verification".[119] However, as Lundkvist, argues, nobody, i.e. neither the entrepreneur nor anybody else, can foresee the future prices on such a real market, and therefore a decision cannot be rational. Confronted with a particular price, there is no way to know, and even less a way to verify, if we are approaching equilibrium, if we have already reached it, or we are departing from it (see POM, 222–23). That is what makes speculation so risky. As Hayek himself later realized, if the market is indeed such a discovery process, there is no way to "ascertain how effective it has been in discovering those facts that might be discovered".[120]

This opens up the scene for some more radical Austrians, who want to go even further to escape what they consider the road to serfdom, not being content simply to think of the market process as merely discovering or bringing attention to something already existing, but understanding the ambitions of market activity, in particular advertising, as the creation of new needs and desires, new tastes and even new virtual realities, which will bring about completely new and unforeseen business opportunities (see, e.g., POM, 227). This radicalizes the idea of the plasticity of needs and desires, i.e. that fulfilment and satisfaction merely imply the emergence of new appetites, which

---

116   Lyons, "Risk, Ignorance and Imagination", in *The Theory of Choice*, ed. Heap *et al.*, p. 54.

117   Lyons, ibid., p. 56.

118   Ibid., p. 56.

119   Friedrich von Hayek, *Individualism and Economic Order* (London, 1949), p. 45; here quoted from POM, 224.

120   Friedrich von Hayek, *New Studies in Philosophy, Politics, Economics, and the History of Ideas* (Chicago, 1978), p. 274; here quoted from POM, 224.

the entrepreneur can stimulate, thus radicalizing the subjectivist value theory even further and developing what is often considered a post-modern perspective on economy.[121]

Even if these opportunities were by chance to be calculated objectively, employing advanced game theory, on the real market it is ultimately up to the subjective agent to decide whether it is worth trusting and acting on such calculations. It is the market agent who decides when and where to buy or sell, and with whom this enterprise should be undertaken. It is their free choice, and in contrast to how it is conceived of in neo-classical economics and modern game theory, this choice is underdetermined by rationality and can be subject to all kinds of whims and distractions. Thus, as Ludwig Lachmann puts it: "No market process has a determinate outcome".[122] We act on the market as through trial and error, but we cannot really learn anything, nor do we really want to.

The radical contingency of the market changes the basic agenda of economics. It no longer makes sense to try coordinating rationally the social economy of a society as a whole. Hence, the coordination problem simply disappears. Economics is still a practical discipline, advising agents on what to do, but given the limitations it must restrict itself to providing the tools for the exploitation and creation of business opportunities. Economics no longer addresses the politician or the citizen, but the business entrepreneur. The main venue for teaching economy is no longer a university department of political science, but business schools. Economy is not, as Keynes, Samuelson, Krugman *et al.* assumed, primarily a political issue to be discussed under the presupposition of common interest in the common good of society. The market economy no longer aims to build its legitimacy in competition with planned economy, demonstrating its social efficiency in distributing goods within society in the best way possible, according to standards of social justice. For the radical Austrians, the market builds its legitimacy on the freedom allotted to the individual economic agent in search of and acting on business opportunities.

To put it in the terms generally used in political philosophy, as done by libertarians such as Nozick, individual freedom is simply considered the sole standard of justice. Hence, merely aiming to realize social justice by measures constraining individual freedom becomes unjust and thus wrong. This is, as Lundkvist affirms, the radical acceptance of the market, including the economic agent in his most anti-social form. It is thus an affirmation of private

---

121   See, e.g., Ch. 2, Sect. C.

122   Ludwig M. Lachmann, *The Market as an Economic Process* (Blackwell, 1986), p. 4; here quoted from POM, 225.

property rights rather than rationality, be that individual or social. Depending on one's political inclinations, what the Austrians try to determine is either the "absolutely free individual" or the "in principle anti-social human being" (POM, 227). However, as mentioned earlier, in reality, i.e. in both cases, it is only the freedom of the property owner we are discussing.

It is part of the monetarist agenda that economics should primarily back up business in pursuit of profit. One often attributes to Friedman the quotation that "the business of business is business",[123] thus signaling that the sole responsibility for business is the pursuit of profit. Friedman, however, still counts on there being a society taking care of the needs of the people, but his point is that it is not the responsibility of private enterprise.[124] Thus liberated from the burdens of social responsibility by the joint effort of neo-classical monetarists and Austrian neo-liberals, the entrepreneurs can pursue unlimited profits without second thoughts. This sets the stage for the post-modern economy, i.e. an economy of chance, games and plasticity of needs and desires, and such a market economy is attractive by being more playful and fun, leaving more room for excitement, challenges and fantasy, or even horror, than the dull political economy of the social democratic neo-classicists, deducing their long-term bureaucratic planification of the whole economic system and threatening to reduce us all to passive clients. Rather than aiming at realizing social and political justice, economics thus offer tools to develop various form of individual aesthetic and poetic gratification.

The means necessary for such adventures is precisely what has been created during the decades of the neo-liberal counter-offensive. All kinds of deregulations have opened up a global financial market, and most important in this context is the creation of the so-called hedge funds, which already in the 1960s began placing capital 'offshore', i.e. in places where normal financial control would not be possible. Already in 1992, this made it possible to accumulate private capital at such a massive scale that an individual speculator such as Soros could bring down Great Britain, forcing it to accept a dramatic decline in the value of the pound.[125] Soros's plan was as simple as it was bold: he made a huge bet that the sterling would be forced out of the European exchange rate mechanism.[126] The British economy was in recession, and the pound was

123   See, e.g., Irving Wladawsky-Berger, "Reshaping Business and Capitalism for the 21st Century", *The Wall Street Journal*, Oct. 11th 2013.

124   See, e.g., Milton Friedmann, "The Social Responsibility of Business is to increase its profits", *The New York Times*, Sept. 13th 1970.

125   See, e.g., Krugman, *The Return of Depression Economics*, p. 50.

126   See, e.g., Gapper and Denton, *All that Glitters. The Fall of Barings*, p. 42.

found to be overrated on the currency markets. As Krugman tells the story, a crisis was probably already on the way. Soros, however, did not wait for it to happen, but provoked it himself.[127]

As a true entrepreneur, Soros thus not only tried to exploit the opportunities of the market, he also created these opportunities himself. The details of how he manipulated the markets are not that important. The point is that Soros and his Quantum Fund were able to lure in other speculators to help ignite a speculative wave so powerful that it made Britain spend billions of pounds in a few weeks, in a vain attempt to defend their exchange rate. This incident made Britain leave the currency scheme; Soros could cash in the winnings of his huge bet, and instantly he became world famous.

Such a story brings back the glory, or least the suspense, to capitalism. The entrepreneur is a figure who can fascinate, mostly of course when being as successful as Soros, but also when we are dealing with a young amateur who, through ambition and serendipity, gets the chance to speculate for billions, discovering at his outpost, i.e. the small Singapore exchange, the enormous opportunities on the financial markets, but is nevertheless brought down by various unfortunate circumstances. Most important was his lack of fortune in speculating in the Japanese economy at a time when the growth of the 1980s was already way past,[128] and the "volatility of the Tokyo market"[129] was a recognized fact. What earned him fame, however, was that in 1995, in the process of covering up his tracks, i.e. hiding his mistakes and enormous losses, he was able to bring down his employer, Britain's by then oldest merchant bank, Baring Brothers. Besides the obligatory 15 minutes of fame, this entrepreneur thus received a sentence of six and half years for having cheated the Singapore exchange.[130]

vi   Crises: Bringing in the Money

Cases such as these, and the recurrent crises cycling around the globe, indicate, however, that maybe volatility was not just a coincidental attribute on one particular market sometime in the 1990s. In fact, I would dare the suggestion that increasing volatility is what characterizes the globalized free market economy as a whole after decades of deregulation. As it is well-known, it was the chain reactions of mistrust caused by so-called derivatives, i.e. obscurely constructed

---

127   See Krugman, *The Return of Depression Economics*, p. 121.
128   See, e.g., Krugman, *ibid.*, pp. 60–82.
129   Gapper and Denton, *All that Glitters. The Fall of Barings*, p. 240.
130   See Gapper and Denton, *ibid.*, p. 339.

bonds and papers, which brought us the 2008 crash.[131] What is alarming is that these derivatives are still highly valued in the international financial markets, being sold for billions and trillions of dollars. As it was emphasized recently by Warren Buffet, another financial entrepreneur and one of the most powerful contemporary financial speculators, such financial papers constitute a "potential time bomb".[132]

The lack of stability and predictability in real-life economic systems is, I think, part of the reason why the neo-liberal idea of economy has gained ground on the neo-classicists, including the monetarists. As Vetlesen summarizes the neo-liberal ideal, it is all about market, freedom, individuals and choice,[133] i.e. words that clearly make sense for the capitalist entrepreneur. Neo-liberalism thus makes sense in the globalized capitalist economy created by the monetarist and neo-liberal economics. As we have seen, the general equilibrium theory simply presupposes equilibrium, full information and complete rationality, and this does not seem strange only to the Austrians. Also when the economic analysis is inspired rather by Keynesian or Marxist ideals, like in the case of Riutort, the critique of these neo-classical presuppositions is ready at hand, aptly characterizing them as "counter-factual".[134]

As Riutort emphasizes, neo-classic economics cannot account for the current crisis, or any other crisis for that matter, simply because it does not recognize the idea of crisis as such. There is no room for it in the theory. This is the implication of Say's law, i.e. that supply always *implies* demand, and the complementary law of Walras, specifying that supply always *equals* demand: "all the agents sell only in order to buy".[135] As Riutort notes, one has to bear in mind that calling them laws does not mean they express generalizations of causal or empirical relations. Rather, they are *a priori* principles or presuppositions, just like the general equilibrium itself. Together they rule out *prima facie* the existence of a crisis, or rather, in monetarist interpretation, they point to only one possible problem, namely that interference from the outside can have affected the equilibrium of the multiplicity of market agents, and here the culprits are typically assumed to be the usual suspects, i.e. the state or the unions.[136]

---

131   See, e.g., Sahra Wagenknecht, *Wahnsinn mit Methode. Finanzcrash und Weltwirtschaft* (Berlin: Das neue Berlin, 2009).

132   Buffet in Marion Dakers, "Derivatives are a potential time bomb for banks, warns Berkeshire Hathaway chief", *The Daily Telegraph*, May 2nd 2016, p. 3.

133   See Vetlesen, "Nyliberalisme – en revolusjon for å konsolidere kapitalismen", p. 9.

134   See Riutort, *La gran ofensiva*, p. 184.

135   See Riutort, *ibid.*, p. 189.

136   See, e.g., Shaun Hargreaves Heap, "Planning", in *The Theory of Choice*, ed. Heap *et al.*, p. 243.

As mentioned, the crisis of the 1930 made Keynes think differently. Insisting that economics was about the real world, Say's law could thus be considered falsified. Behind the lack of effective demand, however, he found other reasons to question the neo-classical orthodoxy. Hence, for the neo-classicists, assuming the laws just mentioned, money was no problem. As already mentioned, the equilibrium of Walras's mathematical equations did not really need money (see POM, 269). Money was merely considered what made the real economy work, hence relieving the friction of the world, just like oil. For Menger, money thus only had exchange-value, no use-value (see POM, 265–66). As Riutort puts it, for the neo-classicists money was considered "neutral".[137]

However, apart from being a medium of exchange (see POM, 288), as already Locke realized, money can be used to store value beyond the time where normal goods decay.[138] Hence, money has to do with time, as also Walras was aware (see POM, 271). Allowing time and uncertainty a more prominent place in economic reasoning, as well as recognizing that money did have use-value, namely in the form of storage of value, made it possible for Keynes to realize that in times of crisis, the real-world rational economic agent had good reason to withhold both acquisition and investment. Believing that the future rate of interest will become higher than the present is a good reason for what Keynes would call a "liquidity-preference due to the precautionary motive".[139]

Furthermore, when there is little confidence in the workings of a particular economy, it becomes clear that savings and investment are not the same, and that the neo-classicists have been wrong in assuming so. Quite the opposite is the case: savings are equivalent to resources, at least as long as the inflation is limited, whereas investments, in a situation with insufficient effective demand, could ruin you. In difficult times, liquid money is in fact more useful than money invested in means of production that may be obsolete. In other words: insecurity in times of uncertainty makes money especially useful, and thus valuable, since it can more easily be converted into other goods and, thus, to use a phrase from Galbraith, minimize the "burden of ownership".[140]

The crisis of the 1930s, apart from demonstrating a lack of effective demand of goods and services, including labour, also exemplified what after Keynes became known as a liquidity trap. The point is that even if money is in fact available, due for instance to expansionist monetary policy, private market agents do not want to lend, spend or invest, because they expect lending, spending

---

137   Riutort, *La gran ofensiva*, p. 192.
138   See references in Ch. 1.
139   Keynes, *The General Theory of Employment, Interest, and Money*, p. 170.
140   John Kenneth Galbraith, *The Great Crash 1929*, 2nd ed. (Harmondsworth: Penguin, 1961), p. 47.

and investment to be low, thus creating a self-fulfilling prophecy. The basic problem is thus assumed to be a matter of psychology,[141] i.e. that there is too little mutual confidence and trust between the agents of the market in a situation of economic crisis. The risk, however, can be very real. Nobody wants to be dragged down by the fall of the others. It is this worry that is addressed by the Keynesian state, either by providing credit, investing or simply spending, all of which with the intent of reactivating in the economy the effects of the self-generating "multiplier".[142]

The post-ww II synthesis of Keynesian macro-economics and neo-classical micro-economics, was considered successful in avoiding most crises until the 1970s, when the stagflation problem occurred. With the monetarist economics now past, as far as I can see, various versions of this synthesis still constitute mainstream economics among decision makers, although the neo-classical element is now much stronger at the macro-level. This has wiped out some of the social concerns that were recognized during the Keynesian consensus, i.e. alienation, unemployment, poverty, etc., making ruling economics even more scientific, more technical and thus more inhumane than ever.

The only apparent attraction left within economics is, as mentioned before, the aesthetic fascination of the Austrian entrepreneur and the chances at the casino. By maintaining the ideology of the self-regulating free market, mainstream neo-classical economics can be said to legitimize setting free the individual economic actor, which creates an oversimplified ideological idea of freedom, i.e. being able to follow one's whims and inclinations. Placing their trust in chance, the Austrians can create a different ideology than the Keynesians and the neo-classicists, namely the ideology of the American dream, idealizing the idea of the luck of the self-made man. Those not ready to do, or capable of doing, what is required by such an ideology can hope for no more than grace in life.

The latter ideology, i.e. that of hope, keeps alive Internet scams, gambling halls and lotteries, making people spend hours and eventually fortunes on the extremely slim chance of a life as the one depicted in the magazines, i.e. the life of the successful entrepreneurs who can afford to visit real casinos. However, there are only few winners in the world of casino capitalism, and as it has always been the case, being on the losing side of the capitalist playing field is no fun. It is a scary world; it does continue producing and reproducing injustice at an ever-accelerating speed, and it is terrifying in its contingency.

---

141   See, e.g., Keynes, *The General Theory of Employment, Interest, and Money*, p. 170.
142   Riutort, *La gran ofensiva*, p. 195.

But contingency is also the possibility to pursue chance, and as long as one is part of the game, i.e. as long as one has something to bet, the casino is also fun, and the desire involved in the prospects of winning can make the losers seem invisible, even when they include oneself. That is part of the aesthetics of gambling, and the problem is that this makes the capitalist entrepreneur an attractive figure.

The main point here, however, is that money is not neutral, even though monetarists have tried to return to this neo-classical idea.[143] As mentioned, money lessens the burdens of ownership, and currently with almost no inflation there is only little rational incentive for speculative capital to risk the investment in real economy.[144] On the contrary: borrowing money costs almost nothing and there is plenty of it around. As mentioned, interest rates are low, and enormous sums have been pumped into the economy by the central banks in Europe, Japan and the USA.[145] Neither is there much ideological incentive to invest in particular local projects, since protestant work ethics, Marxist workers' ideology or nationalist populism are not among the favoured ideologies of contemporary business people.

With neo-classicists and neo-liberals now in power, worldwide we have seen a strong tendency to restrict local fiscal policy, thus reducing the welfare provisions that function as indirect salaries. Instead, the focus has been on monetary politics, trying to regulate everything with the money supply. In times of crises, this means stimulating investment by lowering the interest rates, and we have recently seen examples of negative interest rates in the EU. Still, only little money is invested productively; what we see is thus an international, almost global liquidity trap. The money is there; since borrowing has been cheap for years, there is so much money in electronic circulation that it is beyond imagination. In fact, money is produced electronically whenever somebody is borrowing money, and the result is the existence of an enormous and ever-growing debt that has been recognized as one of the main reasons why financial bobbles and thus crises occur.[146] Hence, worries about the debt in the USA were already prevalent before the 2008 crash.[147]

---

143   See, e.g., Riutort, *ibid.*, p. 205.
144   See, e.g., Paul Lewis, "Cash v. Stocks: the winner may surprise you", *FTMoney* (*Financial Times*), June 18th 2016.
145   See, e.g., Róin, "Når penge ikke er nok" and "Hvor super er Mario Draghi?"
146   See, e.g., Riutort, *La gran ofensiva*, pp. 212–13.
147   See, e.g., Martin Burcharth, "Valutaparadoks skaber ubalance i verdensøkonomien", *Information*, December 21st 2006.

With the coming of modern information technology, the consequence of all the deregulation has thus been a growth in international financial transactions which is simply beyond imagination. Add to this that the increased possibilities of short-term speculation, and the casino image of economy, have raised the rational expectations of returns way above what can be expected of long-term investments in real economy. Thus, due to the removal of all kinds of restrictions on money production and transfers, as well as the inflated expectations of returns, international capital is so enormous and volatile that it can bring down any country.

This makes it rational for politicians, even if they do not like it, to adjust to what they take to be the realities, i.e. TINA: There Is No Alternative. The result is that each country competes in providing for the anonymous flow of capital even better conditions by removing any obstacle that can be thought of, thus facilitating entry but also exit, ultimately accelerating what has nowadays become known as the 'race toward the bottom'. But realities change. It is no more than a few decades ago that money could not be sold across borders, i.e. it was illegal and punished severely by many countries, and in fact we still see China having chosen isolation in relation to the international financial system. This is just to bring back to attention the fact that we are dealing with things that are human made, historical, and can therefore also be changed.

F   Wrapping Up

This is as far as I can get for now in the investigation into the economic, social and ideological realities of contemporary globalized capitalism. The outset has been the classicists and the neo-classicists of political economy, who have been accused of not taking into account the economic realities by Marxists, Keynesians and, most recently, neo-liberals. They all claim to be realist, but obviously that must imply that realism can mean very different things. The realism involved in acknowledging a crisis is the condition on which the general equilibrium theory can be shown to be ideological and false. Quite another kind of realism is necessary for governing politically a complex national economy, and they are both very different from the realism involved in being a free market entrepreneur looking for business opportunities.

However, maybe my critique of political economy and capitalism has focused on issues that only convey a very superficial and distorted representation of the real realities. Hence, by focusing on the market, I have been led to make my analysis depend on the subjective concept of value, and at least so far restricting my arguments concerning capitalism to the sphere of circulation and distribution. According to Postone and Kellner,[148] this makes me an accomplice of the classical critical theorists, i.e. Pollock and Horkheimer. In a more orthodox Marxist perspective, the problem is that this neglects the sphere of production, where value according to the classicists is produced, and from which the idea of an unjust exploitation draws its rationale. So without the labour theory of value, criticizing the exploitation of the workers becomes less straightforward. One can still criticize the reification and alienation produced by instrumental action, but without a comprehensive Hegelian-Marxist concept of work, it is not work that brings us beyond mere labour, but something else, which is not already an inherent necessity in capitalism, e.g. communication in the case of Habermas. Without the comprehensive idea of work and the labour theory of value, the idea of a transformative immanent critique of capitalism, through a determinate negation, is severely weakened.

My cultural Marxism may in fact have a very strained relationship to many interpretations of Marx's critique of political economy. Not only does my argument make the coming of a more reasonable society improbable; it might not seem possible at all. This was where Horkheimer ended up,[149] but I would be most unwilling to accept such a conclusion. Still, it seems that it would require some argument to avoid it; however, presently I am not sure which direction to take. One possibility could be to explore a broader concept of value, e.g. labour for production, utility for circulation and then surplus for accumulation, thus including both subjective and objective aspects in the same concept of value.[150] For now, however, like Horkheimer I am just left with the will to continue pursuing the political possibilities of bettering the world.[151]

As Marx did in the aftermath of the great crisis of 1857, I have now taken the first few steps to write my *Grundrisse* to a critique of political economy, allowing myself to reflect continuously on the basics of contemporary capitalism. As yet, I have only scratched the surface of market economy, still having to struggle with further details and intricacies of money, finance, interest and last but not least capital. But: time and space are, as always, limited. I must stop for now, but capitalism does indeed seem to remain here for a while. So I will return ... maybe I will eventually arrive at something like *Das Kapital*.

---

148 See, e.g., Kellner, *Critical Theory, Marxism and Modernity*, p. 62, and Postone, "Critique, State, and Economy", p. 175.

149 See the Interlude above, Sect. C.

150 Hence, I am still stuck in the concept of value that set me off for Ch. 1 above, and this is also an issue that will continue to occupy me in DDD II.

151 This will is also reflected in the works collected in DDD III.

Name Index and Bibliography

The present index only lists names of persons (for other names, please see the Subject index). The name index also functions as a bibliography. Where relevant, the name of a person is followed by a page and note number in *italics*, indicating a footnote that provides full bibliographical information about a work authored, edited or translated by the person in question. Full bibliographical information about a work is provided the first time the work is referred to in each chapter. Some works, however, are referenced with abbreviated titles and page numbers in brackets in the text (please see the List of Abbreviations above for more information).

• • •

Subject Index

Detailed List of Contents

PART TWO
Dialectics